SCIENCE AND CULTURE SERIES
JOSEPH HUSSLEIN, S.J., Ph.D., GENERAL EDITOR

MAKERS of the
MODERN MIND

MAKERS of the MODERN MIND

THOMAS P. NEILL, Ph.D.

ASSOCIATE PROFESSOR OF HISTORY

ST. LOUIS UNIVERSITY

THE BRUCE PUBLISHING COMPANY
MILWAUKEE

TO MY FATHER AND MOTHER

PREFACE BY
THE GENERAL EDITOR

THE subject of this book, MAKERS OF THE MODERN MIND, cannot fail to exercise a strong attraction upon numerous present-day readers. It is something novel in the field, not written for the specialist scholar, but for the overwhelmingly larger number of intelligent men and women desirous of correct information on the important matters dealt with here. They are the men and women who, in particular, deserve more attention than has so far been given them, and something more substantial, the author believes, than the intellectual pabulum hitherto handed them by most popularizers. It is to such readers, therefore — more numerous than either the college professor or movie producer will admit — that this book is directed. The scholar, in turn, cannot afford to miss it.

To weigh the importance of its subject matter and gauge the interest attached to its pages it suffices only to read the familiar names that serve as chapter headings: Luther, Calvin, Descartes, Locke, Newton, Rousseau, Kant, Bentham, Darwin, Marx, and Freud. Attention is given to each in turn, with all due discrimination between the good and evil, the false and true, that may be found in the work and writings of these men.

Familiar, no doubt, to every reader are most of these eleven names whose bearers have in general sought to influence the modern mind. They are largely the names of men in whose defense or condemnation thousands are still ready to range themselves. Truly, then, intelligent readers of every class must obviously be more than moderately interested in the bearers of these names. Moreover, the knowledge of how the modern mind has been affected and developed through them will enable us to comprehend more readily how it works in this our day.

Such, then, is the moving panorama with which every intelligent reader who follows the course of world events will wish to be acquainted. The author himself can be relied upon to remain undeviatingly fair in his treatment of each individual, in his discussions and final implications, giving due reasons for praise or blame, preserving invariably his peace and balance of mind, and withal that saving sense of humor which prevails throughout.

JOSEPH HUSSLEIN, S.J., PH.D.
General Editor,
Science and Culture Series

Saint Louis University
January 20, 1948

ACKNOWLEDGMENTS

GRATEFUL acknowledgment is made to the following for their patience in reading the entire manuscript: Professors James Belton, James Collins, and Charles Dougherty, of St. Louis University; Professor Emerson Hynes, of St. John's University; Miss Barbara Brennan; and Mr. Arthur R. Kuhl. Their wise criticisms and their helpful suggestions have saved the author from many blunders, and they have made the following pages easier on the reader. Other professional friends are also to be thanked for reading individual chapters which they were particularly qualified to criticize. They have all been tolerant, kindly, and helpful.

Acknowledgment is also made for permission to quote from the following books, permission generously granted by the publishers, authors, or estates controlling the copyrights on the works listed: George Allen and Unwin, *Sigmund Freud*, by Fritz Wittels, and *Totem and Taboo*, by Sigmund Freud; Appleton-Century, *Darwiniana*, by Thomas H. Huxley; J. M. Dent and Sons, *Puritanism and Liberty*, edited by A. S. P. Woodhouse; E. P. Dutton, *The Quintessence of Capitalism*, by Werner Sombart; Harcourt, Brace and Company, *Religion and the Rise of Capitalism*, by R. H. Tawney; Harvard University Press, *Freud*, by Hanns Sachs; Hodder and Stoughton, *John Calvin*, by Hugh Y. Reyburn; Henry Holt and Company, *The Age of the Reformation*, by Preserved Smith, *John Calvin*, by Georgia Harkness, and *Political Thought in England*, by William L. Davidson; Houghton Mifflin Company, *Making of the Modern Mind*, by John H. Randall, Jr.; Little, Brown and Company, *Darwin, Marx, Wagner*, by Jacques Barzun; Liveright Publishing Corporation, *A General Introduction to Psycho-Analysis*, by Sigmund Freud; The Macmillan Company, *Isaac Newton*, by J. W. N. Sullivan; W. W. Norton Company, *Marxism: Is It Science?*, by Max Eastman, and *Autobiography,* by Sigmund Freud; Philosophical Library, *The Dream of Descartes,* by Jacques Maritain; G. P. Putnam's Sons, *Protestantism and Progress,* by Ernest Troeltsch; Charles Scribner's Sons, *Three Reformers,* by Jacques Maritain, *Some Turns of Thought in Modern Philosophy,* by George Santayana, and *Isaac Newton,* by Louis T. More; Simon and Shuster, *Men of Mathematics,* by E. T. Bell; and Yale University Press, *Charles Darwin,* by Geoffrey West.

CONTENTS

MAKERS of the
MODERN MIND

I

INTRODUCTION

SEVEN MEN ON AN ELEPHANT

THE dizzy pace at which the world has progressed in all branches of applied learning this past century has given rise to a disturbing paradox. Never before in history have men known so much about so many things, and never have they been so confused on such basic questions as whether the world is what it seems, or even whether they have minds. As scholars probe more deeply into the secrets of nature and encompass ever wider fields of knowledge, they find it necessary to specialize more and more exclusively on smaller and smaller areas of knowledge. Thus collectively they have pushed back the frontiers of knowledge and multiplied many times over the sum of facts known by mankind. But in the process each specialist has necessarily closed his mind to everything except his own little specialty. He lets the rest of the world go by.

Two hundred years ago, for example, the average physician did not have too profound a knowledge of medicine; but he understood other aspects of life well enough to act as friend and counselor to his patients on a hundred various problems. A century ago doctors tended to see all human problems in terms of physiological upsets, because they had learned more about medicine and had closed their minds to the intricacies of agriculture, finance, and human relationships. Today, as the result of increased specialization, the heart specialist tends to see every human disorder in terms of cardiac disturbances, and the psychiatrist sees the same illnesses in terms of neurosis.

1

In days gone by, to take another example, the competent historian knew the general story of man's past fairly well; today no historian is considered respectable unless he has specialized in the events of a single decade within a single country. About the rest of history he may be as ignorant as the physician or the lawyer. So it necessarily is, of course, in all branches of learning. Because there are only twenty-four hours in the day and about twenty-thousand days in a lifetime, such specialization as we have in the modern world can be accomplished only by sacrificing wide knowledge for deep learning in a tiny area.

Modern scholars therefore remind one of that little jingle most of us learned as children.

> It was six men of Indostan
> To learning much inclined
> Who went to see the Elephant
> (Though all of them were blind),
> That each by observation
> Might satisfy his mind.

Each man, the fable runs on, took hold of the elephant at a different place, and each concluded from his limited experience what sort of animal this wondrous elephant was. One bumped against its side; so he decided that "the elephant is very like a wall." Another took hold of its tusk and therefore concluded that it was "very like a spear." A third thought the elephant was similar to a snake, because he had grabbed its squirming trunk. A fourth, who clasped it by the knee, thought it "very like a tree"; another felt its ear and thought it like a fan; and the sixth blind man, grabbing its tail, concluded it was "very like a rope."

> And so the men of Indostan
> Disputed loud and long
> Each in his own opinion
> Exceeding stiff and strong,
> Though each was partly in the right
> And all were in the wrong!

The two important points behind this little jingle are obvious. In the first place, the six men of Indostan argued loud and long about an animal none of them had ever seen. Each had, so to speak, become a specialist on one part of the elephant's anatomy; each was therefore competent to talk about his specialty, but none was qualified to generalize correctly about the elephant as an animal. Each was therefore partly right, but all were wrong. Because none of the men could step back a few paces to see the whole elephant, the six fields of specialization created confusion about the animal as a whole.

But there is still a seventh man, so horrified at the findings of the blind men and their acrimonious debate, that he is content to see the elephant from a distance. His vision remains intact, but he learns little that is exact about the elephant.

Closer inspection of the contemporary mind reveals how men today are faced with the dilemma of the seven men on the elephant: of giving up specialization to preserve sanity, or giving up a rounded knowledge of things human to learn ever more about smaller areas of knowledge. For closer inspection reveals how striking is the paradox between the modern mind's wonderful accomplishments and its awful shortcomings. Freedom of controversy and tolerance of almost any opinion are accorded to all people, at least in this country. This is a possession which we of the modern world are likely to take for granted without reflecting how it was won by bitter struggle through the long years of modern history. It is a priceless heritage through which man can arrive at truth more surely and more readily than in any other way.

Modern humanitarianism, again, compares favorably with the way man has dealt with man any time in the past. It is good to try rehabilitating criminals instead of torturing them. It is good to assure medical services, education, old-age assistance, and unemployment relief to the less fortunate members of the human race. It is good, moreover, not to abandon the alleviation of suffering to the chance offerings of private charity alone. It is good to hate dictatorship for its demoralizing attack on human persons, and it is good to prize democracy for the dignity and worth it accords a man simply because he is a human being. These are all good things, and they are all the fruit of long, hard struggles in the past.

Man's recent accomplishments in the fields of science and medicine are wonderful. His life span has been lengthened many years, and it has been made more comfortable than ever before. The utilization of water power, of electricity, and now of atomic energy are in themselves all good things, for they are victories for man in his struggle to subdue the forces of nature and to use them for his welfare. Even man's study of himself has revealed much that was undreamed of in the past. It is good to know how the mind of man works, how his decisions are made, how unconscious drives affect conscious activity. Man's self-analysis and self-criticism have developed tremendously in the past century, and this development has opened up amazing possibilities for social control and for individual betterment in the future. All these things, it must be remembered, have been accomplished because of specialization.

These findings of the specialist are good, but few of them have been as fully utilized as possible because men lack the wisdom and the self-control to use them to the best advantage. To cite a currently overworked example: atomic energy is potentially man's greatest servant, but at the same time it can be employed to destroy millions of human beings. So it is with every other modern accomplishment. The radio is potentially a means of contributing to the education, the culture, and the pleasure of the human race — but it is also potentially a means of stirring up hatred among men, or rousing them to blind fury and to animal-like action. The press can be used to make the public a well-informed citizenry in every country in the world, but at the same time it can misinform and beguile its readers and hide from them the truth they have a right to know. Forces created by the specialist are always potentially good or bad, depending on the wisdom shown in employing them.

But unfortunately in the process of specialization we have sacrificed wisdom for learning. We have, indeed, tended to dehumanize ourselves and to lose the rational self-possession that characterized educated persons in days gone by. For paradoxically, insanity increases as man learns more about the world; neurotics multiply as man learns more about himself; confusion closes in on his mind as it obtains a clearer picture of atomic fision or of the action of antibodies in the blood stream. Never before in history, in fact, have there been so many people suffering from mental disorders as there are today — eight million of them in this country alone, according to the estimate of Surgeon General Thomas Parran in 1947. Millions appear more interested in their own minds than in anything else, and, though intro-spection has helped us discover much about ourselves, in its general effect it appears corrosive instead of salutary. It seems to have caused more neurosis than it has cured.

So it has been with other developments in human thought. Each appears, paradoxically, to walk arm in arm with its own ne-gation. At the same time that humanitarianism has won the modern mind, humanitarians are discovered holding an extremely low opinion of man. The English Canine Defense League, for example, requested President Truman to save animals by using convicted war criminals in the Bikini atom bomb tests. Protesting against the use of "innocent animals" for this purpose, it re-quested the president to substitute "subhumans in the shape of humans" in their place. There are almost daily press reports of dogs and cats receiving large bequests from persons unmoved by the human poverty in their neighborhoods, or of people opposed to sending relief to children in a war-stricken Europe but enthusiastic about feeding undernourished kittens at home.

Sincere thinkers are concerned about this paradoxical situation of the modern mind in doing so much for concrete, practical science, and yet remaining so confused on many of the basic problems of human existence. They therefore try to resolve it in either of two ways. If specialists, they may tend to concentrate ever more fiercely on the elephant's tail or trunk — or whatever their specialty may be — trying to convince themselves that this is the one thing of most importance, while ignoring the rest of the world or viewing it largely in the narrow terms of their own specialty. The other alternative is simply to stay aloof entirely from this paradox of the modern mind and to deny at the same time the validity of the specialist's observation. Neither of these two classes can be right.

If the fable of the six men and the elephant is to have a happy ending, we need still another man — an eighth — to stand back a few paces, study the elephant as an integral whole, find out what the blind specialists are doing, and then correlate their findings into a unified picture. This eighth man, then, must be one who welcomes sincerely the genuine discoveries of any specialist, but who never loses sight of the whole animal that is being studied piecemeal by the six blind men.

It would therefore be well to draw back historically from this "elephant problem" to see how it came to be the confusing thing it is today. Such was always the advice of Aristotle, who said more than twenty centuries ago: "He who considers things in their growth and origin will obtain the clearest view of them." As contemporary a philosopher as Santayana wrote in the same vein not so many years ago that a grasp of tradition is "a great advantage, conducive to mutual understanding, to maturity, and to progress."

Seeing these problems grow would at least reveal to us that what we consider peculiar shortcomings in the modern mind, as well as its various strong points, are not nearly so novel as they seem to us today. We would see, for example, how men have never been moved by pure reason alone; how they have always been emotional as well as rational beings; how prejudice and various kinds of pressure groups have always forced decisions in one direction or another. We would see how toleration of others' views grew slowly and was brought out not only by much bloodshed but also by unfortunately developing a kind of intellectual indifferentism which is inimical to clearly defined thinking. We would see how the difficult balance between the head and the heart has been tipped historically, now in favor of the head and now of the heart; how one extreme almost always begets the other within a relatively short time. Such a story, however, would be too full and too complicated for the compass of a single volume. But by following the intellectual development of certain foremost makers of the modern mind we may hope to throw light on the paradox which contemporary man creates by solving intricate intellectual problems while denying that he even has a mind.

The eleven men selected for treatment in the following pages serve a double role in helping us to understand the modern mind. In the first place, their contributions to the fund of human knowledge bulk large. They are the master builders in making the modern mind; and though there are hundreds of other thinkers who made their individual contributions to the history of ideas; nevertheless the thought of these men added together comes close to giving an accurate and complete picture of what is here called the modern mind. In the second place, the eleven men treated in these pages serve handily as pegs on which to hang a number of pertinent truths in the development of modern thought, for they exemplify intellectual currents of their age. Change in intellectual climate, of course, is gradual, and it is effected as much by a concatenation of economic, social, political, and human causes as it is by the mighty mind of an individual thinker. The makers of the modern mind selected for treatment here therefore serve the secondary purpose of being milestones in the Western World's intellectual history these past four centuries. The road goes on between them without sharp turns. They show us, from time to time, whither the road is leading.

The men treated here are chosen, then, not for the intrinsic worth of their thought but for their importance in making the Western mind what it is today. There are other more profound and other more original thinkers. But there are none more influential on subsequent generations and consequently, directly or indirectly, on this. Our eleven makers of the modern mind were almost always influential, as we shall see, because they said what the world wanted to hear at the time they spoke; they were sometimes influential, as Locke and Darwin were, precisely because they were not profound thinkers. Yet because they struck up sympathetic vibrations with their own or with succeeding generations they are important. For this reason they merit serious attention by those who would see how the modern mind has grown in order to understand how it functions as it does today.

II
LUTHER

EVERYMAN HIS OWN PRIEST AND PROPHET

MARTIN LUTHER is very much a modern man. Where Calvin would look coldly on the modern world and pierce its confused hubbub with his icy eye, Luther would enter into the confusion with gusto. Where Descartes would retire to his ivory tower to shut out noisy men and withdraw into the world of his own thought, Luther would descend into the market place and the tavern, rub elbows with laborers and shopkeepers, argue with amateur politicians, and appear on quiz programs. Where Karl Marx would look for the universal world scheme behind the day's iniquity, Luther would declaim against the price of wheat and the quality of men's shirts, and he would discover an easy formula as a means of fixing irreparable guilt on the heads of his enemies.

The ex-Augustinian monk can easily be imagined at home as a leader in the contemporary world. He would fit in nicely as a labor chief or a self-made industrialist; as a senator or the big

8

man in the local Rotary Club. He would be a restless but effective figure in the modern world, one continually in the headlines, one always getting things done. He would be sharply criticized by some, but he would be a hero to his followers. He would be a rough and tumble figure in public life. And he would love it. He would revel in the confusion and the scurry of the modern atomic world — except when it grew very dark and a little quiet. Then he would be afraid.

Luther would be a successful figure today, for he possessed qualities of leadership and of dynamic forcefulness that make for success in a disjointed world. He was important, in fact, precisely because his age was out of joint and out of temper. Europeans felt the need of leadership early in the sixteenth century when the medieval world was disappearing and the dim outlines of the modern world were yet but vaguely seen. Leadership fell to Martin Luther, a German who knew the German people, their hopes as well as their hates, who felt as they felt and spoke their rough Germanic tongue. Luther was truly *volkstümlich* — sprung from the people — and he never let the people forget it. He achieved historical importance because he expressed certain powerful but suppressed feelings of the German people, because he appealed to the cupidity of the nobles and the ambition of the princes, because the time was ripe for such a revolution as his, and he instinctively knew how to utilize the forces of change at his disposal.

Of Luther's importance there is no question. His was the first permanent break from the Roman Catholic Church. His was a religion which stressed blind trust and deprecated philosophy, a homocentric religion which was much more in tune with the succeeding individualistic ages than was the Catholic religion from which it broke. Luther's attack on reason, his insistence that every man is his own priest and prophet, his outlook on man as an essentially depraved creature, were all to bear their bitter fruit in later, more auspicious days. More immediately, Luther justified and promoted the absolute power of the prince; he furthered religious divisions along national lines and thus helped usher into European history the truly bloody religious wars of the sixteenth and seventeenth centuries.

Had Luther never lived, it is true, there would likely have

arisen another figure who would have led such a movement as his. But there was a Luther, and the fact remains that it was he who initiated the break, who gave it the direction it took and the tone it possessed. Luther did not control the movement, however, after it got under way. The princes did that. Nor did he formulate final Lutheran doctrine; the Augsburg Confession of 1530, the basis of Lutheran doctrine, is more Melanchthon's work than Luther's. But Luther remained the leader and the public-relations man of the movement throughout his lifetime. And his influence on European mentality is decisive. His famous *pecca fortiter et crede firmius* (sin boldly and believe more firmly), as well as his insistence that each man is his own priest and prophet, was rejected by princes and by later Lutherans. But, as Jacques Maritain puts it, "the spirit of Luther went on travelling underground, for new upheavals and new crises."

In justice to Luther and to later Lutherans, therefore, we must distinguish Luther's teaching from its results. Like every founder of a school in modern times, Luther deplored the conclusions to which his theories were reduced in his own lifetime; he would, indeed, have thundered out a century later, "If this is Lutheranism, I am no Lutheran." The results to which Luther's theories were reduced were in some respects better and in others worse than his own teaching. Certainly the Lutheranism of Melanchthon was not what Luther envisaged when he first propounded his doctrine after breaking from Rome. But we are more interested in the results of his teaching than in the teaching itself. We must see what happened to the modern mind because of Luther's theories — but we must not assume that he either foresaw or desired those results.

1

Luther could have made his mark only when society was in flux — as it is today — when there was discontent deep in men's hearts; when the existing powers abused their trust. He could have come to the fore only in a world where things were changing; where there were rumblings beneath the surface of society; where men's minds were not at rest; and where their hearts were not at peace. Luther lived in such a society.

The scholastic philosophy, which had reached a high point in the thirteenth century and had guided the thought of most educated Europeans at that time, had come upon sorry days. There had developed many varieties of scholasticism, and their rivalry was intense — as rivalry so frequently becomes in philosophy and theology. By the time Luther was ready for school the Occamist variety of scholasticism had triumphed in most places. Aristotle was still supposed to be the Philosopher, but it was a caricature of Aristotle that the Occamists passed out to their students. The validity of abstraction, a key point with Aristotle and the scholastics, had been denied by the Occamists, who propounded a nominalism instead — the theory that there is no reality except concrete reality, that such terms as "man" and "good" are only labels, or names, attached for the sake of convenience to certain concrete things in order to group them under various handy headings.

Philosophy was thus becoming a science of name calling, of terminism. Men naturally reacted to such a system of thought. Either they tended to become skeptics, insisting we can have sure knowledge of nothing, or they threw the whole business of philosophy overboard and insisted on good living instead of good thinking. They asked with Thomas à Kempis, "What signifies making a great dispute about hidden things which for having been ignorant of we shall not be reproved in the judgment?" And they answered, "Nothing."

Europe was cracking up, prior to Luther's coming on the scene, cracking up not only intellectually but also religiously. The authority of the Catholic Church, the governess of the universities and the mistress of truth in medieval days, had been badly shaken by a long series of events in the fourteenth and fifteenth centuries. First had come the quarrel with the newly founded national monarchies over the taxation of the clergy. The last medieval pope, Boniface VIII, had hurled defiance at Philip IV of France and Edward I of England. Neither king gave way. Neither did Boniface, who died shortly after being manhandled by Philip's envoys sent to Anagni to arrest him. But his successors found it convenient to back down before the kings.

Then came the popes' long "Babylonian Captivity" at Avignon, where they appeared to be under French control through a large part of the Hundred Years' War, surrounded as nominally sovereign Avignon was by French territory. In this age of developing national feeling, popes were condemned by the French for not being sufficiently French and by Englishmen, Germans, and Italians for being too French. In 1377, the pope returned to Rome, and in the next year began the worst divisive force of all for the Catholic Church — the Great Western Schism. There came to be two claimants to the papacy, two rival colleges of cardinals, two appointees for each vacant bishopric, two obediences, and two Peter's Pence collections to support the two rival "popes." This internal struggle within the Church lowered the papacy in the eyes of the faithful throughout Europe — and all Europeans were Catholics then — to the level of a kingly crown about which rival dynasties warred.

When the schism was ended and unity was established in the Catholic Church again, the pope found that he could not effect reforms he saw were necessary. Any talk of reform in the high places of the Church, where it was most severely needed, provoked talk of another schism, and the reform proposal was quietly dropped. The Church never recovered the prestige lost through the long Babylonian Captivity (1305–1377) and the Great Western Schism (1378–1415). For new attitudes had been in the making in these years. A new worldliness had developed, a new skepticism had crept into men's minds, a new standard of morality and a new hierarchy of values had been formulated. The Renaissance had come to Europe, and it had taken hold of the best educated men of the time, laymen and churchmen alike.

Men of the Renaissance had thrown off the tutelage of the Church and the protection of the nobility. They had decided to think as they wished and to protect themselves as they could. They lowered their gaze from the clouds to the earth at their feet — and they discovered many things. They quit looking for pie in the sky, and they found in their midst something that has passed for pie from that day till this. They concentrated on themselves and created for themselves an anthropocentric morality and an individualistic society to replace the theocentric world of medieval times. They let those who liked that sort of thing contemplate playing a harp forever on the edge of a wet cloud, but they tried to achieve immortality in the memory of man. They decided to get ahead down here below and not think too much about what might happen after they died. Worldly success became self-justifying. Restraints were cast off, sometimes openly denied and sometimes just conveniently forgotten. The Renaissance was an age of rugged individualism for artists, businessmen, and princes alike. The strongest survived and were held up by mothers and schoolmasters as models for children of the next generation.

Men of the Renaissance looked for a new moral code that would justify this restless, ruthless sort of life. And they found it in the humanities of the classical past. So there was a revival of classical Greek and Roman culture, which had never been blacked out completely, and the ancients soon became models not only for style but also for standards of conduct. The murder of Caesar, for example, was repeated with monotonous regularity — almost whenever a reasonable duplicate of the stalwart old Roman could be found by a group of young men anxious to live forever in the memory of posterity. Life became laxer and freer, especially among those who drank deep of the wine of antiquity. And among these were, in high proportion, the higher clergy of the Church.

This return to frankly pagan living was most ostentatiously accomplished in Italy, the most cultured part of the European world. In the German countries the old scholasticism had degenerated into nominalism and terminism in the schools and into a frank rejection of reason among many learned, pious people. But along with rational thought they also rejected pagan morals. Instead, they developed a mysticism — especially in the Low Countries — which gave them a direct wire to heaven, to truth, and to morality, without plugging in through the switchboard of reason. They were ready, before Luther was in school, to attack both the loose living and the speculative thought of Rome. They had their weapons of a false mysticism and a false asceticism; they only needed someone to wield them effectively.

The days of Luther's youth were days of unrest socially and politically. In Western Europe — Italy, Spain, France, and England — anarchy created by the rugged individualism of the early Renaissance had given way necessarily to absolute rule. Little despots set themselves up in various Italian states, and soon they were copied on a grander scale by national despots in Spain, where Isabella and Ferdinand established absolute rule; in England, where Henry VII ushered in the Tudor despotism by putting the royal crown on his own head after the battle of Bosworth; in France, where the successors of St. Louis finally brought the various parts of the country under their autocratic sway. These new states capitalized on national differences of language, traditions, and way of life. National feeling, dormant through the Middle Ages, was exploited by the new rulers, and it was found to be a dynamic element that could no longer be ignored by those who would do things in European history.

There was relative peace and relative prosperity under these new national despots. People were thankful for the protection given to them by the strong ruler; the middle class, which had been the dynamic group in the social upheaval of the Renaissance, was glad to enter into an alliance with the absolute king in order to make secure the wealth and the position they had recently won. In much of Western Europe the new social pattern which was to last until the eighteenth century had been cut. The bourgeoisie had sold out their ideal of liberty for the more comfortable commodity of security.

But in the Germanies no such development had taken place. In that section of Europe there was neither a large middle class with money to pay for security nor a single ruler with both the ability and the desire to assert absolute control over the German states. The Holy Roman Empire was only a loose organization of jealous princes theoretically under the severely limited control of an emperor. These princes were anxious to assert their complete independence of the emperor and to become petty despots in their respective states; they were predisposed to welcome any disruptive movement that might embarrass the emperor and weaken his already tenuous hold upon them.

More important, perhaps, was the lack of a strong king to protect the German people from the onerous exactions of unscrupulous churchmen. Throughout the generation before 1517 bitter complaints were continually made about the tithes sent to Rome and to the various dioceses in Germany. Bitter, too, were the complaints about the lax living of the clergy. Such was the social and economic discontent with church organization in Germany that the papal nuncio complained, in 1521, that nine tenths of the people were crying "Long live Luther," and the other tenth "Death to the Church." There was no discontent with church doctrine, but Germans were ready to back any spokesman who would denounce ecclesiastical practices and inveigh against Rome's exactions.

This discontent was deepened by the fact that Germany was suffering economically. For some time a gradual drift of trade routes westward had been shifting prosperity from German and Italian cities to the Atlantic seaboard of Europe. An increase in the amount of bullion caused a general price rise in a day when German income did not increase at all. Particularly princes, whose fixed revenues were pitifully inadequate to meet the higher cost of living, found themselves in bad economic straits. They tried every method possible of increasing their incomes — which meant discovering additional ways of squeezing money from their serfs and peasants. All of this made for social unrest. The Germanies were restless in 1517; they were seething with social and economic discontent, and the masses of illiterate peasants were ready to grasp at anything which offered the slightest hope of change. Any change, they felt, would have to be for the better. They were a religious people in the Germanies, more so than in Italy or France, but in a mystical and emotional way. And they were discontent.

2

This was the stage on which Luther appeared when he nailed his ninety-five theses to the church door at Wittenberg on Halloween of 1517. But to evaluate Lutheran theory properly it is much more important to understand its author than its background, for Luther's doctrine is essentially the projection of his personality and a solution of his peculiar individual problems. It was because he was so troubled about his own salvation that he developed the satisfying doctrine of justification by faith alone. This was his only way of obtaining absolute assurance of salvation. It was for this reason, he frankly tells us, that he denied man freedom of will. "Without this doctrine [of determinism]," he says, "I believe I would be constantly tortured by uncertainty and compelled to expunge all my work. My conscience would never enjoy certain ease. . . . If free-will were offered to me, I would not accept it at all." Luther's main concern was to formulate a creed that satisfied and assured his abnormal mentality. That is why it is important to know the man and his strange mind, to see something of his personal background.

Luther was born of peasant stock in Saxony. His boyhood seems to have been gloomy and joyless, pervaded by an overwhelming fear of death, damnation, and the devil. His parents were unduly severe. "My mother flogged me until I bled on account of a single nut," is one of his complaints in later life. There was little sunlight in Luther's boyhood. His father Hans, however, was industrious and, in a practical way, quite intelligent. Within a few years after Martin's birth, in 1483, the Luther family was fairly well fixed financially. Hans, who had risen from his peasant status to that of a petty capitalist owner of a copper mine, decided to send Martin through law, the surest road to social preferment and financial security for a German of base blood in the early sixteenth century.

Martin's youth was that of a typical German peasant — wrapped in melancholy, pervaded by popular local superstitions. But he showed himself to have a good mind, though not a deep one. He did well in his studies, obtaining his bachelor's degree in the minimum time in 1502, and three years later ranking second in a class of seventeen who received the master's degree. At the University of Erfurt, where he did his work, he was subjected to the "modern" Occamist philosophy with its useless hairsplitting and its barren terminism. Though the new humanist studies were then offered at Erfurt, Luther does not seem to have taken to them seriously.

His father had picked Martin out a wife and enrolled him in law school. But all at once the young man was in an Augustinian monastery preparing to become a priest. What happened in the summer of 1505 illustrates the cardinal point of Lutheranism and of Luther's effect on subsequent generations — the supremacy of emotion over the intellect. Moved by uncontrollable fear when he was almost killed by lightning on July 2, Luther took an oath to become a priest if his life was spared. Thus he entered the monastery an undisciplined young man, strong willed and highly imaginative, capable of sharp reasoning on purely practical matters, but beneath the surface a simple, emotional peasant lad who was concerned with only one problem — the problem of his own salvation.

For more than ten years this problem ate at his heart; he wrestled with it continually, but he never felt that he had overcome it. He lived in perpetual fear of eternal damnation, in continual dread of dying. Terror besieged him almost always. His novice master tried to comfort him by telling him to have faith; after he was ordained, his superior, Staupitz, tried to soothe his wretchedness by advising him to put confidence in Christ the Redeemer who could not have died vainly for man's salvation. From this advice Luther took a small measure of consolation. Uncertainty remained nonetheless, and Luther still searched for an irrevocable ticket to heaven. He wanted his reservation assured at once so that he could dismiss the problem of his salvation and turn to other matters.

This unhealthy, inward bent of his mind upon himself, this concern with himself and his own problems alone, continued to occupy Luther until about 1515 or 1516. His flurry of activity — preaching, caring for fish ponds, teaching — was only to escape from himself. By 1516 he had worked out his doctrine of salvation, a foolproof one that took all the burden off his own shoulders and put it all on Christ's. From St. Paul's Epistle to the Romans, Luther evolved his theory that all men's efforts are sinful, that he has no free will, that he is an animal governed either by God or the devil — depending who is in the saddle. Completely depraved animal that man is, he can of himself do nothing to earn salvation. It comes to him only when he puts blind trust in Christ. *Pecca fortiter et crede firmius.* The first part is unimportant; it is the second part that counts. Believe — Luther really means trust — always more firmly and blindly. Do not worry about good works, for man can do nothing of himself to earn salvation. Christ has done it all.

This doctrine satisfied. Luther had convinced himself of it and was teaching it in his classes when the momentous indulgence controversy broke on Europe late in 1517. Indulgences, as good works in the Catholic system, had no place in Luther's doctrine of salvation by trust alone. He therefore rose to attack them. Wisely for his cause he concentrated on the all too-apparent abuses in the preaching of indulgences. But he had composed another set of ninety-seven theses seven weeks earlier, in which he clearly set forth the essential differences between his teaching and the traditionally accepted teaching of the Catholic Church. In these theses he asserted, among other things, that man can "desire and do only evil," that "his will is not free," that "the sole disposition for grace is predestination, eternal election by God," that "the only good law is the love of God."

Luther's theses attracted scant attention at first, for it seemed, after all, this was just another of those "monkish squabbles" so common in sixteenth-century universities. Before long, however, the theses were printed and circulated widely in monastic circles. Because they attacked such obvious and such annoying abuses in such bold language, they appealed to many good German clergymen — and some not so good. Sides began to form, and for a while it seemed that this would become a quarrel between the Augustinians and the Dominicans.

For a few years, indeed, there was reason to believe that Luther did not want to break from Rome, that this was just another healthy difference among theologians which could be debated and eventually ironed out. Luther himself protested his sincere Catholicity to the pope: "I cast myself at the feet of Your Holiness, with all that I have and all that I am. Quicken, kill, call, recall, approve, reprove, as you will." But neither Luther's peculiar mentality nor the spirit of the German princes and people was conducive to a peaceful settlement. Nor did the Catholic Church's representatives deal as capably as they might have with the new heretic.

Luther was, indeed, pushed from holding a moderate position to an extreme one in defending his original doctrine of salvation by trust alone. His debate with John Eck at Leipzig was typical of both his stubborn pride and his intellectual inconsistency, and of Eck's lack of prudence. Luther had held that a Church council was superior to the pope, for he hoped to appeal to a future council for approval of his teaching. When Eck pointed out that ecumenical councils had specifically denied this point, Luther came to insist that final authority was in Holy Scripture alone. A strong stubborn streak and an obstinate pride on Luther's part, concomitant with social and spiritual unrest in the Germanies and a bad handling of the crisis in Rome, made this monkish squabble grow into the Protestant Revolt. The debate at Leipzig in 1519 focused attention on this relatively obscure heretic. The papal bull of excommunication issued the following year made him a national German hero.

3

What sort of person was this man who had managed to become a German hero against the Roman churchmen? By disposition, by temperament, by personal equipment, he was a natural leader of men, for his was a forceful personality which few could resist on close and continuous contact. His enemies spoke of the "demoniac" power of his eyes; his followers marveled at the "divine sparkle" in them. Luther impressed people. He never argued; he never reasoned. He thundered denunciation or shouted down opposition, steamrollering his opponents, and smashing them under strong accusations or withering them with his biting, satirical wit. His coming out of seclusion to Wittenberg, for example, was impressive. Disguised as "Squire George," he had hidden at the Wartburg Castle after he had been declared an outlaw by the Edict of Worms in 1521; but when the religious situation got out of hand at his home town of Wittenberg, Luther did not hesitate to enter the village boldly, preach eight sermons on consecutive days, and overwhelm the "radicals" who were trying to snatch the leadership of the religious revolt from him. It took courage and it took bluff. Luther had both, and the people admired him for it.

He was strong, then, and forceful in a nonrational way. But he was more than that. He was courageous. When the plague came to Wittenberg and when most men who could do so fled the city, Luther stayed there to tend the sick and dying. Later, when the "English sweat" broke out in 1529, he showed the same courage by staying in the city and exposing himself to the disease. His courage and his impressiveness were those of a rugged individualist who struck blindly at his opponents, who heaped abuse on his enemies, who loved excitement, unrest, and turmoil, who never flinched from a struggle which required physical, animal bravery.

Luther was proud. This was perhaps his worst fault. Certainly it was pride that drove him further and further from Catholic teaching, and prevented him from working with Melanchthon for a formula that could be accepted by Rome. Pride, moreover, was at the bottom of his refusal to reason with either followers or opponents. *Ipse dixit* was reasoning enough for him. "*Sic volo*," he answered when asked the reason for his teaching as he did, "*sic jubeo, sit pro ratione voluntas.*"* Or again: "Whoever teaches differently than I, though he be an angel from heaven, let him be anathema." He was inordinately proud of his translation of the Bible — which was, indeed, a considerable accomplishment rendered into excellent colloquial German. But there is pompousness and perhaps not too much real conviction in his claim that "Saint Jerome and many others have made more mistakes in translation than We." Or in his insistence that "I know that I am more learned than all the universities, those sophists by the grace of God."

Luther deluded himself and he was proud of himself, but he did not thereby achieve tranquillity of mind. He was never at peace with himself or with his neighbor. He hated contemplation, and he feared the quiet. He had always to be throwing his weight about, either intellectually or physically. He loved the fury of combat, and many times he spoke eagerly of using his fist instead of prayer when the going was rough. When he advised the princes to take up arms against the monks in 1540, for example, he added: "I shall join in too, for it is right to slay the miscreants like mad dogs." He loved a rough and tumble fight; it made him forget himself. Work of any kind was, indeed, the way that Luther escaped from himself and his scruples.

In this respect, Luther had both the strong points and the weaknesses of men today. In the midst of conflict, in the public arena of controversy, and in the face of a plague he was admirably courageous. But he was deathly afraid of the dark, and silence was more than he could endure. In one of his last letters to his ex-provincial, Staupitz, he exults: "The confusion rages splendidly. It seems to me that it can be quelled only by the break of doomsday." Luther is in fine fettle here. But when he

---

* This is a typical nonclassical Latin construction of Luther's day. It can be translated: "Thus I wish it, thus I command it, simply because I will it so."

is alone he cringes in fear. He sees devils who grab him by the hair; his mind is in a turmoil, and temptations become too strong for him to stand them. Quietude, he tells us, "calls forth the worst of thoughts." His only solution is excitement, his only formula for peace with himself is distraction. He must conjure up an enemy in a hurry. His sure-fire remedy is to think of the pope and to fill himself with hatred against that man in Rome. "Then my mind is completely refreshed," he assures his listeners, "the spirit is quickened and all temptations flee."

He was an excitable, highly imaginative person, then, who was bothered all through life by lively phantoms of his own creation. Many times he "saw" the devil, sometimes in disguise and sometimes not. His bouts with the devil were physical fights to him, and they aroused in him a physical fear. He was once called upon, for example, to drive the devil out of a girl about eighteen years old. She was brought into the sacristy of the parish church at Wittenberg, and after she entered someone locked the door and mislaid the key. When Luther kicked the girl to scare the devil from her, she turned on him with a threatening eye. Luther was so terrified, according to a witness, that he was in utter despair. "He ran about," Straphylus reports, "hither and thither, seized with fright," until finally someone found the key.

Luther had none of the calmness and coolness that come with rational self-possession. Excitable, energetic, and bombastic, he emoted rather than reasoned when he pretended to be arguing his case. His answer to the attack made by the faculty of the University of Paris on his teaching was typical. Instead of replying to the attack, he denounced the faculty as "the greatest spiritual harlot under the sun and the back-door to hell." Luther was all heat and noise. Every argument was intensely personal with him, as was every doctrine. He could not disassociate a statement from the man who made it; he attacked not the man's argument but the man who argued.

As a matter of fact, Luther never tried to be consistently rational. Indeed, he refused to reason, and he was quite happy with his many contradictions and his constantly exposed inconsistencies. He took pride in not being rational like the rest of men. This weakness was, it would seem, a cause of his strength and his success. He was not a good man for society, though he was extremely sociable. He did not deal with men as a rational human being treats with other persons. He forced himself on society; he hammered it to his own pattern through his animal power alone. Instead of reasoning with his associates he battered their heads against the wall till they conformed. Bossuet, a Frenchman and a bishop in the Catholic Church, no mean orator himself, depicts Luther in a single sentence, as only a Frenchman can do, so as to account for both his surprising success and his fundamental shortcomings: "There was strength in his genius, vehemence in his speech, a lively and impetuous eloquence which carried crowds off their feet and enchanted them; extraordinary boldness when he found himself supported and applauded, together with an air of authority which made his disciples tremble before him, so that they dared not contradict him in anything big or little."

Like so many individualists in the contemporary world, Luther had a gentler and kindlier side reserved for his relatives and his intimate friends. He was — despite the stories of his calumniators — a good family man (whether he should have been a family man at all is another point) who spent his evenings at home, whose house was home to students and whose board was open to wayfarers at all times. His generosity and his compassion are well-known and well-advertised traits. He gave bountifully of what he possessed, and his heart was as easily opened as his purse. He was moved to tears by a limp violet he found in the snow; he loved the blue sky and the harvest season; he was moved by the sight of birds in the sky and by flowers in the spring.

Luther possessed virtues, then, which make men popular in the modern world. He was generous and cordial, jovial and familiar, possessed of a rough humor and the ability to tell a good story. Maritain probably gives as fair a brief summary of Luther as anyone when he states that he "was gifted with a nature at once realistic and lyrical, powerful, impulsive, brave and sad, sentimental and morbidly sensitive. Vehement as he was, there yet was in him kindness, generosity, tenderness, and, with all, unbroken pride and peevish vanity. What was lacking in him was force of intellect."

4

Luther's bent of mind was eminently practical. Concerned as he was with himself, he still had the ability to study and the keenness to know his German neighbors. In his struggle with Rome he played upon the German people as a virtuoso plays upon the harp. And the German people responded. Luther knew their weaknesses and their virtues, their peculiarities and their moods. He took advantage of them all — with such success that he was soon looked upon not as the leader of a new religion but as the German champion against pagan, corrupt, grasping Rome.

His *Address to the Christian Nobility of the German Nation* was, in the words of his friend, John Lang, a "trumpet of war that resounded throughout Germany." In this pamphlet — written in colloquial German rather than in the customary Latin — he stressed Roman abuses in the collection of revenue and insisted that Germans were losing both their money and their honor. He called upon the nobility to drive the Catholic hierarchy from the land, and he appealed to them to use the sword if necessary. This appeal to the nobles cleverly combined, perhaps not intentionally but nonetheless effectively, a play upon their strong national inferiority complex, upon their swashbuckling defense reaction, upon their anticlericalism, and most of all upon their hunger for wealth.

"Let the territorial lords dispose of them as they see fit," Luther proclaimed of the churches and monasteries in German lands. Münzer, an early follower of Luther's who broke from him later when he deserted the peasant cause, observed bitterly that Luther had "cajoled and honeyed" the nobles, and "they fully expected that by your preaching you would obtain for them Bohemian gifts of monasteries and foundations, which you now promise to the princes." For a time, there is no doubt, Luther was consciously the prophet of the Germans. After 1525, when the Peasants' Revolt split the Germanies socially, Luther took the better part and remained always the prophet of the German princes. He was an adroit political maneuverer.

His appeal to the clergy was equally successful. He offered them wives, and they wanted wives. He withdrew them from the monasteries and put them in the public square, and they wanted to live in worldly society. Erasmus could thus observe wittily: "Many speak of the Lutheran affair as a tragedy; to me it appears rather as a comedy, for the movements always terminate in a wedding." The clergy preferred comedy to tragedy, and Luther knew it well. His appeal to the German-in-the-street again was an effective combination of nationalism, resentment over ecclesiastical exactions, and the purer desire for an unadorned, evangelical religion.

All this, Luther insisted, was to be done without shocking people. The Catholic services were altered in their essential parts, but it was done, at Luther's direction, so that the common people "would never become aware of it." Luther was a practical man, and he was remarkably successful in his practical way. The core of his doctrine was itself eminently enticing. His was a religion made for men, for such men as Luther himself, and its appeal was both to the weak side of man's nature and to his innate striving for perfection. George Witzel, himself a Lutheran for a time, wrote at a later date: "Oh, what a grand doctrine that was, not to be obliged to confess any more, nor to pray, nor to fast, nor to make offerings, nor to give alms." It was a grand doctrine from the German point of view, and Luther knew how to package it and sell it.

But more than knowing how to sell it, he knew to whom to sell it. Until about 1525, Luther stressed unrestrained freedom for everyone to believe what he wanted. Each man was to be his own priest and prophet. Since man is saved by trust alone, no intermediary priesthood, no services or ritual were necessary. When he was appealing for popular support Luther could insist: "Neither the pope nor the bishop nor any other man has the right to dictate even so much as one syllable to a Christian believer, except with the latter's consent." The whole rule of faith was to be found in the Bible, he asserted, and the Bible was to be interpreted by everyone for himself, even by a "humble miller's maid, nay, by a child of nine if it has the faith."

Early in 1525 Luther thundered: "The authorities are not to hinder anyone from teaching and believing what he pleases." But in 1530, after the Anabaptists had broken from his following, he ordered that "the authorities shall hand over knaves of that ilk to their proper master, to wit, Master Hans [the hangman]." Be-

tween these two dates Luther the libertarian had sold out his
doctrine of freedom of religion to the princes in return for their
protection of his new religion. He had cut himself loose from
his radical following of the German peasantry and turned them
over to the tender mercies of the German princes. "It does not
do to pipe too much to the mob, or it will too readily lose its
head." "The ass wants to be beaten, and the mob ruled by force."
He therefore appealed to the prince to beat the peasants, to
rule them by force, to "cut and thrust, strangle and strike at
random, as if he were in the midst of mad dogs."

So although Luther made use of peasant grievances to popularize his revolt, and inadvertently aroused the poorer classes to
a rebellion that had long been cankering in their hearts, still
he did not hesitate to disavow them when their rebellion took a
radical turn. He cut himself and his revolt loose from the albatross
of social upheaval that the peasants had hung about his neck;
he allied himself to the princes and advised them that because
the peasants "rob and rave and act like infuriated dogs . . . dash
them to pieces, strangle them, and stab them, secretly or openly,
just as one is compelled to kill a mad dog." Luther staked the
success of his religious revolt on the princes, and events proved
how shrewd a choice he had made. Wyclif, Hus, and other of
his predecessors had identified themselves with discontented
peasants, and they had been cut down "like mad dogs." Luther
did not let a compassionate heart lead him to a similar fate.

Such a change of front did not bother Luther, for he never
believed in consistency. He did, however, back up his change
with biblical support. "Christ does not wish to abolish serfdom,"
he argued. "What cares He how the lords or princes rule?" Moreover, he wrote, one should remember that "it is God who hangs,
quarters, decapitates, slaughters, and makes war." Thus he had
given full power to the princes and denied liberty to the peasants
who first followed him. Even freedom of religion was denied to
all but the princes. "Only one kind of doctrine may be preached
in any one place," was Luther's statement of the *cuius regio eius
religio* [the ruler chooses the religion] principle long before it
was formally adopted at the Peace of Augsburg in 1555. Thus
had Luther introduced the elements of subjective individualism
and religious liberalism into religion only to deny them in favor

of the absolute prince who now becomes pope as well as secular despot. By doing so, however, he secured the permanency of his new religion.

5

Lutheran doctrine, Luther's direct contribution toward making the modern mind, was intensely personal. It was formulated to satisfy Martin Luther; it was preached to keep him happy. This subjective strain in religion remains the essence of most religion in the Western World today. Religion thus is a morale builder; its purpose is to fill some sort of craving in the human spirit. If it tastes good spiritually, if it is palatable and it satisfies, then it is rated good. Now Luther had a peculiar mentality to satisfy; his spiritual hunger was not that of a normal man. His contribution to our mentality is consequently one that tends to make the neurotic a normal rather than an abnormal man; it makes for unhealthy introspection and nonsensical self-analysis; it makes for wishful thinking and the creation of beliefs to satisfy our mental quirks rather than to correspond to objective reality.

It is because he created doctrine piecemeal to satisfy himself that Luther was essentially inconsistent. Because his doctrine flows from his personal problems and his solution for them, it is necessary to remember the kind of man he was in order to grasp the true meaning of his doctrine. For one must credit him with having harmonized in his own peculiar mind contrary and even contradictory elements. Although he could never utter the petition "Hallowed be Thy name," without adding "Accursed, damned, disgraced shall be the name of all papists," he could still say of himself — and mean it — : "I maintain a kindly, friendly, peaceable, and Christian heart towards everybody." Again, when he thought he was about to die and therefore had every reason to be honest with himself, he prayed thus: "O God, Thou knowest that I have taught Thy Word faithfully and zealously. . . . I die in hatred of the pope." He could cry for princes to come forth with the sword to cut up the peasants "like mad dogs," and still he could insist he loved all men as his brothers. Luther believed this; he deluded himself more successfully, it would seem, than a twentieth-century millionaire who pleads inability to pay living wages.

The works of Luther are full of strong statements and moving passages, but they are also full of contradictions with which Luther seems quite content. When he is faced with a difficult problem that he cannot solve by a simple declaration, he finds it more agreeable to flee from the problem than to tackle it. When he found the problem of deciding on marriage cases too complicated, he threw up the intellectual — and doctrinal — sponge. "I have cast it from me," he wrote, "and have written to several persons that, in the name of all the devils, they should do as they see fit." At the same time, nevertheless, he insists that those who inveigh against the marriage of priests and nuns are "public assassins, robbers, traitors, liars and miscreants." Again, he dismisses arguments against his teaching on salvation by trust alone thus: "I would not answer such asses, nor reply to their vain, monotonous babbling about the word *sola,* otherwise than to say: Luther will have it so and says so, he is a doctor superior to all other doctors in popedom. Thus shall it be."

Erasmus, who at first hailed Luther as a champion of light, soon rejected him for his attack on man's mind and freedom of the will. Of Luther he wrote: "The world will believe that Martin has become demented through hatred, or that he suffers from some other mental disorder, or is dominated by an evil spirit." Nor was Erasmus the only one to condemn Luther for his lack of logical reasoning. John Cochlaeus, one of the leading defenders of the Catholic position, subtitled his *Seven-Headed Luther,* "Luther everywhere in contradiction with himself." As a matter of fact, Luther made no attempt to be logical or even rational in his writing. He summed up his attitude toward the rational approach in this statement: "No good work happens as the result of one's own wisdom; but everything must happen in a stupor."

Now there have been many persons — many, like Luther, with doctor's degrees — who were happily nonrational. But there are few, indeed, who have made as vicious an attack on reason as did this first maker of the modern mind. All philosophers were anathema to him. He calls Aristotle an "urchin who must be put in the pig-sty or donkey's stable"; the Sorbonne is "that mother of all errors"; the theologians of Louvain are "coarse donkeys, cursed sows, bellies of blasphemers, epicurean swine, heretics and idolators, putrid puddles, the cursed broth of hell." Not only philosophers, but philosophy itself is viciously attacked by Luther. In 1536 he wrote: "I shall have to chop off the head of philosophy." Again: "One should learn philosophy only as one learns witchcraft, that is to destroy it."

Luther carries his assault to reason itself by attacking man's very mind. "Reason," he wrote, "is contrary to faith. . . . In believers it should be killed and buried." He condemns reason more specifically because he thinks it "is the devil's handmaid and does nothing but blaspheme and dishonor all that God says or does." All through his mature life he dealt his heaviest blows at man's reason, but he found it hard to overcome, as he complains in his commentary on the Epistle to the Galatians: "Alas, in this life reason is never completely destroyed." But he fought it furiously to the very end. In one of his last sermons he warned his listeners of the arbitrary interpretation of Holy Scripture by "that prostitute, human reason."

Thus Luther's first permanent contribution toward the making of the modern mind was an attack on the mind itself, on reason, "the devil's greatest whore."

6

The key doctrine of Luther's theology is the doctrine of trust in Christ, the importance of which Luther fully realized. "It is not allowed," he proclaimed, "either to deviate from, or to surrender this article, even though heaven and earth should fall. Everything is founded upon this article, which we teach and by which we live in defiance of the pope, the devil, and the world." Luther's new theology of trust was made for man. A human desire for spiritual security was its point of departure; man's spiritual satisfaction was its purpose. Man remains supreme within its system, moreover, for it is a homocentric rather than a theocentric religion. Man, whose worldly supremacy had been reasserted by the Renaissance, is given spiritual sovereignty over his soul and the very heavens by the Lutheran system. By blind trust he overcomes even God. "The Christian," Luther wrote, "becomes by faith so exalted above all things that he is made spiritual lord of all; for there is nothing that can hinder his being saved. He may snap his fingers at the devil, and need no longer tremble before the wrath of God."

In the new religion, indeed, everyone becomes his own priest and prophet. Each man's revelation from God is to be found in the Bible; each is empowered to interpret the word of God as he feels fit. "We are not only kings and the freest of all men," is the way Luther put it, "but also priests forever, a dignity far higher than kingship, because by that priesthood we are worthy to appear before God, to pray for others, and to teach one another mutually the things which are of God." Again: "If we all are priests, how then shall we not have the right to discriminate and judge what is right or wrong in faith?"

That individualism, which is to remain a principal element of modern life down till yesterday, is now projected by Luther into the religious field. Before his day it had been asserted culturally, socially, and intellectually. After him individualism comes to pervade all fields of thought and endeavor in the Western World. That superindividualist, Carlyle, saw the part Luther played in making inevitable Carlyle's world of Heroes or superindividuals. "In all this wild revolutionary work, from Protestantism downwards," he wrote, "I see the blessedest result preparing itself: not abolition of Hero-worship, but rather what I would call a whole world of Heroes." Luther makes the Hero not only self-sufficient intellectually and socially, but also religiously. He ushers in the age of theological rugged individualism.

From this individualism came, in Luther's lifetime, sorry and unforeseen consequences. Luther had believed that if man trusted in Christ's merits he would live by Christian principles. Although his *pecca fortiter et crede firmius* was not an encouragement simply to sin boldly, nevertheless it was so understood by many of his followers. If salvation is to be achieved solely by trust in Christ's merits, if good works have nothing to do with sanctification, why then should not one have his religious cake and eat it too? Luther had propounded the theory that trust was sufficient for salvation, and he had uttered many phrases that could be interpreted as encouraging license in worldly affairs. In cities and principalities which accepted Lutheranism there was generally a period of moral turbulence — so much so that

Luther came in later life to stress authority more and more. He insisted on doctrinal uniformity, and he insisted on living according to the Gospel. But because he had destroyed religious authority he had to appeal to the prince to end religious anarchy and moral chaos. Man was to live according to Lutheran standards under his system, not because they were objectively good or bad, but because the prince so decreed.

Most important among his contributions to modern mentality was Luther's pessimistic view of man. His picture of man is essentially the same as Hobbes', or Machiavelli's, or Hitler's. Man is at bottom wicked, according to Luther; he is sinful to the marrow of his bones. Not only is he weak and inclined to vice, as the Catholic theologians of the time held, but according to Luther he is utterly depraved, thoroughly vicious. He can "desire and do only evil." In man, says Luther, "the spiritual powers have been not only corrupted by sin, but absolutely destroyed; so that there is now nothing in them but a depraved reason and a will that is the enemy and opponent of God, whose only thought is war against God."

If man can do only evil, if "the just man sins in every good work," then the distinction between good and evil is meaningless. Then there is no reason for not following Luther's often repeated advice: "Seek out the society of your boon companions, drink, play, talk bawdy, and amuse yourself." Luther had reason for being pessimistic about this creature Man. He had degraded his reason and had freed the animal in him. And he had denied him free will. His famous analogy on will was given to the world in these words: "The human will stands like a saddle-horse between the two [God and the devil]. If God mounts into the saddle, man wills and goes forward as God wills. . . . But if the devil is the horseman then man wills and acts as the devil wills. He has no power to run to one or the other of the two riders and offer himself to him, but the riders fight to obtain possession of the animal."

Thus the animal in man is irresponsible for his so-called human actions; responsibility can attach only to whichever rider is in the saddle — God or the devil. And if you have trust in God, then He is in the saddle. Whatever you do is good, not through the animal merit of the depraved man-horse, but through the

merit of the God-rider. The great drama of salvation is played
out between God and the devil. Men are only passive instruments, the *loci* of the drama; they are not *personae dramatis*.

7

Debasing man, the new Lutheran religion blessed and glorified the state. John Neville Figgis, the late eminent British
authority in the history of political thought, goes so far as to
claim that "the supreme achievement of the Reformation is the
modern state." Luther plays a major role in that achievement.
His original intention could hardly have been to help create
absolute rule, but he was pre-eminently an opportunist, and he
did not hesitate to adapt his political theorizing to the necessities
of the moment. He needed the support of German princes to
make his revolt succeed; moreover, he was fearful of the excesses
to which his early doctrine of liberty had been carried by people
like Münzer and Stübner. So he invoked the protection of the
secular arm — not only to preserve his gains up till about 1525,
but also as an inducement for other princes to adopt the Lutheran
religion.

"We must firmly establish secular law and the sword," he
therefore wrote, "that no one may doubt that it is in the world
by God's will and ordinance." The perfect Christian, it is true,
would be good without the sword hanging over his head. But
there are no perfect Christians; man is essentially bad. "Since,
however, no one is by nature Christian or pious, but everyone
sinful and evil, God places the restraints of the law upon them
all, so that they may not dare give rein to their desires and
commit outward, wicked deeds." Everyone, therefore, is subject
to secular rule. Of course only anarchists have ever denied this,
but few have gone as far as Luther in extolling the sword and
debasing the man over whose head it hangs. "Stern, hard civil
rule is necessary in this world," he insisted. "No one need think
that the world can be ruled without blood. The civil sword shall
and must be red and bloody."

His little work *On Secular Authority*, written in 1523, remained
a source of satisfaction to him all through life. "I would fain
boast," he said later, "that, since the age of the Apostles, the

secular sword and authority have never been described so clearly or praised so splendidly, as by me." Luther insisted continually and vehemently on passive obedience to the secular prince. "There are no better works than to obey and serve all those who are set over us as superiors. For this reason also disobedience is a greater sin than murder, unchastity, theft, and dishonesty, and all that these may include." Even injustice must be suffered passively if it comes from the prince. "It is in no wise proper for anyone who would be a Christian to set himself up against his government, whether it act justly or unjustly." "A Christian," indeed, "ought to be ready to suffer violence and injustice, more particularly from his own ruler." Under no condition, then, may the prince be resisted or disobeyed.

Luther did not content himself with merely stating the principle of passive obedience. He made it abundantly clear that he contemned the people and revered the prince. Luther was pragmatic, and the princes held the sword to which the masses only aspired; the princes, moreover, knew how to use the sword, whereas the masses hardly knew how to use a plowshare. In his *Sincere Exhortation to all Christians to Guard Against Rebellion,* Luther asserted that the authorities alone, and not *Herr Omnes* had the right to enforce the truths of the Gospel. For *Herr Omnes* — the mob — Luther has nothing but contempt. "The princes of this world are gods, the common people are Satan. . . . I would rather suffer a prince doing wrong than a people doing right."

Luther was consistent in glorifying the prince and in justifying his every action. When the peasants revolted he cursed them thus: "You powerless, coarse peasants and asses, would that you were blasted by lightning!" He insisted, moreover, that it would be well if serfdom and slavery were revived. To the princes he appealed for strong measures with the sword. "Let him who is able, in whatsoever manner he can, cut and thrust, strangle and strike at random, as if he were in the midst of mad dogs." This was literally a consistent stand for him to take; it was the reverse side of his low estimate of depraved man's inherent viciousness. Man had been deprived of his free will, and his reason was only "the devil's greatest whore." He was only a special kind of animal, who was to be under the absolute prince and ruled like a "mad dog." Man could not consistently claim rights against the prince; he could only assert superior force. There remained no ground for resisting the whim of the absolute prince.

Luther allotted more and more specific functions to the rulers of his day, and thus he made significant contributions toward building the modern state in actuality as well as justifying it in theory. Church properties and the functions attendant upon them were assigned by Luther to the princes. Among these the most important were the control of education and the promotion and regulation of religious worship. Other less important functions were turned over to the prince, such as marriage, which Luther claimed as "a purely temporal matter, such as raiment and food, house and courtyard, subject to secular authority." All these functions strengthened the prince's control over his subjects, emasculating education and religion, the two strongest remaining fields of independent human endeavor not then under secular authority. Luther denied the individual, as a man, the right to stand up against the prince; he further weakened opposition to absolutism by putting education and religion in the prince's hand.

In Luther's day the national state was in formation throughout Western Europe; national feeling had been aroused to demand that state boundaries coincide with national divisions. Luther consistently advocated absolute control of *Herr Omnes* by the princes, but though he appealed to German national sentiment he did not advocate a national German state. Such a national state would at that time have had to coalesce under the aegis of the Hapsburg house — and the Hapsburgs were Catholic. Luther therefore appealed vaguely to German national sentiment without advocating the formation of a national German state.

One strong nationalist note running consistently through his utterances after the first few years was Luther's violent antisemitism. Originally he had wished to win the Jews over to his cause, but when he failed to convert them he turned on them with terrible blasts of scorching language. Nazis, incidentally — and erroneously — looked to Luther as a glorious German predecessor of Nazi antisemitism. But Luther's attack on the Jews was, like that of medieval Catholics, based more on religious than on racial grounds. Its practical effects, however, were nationalistic. With Luther's approval, John Frederick expelled the Jews from

Electoral Saxony in 1536. From that time on, Luther's attacks were frequent and violent, the best known perhaps being his *Epistle Against the Sabbatarians,* the tracts *On the Jews and Their Lies,* and *On the Last Words of David.* His last sermon, preached at Eisleben shortly before his death, contained an attack on the Jews in which he advised: "You rulers ought not to tolerate, but to expel them."

8

The results of the Lutheran movement on history and on the modern mind proceeded independently of Luther's desires. Although these results were not what he envisaged, nor were they due to him alone, they occurred as they did principally because of the tone Luther gave to the Protestant revolt and the religious sanction he put upon movements already under way. These results can be summarized in this fashion:

1. European unity, already wearing thin, was precariously weakened. It is perhaps too much to say, with many European historians, that it was destroyed. A consciousness of some kind of watery unity will remain among Europeans; they will continue to know that they hold certain common possessions which are theirs alone and which therefore distinguish them from non-Europeans. But religion is no longer one of those possessions, whereas formerly it was perhaps the most vital of them all. Divisions among the various Christian religions led to a period of the bitterest and bloodiest warfare Europe knew till recent years — the period of the religious wars.

The Protestant revolt, then, inaugurated by Luther and carried on by many others, divided Europe into religious segments which generally coincided with national boundaries. National divisions became deeper and harder to span. This new religious division added to the fierceness and bitterness of the wars between the European nations. The Spaniard could now kill a Dutchman with greater gusto — for he was a heretic as well as a rebel. The Spaniard was now doing God's work, as well as the Hapsburgs'. So it was with the Englishman and the Swede and the Dutchman and the others. They were all fighting against blasphemers and heretics in the first place — and incidentally against national enemies. It is easier to fight a war for theological reasons than for economic or dynastic interests. It makes more sense. And it makes the warfare more terrible, more inhuman, bloodier. Hatreds were therefore increased by the religious divisions within Europe, and another note of difference between national groups was added to an already long list. Englishmen were now Anglican as well as English; Spaniards were papist as well as Spanish; Swedes were Lutheran as well as Swedish.

2. Although Luther was not himself an individualist, he furthered that attitude of individualism which was to pervade the history of the Western World till recently. Luther's creed was religious individualism, for it did away with an intermediary priesthood, with a hierarchical organization in the church, with a sacramental system, with a body of the faithful in communion with each other and with those already saved. It put each man completely on his own resources and left him to achieve his own salvation by a simple act of trust; it left each man free to decide what is a matter of faith and what is heresy. He need only read the Bible and be his own infallible interpreter. Each man stands, in the field of religion, isolated from his fellow men and in direct touch, through trust, with God. Luther cut man loose from spiritual and religious restraints, as the Renaissance had cut him loose from social restraints.

3. Luther's attack on reason had lasting results. Although, as he himself complained, "in this life reason is never completely destroyed," nevertheless there is a strong anti-intellectual undertone throughout modern history. Luther's distrust of human reason will crop out time and time again. Occasionally even his hatred of the mind will come to the surface. A direct connection with modern subjectivism can easily be traced to Luther's pen. Voluntarism, wishful thinking, thinking with your blood, and sentimentalism are all legitimate progeny of Luther's attack on reason, though they couple through the generations with many strange mates. But Luther's paternity cannot be denied.

In one way Luther contradicted a development of the preceding age. Most men of the Renaissance had put man, as a human being, on a pedestal. They had exalted human reason, and they had glorified human freedom. They had insisted that man was naturally good, that he was capable of accomplishing untold wonders through the use of his natural faculties. They had made the world a place of wonderful adventure where the brave and the ruthless could cut their way through the forests — and through other men — to arrive at the desired goal of immortal fame in the memory of posterity. They had gone to an extreme in stressing man's innate goodness and his self-sufficiency. Luther answered by going to the opposite extreme in stressing man's depravity. The Renaissance exalted the intellect, Luther attacked it as vicious; the Renaissance glorified free will, Luther flatly denied it; the Renaissance praised wordly human endeavor, Luther asserted that all human actions are essentially vicious, that "the just man sins in every good work." Here he agreed with and strengthened the case of the pessimistic minority group who, like Machiavelli, had a low opinion of man.

4. Lutheranism was the first distinctly modern religion, the first step toward what religion is today. For Luther's religion was built around man's desire for subjective spiritual security. Its immediate aim was to assure man of his salvation and thus to put his mind at ease. From this revolutionary, subjective approach to religious doctrine it is not too long a step to make religion nothing but a morale builder, with doctrine accepted or rejected according to the worshiper's spiritual constitution. He accepts what agrees with him, what soothes him and makes him happy. The rest he ignores — or denies, if that makes him happier.

5. Luther's contribution toward the building and the justifying of the absolute state is large. He glorified the prince and, as prince, blessed his every action, just or unjust. He took from under man the platform on which he had stood as a human person and on the basis of which he could defy unjust aggression by the state. In theory Luther insisted on passive obedience and left man isolated and naked before secular authority; in practice he handed over to the prince many functions formerly reserved to the individual or the church or the local community. He both helped build the modern state and assisted the modern prince in becoming an absolute ruler.

6. Finally, Luther's contribution toward building modern capitalistic society is not negligible. His specifically economic teaching is only incidental to his principal work, and what there

is of it is reactionary rather than progressive. Luther, says R. H. Tawney, "is like a savage introduced to a dynamo or a steam-engine" when he turns to the complexities of finance or of foreign trade. Certainly in emotional tirades he denounced the taking of interest; he inveighed vehemently against the commercial developments of the previous two centuries and advocated a return to medieval economic arrangements.

But Luther's belief in salvation by trust alone, his writing off of good works as unrelated to salvation had staggering social and economic consequences. Luther separated heaven and earth by means of his revolutionary religious doctrine. He put the soul of a trusting man into heaven and left the body free for unlimited, religiously uncontrolled activity on earth. It was only natural for those who could not help themselves to heaven by good works to turn their energy into activity that would be rewarded here on earth. Man's energy formerly had been divided between earning salvation and earning a livelihood. Now it is to be directed into the single channel of worldly activity. Tawney can therefore well assert: "Monasticism was, so to speak, secularized; all men stood henceforward on the same footing towards God; and that advance, which contained the germ of all subsequent revolutions, was so enormous that all else seems insignificant."

Luther had removed the religious sanction from the regulations that governed economic activity. He had, in his way, removed the moral stigma formerly attached to money-making and had sprinkled holy water on the countinghouse. That is why Max Weber observes that, "like a ghost of its former religious content, the thought of *Berufspflicht* haunts our lives." It was not so much Luther as Calvin, however, who was destined to be the businessman's preacher. Luther, after all, was of peasant stock; Calvin came from the bourgeoisie and was predisposed to take their point of view. Calvin was prepared to preach to those who were soon to take over the earth — the middle class.

III
CALVIN

AND THE GOOD SHALL PROSPER

JOHN CALVIN was born in 1509, two years after Luther had
been ordained an Augustinian monk. He was eight years old
when Luther posted his theses on the church door at Wittenberg,
and by the time Calvin was ready to attend the universities
of Orleans and Bourges some professors in both schools had
espoused Luther's teaching. When Calvin experienced his "conversion" in 1533, the success of the Lutheran movement had
been assured, Zwingli and various Anabaptist groups had already
followed in Luther's path, and the Protestant movement was
approaching a swell it never again reached in European history.

Calvin entered the Protestant ranks a relatively unknown
youth of twenty-four, but when he died thirty-one years later
he had stamped his personal mark on the biggest and most important division in the Protestant ranks. Although Calvin bor-
rowed much from his German predecessor, the finished product
of his Reformed Christianity had a completely different tone

and flavor to it. Both Luther and Calvin claimed to offer a way of salvation outside the Catholic Church; both placed supreme authority in the Bible and made a priesthood unnecessary; both looked upon man as depraved and invoked the power of the state to keep him orderly and passive. The Lutheran God was a loving and forgiving God who overlooked man's weakness and receded into the background to make room for His sinful creature. But where Luther's God served man, Calvin's God tyrannized over him. Calvin's God was an absolute, arbitrary sovereign who had no love for his wicked creatures. Man was created, indeed, to glorify and exalt God by his suffering in this life and hereafter. Luther's is a God of mercy, Calvin's a God of strict justice.

Personally Calvin and Luther had even less in common than they did doctrinally. Luther was capable of stirring up rebellion, but not of leading his followers to victory; Calvin was not a rebel by nature, but when once rebellion was under way he was able to sustain it, invigorate it, and lead it to victory. Luther was wild, hot, impetuous; Calvin was cold, calculating, self-disciplined. Luther tells us how he felt his blood boil; Calvin's blood was cold as a mountain rivulet. But he did say that he felt bile take possession of himself. Luther worried incessantly about his own salvation, for he felt sinful to the marrow of his bones, and so he made trust the key doctrine of his religion; Calvin righteously assured himself that he was predestined to salvation, and he organized, logically and systematically, a terrifyingly strict moral code for such Elect as himself.

Lutheranism and Calvinism were born in different settings, and neither religion completely outgrew its birthmarks. Lutheranism began as a clerical revolt, a rebellion of priests against their pope in Rome, whereas Calvinism was a layman's revolution. It produced a lawyer's religion characterized by its narrow legalism. Lutheranism was not, at least with Luther, a consistent body of doctrine; it was rather a curious collection of beliefs and practices which appealed personally to its creator. Calvinism, on the other hand, was a thoroughly systematic body of doctrine that gave satisfaction to man's intellect rather than his passion. One who agrees with Calvin's three or four basic doctrines is reasonably forced to agree intellectually with his logically harsh conclusions, even though instinctively one rebels against them.

Although the difference between Calvinism and Lutheranism are marked, and each group cordially hated the other — Lutherans for a long time referred to Calvinists as "Christian Turks" — yet the two movements supplemented and sustained each other in an age when Luther's revolt alone might have collapsed or disintegrated. At a time when Lutherans were content to go on the defensive before a revived Catholicism, Calvin's followers became militantly aggressive. It was Calvin who forged a race of crusaders with souls of steel, the Ironsides of the Protestant movement; it was Calvin who gave Protestantism the tremendous energy to carry on successfully and to win over for his doctrine the most prosperous sections of European society.

There is, indeed, more of John Calvin in the contemporary mind than there is of any other one figure. We are not as conscious of Calvin as we are of Marx or Freud, but his influence, watered down through the centuries as it is, has permeated our very being. Modern man may consciously wear Marxian or Freudian clothes; he is Calvinistic in his bones and blood.

It is generally agreed that until fifty years ago the modern mind was fundamentally puritan — and puritanism is one aspect of Calvinism; but it is not generally appreciated that the strong reaction to puritanism during these last two generations transfers many old puritan traits into new channels. It is not generally appreciated that Lenin was the puritan of the Russian revolution, as Robespierre was of the French revolution and Cromwell of the English. It is not generally appreciated that the puritan conscience, or at least its heritage, persists in most parts of Europe and here in America. It is not generally appreciated that Wall Street, and the awe in which we hold it, are logical conclusions from Calvinism. The prestige of porcelain bathtubs, the luster of tiled kitchens, the appeal of shiny linoleum, the hushed, templelike atmosphere of the average bank, the aphorism that "cleanliness is next to godliness" all stem historically from John Calvin. Local clean-up campaigns, village reformers and county judges, prohibitionists and Boston book indexes are all influenced more by John Calvin than by any other maker of the modern mind. Calvin's spiritual children, indeed, made the modern world what it is today.

Calvin, of course, was only partly a puritan. There have always been puritans of different hues and varying strictnesses, and there would be puritans today had Calvin never existed. But Calvin justified the puritan attitude toward life. He apotheosized it so that, whereas puritans were formerly considered cranks, after Calvin they were the respected people of the community. Calvin harnessed the puritan spirit and set it about its work of making money with religious zeal and of forcing everyone to conform to its standards. So although there would have been puritans throughout modern history even if there had been no Calvin, it remains that he is responsible for the form puritanism took since his day — and for the energy it possessed. The puritan spirit, of course, is found in purest form among those Protestants who trace their ancestry directly to Geneva. But it is by no means confined to them. It has seeped into all religions in varying degrees. It long set the standards of respectability to which Catholics, Jews, and atheists, as well as Protestants, had to conform. It permeated Western society, and until recent years the puritan extract flavored everything respected people touched.

For all of this Calvin is neither solely nor directly responsible. He brewed up spirits in the sixteenth century which his successors could not control, spirits that got out of hand and have plagued Western people ever since. Calvin did not know the form that these spirits would take, nor could he realize the superhuman strength they would possess. He did not know that in his day there were at work political, social, and economic factors whose growth his doctrine would aid, and whose success would pervert many of his teachings. Calvin's religious doctrines fitted in perfectly with the desires and the hatreds of the rising bourgeoisie, and the two of them, the Calvinist spirit and the middle class, marched through history arm in arm, leading and sustaining, strengthening and justifying each other.

We must therefore distinguish Calvin's doctrine from the conclusions to which it was pushed by later Calvinists. For Calvin would never be at home on Wall Street. He would certainly disown Benjamin Franklin and the Wesley brothers and all those Calvinist offspring of the seventeenth and eighteenth centuries. But these second-generation descendants — Methodism, Baptistism, and the like — are all his legitimate grandchildren, and Calvin's disapproval of them does not absolve him from paternal responsibility.

Calvin's concept of God, plus the doctrine of election, plus the puritan conscience, made a dynamic mixture that was to impel the Ironsides of the Protestant movement with awesome energy. Because there were some basic paradoxes in Calvin's body of thought, however, his followers could logically drive in divers directions without renouncing their Calvinistic paternity. Calvin insisted, for example, upon passive obedience to all rulers, good or bad. But his doctrine of the Elect, aristocratic in his own hands, worked through modern history as the yeast of democracy. For the Elect stood self-righteously before "wicked" kings and, with the assurance of God's approval, overthrew them in England, in Scotland, in America, and in France. Even while asserting the divine right of established government, Calvin knocked the props out from under the king when he wrote: "Earthly princes lay aside all their power when they rise up against God, and are unworthy to be reckoned in the number of mankind. We ought rather to spit on their heads than to obey them when they are so restive and wish to rob God of his rights." And no puritan ever doubted that the king he opposed had risen up against God.

So it worked out in other respects. Calvin insisted more rigidly than anyone before him on the doctrine of predestination, teaching that the Elect could not resist God's saving grace, nor could the reprobate escape eternal damnation. He denied freedom of the will in unmistakable terms. No religious group in history, however, has held men as strictly accountable for their acts as have the Calvinists. Calvin's critics who revel in this inconsistency do not realize that he was logically following out the consequences of another of his basic doctrines — that man's sole purpose in life is to glorify God by living according to the divine norms found in the Bible. Man could be held strictly accountable for doing God's bidding whether he had free will or not. Indeed, Calvin does not seem to have considered the reconciliation of moral responsibility with predetermined activity a problem at all.

Calvin's insistence on diligent labor at one's calling likewise developed, logically enough when you remember man's weak

nature, into a justification of vices Calvin himself vehemently
denounced. He insisted, for example, on incessant work as a
means of avoiding temptation, and most of all as a way of
glorifying God. But in the minds of his successors hard work
became an end in itself, and the wealth which it earned was
taken as God's approval of industriousness. Prosperity and virtue
became interchangeable terms — the former was the exterior sign
of the latter's dwelling within. Such vices as avarice and fraud,
which Calvin warned his disciples to avoid, were soon rational-
ized into virtues. Thus, for example, the *caveat emptor* attitude
can be traced indirectly to Calvin, though he would have denounced its iniquity. Thus, too, it is no accident that Calvinist
groups in this country have always been more vigorous advocates
of prohibition than of a living wage.

In her well-balanced biography of John Calvin, Georgia Harkness sums up the way that Calvin's teaching came to be perverted within a century — but logically perverted, and Calvin
cannot be completely freed of what his followers said. "Had
Calvin's followers heeded all his words about the unrighteousness
of exploitation and the moral dangers of prosperity, Calvinism
might have been a deterrent, rather than a promoter, of the
capitalistic spirit. His injunctions to industry, frugality and docil-
ity were heeded; his warnings against avarice were forgotten.
The explanation lies in the almost irresistible power of economic
forces and in the tendencies of human nature. Competition,
acquisitiveness, and social conservatism reinforced the one set
of teachings, nullified the other."

Had Calvin been interested only in making Geneva the
civitas dei of this world, historians could dismiss him in a
paragraph. But he was interested in making the entire Christian
world conform to his reformed teaching. Particularly did he
want to win over his native France, where he sent hundreds of
missionaries to spread his gospel. Geneva became the training
center for thousands of reformed ministers who fanned out from
"the Protestant Rome" into all the countries of Europe, sometimes
to suffer humiliations and martyrdom, sometimes to win smashing victory, sometimes only to stir up bloody rebellion that
ended in a religious stalemate.

Scotland was won over to Calvin's reformed religion by John

Knox, who studied at Geneva and imported Genevan theology and morality into Scotland as Presbyterianism. The Netherlands became another center of pure Calvinism, when Genevan religious belief and practices were tied in with the Hollanders' revolt from Catholic Spain in the latter sixteenth century. The Presbyterian and the Dutch Reformed religions have remained two of the least adulterated expressions of Calvinism in modern times.

But Calvin's teaching was adopted by dissenting groups in almost every country of Europe. It spread to England under various headings — Puritan, Congregationalist, Independent, Separatist — and it spread among a strong, wealthy minority in France who were known as Huguenots. It spread into Germany, along the Rhine chiefly, and even off into Hungary, Transylvania, and into a few places in northern Italy. Most important, it spread among the people and among the classes that were to dominate European history from Calvin's day down till yesterday. Finally, it spread to America with the New England colonists, and it traveled with them westward across the country to Oregon.

Indirectly Calvin influenced also religious groups in Europe. Unlike Lutheranism, which was confined chiefly to sections of Germany and to the Scandinavian countries, Calvin's was a religion for export, and it even sold many of its ideas and attitudes to various religious groups. In fact the most rigid of French Catholics, the Jansenists, have indeed been called by some Catholic historians "Calvinist heretics within the Church." Catholics in any country where there was a numerous Calvinist group, as in England, in France, or in this country, rejected Calvin's theology but were liable to be influenced by his morality. So it was with other religions. Anglicans refused to submit formally to puritan reform, but the puritan morality worked its way into their life. And most of the later Protestant groups, such as Methodists, Quakers, and Baptists, accepted Calvin's moral code, no matter what theology they happened to adopt.

Socially, Calvin's ideas appealed chiefly to the commercial class. It is not inaccurate to say that Calvinism followed the trade routes as it spread through Europe and America — to commercial Holland, along the Rhine River, in the parts of England around London and other port towns, to New England, to the western parts of France. It never appealed to the old nobility, but they became a diminishing force in European affairs, whereas the middle class grew increasingly important with the turn of each decade and the success of each revolution. Nor did it appeal so much to the peasantry and the artisan class in the cities, but through the bourgeoisie it set the standards to which all respectable, ambitious artisans or peasants who hoped to make a million dollars quite naturally conformed. Such adages as "Time is money," "A penny saved is a penny earned," "The standing pool is prone to putrefaction" were all pounded into the poor boy's head, and he came to live by them. Horatio Alger stories are the logical conclusion of Calvin's model experiment in Geneva. Thus by education and propaganda did the Calvinistic middle class push its ideas, like leaven, through the masses of Western men.

Only a few nations, and a single class, were immune to Calvin's puritanism. And these people were unimportant in modern history — the Italians, who generally had too fine a sense of proportion to accept puritan standards; the old nobility, to whom the new morality made neither an economic nor an aesthetic appeal; most inhabitants of the Balkan peninsula, who were long immune to almost everything Western. These were the people who went on living as though there had never been a Calvin; and these were the people who had almost nothing to do with making modern history or creating the modern mind.

1

What kind of man was John Calvin? What sort of personality did he stamp upon the modern mind? A fair estimate of Calvin the man is doubly hard to make, for, in the first place, until recently his biographers have been either lavish in their adulation or unfairly harsh in their condemnation; and in the second place, Calvin was himself such a combination of apparent pettiness and seeming selflessness that the biographer is given some factual data for any conclusion he wishes to reach. Harkness therefore well observes that "no man . . . has been more admired and ridiculed, loved and hated, blessed and cursed."

There can be no doubt that Calvin frequently appeared

miserably petty. Typical of this pettiness was his refusal to mount the pulpit until the Genevan council punished a man who, when tipsy in a tavern, spoke against him. Even when Ameaux, upon sobering up, offered to apologize and retract his statements, Calvin remained adamant. Ameaux must suffer. Again he appears small in insisting on Gruet's death, largely upon the evidence of the latter's having written "all nonsense" in the margin of one of Calvin's books. And it seems petty for him to will his nephews, Samuel and John, 400 gold pieces each and his nieces, Anna, Susanna, and Dorothy, 300 apiece, while cutting their brother David off with only 25 gold pieces "in reprehension of his juvenile levity and petulance."

But at the same time Calvin was not at all selfish. He gave unstintingly of his time to those who asked his aid, and he required nothing in return. He could have amassed great wealth; he could have acquired even greater power than he did. But he seems to have devoted himself selflessly to what he considered his life's work. In him there was, indeed, combined a meanness of character with a selfless devotion to duty, a smallness and a generosity that would reflect on the ordinary man's character if he possessed them. But in Calvin it was different. And this must be appreciated if we are to do him justice.

This apparent contradiction in Calvin's character dissolves when you remember that Calvin always insisted on God's arbitrary sovereignty and on man's essential depravity; that he identified his word with God's, so that one who wrote "all nonsense" in the margin of his book had slapped God in the face; finally, that man's sole purpose is to glorify God by living according to His rule, which is Calvin's rule. Sleeping while Calvin preached was closing one's mind to God; smiling during Calvin's sermon was snickering in God's face.

Calvin's simple identification of himself with God, and the opposition with the devil, explains away his apparent meanness. But it is dangerous business. It relieves Calvin of mere pettiness, but it leaves him self-righteously intolerant. It gave the puritans an amazing energy to do what they wished, for their will was God's will, and they were God's chosen agents here on earth. Cromwell, for example, never doubted that he was glorifying God in the needless massacre of the Irish at Drogheda, as Calvin never doubted that he was justified in using questionable evidence to obtain Servetus' death for heresy.

Yet through all this there runs in Calvin an undeniable, though hard, sincerity. All he wrote and all he did indicate that Calvin was sincerely convinced of his God-given commission to reform the world, to tell men how to glorify God on earth, to create a model community in Geneva where God's rule would be ruthlessly enforced by the law and the sword. There is no streak of mercy in Calvin's stewardship. He was harsh, cold, unmerciful with all men, himself included. He was unmercifully stern with others, whom he drove as befitted his tyrannical God's prosecuting attorney; but he was equally harsh with himself, for he never gave quarter to the demands of a sickly body as he drove himself relentlessly through life.

He carried to the logical extreme his idea of base man's glorifying God. In doing so he showed clemency to no man, made allowance for no weakness, mixed not a bit of mercy with strict justice. He summed up his method in one place thus: "We ought to trample under foot every affection of nature when it is a question of his [God's] honor. The father should not spare his son, the brother the brother, nor the husband his own wife. If he has some friend who is as dear to him as his own life, let him put him to death." Most Calvinists accepted in theory the thesis that man should gladly will death itself for God's glory.

There are some traits of Calvin's character and personality that none deny today. To begin with, he was never a well man. All through his life he seems to have suffered from a million aches and pains — and they were the kind, as well as we can diagnose them, that particularly embitter one's disposition. Throughout life he suffered from dispepsia; as he grew older he was bothered by ulcers and kidney stones; and in late life he apparently had tuberculosis. Calvin drove his frail body with an iron will that brooked no physical debility, a symbol, Preserved Smith says, of the way he ruled a morally sick world. Certainly his physical frailty soured his disposition and hardened his will to overcome all obstacles.

In one of his letters to Farel, Calvin confessed that "bile had taken such possession of me that I poured out bitterness on every side." In other letters he complains that scoundrels in Geneva took advantage of his irritability. Even such a sympathetic biographer as Reyburn must therefore conclude: "It would be a mistake to claim for Calvin the jovial disposition that so often manifested itself in Martin Luther. . . . He was too intense to be generally amiable, and he was oftener feared than loved." Calvin's outlook was always bilious, his disposition always dour. And his religion did not escape the effects of its author's choleric outlook.

Calvin had no sympathy for weak man. Whereas Catholics before him asserted that as the result of original sin man was deprived of grace and inclined to evil — although by the proper means he could regain the grace thus lost — Calvin insisted that men were depraved, that they were wicked in essence; but that they deserve no sympathy. Calvin was known among his fellow students as "the accusative case" because of his faultfinding propensities, and he remained in the accusative case till the day of his death. He could stay in the accusative case because he had no sense of proportion, no relieving humor. He could never see the point in ridicule leveled at himself by the citizens of Geneva, as when they took to naming their dogs "Calvin." His treatment of Ameaux and of little David shows a lack of sympathy and a dearth of humor that is dangerous in a reformer. His having a man prosecuted for refusing the name "Abraham" picked out by a minister for the man's son indicates his consuming seriousness and his failure to adapt himself at all to human vagaries.

Calvin's reason was as much disassociated from his body, his passions, and his emotion as the mind of man can be. His enjoyment of natural beauty, for example, was intellectual rather than aesthetic. He enjoyed the things of nature as a mechanic enjoys an effective engine. Even his attitude toward women seems to have been coldly rational and calculatingly practical. In a letter to Farel he wrote: "The only beauty which can please me must be that of a woman who is chaste, agreeable, modest, frugal, patient, and affords me some hope that she will be solicitous for my personal health and prosperity." After his wife died he gave her his warmest possible compliment by observing that she had never interfered with his work.

Calvin's reason was quite independent of his body, and his

body was always in complete subjection to his reason. However, he was often consumed by anger — not an instinctive, emotional rage, but the white-hot, holy anger of the mind. He admits, indeed, that he sometimes became so angry that he became ill. Thus Palm can describe Calvin as a "determined man with a cold heart and a hot temper." Moreover, though he was coldly rational in all his activity, Calvin by no means enthroned reason on a pedestal. Superior to all reason, he taught, is the inward testimony of the Spirit. Neither Calvin nor his direct descendants, however, took this inward testimony of the Spirit too literally — as did Methodists and various other later stepchildren of Calvinism. Calvin himself asserted that it was not proper for one man to set up his conclusions against the beliefs generally accepted by others. Nor did he ever inquire whether Servetus or Gruet or any of the other "idolaters" had felt the inward testimony of the Spirit.

Calvin's mind, finally, was not philosophical. His search for truth was never metaphysical; he arrived at ultimate truth by going directly to God through the Bible. Calvin's mind was theological rather than metaphysical, and above all it was legal. He approached all matters as a lawyer. Thus he could brief a theology much more consistent than Luther's and draw up a moral code essentially legalistic in nature.

Where Luther came from rough peasant stock in Saxony, Calvin came from a middle-class family that enjoyed a certain measure of prestige in Noyon, France. Calvin's father was a lawyer by profession; he was, according to Theodore Beza, Calvin's close associate and first biographer, "apostolic notary, fiscal agent, scribe in the ecclesiastical court, secretary to the bishop, and promoter of the chapter." The father, at any rate, had influence enough to secure a petty church benefice for John, and money enough to send him to college in Paris and then to the universities of Orleans and Bourges. He had decided that John should take up law as his profession because, Beza informs us, "the father thought the law opened a surer road to riches and honors."

In college young Calvin was known for marked ability, strenuous morality, and intense earnestness. He was apparently looked upon as an especially promising young man by his instructors, several of whom took special interest in him. Because some of these professors were Lutheran, there is every reason to believe that Calvin had become acquainted with Lutheran doctrine before he was graduated. When John was seventeen, his father was involved in a financial scrape as a result of which he was excommunicated from the Catholic Church. This event is usually thought to have embittered young Calvin and predisposed him to accept Lutheran teaching.

His first work, a commentary on Seneca's *De Clementia* published in 1532, shows him still to be a Catholic of the Erasmus stamp. Sometime in the next year he experienced his "conversion," about which he tells us only two things: that it was sudden, and that it came directly from God. The first overt expression of his break from Catholic teaching is found in the presidential address he helped Nicholas Cop prepare for delivery at the University of Paris on November 1, 1533. When action was taken against Cop by the Parlement of Paris and by the king, Calvin fled from Paris, broke from the Erasmian humanists, and devoted himself to furthering the Protestant cause.

He traveled in Switzerland, France, and Italy for the next three years, eventually settling at Basle, where he wrote his *Institutes of the Christian Religion* in 1536. This work, first written by Calvin when he was only twenty-seven, went through five editions in his lifetime and grew from an original six to eighty chapters. It gathered various Protestant beliefs into a coherent system and attempted to give a rational defense of a movement that till then had been largely voluntaristic and nonintellectual. Reyburn in an enthusiastic summary of the qualities of the *Institutes* concludes: "Everything that the controversialist with Rome needs is found here, scholarship, argument, scripture proof, invective, denunciation, ridicule, and above all the systematic exposition of fundamental religious principles."

In the summer of 1536, Calvin stopped off in Geneva for, he thought, an overnight visit with Guillaume Farel, the fiery reformer who had led the Genevese in their break from the Catholic Church. Farel harangued Calvin heatedly, insisting that God had sent him to Geneva to save the newly established church, and that if he should ignore God's call he would suffer everlasting punishment. Calvin tells us that Farel's importunity "so frightened and terrified me that I desisted from the journey which I had undertaken." Except for a three-year period of banishment, he spent the rest of his life ordering the religion and regulating the morals of Geneva.

Geneva was remodeled and refurnished and repainted according to Calvin's doctrine. So complete was the rehabilitation that for the last ten years of Calvin's life Geneva could be looked upon as an almost perfect earthly city ruled by the word of God as Calvin interpreted it, a city where God's will was done and where man's sinfulness was completely repressed. Geneva was the city about which Protestants could wax eloquent, a city for which, from their point of view, they need never apologize, the city they set off against Rome.

But Calvinist reform was not accomplished without a struggle, without bloodshed and pillory, without acrimonious dispute over petty things. Calvin's iron will was sorely tried, but it crushed all opposition, and by 1555 Calvin controlled Geneva as despotically as he controlled his own frail body. Calvin's vigorous reforms, first forced upon Geneva in 1537, were far from popular. In the following year Calvin was exiled from the city, and for three years he stayed in Strassburg. In desperation, however, the city council of Geneva recalled him in 1541 to bring order to a city torn by internal dissention during his absence. From 1541 till his death in 1564 Calvin labored incessantly to enforce the word of God among the Genevese. Eventually the "libertines" were suppressed and Calvin's rule was unopposed. Of his reform Palm observes: "Legalistic, mechanical, without imagination or compassion, the work of a jurist and organizer of genius, Calvin's system was more Roman than Christian, and more Jewish than either."

Geneva became a city of glass, where every family was under the supervision of a spiritual gestapo which visited the home and pried into family affairs as no group has ever done till contemporary times. Laws, civil in form but religious in origin, were drawn up to enforce Calvin's interpretation of the word of God. Officially, Calvin remained only a preacher, but his influence over the city council was such that he can be called the dictator of Geneva. His laws were harsh, and they were strictly enforced. Penalties were meted out for laughing during the sermon, for dancing, cursing or swearing, for playing cards on Sunday, for staying too long in the tavern. A woman was punished for saying *requiescat in pace* over her husband's grave. Others were punished for saying the pope was a good man, for betrothing a young lady to a Catholic, for arguing against the death penalty for heretical opinions, for singing a song defamatory to Calvin, for saying there is no devil or hell.

Calvin insisted on the harshest of penalties. A child, for example, was beheaded for striking its mother; men were burned at the stake for interpreting the Bible differently from Calvin. Although Calvin insisted on severe punishment, he wanted it inflicted with as little torture as possible. We should remember, too, that he was driven to desperation by the so-called libertines who took advantage of his cranky disposition and his lack of humor. They nicknamed him Cain, named their dogs after him, sang songs ridiculing him, and subjected him to many annoyances which he interpreted as devilish attacks upon God Himself. Reformers seldom see themselves as funny; and Calvin had even less humor than the average reformer.

One by one, leaders of the opposition were burned or banished, until by 1555 Calvin was an autocrat whom none in Geneva dared oppose. He pursued the recalcitrant with relentless vehemence, for he looked upon himself as the anointed agent of God driving the children of Satan into the exterior darkness. Between 1542 and 1546 — the worst years of his persecution — seventy-six persons were banished and fifty-eight were executed in the little city of about 16,000.

When, in the last months of his life in 1564, Calvin was carried to the pulpit to preach, he could look out upon a reformed citizenry peopling a model city where all lived in outward conformity to God's law — which was as much as Calvin ever hoped to achieve in this world of damned mortals. The Elect governed Geneva; the reprobate glorified God by outwardly conforming to the divine plan for earthly life enforced by God's anointed few. In his primary mission in life, to convert Francis I and the French nation to his reformed religion, Calvin was a complete failure. In the task he set himself to in 1536, however, he was fully successful. Geneva's way of life had been changed. A city in the heart of Europe had been puritanized.

2

The reform of Geneva turned out to be Calvin's minor contribution to history. Geneva was only a place where his ideas were put on the statute books and where life conformed to them. It was his ideas that were really effective, ideas which he spread by preaching and writing, ideas which were carried forth from Geneva by zealous missionaries into the four corners of Europe. It was Calvin's body of doctrine that sustained the men of the Protestant revolt, that made them martyrs when they were weak and tyrants when they were strong, that gave them amazing confidence in themselves and disdainful disgust for all who disagreed with them.

Calvin sent out from Geneva the Ironsides of the Protestant movement, men with souls of steel, men convinced of the rightness of their cause and of the necessity of sacrificing everything for its success. These are the men whom Preserved Smith characterizes as "a strong and good race. . . . Believing themselves chosen vessels and elect instruments of grace, they could neither be seduced by carnal pleasure nor awed by human might. Taught that they were kings by the election of God and priests by the imposition of his hands, they despised the puny and vicious monarchs of this earth. They remained in fact, what they always felt themselves to be, an elite, 'the chosen few.'"

Armed with Calvinist ideas they conquered the world of weak mortals and strong natural forces before them. They subdued and slaughtered the Indians in this country, never asking whether they had claim to the land on which they lived; they put the head of Charles I on the block because he tried to rule the chosen few as he did the millions of lost souls; they toppled Mary Stuart off the throne of Scotland because she did not respect the covenant of the Scottish Presbyterians; they underpaid their workers to keep them sober, and worked them sixteen hours a day to keep them out of temptation's way. Their confidence, their energy, their ruthlessness were never shaken, even momentarily, by the disquieting suspicion that they might be wrong, or by the annoying suggestion that even the damned might have rights against the Elect.

They were a race of iron men clothed in an armor none in modern times could penetrate — the armor of Calvin's ideology. This is a point which the French syndicalist, Sorel, thoroughly appreciated late in the nineteenth century when he tried to furnish his followers with an equally invulnerable set of ideas. He refers respectfully, almost reverently, to the Huguenots of France and to their Calvinist brethren everywhere as the only men in modern times who were armed with a "myth," which, Sorel explains, is a body of ideas accepted instinctively without being subjected to rational criticism. It is an ideology, in Calvin's case, which of its very nature is a pure assertion, but an ideology capable of arousing its possessors to irrational, heroic action by identifying their views with the highest truth and the highest good, and with the judgment of God Himself.

Such a body of doctrine Calvin forged, not so much by creating new articles of belief as by systematically arranging a collection of doctrines his predecessors had already popularized. He briefed others' ideas into an almost irrefutable case for the reformed faith. It is too much to agree with Palm and many other historians who assert that "there is not one original thought in any of Calvin's works." But they are close to right. Calvin seems to have only one really original idea. It was, however, the basic point of his theology — his concept of the absolute sovereignty of an arbitrary God.

Calvin's God is anthropomorphic — made to the image and likeness of man. The man who modeled for Calvin's God was Machiavelli's prince, the despot who ruled absolutely, amorally, arbitrarily. For Calvin posits an almighty, unlimited God like that of the Catholics before him; but whereas the Catholics had stressed God's intelligence and necessary justice, Calvin stressed His will, a will which he made as arbitrary, as erratic as the earthly despot's whim. "The will of God," he wrote, "is the highest rule of justice. What He wills must be considered just, for this very reason that He wills it. Therefore when it is asked why the Lord did so, the answer must be, because He would."

This sovereign God rules the world exactly as He pleases — and it is not for man to inquire into the nature of God's rule or into its justice. Christians had till Calvin's day insisted that God could, of His very nature, do no injustice or no evil, for such action would be self-contradictory — like a circle being square. Calvin's God, however, does not seem to be limited to doing what is reasonable, just, and good. He does whatever He wants, and there seems no way of knowing what He will want. The Christian God of mercy becomes in Calvin's hands a tyrant whose sole concern is His own satisfaction and glory. This is the God that came to hold sway throughout most of the Protestant world after Calvin's day, the God against whom moderns react when they consider the problem of evil. For Calvin's God apparently enjoys watching His hateful creatures squirm in anguish here below. This is why so mild-mannered a man as John Stuart Mill can label the Calvinistic God "loathsome" and write of Him: "If such a being can sentence me to hell, to hell I will go."

Such is Calvin's God. Man's relation to Him is simple, for man exists only to glorify God. This is his only purpose in life. His soul is already predestined either to heaven or to hell, and man can do nothing to change the label God has put on him. He was created, in fact, not for his own salvation but for God's glory, which he promotes by his suffering if he be of the reprobate and by his prosperity if he be of the Elect. God has, however, laid down certain rules of worship, and these are to be found in the Bible. Man therefore has the obligation to glorify God by worshiping Him in the way God has chosen and shown to mankind. To worship God in any other way, or to worship a false God, is the worst of all sins. For Calvin tells us: "The first foundation of righteousness is certainly the worship of God; and if this be destroyed, all the other branches of righteousness, like the parts of a disjointed and falling edifice, are torn asunder and scattered." And again: "Whatever crimes can be thought of do not come up to this; that is, when God himself is involved in such dishonor as to be made an abettor of falsehood. . . . Now to corrupt pure doctrine, is it not the same as if to put the devil in God's place?"

Therefore Calvin concludes that "the mockers who would suffer all false doctrines and let any one disgorge what he likes are not only traitors to God but enemies of the human race." Therefore idolatry, "whether in man or woman, ought to be a mortal and capital crime." These are harsh conclusions to which Calvin comes — but they are logically harsh, for in his system men count for nothing except as creatures made to glorify God.

Theirs is never to reason why, theirs is only to obey blindly and die. Calvin, unlike Catholic theologians before him, was not metaphysical. He did not inquire into the nature of God. He did not even admit the right to inquire. His was a legalistic religion laid down by an arbitrary God through His secretary and prosecuting attorney, John Calvin.

Calvin was creator of the reformed Christian religion. The exaltation of the human person, always to the fore in Christ's message, is essentially foreign to Calvinism. His stress is on the Decalogue, not on the Sermon on the Mount; the first of Christ's two great commandments is so stressed that the second is almost forgotten. The Jehovah of the Jews, presented in a distorted image, becomes the God of Calvin, while the Elect have replaced the Jews as God's chosen people. Calvin is the second Moses. Christ is not denied, but He becomes quite unimportant. Those elements of Christianity which were distinctly Christian recede into the background. God no longer loves man as his creature; He hates him as a sinner. God's justice is no longer tempered with mercy.

Calvin's second basic doctrine was predestination, which, he believed, followed of necessity from his doctrine of God's absolute, unlimited sovereignty. For to allow men to achieve salvation through their own efforts is to place limits on the divine sovereignty. All men deserve eternal punishment, Calvin insisted, but for His own pleasure and as a means of glorifying Himself God selected some — relatively few, it would seem — for salvation. These Elect have neither done anything in the past nor can they do anything in the future to deserve their selection. They are lucky in the same way that a lottery winner is lucky, for God's choice, Calvin says, "is founded on His gratuitous mercy, totally irrespective of human merit." More than that, those who have been selected for salvation cannot resist God's choice, nor can they do anything to make God change His mind and condemn them to eternal punishment. It is all arranged by God Himself, acting with absolute independence of the creatures He has either condemned to hell or assigned to heaven. There is absolutely nothing you can do about it.

It follows, therefore, that man does not possess free will. On this point Calvin was explicit and positive. His followers, though they held men strictly accountable for their moral actions, never deviated from this view — as long as they remained Calvinists. William Prynne stated this belief in two of his seven "dogmatical conclusions" of Calvinism: "4. That there is not any such free will, any such universal or sufficient grace communicated unto all men, whereby they may repent, believe, or be saved if they will themselves. . . . 6. That the Elect do always constantly obey, neither do they, or can they, finally or totally resist the inward powerful and effectual call or working of God's Spirit in their hearts, in the very act of their conversion: neither is it in their own power to convert, or not convert themselves, at that very instant time when they were converted."

Man, in Calvin's system, is a lowly creature essentially depraved by the sin of his first parents. He is thoroughly corrupted, and he is impotent even to will, much less accomplish, a good act. He has been cast by God into this arena of black sin, and if he is of the Elect he must battle through this wicked world alone, unaided by other men. He is not, except incidentally, a social person. He fights for God's glory and does His will as an individual crusader who relies only upon his own resources and upon the God who has marked him for salvation. "His life," Tawney well says, "is that of a soldier in hostile territory."

But can you know you are on God's side? Is there any proof that you are of the Elect? This is a question that would quite naturally bother any Calvinist. And Calvin had a double answer for it. One knows if he is of the Elect through the "witness of the Spirit" within him, which seems to be an overwhelmingly powerful inner conviction of God's assurance that you are good and what you say is true. This witness of the Spirit, however, serves as proof only of one's own election. It does not tell you who else has been marked for salvation, who are your brethren in the company of the Elect, and yet, practically speaking, with the Calvinists a man's neighbors constituted themselves the judges of his spiritual health.

In the second place Calvin and his followers come to believe that prosperity in this life was the best possible indication of salvation in the next. The connection between worldly success and election to heaven was not necessarily foolproof, but Calvinists all came to feel that God would surely help His chosen people in their worldly pursuits and that you could therefore adjudge a man's election to salvation by his godliness here below — and by the size of his bank account. Surely, if all men are essentially wicked and hateful in the sight of God and if God has freely marked a few for salvation, then those few must enjoy God's blessings on earth. Surely the good must prosper — for they have nothing else to do with their time and their energy; they are already saved, and their activity on this earth has no connection with their salvation.

Calvin himself frequently stated this idea of divine favor attached to the Elect. In the *Institutes* he told his readers: "Whatever a man possesses has fallen to his lot not by a fortuitous contingency, but by the distribution of the supreme Lord of all." In other places he asserts: "Though some seem to enrich themselves by vigilance, nevertheless it is God who blesses and cares for them." "Goods sometimes come to His children as they sleep. And this shows that men err if they think they enrich themselves by their own merit." Thus the prosperous man can congratulate himself on having found favor with God. For the good prosper. And there is no prosperity without God.

Calvin's doctrine of predestination gave immediate impetus to wealth-seeking as an end in itself. For if you know you are already consigned by God either to heaven or hell and there is nothing you can do about it, and if you are curious about your destiny, then you will naturally concentrate very earnestly on the exterior mark of prosperity that will indicate your salvation. It will, moreover, cause you rationally to direct all your energies into worldly work, for the business of your salvation is already determined. You cannot save your soul by making a million dollars, but you can obtain the comforting assurance that God is on your side and has almost certainly pinned the "Elect" label on your soul.

The absolute sovereignty of God and predestination are the two pillars of the Calvinist system. A third important point is his bibliocracy. The Bible, read literally, contains God's blueprint for the running of the universe. In it is to be found everything God had ordained for His own glory and for man's life on earth. "In his [Calvin's] hands," Reyburn states, "the Bible became a manual of dogmatic theology, a directory for public worship, and a scheme of Church government. Nothing in religion was permissible except what was sanctioned in Scripture or might be deduced from it by necessary inference."

It was not really the Bible, but Calvin's interpretation of it, that ruled Geneva. Calvin was supreme, rather than the Bible, for any interpretation of a scriptural passage that conflicted with Calvin's was anathema. So the Bible served more as a constitutional check on Calvin than it did as a source of law and religion. Even as a check, the Bible was as putty in the indomitable Frenchman's hands. He interpreted what Jesus said to the adulterous woman, for example, so as to eliminate mercy altogether. It is not too far amiss to say that the Bible in Reformed churchmen's hands said what Calvin wanted it to say. To hold, then, that Geneva was a bibliocracy is correct only if you remember how strong a personal flavoring Calvin gave to his scriptural exegesis.

3

From Calvin's theological system and from his bibliocracy came his hard ethic. For this, indeed, are the Calvinists best known. It is this hard ethic which distinguishes them most sharply from Catholics and from non-Reformed Christians. Calvin was by no means an ethical theorist, but no man in history has had a clearer or sharper set of moral ideas than he. His ethic was a lawyer's code based upon precedents in the Bible, and never did Calvin doubt the correctness of his view nor his duty to impose it upon all men for the glory of God. "*To hurt* and *to destroy*," he says, "are incompatible with the character of the godly; but to avenge the afflictions of the righteous at the command of God, is neither *to hurt* nor *to destroy*. . . . I sincerely wish that this consideration were constantly in our recollection, that nothing is done here by the temerity of men, but everything by the authority of God, who commands it, and under whose guidance we never err from the right way."

He briefed a powerful, driving ethical code for his followers, and it gave them all the energy of prosecuting attorneys in God's battle against wickedness. It was an ethic based upon biblical texts as culled and interpreted by Calvin rather than upon reason, upon the Decalogue as likewise interpreted and applied by him rather than the Sermon on the Mount. "The Bible," Calvin wrote, "ought to affect the whole man with a hundred times more energy than the frigid exhortations of the philosophers." And it did. Certainly — and logically — the Calvinists were intolerant to the very marrow of their bones. When Calvin believed that man's sole end in life was to glorify God, that the Bible contained all the rules for doing this work, and that his interpretation of Scripture was the only correct one, then he could not logically be tolerant.

Georgia Harkness sees this well when she observes: "When one is convinced that God's glory transcends all earthly considerations, and when one is also convinced that God's glory is being fouled in the dust and men's minds poisoned by false doctrine, one can bring himself to kill for God. . . . Calvin's doctrine of persecution was the coolly reasoned product of a theology which combined God's sovereignty, man's littleness, Biblical literalism, and Hebraic ethics" — all, of course, as interpreted and applied by Calvin.

The rise of religious tolerance after Calvin's day owes absolutely nothing to Calvinistic theory. Where they controlled the machinery of persecution, Calvinists were more energetically intolerant than any religious group in modern times. Where they were a minority, however, they devised theories in favor of tolerance — as did Catholics in England or Anabaptists in Switzerland. Champions of toleration did not come from Geneva.

Calvin's morality was essentially a lawyer's. It was a purely exterior morality that dealt with acts rather than with desires. Sobriety, frugality, honesty, prudence were all virtues which in their working out soon came to be practical and financial rather than spiritual. Sombart has caught the spirit of the Genevan's ethic in his description of Calvinistic honesty: "In essence, this meant — eschew all irregularities; appear in respectable society; avoid drinking, gambling and women; go to church regularly; in a word always wear the aspect of true respectability, and all for the sake of your business. Such a moral rule of life will ensure your credit." Calvin's ethic was a form of moral mathematics whereby you could assign your neighbor to heaven or to hell by means of a calculus of his exterior virtues and vices. To his credit would be listed such things as a sober demeanor, a dour countenance, clean apparel, a frugal way of life, unlimited industriousness, dearth of humor, and consuming seriousness about the practical affairs of life. Such a man was a good man; such a man had evidently been labeled "Elect" by God.

Virtues, in the Calvinistic ethic, were all those virtues that have been associated with the middle class. Throughout Calvin's writings there is constant stress on reverence, chastity, honesty, sobriety, industry, and frugality — those virtues which make for much production and small consumption, for the amassing of wealth and for hoarding rather than spending it. Calvin resurrected, in perverted form, the neglected Catholic virtue of asceticism and self-discipline, making it more rigorous than the Catholics ever had and applying it exclusively to mundane matters. Where Catholics before Calvin had insisted that worldly pleasures, in their proper place, are good and are to be denied only for a higher spiritual good, Calvin insisted things of this world were bad in themselves and had to be avoided as evil. "Either the earth must become vile in our estimation," he insists, "or it must retain our immoderate love." Again, he condemns pleasures of the senses in such sentences as this: "Those who have much variety in order to satisfy the appetite have surely offended God, and ought to be despised. . . . It could be wished that such people had died before they were born."

Where Catholic asceticism had meant withdrawal from the world for contemplation, Calvinist asceticism meant method and discipline in worldly life. Rather than prayer and contemplation, it meant an ascetic life in business and in social relationships. It meant, in the long run, cutting away from all foolishness and lightheadedness that interfered with serious, practical business activity. This asceticism is well described by Troeltsch as, "the demand for ascetic conduct and of work-activity as the best means of spiritual and corporal discipline . . . the utmost simplicity of life with regard to clothing and comfort; the practical capacity, assurance, and honor in all callings, which lead to a very practical social, political, and business activity."

Frugality was treated by Calvin and his followers as a necessary virtue. The frugal life is the saintly life; extravagance, a manifestation of ambition and pride, is a devilish thing. The Elect are to receive God's blessings, it is true, but Calvin reminds his followers that, when God sends prosperity, "the affluence of our blessings is to try our frugality." The Elect must know how to live penuriously, no matter what material blessings God has sent their way. The Calvinist cannot be guilty of ostentatious waste or even of unbecoming display. "To restrain ourselves in the midst of abundance is a virtue well-pleasing to God, and reveals a grateful heart."

Industriousness, labor for its own sake, is another virtue stressed by the great reformer. Calvin was temperamentally opposed to any kind of softness, and idleness was for him a vicious form of softness. "It is certain," he avers, "that idleness and indolence are accursed of God." And in one of his most frequently quoted passages he tells us that "nothing is more unseemly than a man that is idle and good for nothing." Work for its own sake, as a sign of salvation, seems to have impressed itself most deeply upon Calvin's associates and on his followers. "And," Harkness sums it up, "the injunction bore its fruits. The combination of frugality with industry made for thrift — and thrift for the amassing of riches. Then with the heaping up of riches came the care of this world and the undoing of much for which Calvin labored."

Calvin briefed the purely capitalistic businessman's ethic. It remained his ethic throughout modern history — with further secularization and with Calvin's limiting counsels forgotten. Calvin's justification of the capitalistic spirit — already in existence, but not yet given full social approval — was perhaps his most significant accomplishment. More than justifying the capitalistic spirit, he gave it impetus and promoted several of the essential ingredients on which capitalism could build and thrive. In the first place, as we have seen, he advocated, through example and precept, the cultivation of the middle-class virtues: prudence, industry, frugality, sobriety, honesty.

Second, he advanced the doctrine that all material goods are bestowed on their possessors directly by God — a belief that connoted a sanctity of private property which has plagued mankind since his day. For among the descendants of Calvin private property is more hallowed than the human beings who possess it — or from whom it is taken. It is a belief that came to absolve the unscrupulous of the means they used to obtain property, for after all it was bestowed by God, and, if God willed that the reprobate be foolish and the Elect prosper, who is the business-man to inquire into the ineffable will of God?

Third, Calvin insisted on the virtue of obedience. Servants were told to submit to their masters, and workers were enjoined to obey their employers. This insistence on obedience, combined with the virtue of industry, helped make for a hard-working, passive class of employees — an essential factor in the centuries to come for the commercial and industrial revolutions. It is not mere concomitance of circumstances that caused these revolu-tions to occur most fruitfully in Calvinistic countries; nor is it mere accident that employers interested in the religion of their workers sought to propagate some form or another of Calvinism among them.

In the fourth place, Calvin permitted the taking of interest, a point which, it seems, has been too much emphasized by eco-nomic historians. The capitalistic-Calvinistic spirit which he gen-erated would soon have got around the problem of interest any-way. Moreover, Catholic theorists had found many grounds to justify the taking of interest by Calvin's time. Calvin, nevertheless, was the first to justify interest in itself, though he stringently forbade his followers charging excessive rates or taking any from the poor.

Finally, more than Luther had done before him, Calvin in-vested the secular calling or vocation with a religious significance. The shoemaker and the farmer are doing the Lord's work as directly as is the preacher. "The Lord commands every one of us," Calvin wrote, "in all the actions of his life, to regard his vocation. . . . He has appointed to all their particular duties in different spheres of life. And that no one might rashly transgress the limits prescribed, he has styled such spheres of life *vocations* or *callings*. Every individual's line of life, therefore, is as it were, a post assigned him by the Lord." One who feels he is doing the Lord's work as he makes shoes will make more shoes and better shoes than if he works only for his supper. The religious significance Calvin gave to secular work helps explain the almost superhuman energy with which captains of industry have carried on in modern times. The Latin American who is bewildered by the Yankee's terrifying energy does not appreciate the effects of the *Institutes of the Christian Religion* on the modern mind.

Like Luther, Calvin gave political advice to his followers. Like Luther's, Calvin's political theories were in favor of established rule and against rebellion. "No Stuart," it has been observed, "ever proclaimed more vigorously the 'divine right' of kings and magistrates to govern." As James I was, in a short time, to speak almost mystically of "The divinity that doth hedge a king," so Calvin proclaimed that "civil magistracy is a calling not only holy and legitimate, but far the most sacred and honorable in human life." Obedience is due even to wicked rulers, for they are visited upon men as a punishment for their sins. They are, moreover, God's representatives on earth and one "cannot resist the magistrate without resisting God."

But at the same time Calvin pushed a wedge into the authority of the prince through which legions of revolutionists were to march. "We are subject to the men who rule over us," he had written, "but subject only in the Lord. If they command anything against Him, let us not pay the least regard to it, nor be moved by all the dignity which they possess as magistrates." This had long been taught by Catholic moralists, but the followers of Calvin gave the command a new significance. For the Calvinist had identified himself with the Lord; he is the Lord's agent, one of God's Elect, and if the prince commands him to act in a way he does not want to, that prince is issuing a command against the Lord. Even here, of course, Calvin sanctioned only passive resistance. But his advice "rather to spit on their heads than to obey them" was taken literally and made a justification for rebellion in Scotland and England, the Netherlands and France, and indirectly in America too.

4

Calvin's teaching resulted in attitudes and actions he could never have dreamed of. First, and perhaps most important, it created a race of hard men, men who would control European politics and business for centuries to come, men who ruthlessly bent all opposition to their indomitable wills, men who believed with the Whig, Mackintosh, that their class had the "largest share of sense and virtue." Until recent decades the middle classes were an iron race among the people of Europe and America, and their hardness derived largely from Calvinist theory. The puritan spirit, according to an eminent Canadian authority, A. S. P. Woodhouse, "nerved the arm and brought an excess of courage, which on any other premise, would have been reckless."

This was a restless, dynamic spirit Calvin forged, and its possessors moved forever like the sea in an otherwise relatively placid European society. This active, practical temper feared rest and quiet as Luther feared the dark. In his famous book of advice, *Christian Directory*, Baxter summed up the Calvinist-puritan feeling when he asserted, "It is action that God is most served and honored by." Henry Robinson in like manner told his readers: "The true temper and proper employment of a Christian is always to be working like the sea, and purging ignorance out of his understanding and exchanging notions and apprehensions imperfect for more perfect, and forgetting things behind to press forward." Milton raised this restlessness to a higher plane. "To be still searching what we know not, by what we know, still closing truth to truth as we find it . . . this is the golden rule in theology as well as in arithmetic." This is nobler than Baxter perhaps, but Milton's is an equally restless spirit.

Second, Calvinist theory armed the middle class with the strongest of all weapons, a powerful idea, and sent them into the world as revolutionary reformers. The Calvinist had to strain every nerve, every muscle to make sound doctrine and good morality prevail in every nook and cranny of life, from the king's chamber to the farmer's dining room. Reform must be accomplished everywhere, in the countinghouse and the tavern, in the meetinghouse and the living room. The word of God must prevail throughout the world. Such was the mission of the Elect. Sometimes this meant revolution; sometimes it meant drastic legal reform, sometimes social reform, again a cleanup campaign. Calvinist groups have been leaders for reform of any kind, good or bad, through modern history. The puritan, Thomas Case, chanted the old reform refrain to the House of Commons when he cried: "Reform the universities. . . . Reform the cities, . . . the counties, . . . the sabbath, . . . the ordinances, the worship of

God. . . . Every plant which my heavenly Father hath not planted shall be rooted up."

Reform of various kinds was accomplished. But at the same time, and again largely because of John Calvin, society came to be impersonalized as it never had before in human history. In the Genevan's system, every man stands isolated from his fellows. Each is a lonely warrior against iniquity, with only God on his side. All struggle is for God's honor and glory. Thus the socially warming quality of brotherly love was looked on as a religious weakness. No one should be logically concerned with his fellow creatures for their sake; any concern with mankind is an impersonalized, legalistic concern that they conform to the will of God in their outward actions. Calvin had himself systematically eliminated Christ's regard for man as a human person. He had neglected the second of the two great commandments — without which society is almost bound to be organized in filing cabinets and card indexes, as it is today.

Calvinists and puritans therefore naturally, though unintentionally perhaps, changed their attitude toward social obligations. For the first time a social and moral taint was attached to poverty. The term "beggar" began to take on the unsavory connotation it still has today, where formerly mendicant priests and university students plied the begging trade with high self-respect. In England, for example, where enclosures had been condemned as vicious social evils by Thomas More and his contemporaries, a century later Baxter and his friends encouraged enclosures as a method to put the lower classes under severe masters who would establish good moral discipline among them. Common lands were condemned as evil, for they encourage that worst sin of all, idleness. Arthur Young smugly summed it all up late in the next century when he pontificated: "Every one but an idiot knows that the lower classes must be kept poor, or they will never be industrious."

A third major result of Calvin's theological and moral doctrines is found in their application to business life. "It is perhaps the first systematic body of religious teaching," Tawney writes, "which can be said to recognize and applaud the economic virtues. . . . Such teaching, whatever its theological merits or defects, was admirably designed to liberate economic energies, and to weld into a disciplined social force the rising *bourgeoisie*, conscious of the contrast between its own standards and those of a laxer world, proud of its vocation as the standard-bearer of the economic virtues, and determined to vindicate an open road for its own way of life by the use of every weapon, including political revolution and war, because the issue which was at stake was not merely convenience or self-interest, but the will of God."

Neither the Bank of England nor Wall Street was foreseen by Calvin, but he made easier the creation of both. The connection between his teaching and the new capitalistic world was observed almost at once. Spaniards spoke of the intimate connection between Calvinism and the commercial spirit of the revolting Netherlanders in the late sixteenth century. Baxter mentioned France in the next century where it was "the merchants and the middle sort of men that were Protestants." And a puritan pamphleteer of 1671 wrote: "There is a kind of natural unaptness in the Popish religion to business, whereas on the contrary among the Reformed, the greater their zeal, the greater their inclination to trade and industry."

The Calvinist was called to practice his business with an almost inhuman seriousness. Business was no longer a task. It became a passion. The puritan divine, Richard Steele, told his readers that, "The Great Governour of the world hath appointed to every man his proper post and province, and let him be never so active out of his sphere, he will be at a great loss, if he do not keep his own vineyard and mind his own business." It was unseemly, indeed, the puritans were told, to spend too much time in prayer when the same time could be profitably spent in business.

Thus the followers of Calvin glorified work as it had never been glorified before. Work was good both as an end in itself and as a means of amassing wealth. Baxter's advice was typical: "Be wholly taken up in diligent business of your lawful callings, when you are not exercised in the more immediate service of God. . . . Keep up a high esteem of time, and be every day more careful that you lose none of your time than you are that you lose none of your gold and silver." The wealthy are not excused from the duty of labor, for in the words of Richard Steele, "The standing pool is prone to putrefaction: and it were better to beat down the body and to keep it in subjection by a laborious calling, than through luxury to become a cast-away." Work is for the sake not only of the soul, but also for obtaining wealth. Baxter tells his readers that it is sinful to choose the less gainful of two possible transactions; and Wesley says bluntly, "We must exhort all Christians to gain all they can and so save all they can; that is, in effect, to grow rich."

Labor, then, is a duty for all. It must be hard, diligent labor that purifies the soul and makes money; it must be systematized labor that is the result of ruthless self-discipline. It is an industriousness that admits of no idleness, no laxity, no rest. "Remember," Ben Franklin told his young tradesman, "that time is money." Thus it follows that since the good work incessantly and live frugally, the good shall prosper. Virtue is more than its own reward; it pays off in dollars and cents. The puritan pamphleteer, Younge, summed up the connection between godliness and wealthiness pithily: "No question but it [riches] should be the portion rather of the godly than of the wicked, were it good for them; for godliness hath the promise of this life as well as of the life to come."

The part played by Calvinism in making the commercial and industrial world now dissolving is summed up succinctly by Troeltsch in this paragraph: "When all is said and done, Calvinism remains the real nursing-father of the civic industrial capitalism of the middle classes. Self-devotion to work and gain, which constitutes the involuntary and unconscious asceticism of the modern man, is the child of a conscious 'intramundane' asceticism of work and calling inspired by religious motives. The 'spirit of the calling,' which does not reach out beyond the world, but works in the world without 'creative worship' — that is, without love of the world — becomes the parent of a tireless systematic laboriousness, in which work is sought for work's sake, for the sake of the mortification of the flesh, in which the produce of the work serves, not to be consumed in enjoyment, but to the constant reproduction of the capital employed. Since the aggressively active ethic inspired by the doctrine of predestination urges the elect to the full development of his God-given powers, work becomes rational and systematic. In breaking down the motive of ease and enjoyment, asceticism lays the foundation of the tyranny of work over men."

If voluntarism was the chief result of Luther's doctrine, puritanism was the main fruit of Calvin's. Luther's voluntarism was soon checked by a long age of rationalism, but it went on living beneath the surface of Western society, and it cropped out to flourish in the nineteenth and twentieth centuries. Calvin's puritanism, on the other hand, always rode high on the crest of Western society, and there was hardly a man of affairs after Calvin's day who escaped his influence. Calvin's influence on the modern mind is not as direct as that of Rousseau or Marx or Freud, but it is more extensive, more penetrating. It is harder to escape. Long ago John Adams warned, "Let not Geneva be forgotten or despised." Even today his warning cannot be ignored.

IV
DESCARTES

PURE REASON'S FAILURE

LUTHER'S revolt came from his inability to solve the personal problem of achieving spiritual security. Calvin found himself immersed in a revolution which he had to control in order to save his life on this earth and his soul in the next. But René Descartes Duperron was not forced by circumstances into his life of revolutionary philosophizing. He deliberately chose his career after calmly surveying the world in which he lived, assessing its shortcomings, and deciding that it was up to him to set men's minds aright. Descartes, it is true, had a passionate craving for intellectual security — and to this extent his personal desires prompted his revolutionary thinking almost as imperatively as Luther's had. Descartes, however, was eminently calm, perfectly balanced. He proposed to himself nothing less than a one-man revolution whereby he would overthrow the old world of ideas and create a better one. It would be his task to start from nothing, for nothing was certain in the mind of man, and from this basis

70

he would create a new world by means of his unaided reason. This he would do alone, unaided by the rest of mankind, and he would complete the task before he died.

Descartes would never want to be judged as mostly right and a little wrong; either he was completely right, he would tell us, or he was wrong. Either he had rebuilt the world of thought on incontrovertibly clear and certain foundations, proceeding by one absolutely unmistakable step after another, or he had failed. With this purpose in mind, openly avowed by Descartes, we must judge him. He had undertaken a gigantic task, and when death claimed him at the age of fifty-four he had not yet completely developed his "marvelous science." Could Descartes have preached his own funeral oration, he would have had to accuse himself of failure.

But Descartes was not the kind of failure who could be ignored or quickly forgotten. For he put his imprint deep on the modern mind and influenced its workings from his day to this. It would not be too much to say, indeed, that Descartes had a hand in the atomic bomb. For Cartesianism is at the basis of European history and European philosophical and scientific thinking throughout the seventeenth and eighteenth centuries, and even after the romantic reaction of the early nineteenth century its influence is still felt in all fields of thought. For at least two centuries no philosopher could afford to ignore Descartes; either he had to carry on Descartes's work and solve the problems he bequeathed to philosophy, or he had to level the Cartesian edifice before erecting his own. Cartesianism was long in possession of the modern mind, and the effects of its long tenancy are only today wearing thin. We can truly say that we are now witnessing the final failure of three centuries of rationalism.

Descartes is the father of rationalism. Malebranche, Leibniz, Spinoza, and others tried to perfect his rationalistic deductive method of thought and to bring to full bloom all the germinal seeds of his innate ideas. They likewise tried to solve the problem of the relation of the body to the soul, which Descartes had so definitively separated. From him stem both the idealism of Berkeley and Hume and the materialism of such philosophers as La Mettrie and Holbach. Descartes left philosophers a spirit which was pure thought and a body which was only a machine.

Some philosophers picked up the spirit and went off into the clouds of idealism, ignoring the body and all things material, denying their cognoscibility and sometimes even their existence; others picked up the body, which was merely a wonderful machine whose only necessary notes were extension and motion, and either forgot about or denied the spirit and the mind.

Most important, perhaps, Descartes turned the world of knowledge inside-out. He concluded that we have immediate knowledge only of our own ideas, and thus he shut up the mind in itself and cut it away from the clouds we see, the rain that beats in our face, the steak we eat, and the chair we stumble over in the dark. All these things we can never know except through our knowledge of God. A man must take it on faith that whiskers grow on his face and he needs a shave. Descartes ended up by making our ideas independent of the world they supposedly picture. This is the element of subjectivism so prevalent through modern history and so strong today — from animal clubs, which prefer local kittens to displaced children from afar, to the Nazi ideologist, who claims that Einstein's theories might be true for Jews but not for Nordics.

1

Descartes (1596–1650) wrote in an atmosphere charged with theological controversy, in an age when philosophy was thoroughly discredited and when the new findings of physical science were attracting men's attention and capturing their imagination. It was an age when the scholastic philosophy of the Middle Ages had discredited itself outside the schools, had long since, indeed, committed intellectual suicide. The quarrels of the schoolmen since the thirteenth century had got out of hand. Each one corrected his predecessors and argued with his contemporaries until it seemed that no two great minds could agree on anything. This sort of argument, healthy when kept within bounds and when there is agreement on basic truths, discredited the very name of philosophy in a day when all thinking persons were concerned with the never-ending and never-settled arguments. As Etienne Gilson so aptly remarks, "There is never too much of a good thing, but there were too many varieties of the same thing." People finally decided that philosophy, by its very nature, was incapable of arriving at certainty and that it was only a game for those who wanted to make bickering their indoor sport.

In the century before Descartes's birth, as we have seen, the nominalistic variety of scholastic philosophy had won the day against the moderate realism of St. Thomas and Bonaventura. Occam's nominalism, which denied the validity of abstraction and generalization, undermined the very basis of philosophy and insisted that such general terms as "man" were only labels stuck on various concrete creatures who seemed to be alike. Such a philosophy led straight to skepticism by denying the possibility of man's transcending sense experience and getting to the essence of things. Philosophers of this age were guilty of most of the abuses commonly associated by the modern mind with philosophy at any time — how many angels can dance on the point of a pin, and all that sort of thing. A common vice of the time was terminism: philosophy had degenerated pretty much into the nominalistic practice of naming and then into name calling. Disputation had become quibbling. The valid method of making distinctions and subdistinctions in the interest of clear thinking had become a game, the purpose of which was to confuse listeners and overwhelm opponents. Truth no longer was the goal.

This suicide of scholasticism led to two general resultant attitudes. One was expressed by Petrarch when he maintained that Aristotle's opinion of happiness was not as good as "the opinions upon this matter of any pious woman, or devout fisherman, shepherd or farmer." Notice how the word "opinion" worked its way into the discussion. If philosophers cannot agree on such a thing as the nature of happiness, then it all becomes a matter of opinion. And why not take the fisherman's opinion, or the shepherd's? So skepticism about man's ability to know, to apprehend reality, set in. At best it was a matter of opinion. Which sounds like Jeremy Bentham in the nineteenth century, or a debate in Congress today.

The other attitude resulting from the decline of scholasticism was narrated in the question of Thomas à Kempis, "What signifies making a great dispute about hidden things which for having been ignorant of we shall not be reproved in the judgment?" This is the intellectual indifferentism which had set in among the Brethren of the Common Life and various quasimystics like Luther at the very beginning of modern history. It matters not what you believe, as long as you believe firmly and die well. This attractive attitude is full of dynamite, for it is based on the comforting, but false assumption that there is no connection between belief and action, between what goes on in one's mind and what follows in his physical movements. It is based on the disheartening assumption that man is not a rational animal, and that he has no rational control over himself.

Skepticism and intellectual indifferentism combined to make men of the sixteenth century feel that right ideas were difficult, if not impossible to get, and that even if you could get them it wasn't worth the effort required. The humanists, with their emphasis on rhetoric and form, had rightly sensed that their archenemy was Aristotle. They had made a flank attack on him with their special weapons of ridicule and scorn and satire. And they had dethroned him. Plato had become the philosopher of humanism, but it was *their* Plato rather than the austere follower of Socrates whom they crowned. Thus before Descartes appeared on the scene the realistic scholastic philosophy had succumbed to attacks from without as well as to the "fifth column" of Occamism within its stronghold.

The great Montaigne, who served as Descartes's philosophic point of departure, had brought this discrediting of philosophy to its logical conclusion. The urbane Frenchman had withdrawn from the world of confusion and incessant struggle, intellectual, political, and religious, to meditate and to write down his thoughts. Montaigne concluded that there was wisdom indeed, but true wisdom consisted in never committing the mind to anything. He thought that the evils of the Protestant revolt and the intellectual anarchy of the time resulted from dogmatism. Everyone was positive he was right, and he knew everybody else was wrong. Montaigne concluded that the wise man would never be sure of anything. Thus, as Gilson puts it, "the only thing we can learn from him is the art of unlearning."

Descartes, who was going to build a new philosophy from scratch, who was anxious to become the Aristotle of the modern world and to replace the learned "father of philosophers" as the Sage of the schools, had to find a knowledge that would stand the test of the skepticism of the Parisan "libertines," followers of Montaigne. Of this he was keenly aware, and for such a knowledge he began to search. It certainly was not to be found in scholastic philosophy. Descartes insists on that. "Of philosophy," he says, "I will say nothing, except that I saw that it had been cultivated for many ages by the most distinguished men, and yet there is not a single matter within its sphere which is not still in dispute, and nothing therefore which is above doubt."

He had no intention, then, of rescuing Aristotle from the skeptics and making the ship of scholasticism seaworthy again by reseaming its hulk and refitting its gear. He would build his own ship. But out of what material? The material of the newly popular physical sciences was at hand, and to it Descartes naturally turned, whether purposively or not. It was new and it was fresh and it was practical. It opened up new vistas, and its accomplishments were concrete and observable. Where the old philosophy had degenerated into endless and apparently useless bickering about seemingly inconsequential subtleties, the followers of the new physical science were making compasses and charting the oceans and directing ships around the world. Where the old philosophy slumbered on, self-satisfied and content with the protection offered by parliamentary decrees and royal armies, the new science was willing to defend itself in the arena of men's minds and prove its claims in the laboratory of the world.

In Descartes's youth enthusiasm for the new Copernican astronomy reached fever heat in scientific circles. New voyages into the unknown were undertaken, new lands were discovered across the sea, and Galileo was even discovering unknown planets. By the time Descartes left school the old geocentric concept of the universe had been thoroughly discredited, and the news of Galileo's discoveries was widespread. The microscope and the telescope had been invented, and they revealed unknown worlds of microcosm and macrocosm. They also may have made Descartes realize what could be revealed by new instruments and by a new method. Within a short time Torricelli had invented the barometer and Galileo the first rude thermometer, and Pascal formulated his laws on the pressure exerted by liquids.

Underlying all these accomplishments was an unbounded faith in human reason to accomplish things of a practical nature, to "get things done." Back of all this, moreover, was something which Descartes was probably the first to appreciate — the formal, logical analysis that preceded any of these improvements. Thus his mind was presented with the possibility of retaining the method of algebra and of divesting it of the material with which it was then associated. From this it would be an easy step to conclude that since mathematics was a purely formal science and was independent of the concrete nature of the terms to which it was applied, there was no reason why it should not be applied to any subject matter whatsoever. It would be an easy step, therefore, to convert philosophy into "Universal Mathematics," and all sciences would become one.

This was the age, then, in which Descartes began to cast about for the materials with which to construct his new philosophy. The old philosophy was thoroughly discredited, and skepticism was the attitude of intelligent men toward any body of ideas. The new philosophy would have to stand the acid test of thoroughgoing skepticism; it would have to be built on incontrovertible bases and would have to proceed by clearly and unmistakably correct steps, one at a time. The material for such a new philosophy that would be unassailable by human reason seemed to lie ready at hand in the mathematical method employed by physical sciences. But it should also be remembered that Descartes, who was as much the child of his age as its sire, wrote in an atmosphere that was, as Maritain puts it, "charged with theology." Because he was a child of his age, Descartes applies the clarities of science and the zeal of religion to his new philosophy. "The philosophy of Descartes," Maritain continues, "came into the world with an appearance of Christian and geometric heroism, measuring the earth and immediately finding God in the soul. . . . [His] thought is cloaked in a double prestige, that of science and of apologetics, of geometry and of spirituality."

2

The father of modern philosophy, René Descartes Duperron, would not make a good Elk or Rotarian. Nor, if he lived today, would he be a politician, a union leader, or a member of the local chamber of commerce. Perhaps he would be an unhappy professor holding aloof from students and fellow professors alike. But at least he would maintain his integrity. Descartes always was that sort of man. He shunned society, except when he moved among men to observe them in a detached way. He refused to marry, because he thought a wife would be a burden on him and would curtail his freedom and because, as he wrote to a young lady, there is "no beauty comparable to the beauty of truth." He worked alone, and his attention never strayed to the world of human beings, whose thought processes he believed he was analyzing. His philosophy suffered from his social isolation, for it betrays his failure to have observed the whole man in whom was the mind he studied.

Descartes is a tragic example of a philosopher who was so interested in truth that he ignored the mouths through which truth and error issue. He was so interested in the mind of man that he failed to learn to what extent and in what way it depends upon the body, upon sight and touch and taste and smell. His philosophy could therefore be predicated of angels, of pure spirits, of ghosts — but not of men. It is a tragedy of history that the father of modern philosophy was so absorbed in philosophy that he ignored the philosopher. Thus his philosophy was not true of man. The first philosopher-maker of the modern mind took the mind out of man and thereby made it nonhuman.

The details of Descartes's life are not too well known. He wrote no autobiography, though scholars see autobiographical strains in his *Discourse on Method,* and he had no Boswell to record his thoughts and deeds for posterity. His associates were few and they were distant, so they can tell us little about the man. It is from his writings, from his letters to acquaintances, and from comments of those who knew him that we must glean information about him.

Descartes was born in 1596, and ten years later he entered the Jesuit college at La Flèche. This was the school of which Descartes observed in 1638 that "there is no place in the world where philosophy is better taught." But as a youth he had little liking for the subject, which, he thought, was a means "of making ourselves admired by others less learned." He apparently put little value on his education at La Flèche, his favorite observation being that it was primarily literary. The subject which seems to have attracted him most strongly was mathematics, partly because of the very nature of the subject, and partly, no doubt, because of the remarkable mathematics teacher then at La Flèche, a certain Father Clavius. Descartes inherited from this "Modern Euclid" the spirit of mathematical learning, an awesome and hallowed regard for mathematical truth as the only kind worthy of cultivation.

In the 1611 edition of his *Mathematical Works*, published when Descartes was still at La Flèche, Father Clavius stated his case for mathematics thus: "The mathematical disciplines demonstrate and justify by the most solid reasons everything they may call for discussion, so that they truly beget science in, and completely drive out all doubts from, the mind of the student. This can hardly be said of other sciences, where most of the time the intellect remains hesitating and dubious about the truth value of the conclusions, so manifold are the opinions and so conflicting the judgments. . . . The theorems of Euclid, as well as those of the other mathematicians, are just as purely true today, as safe in their results, as firm and solid in their demonstrations, as they already were in schools many centuries ago. . . . Since, therefore, mathematical disciplines are so exclusively dedicated to the love and cultivation of truth, that nothing is received there of what is false, nor even of that which is merely probable . . . there is no doubt that the first place among Sciences should be conceded to Mathematics." Descartes came away from La Flèche at the age of eighteen convinced not only, with Father Clavius, that mathematics was the queen of the sciences, but that it was the only science deserving of the name.

After leaving school in 1614, Descartes decided to travel in order to "read in the great book of the world." He joined the army of Prince Maurice of Nassau and traveled, but he read not in the "great book of the world" but in the mirror of his own mind. His notes reveal three important dates in his mental development, dates in which can be found his "marvelous discovery" which was to determine the course of modern philosophy for centuries. And, rather annoyingly for the cold rationalist who refuses to see any magic in numbers, these dates were the three successive November 10's of 1618, 1619, and 1620.

On the first of these dates Descartes met Isaac Beeckman, a Dutch doctor eight years older than himself, who provoked him to thinking afresh. He conversed with Beeckman and found that they had in common that love of mathematics which he had found in no other person since he left college. "I slumbered and you awakened me," he was to write to Beeckman at a later date. Together they talked, and together they planned to create a new science by applying the method of mathematics to the science of physics, then a part of philosophy. On the second of these dates he observes: "10 November, 1619: I discovered the foundations of a marvelous science."

The way Descartes had stumbled — for it was practically a case of stumbling — on this "marvelous science" was as follows: Since his army had nothing to do that day, he stayed alone in a small stove-heated room occupying himself with his thoughts. And that night he had a dream in which the Angel of Light visited him, a dream which he was to hold to his dying day the most important event in his life. For in that dream Descartes discovered his "marvelous science," which he was to work upon and perfect the remaining thirty-one years of his life. Ironically, then, modern rationalism was discovered in a dream in which the human mind played at most a subconscious part. What Descartes had done was to make the important discovery of applying algebra to geometry and creating what is today known as analytical geometry. Descartes saw at once, however, that he could also apply mathematics to physics so that "physics that had till then been connected with medicine and philosophy were now shown reducible to number."

It was a discovery worthy of genius. But Descartes did not stop there. He believed that he now saw his way clear to applying the mathematical method to all sciences and thus developing a single science, constructed along the lines of mathematics, which was to embrace all knowledge and reduce all sciences to the level of abstract number. God and angel, the mysteries of time and space, of plant and animal, complex social relationships, even that elusive creature man, were all to be rendered as abstract, as clear and distinct, as mathematical quantity and plus-or-minus relationships.

"All the sciences," he tells us, "are interconnected by a chain; no one of them can be completely grasped without the others following of themselves and so without taking in the whole encyclopaedia at one and the same time." Again: "Such a science should contain the primary rudiments of human reason, and its province ought to extend to the eliciting of true results in every subject." The world, then, and all knowledge will be knowable by the new method. It will be known in a flash, immediately by intuition, and not by the laborious process of taking information in through our senses, reflecting upon it, and resolving it into organized bodies of knowledge. Moreover, it will be a single science, including all knowledge and reducing it all to the same level and to the same method of treatment.

"10 November, 1620"; Descartes wrote the next year, "I begin to understand the foundation of a wonderful discovery." Through the year he had meditated on the ramifications of his discovery and had arrived at conclusions which he was to elucidate throughout the rest of his life. In 1622, he sold his estates at Poitou in order to obtain an independent income on which he could exist while devoting himself heart and soul to the completion of his new science. In 1628, he moved to Holland, where he was to remain for the following two decades. Here he lived in a land of intellectual anarchy, a land of businessmen scurrying about the market place and allowing Descartes to pass almost unseen while he prepared the new science of Cartesian rationalism that would plague the world long after the accomplishments of these busy Hollanders, who never had time to notice Descartes, had melted into insignificance.

In 1642, however, the University of Utrecht condemned his teaching, and he had to appeal to the Prince of Orange for protection. Fearful of arrest, he sought safety at the Hague, and then he began to think of returning to France, a land not noted in those days for the toleration of unorthodox opinions. At this time, however, he received an invitation to serve as instructor for Queen Christina of Sweden. He took the position gladly, for it offered him the double advantage of royal protection and princely patronage. But Queen Christina had a bad habit which proved fatal for Descartes. The royal lady arose at an unearthly hour, and because she felt that her mind was most active at five in the morning Descartes had to rise early too. One morning in the winter of 1650 he contracted a severe chill on his way to tutor the queen. He died a week later at the age of fifty-four.

3

The father of modern philosophy was an innovator by profession. He was the first philosopher in centuries who was not content to correct his predecessors and to make his small addition to the deposit of human wisdom handed down through the ages. He was the first to set out consciously to build the house of philosophy anew from its foundations. But he was a circumspect innovator. There was nothing boldly defiant, nothing dashing about Descartes. "It is not my temperament," he wrote to Pollot, "to sail against the wind." He had a new destination in mind and he was sailing on a new course, but he would tack circumspectly rather than sail straight into the wind of learned opinions. In his *Passions of the Soul* he applies the inglorious but safe rules of the professional soldier of his day: "It is imprudent to lose one's life when one can save oneself without dishonor; if the odds are heavy against one, it is better to beat an honorable retreat or ask quarter than to expose oneself unreasoningly to certain death."

So Descartes decided to choose his words carefully and to phrase his thought, so inimical to the Aristotelian philosophy still taught in the schools, in language that he could explain away if called upon to defend himself. "Now that I am to be not only a spectator of the world," he wrote, "but am to appear as actor on its stage, I wear a mask." The mask he wore was that of accepted philosophical and religious teaching, but the face beneath the mask was that of the sapper of scholasticism. And the words he uttered, when added together, could not be reconciled with the older and then decadent scholastic philosophy. "The truth must be veiled," Descartes had said. From his point of view as author of new theories he was no doubt right. Galileo's fate had warned him of that.

Descartes was passionately interested in truth, but he was

willing to veil her face in order to smuggle her, uninvited, to the feast of reason. Descartes was interested in smuggling truth to the feast, but he did not sit beside her at the banquet table. He was ready to disown her if she should be discovered and he should be named her escort. He did not sign his famous *Traité de monde*, for example, because he was afraid that inasmuch as some of Galileo's conclusions were stated in the *Traité*, Galileo's fate would also be his. He withheld the work from publication altogether, telling Catholic friends that "obedience to the Church" restrained him, "a dutiful son and subject," from publishing what seemed to be against the commonly received teaching of churchmen in France. He was wearing his mask, however, for he informed his faithful friend, Mersenne, that his problem was "to find an expedient by which to speak the truth without startling anyone's imagination or shocking opinions commonly received." Descartes, of course, is hardly to be censured for prudence. But neither is he to be eulogized for a heroism he did not possess. He was simply cautious, careful in an unheroic, pedestrian way, like most men throughout modern history. He liked to look upon himself as the great innovator and the daring new architect of the modern world. But it was not his temperament to sail against the wind, or to fly square in the face of public opinion.

Throughout his life Descartes remained aloof, both socially and intellectually. We find he had friends, it is true, but they invariably turn out to be men whom Descartes was using at the time: Beeckman, the physician, for example, or Faulhaber, the mathematician, or Mersenne, who acted as his contact man with the learned minds of the day. None of them was really a friend. Descartes was indeed incapable of friendship. The motto that he selected to guide him through life was *Bene vivit qui bene latuit*, a good life is spent in seclusion. It is safe to say that, although he did correspond considerably with men interested in his work, he seems to have depended very little upon outside stimulus for his thinking. Neither did he depend upon outside advice or criticism to guide him in his work or to check him against possible error.

He was sufficient unto himself; his reason alone was enough, both as subject and object, to reveal the whole world to him if he used the right method of procedure. No one, he was convinced, had ever yet possessed certain knowledge of anything; nothing, properly speaking, had yet been known. His science, which must be his work alone, would give him true knowledge for the first time in history. He need only have recourse to his reason alone and follow the right rules of methodology. No one's help is needed. No one's help is wanted. Descartes would brook no interference in his work of building his new "marvelous science" from and by his unaided reason.

If there was any one moral vice which Descartes exhibited strongly, it was pride. It was an intellectual pride that possessed him, a pride which enabled him to put himself up against the wisdom of the ages and against all the great philosophers of the past and to conclude that he alone could achieve what he was convinced the great minds of the past had groped for in vain. Maritain's words are both apt and just: "The pride of human knowledge appears thus as the very substance, solid and resistant, of rationalist hopes. Pride, a dense pride without frivolity or distraction, as stable as virtue, as vast as geometric extension, bitter and restless as the ocean, takes possession of Descartes to such an extent that it would seem the universal form of his interior workings and the principle of all his suffering. We know what bitter, dark envy he fostered against Aristotle, and what torment he suffered at still not having supplanted him in the schools."

So much reliance had Descartes placed in his discovery, in his method of arriving at certain knowledge, that he was convinced all people could use it effectively and surely. The new science, he believed, was for all, even for those who had never studied, even for women who would take the time to read his works. Clear ideas are easy ideas, and his was a science of clear and distinct ideas. As a matter of fact, Descartes was anxious to be the one teacher of humanity. He wanted no interpreter to stand between himself and the masses of mankind whom he would instruct. "Those who avail themselves of their natural reason alone," he asserted, "may be better judges of my opinions than those who give heed only to the writings of the ancients." So he wrote in such fashion as to catch the eye and win the assent of the man-in-the-street. He was the first important philosopher to use the vulgar tongue of French rather than the accepted

Latin. He took his composition very seriously and wrote many drafts of each work, for, he tells us, he wished to make himself "understandable even to women."

There is a truly modern note in his writing. Proud man that he was, hostile to philosophers and eager to catch the attention and win the assent of nonspecialists, he quite naturally fell into an out-and-out dogmatism. Descartes does not reason with his reader, as at least the better philosophers had done in days gone by. He does not proceed, as ordinary men do, reasoning his way step by step. He dogmatizes instead. He reasons, it is true, but not with the reader. He meditates; he reasons with himself. The reader must follow, and the implication always lurks in his pages that if you do not follow, if you disagree, there is something wrong with your mind. Descartes is always dogmatically right.

Descartes was undoubtedly a man of genius. His mind was keen, and it cleft boldly through the realms of thought; it cut sharply and incisively and to the point. He was a headstrong genius of heroic proportions who was capable of becoming the father of modern philosophy and engendering the system of rationalism which many less gifted and less heroic thinkers will try to complete in the centuries to follow. Of him Gilson observes: "Indifferent to the life of the court, to military glory, to the pleasures of society and superstitions of social rank; desirous, certainly, of seeing his philosophy triumph over error, but setting the passion for research and the joy of discovery at a far higher price than the pleasure of publishing and the satisfaction of success, Descartes conceived no other ideal than that of a perfectly disciplined will placed at the service of a perfectly clear reason. 'Seek peace in wisdom' was the profound aspiration of this man who lived by thought alone for thought alone." Descartes was one of nature's noble intellects — in an austere, unapproachable sort of way.

4

Method is the important thing in Descartes's thought. If you have that right, everything will follow. If you truly desire the truth and you use the right method in pursuing it, you cannot go wrong. For error is a matter of using the wrong method or of having a bad will. So we must, in fairness to Descartes, observe carefully how he sets about perfecting his method.

He had observed how philosophers agreed on nothing. He had seen how their disagreement had led to the universal skepticism of persons like Montaigne, for when five philosophers disagree on a certain point it stands to reason that at least four must be wrong. And the fifth is likely wrong too. Descartes's problem, then, was to find a method of verifying opinions which would stand the test of Montaigne's universal skepticism. This he believed he could do only by resorting to his system of "methodic doubt." He decided to ignore everything that philosophers had done in days gone by, to pretend that no one before him had ever come to a conclusion. If he took absolutely nothing from other thinkers it stood to reason that he could receive no error from them.

But what about being mistaken himself? Descartes admitted the likelihood of his having made mistakes up to this point. So he decided to adopt the skeptical attitude of not admitting he knew anything at this point. "As for the opinions which up to that time I had embraced, I thought that I could not do better than resolve at once to sweep them wholly away, that I might afterwards be in a position to admit either others more correct, or even perhaps the same, when they had undergone the scrutiny of reason." He did not doubt for the sake of doubting, as did the skeptics, Descartes tells us, "but simply to find ground of assurance, and cast aside the loose earth and sand that I may reach the rock or clay."

He will pretend, then, that his mind is an absolute blank, that he knows absolutely nothing. He will then proceed to receive into his mind only those ideas that are truly certain, which for Descartes meant clear and distinct. The founder of rationalism here seems to involve himself in a very obvious error, one which does irreparable harm to philosophy from his day till this. For this criterion of an idea's truth is a subjective clarity and distinctness which refers to his idea of a thing, not to the thing itself. What is clear and distinct to the mind, according to the Cartesian philosophy, is thereby true and certain. But nothing is more patently wrong, nor more patently egoistic. There are many things in the world of which we have very fuzzy and confused ideas; but to deny their existence because we do not grasp them clearly is egoistic nonsense. So, too, do we sometimes have crystal-clear ideas that turn out to be absolutely wrong. Reality is bigger than our minds, not, as Descartes would have it, limited by them.

Descartes will start with nothing, then, and accept only what he knows by clear and distinct ideas. This criterion, he decides, eliminates all sense knowledge, for his senses have deceived him in the past and he has no guarantee they will not deceive him again. "I observed that the senses sometimes mislead us; and it is a part of prudence not to place absolute confidence in that by which we have even once been deceived." Let us suppose, he requests of us, that we have no eyes with which to see, no hands with which to feel, no nose nor ears with which to smell or hear. Thus Descartes rules out the world of sense knowledge and forever closes the gate through which Aristotle and St. Thomas — and the world of common-sense men — have their knowledge come. When the rain beats in our face we are not to assert that it is raining, or even that we have faces; when we bump a door in the dark and feel blood on our cut lip we are not to assert that we have bumped anything or that we feel pain or that we have a lip that has been cut or even that there is a door which has been bumped.

Where, then, can Descartes turn to find these ideas that will be clear and certain? He turns to the recesses of his own mind, and there he gropes for ideas that exist independently of sense knowledge, ideas which, therefore, have always been in his mind. These must be ideas with which he was born, for unless they are innate they can come into the mind only through the senses — or through direct illumination from God. Now then, if we blot out all knowledge received through the senses what can we possibly know? Descartes answers thus: "We . . . suppose that there is neither God, nor sky, nor bodies, and that we ourselves have neither hands nor feet, nor finally, a body, but we cannot in the same way suppose that we are not, while we doubt of the truth of those things."

He therefore concludes: "Whilst I wished that all was false, it was absolutely necessary that I who thus thought, should be somewhat, and I observed the truth, 'I think, hence I exist,' was so certain and of such evidence that no ground of doubt, however extravagant, could be alleged by the sceptics capable of shaking it."

From this first principle that he exists and that he thinks, Descartes hopes to deduce his whole philosophy. This must be done deductively by his reason, drawing upon itself alone with no reference to things outside the mind or to the experiences of his senses. He will admit as certain, one by one, those ideas which he can deduce clearly and distinctly from his existence and from the fact, of which he has immediate experience, that he thinks. Only these things, and nothing more, are to be admitted to his body of knowledge. Thus he will preserve it from all taint of doubt and safeguard it from the attacks of the most rigid skeptic.

This deductive method, applied rigorously by Descartes, makes of him an obstinate divider. By his analysis he breaks down apparent wholes into simpler, distinct units between which the connection is clearly seen. With Descartes's followers, however, these units tend to separate from each other, each standing out strongly in its individuality, each being clearly and distinctly an independent unit. Thus Cartesians, by the deductive method, divide the world up into a mosaic of things corresponding to their clear and distinct ideas, a mosaic of independent things whose interconnections cannot be known and whose existence, therefore, can all be postulated as mutually exclusive and independent of each other. It is in this way that Descartes made an unconscious contribution to the scientism of the modern world. This is what Maritain means when he says that because of the Cartesian method, "Henceforth, to understand is to separate; to be intelligible is to be capable of mathematical reconstruction. To take a machine to pieces and put it together again, that is the high work of the intelligence. The mechanical explanation becomes the only conceivable type of scientific explanation."

The Cartesian method will be the method of mathematics, the one science Descartes thought was capable of yielding certain truth. The mathematical method, he insisted — and this was his "marvelous discovery" — would be applied to all things. Men, chickens, stones and ideas, atoms and dreams will all be rendered into abstract numbers. This method, by means of which much can be accomplished when the statistician-philosopher remembers what he has done in rendering dollars and men and children into numbers, has by its abuse fostered much of the intellectualist tyranny of modern scholarship. It is at the source of the cold inhumanity of modern science where human beings are turned into "cases" in the clinic, where human students are put through a battery of tests and "classified" in filing cabinets, where stark tragedy, the utter despair of parents and the pathetic wretchedness of little children is computed in so many million missing calories, where the pathos and the crime of war are computed in so many casualties and so many billions of dollars.

Descartes worked, like the mathematician, in pure abstraction. And he rendered everything he knew into the three components of thought, extension, and God. These become the only three elements with which he works and in terms of which he evolves his whole philosophy. Like the mathematician, too, Descartes goes from ideas to things, rather than following the philosopher's method of going from things to ideas. What he posits of his clear and distinct idea he will posit of the reality which it represents. This is the easy way of building the temple of knowledge, for it is all done in the mind. Following the Cartesian method, it is only necessary to build a temple inside your mind out of clear and distinct idea-bricks — and behold you can assert its existence outside your mind.

5

Such was Descartes' method for building his temple of knowledge. What are the characteristics peculiar to his work? By what marks can it be distinguished from the works of other philosophers? Cartesian knowledge can be said, without too much oversimplification of the truth, to have three principal marks: it is innate; it is intuitive; it is independent of things. These are the marks of Cartesian rationalism, and they are the marks by which philosophy was universally recognized in Western history until the time of Locke; they are marks peculiar, to some extent, even of Locke's successors who complete the Cartesian experiment by reverting logically enough to a complete skepticism — right back to the position of Montaigne from which Descartes thought he had rescued man's mind in the nick of time.

These are inhuman attributes, all of them, which characterize Cartesianism. The father of modern philosophy holds, in the first place, that knowledge is innate, that we are born with a natural inclination to form certain ideas and make certain judgments, that knowledge more or less lies deep in the recesses of our minds until, by probing in the right way, we draw it to the front of our minds where we come to know it and to be fully conscious of it. We are born with certain fixed principles planted in our minds by God; they are an inherent part of us. The first of these principles, of course, is that "I think, hence I exist." Other ideas, eternally true and unchangeable in their essences, as that of a triangle, or the principle of identity, are easily discovered in the mind. Now by the proper method of deduction we can build our whole temple of knowledge. The brick-ideas are all in the mind, put there by God when He created us. We need only uncover them, clean them up, recognize them for what they are, arrange them properly, and our temple will be built — orderly, symmetrical, perfect, straight from the hand of God.

But to assert that ideas are innate is to fly in the face of human experience and to deny the process by which we actually obtain knowledge. Descartes's temperament may not have been "to sail against the wind," but his theory of innate ideas is certainly buffeted by anyone's everyday experience. No one is born with the idea of war or of man or of strikes or of fire in his mind, even hidden deep in its innermost recesses. He reads about war, sees the bombing of villages as a youngster, sees soldiers transported to the front and sees veterans, perhaps missing a leg or a thumb, return to civilian life. And he gets a pretty good idea of war. In the same way he sees what fire can do when he burns his finger with a match, and he reads what chemists say about the nature of fire. Thus he forms an idea of fire.

The inhumanity of Cartesian innate ideas is perhaps best shown by seeing a good Cartesian apply them to life about him. One of the physiocrats, an eighteenth-century rationalist who drew up plans for a perfect society to replace the disjointed France in which he lived, tells his readers that his method will be deductive, the only valid method, and that he must deduce social laws from his mind alone. "As truth exists by itself and is the same in all places and all times, so by reasoning and examination we can arrive at it and all the practical consequences which result from it. Examples which appear to contradict these consequences prove nothing, for it is only that men have lost the way and do not have certitude and full knowledge of the truth." If, in other words, you deduce that a *laissez-faire* economy makes for perfect society, the fact that millions of men and women starve while little pigs are thrown into the river and wheat is burned and rice rots in the field are "examples which . . . prove nothing, for it is only that men have lost the way and do not have certitude and full knowledge of the truth."

The second characteristic of Cartesian knowledge is as inhuman as the first. The ideas of Descartes are not only born in the mind; they are known intuitively, grasped, as it were, in a flash of intellectualism. Now this might be the way angels know the truth, or even, perhaps, the way mystics sometimes, by an extraordinary and unexplainable flight of the intellect, arrive at a conclusion. But it is not the way the mind of man ordinarily works. Men reason more or less laboriously, proceeding from principle to principle, from fact to fact, from cause to effect, step by step in logical fashion. This is the way of man's mind. We see that under certain conditions two atoms of hydrogen combine with one of oxygen to form water. From this we arrive at a knowledge of the composition of water, and we then go on drudgingly to study its properties. But Descartes would not have us proceed thus. He would have us go by flashes, like lightning in the night sky, suddenly apprehending new truths like newly revealed vistas hitherto completely in the dark. Thus Descartes disowns reason, does violence to its nature, denies the normal conditions of its activity. His analysis of reason simply does not apply to man.

The third, and perhaps the most damaging characteristic of Cartesian knowledge is its independence of things. Our ideas do not depend on realities outside the mind; they do not depend on the senses. They depend only on the mind itself, and, of course, on God their Creator. An idea is no longer true if it corresponds to a reality outside the mind; it is true independently of outside reality if it is clear and distinct. One's idea of Da Vinci's *Mona*

Lisa no longer must correspond, to be true, to the picture painted by the great Italian artist and now hung in the Louvre. Descartes has completely reversed the order of truth and of reality. He has turned knowledge inside out by cutting it away from things. By breaking loose from its moorings in reality such a theory of knowledge takes free flight in the world of fancy.

Such intellectual irresponsibility is bad enough — and has wrought enough damage in the modern world. But even worse is the tyranny of Cartesian idealism. For such a theory of knowledge seals the mind up into an airtight compartment and cuts it away from contact with anything outside of itself. Its object of intellection is the idea itself, and nothing more than the idea. "My natural intelligence," Descartes tells us, "enables me to know evidently that my ideas are in me like pictures." It is only the picture that the mind sees, never the reality portrayed by the picture. Thus Descartes has put his picture-ideas between the mind and the world, and he has made it impossible for the mind ever to peek around the pictures to see what is behind them. It is for this reason that the problem of existence takes foremost place in Cartesian philosophy, as it does in all modern philosophy. If we know only our ideas, how can we be sure that there is such a thing as rain or a typewriter or this book?

Descartes will not let us know the rain or the typewriter or the book. We know only the idea of each of these things, and now our problem has become the terrific one of proving whether such things do exist. We have not denied them, but neither do we know them. This is the problem, of course, which has never bothered the farmer or the bricklayer or the shoemaker. The farmer knows that it rains and that there is ground under his feet and that out of that ground he has nurtured crops in good years and failed to bring them forth in bad years when there was no rain. But the Cartesian theory of knowledge will only admit that the farmer has ideas of all these things. It will not admit that he can be certain of their actual existence outside of his mind.

But how, in the Cartesian philosophy, are we to account for the ideas of rain and earth under our feet and crops ready to pick in the autumn? These ideas are not dependent on real things. They have not come into the mind through the senses, for the mind is a closed compartment into which no sense knowledge can leak. These ideas, Descartes concludes, could come only from God. It is He who put them in the mind, and they are known, as we have seen, intuitively and independently of things outside the mind. Descartes was convinced that God was a good God, as we shall see, and that He would not deceive mankind. Therefore, he argued, if God has put such ideas as those of rain and earth in our minds and has given us the irresistible conviction that they actually do exist outside of us, then such things must actually exist. Otherwise God would be a deceiver. And Descartes had already decided that God was not deceitful.

What Descartes is really saying is that we do not actually know things in the world. We know only our ideas. But because God is good and could not deceive us, we take it on faith that there are things outside the mind which correspond to our clear and distinct ideas. Strange it is that the father of rationalism should make us accept the whole world, even our hands and eyes, our wives and children, on simple faith! But this is the only way out of his dilemma created by a theory of knowledge cutting the mind off from reality and from sense knowledge. Objects can be known only through God and through our knowledge of His goodness. They exist only because the idea is in our mind, and God, who is good, has given us the idea. The same irresponsibility and the same tyranny remain. The world of reality must more than ever conform to whatever clear and distinct ideas we have. For otherwise God would be deceitful.

6

Descartes convinced himself of the existence of God by following out his idealistic method in logical fashion. The proof, reduced to its simplest form, runs like this: I have an idea-picture in my mind of an infinitely perfect Being. I cannot have created this idea-picture myself, for I am a finite, imperfect creature. This idea must come from a being of infinite perfection, namely, from God Himself. Therefore God exists. This proof for God's existence is corroborated by another Cartesian proof which is equally invalid. The idea of God, Descartes maintained, contains all perfection. But existence is a perfection. Therefore, he concludes, God exists.

The Cartesian proof for God's existence is no proof at all, for it is based on the illicit transition from idea to thing. It is the tyranny we mentioned above of concluding that the world of reality must conform to my ideas. I have an idea of God; therefore there is a God to correspond to my idea. Descartes only proved that he had an idea of God. But he skips sophistically from the idea to the thing. His idea of God includes the note of God's existence. But this only proves that "existence" is a quality of the idea — and not, as Descartes concluded, an attribute of the thing outside the mind.

Such a quick skip is understandable, of course, for more reasons than one. In the first place, it follows logically from the Cartesian method and from the innate, intuitive, and idealistic quality of his knowledge. Cartesian rationalism always goes backward — from ideas to things. In the second place, we should remember that Descartes's greatest concern was to establish an objective world. We know our ideas, he believed, but we must establish the existence of the world which we cannot know directly. Now the only way to do that was to postulate the existence of a benevolent, perfectly good God. So Descartes rushed into any proof he could find. The proofs were bad, but the conclusions were necessary for Descartes's system and for his peace of mind. So they were accepted.

God was of little account in Descartes's system except as the guarantor of material things. After His existence and His perfection had been postulated, and thus the reality of the material world guaranteed, God could be forgotten in the Cartesian system. He withdraws into His heaven and leaves the world to Descartes. The father of modern philosophy had, indeed, resolved to devote "only a few hours a year" to metaphysics, for he believed he had completely mastered the subject in a single analysis; the rest of his time he would spend on much more practical applications of philosophy.

Descartes's picture of God did Him harm in several ways. In the first place, it was anthropomorphic. God is conceived of as a human monarch raised to the absolute of perfection; His qualities are man's good qualities without limitation. And thus His laws will be like the monarch's laws, depending upon His good pleasure alone. He thus comes to be the arbitrary lawmaker, with emphasis on His will rather than His intellect. Divine law, eternal law, natural law become not so much the *ordo rationis* of earlier philosophers as the *lex voluntatis* of modern times. Law resides now not in the nature of things but in the fanciful and arbitrary will of the supreme lawmaker. Thus Cartesian philosophy reinforced Calvinist theology, and carried along the voluntaristic trend of later medieval philosophers.

At the same time it prepared the way for the deism of later rationalists by pushing God back into His heaven and leaving the world to man alone. Even more important — and certainly ironic, coming from the father of rationalism — another field of reality is marked "out of bounds" for human reason. Descartes had made man take the world of material things on faith. Now he insists that, while God's existence and perfection are proved by reason, the field of theology is not to be entered by man. Descartes apparently wanted to safeguard faith by isolating it from reason. But what can reason do, in the Cartesian system of clear and distinct ideas, in a field of mystery and of speculation? There is no room for such speculation about God and the mystery of the infinite in the Cartesian system. In this system, to quote Maritain, "theology if it is not reduced to philosophy itself, is only an exercise of ignoramuses chattering about the unknown." The whole field of theology, then, is marked "out of bounds" for reason, and man is told to rely on revelation alone for his theological knowledge. Theology and philosophy are sharply separated by the father of modern rationalism, and philosophy alone is the province of reason.

7

Descartes was an obstinate divider. His clear and distinct ideas necessitate a dividing and a subdividing into atoms of knowledge which, when once they are divided, can never be brought back together. The most important single cleavage which Cartesian philosophy accomplished, however, was within man himself. For Descartes cut man's mind away from his body, wrenched it out of its habitat, and never managed to get it back again. He had started to build his philosophy, we will remember, by clearing everything out of his mind and imagining that he knew nothing. Then he came to the conclusion that he could not doubt that he thought. He knew his thought by an immediate act of the intellect. But that is all he knew. He could therefore say of himself nothing except that he knows himself as pure thought. And this he says: "I, that is my thought." Again: "I, or my mind." Descartes therefore knows himself as pure thought, and he defines himself as a thinking machine. This is a clear and distinct idea, and therefore Descartes concludes that there is a reality corresponding to this idea in the world. It is the reality of a thinking machine, which is himself. He did not claim he was mind alone, of course, but the mind is distinct from the body — and the mind alone is known directly. His body Descartes must take on faith.

The mind for him is nothing but thought. It is clear and distinct. And it has no connection with the body, no matter what seems to be the case. What, then, of sensation? Bodies cannot be the causes of our ideas, for ideas are innate. So sensation comes to be considered by Descartes as an idea awakened within the mind on the occasion of a change taking place in the body. How to connect changes in the body-machine with ideas in the mind becomes a problem to plague Cartesians through the centuries. Since there can be no causal connection between the body and the mind, which Descartes has so cleanly and so definitely separated, and since the mind is pure thought and the body is mere extension, their only possible point of connection must be in God.

Various explanations of this union are proposed by Cartesian followers. But not by Descartes himself, for as Leibniz put it, "at that point Monsieur Descartes withdrew from the game." Leibniz himself sought to explain the union by his system of pre-established harmony, whereby God, in His perfect wisdom, had ordered all things from the very beginning in such a way that every modification within a body would be accompanied by a corresponding modification within the soul or mind. There is no causal connection between these modifications except in God. Spinoza resolved it in a different way. Pantheist that he was, he had concluded that God was the only true substance, and He was therefore the common source of the parallel attributes of thought and extension which had to flow from that substance with the same necessity so that every mode of extension had to have an equivalent mode of thought. A third explanation was offered by Malebranche. His occasionalism stated that God directly causes us to have an idea on the occasion of a change occurring within our body. When I see this book, which is a sensation, God gives me the idea of book to correspond to the sensation I have received.

These are, of course, all rather complicated and uneconomical explanations of a problem that Descartes had created and failed to solve when he said, "I, that is, my thought." Now as the mind is pure thought in Cartesianism, so the body is mere extension. The consequence of this dualistic concept of man is put well by Gilson when he concludes: "Metaphysics then is pure spiritualism, and physics pure mechanism." The body becomes a mere machine, a clock made up of wheels and wires and springs and locks. This is one of the terrible, inhuman results of Cartesianism from which we suffer today. Man's body is no longer human. It is the machine in which "I, that is, my thought" is somehow located. The thought rents the body as the tenant rents a house. It lives there for a while, but no real union, no intimacy develops. It is merely a matter of convenience. The soul is not affected by the body it inhabits, nor does the body take on anything from its tenant.

This body-machine which the mind is said to inhabit has, under Descartes, been stripped of its dignity, its sacredness, and its intrinsic worth. It has become a machine or a retort or perhaps a vacant house. It is to be experimented with, scrutinized, analyzed. It is to be retarded with sedatives, speeded up with stimulants, and its reactions are to be studied like those of a racing motor or a doped race horse. A straight line of connection can be drawn from Cartesian mechanism down to the inhuman experiments conducted in concentration camps by Nazi physician-mechanics, experiments to which the human body was subjected as guinea pigs and rabbits had been in days gone by. The world was horrified to see what was done. Descartes would have been horrified too. But he could hardly have opposed it on the grounds of his philosophy about man. He said the body was a machine. The Nazi physician-mechanic — or even his American brother scientist — takes Descartes at his word and, like a good mechanic, takes the body apart to see what makes it tick.

Descartes's concept of the body as a machine whose essence was extension was taken literally. In his *Man A Machine,* published in 1768, La Mettrie insists on giving Descartes credit for engendering the view that the body is a piece of machinery. "This celebrated philosopher," he says, ". . . was the first to prove completely that animals are true machines."

Descartes had treated man in rough fashion. And the idea-picture he created in his mind — two separate clear and distinct idea-pictures rather — showed little resemblance to man he exists. The man of Descartes's mind was broken into two complete substances, joined to each other no one knew how — neither Descartes nor anyone else. There was the mind or the soul, which was nothing but thought, on the one hand; and on the other was the body, which was nothing but geometric extension to which God had added motion from all eternity. The Cartesian picture of man can be likened to an angel in a machine. The angel was in the machine — in the pineal gland Descartes thought — about the way the driver is perched in the cab of a bulldozer. But Descartes had never seen a bulldozer. So we might keep the body-picture Descartes undoubtedly saw in his mind and say that he saw man as a pure spirit in a lifeless body. Man, to Descartes, was a ghost in a corpse.

8

Descartes is of tremendous importance in the intellectual history of the modern world. From him flowed all philosophy initiated in modern times. Rationalists carried on his work and tried to perfect the temple of knowledge he had not finished when death overtook him in 1650. They tried to show how ideas are innate, how we know nothing but them, and how we can still give an adequate account of the world about us. They tried vainly to bring about some sort of connection between the body and the soul, and their failure made impossible the equilibrium between the spiritual and the material formerly ascribed to man.

Some philosophers carried on Cartesian spiritualism, and they soon came to the utter absurdity of denying the world, and in time even their own minds. In this way philosophy committed suicide. Other philosophers concentrated on the body-machine, and they ended up materialists by denying the reality of the spirit and of everything except matter and motion. In this way philosophy died of malnutrition.

More specifically, Descartes's break from the intellectual tradition of European philosophy was a serious loss. For this was a tradition which went back to the Greeks and included such names as those of Plato, Aristotle, Cicero, Seneca, St. Augustine, St. Thomas, and St. Bonaventura. Though it was in a bad state of degeneration when he repudiated it, nevertheless there was much that was good and much that was valuable in the remains of scholastic philosophy. This, too, Descartes threw overboard. Had he rescued nothing more than the realistic, common-sense attitude held by these scholastics toward philosophical questions he would have done the modern world a great benefit and saved it from much madness. But to get rid of the mice on the ship of philosophy — and it was full of mice — he blew up the ship and watched with smug satisfaction as it settled into the sea of oblivion, mice, men, and all. Valuable stores of knowledge were lost; the wisdom of generations was blotted out of modern man's mind; the lessons of the past were discarded; techniques and methods, attitudes and viewpoints built on centuries of experience were destroyed. Descartes was an obstinate divider. He cut modern philosophy off from the past, and he made the break clean and sharp and complete.

He created a self-contained system of thought which was bad enough in his own day but was not to bear its bitter fruit of frustrated thinking and of skepticism for many generations. It was an inhuman system which cut man away from the world about him and shut his mind up within itself, which made it impossible for the philosopher to look out on the world from his ivory tower and see whether there was any connection between his golden threads of theory and the world of men plodding wearily through the mud at the base of his tower. He could no longer check his thought by experience. Neither could he derive fresh material for thought from the world of men pushing about him. He could not even rely upon his own senses to furnish him with material for ideas. He had to retreat upon his mind and find therein the universe of thought from which he sought to derive a universe of reality.

His view of man did violence to human nature and gave to the modern mind a twisted concept of man. Man is made a creature of pure thought, who happens accidentally to inhabit a corpse. The complicated but undeniable interaction of the body and the soul on each other is made an insoluble problem. The senses become unimportant, and sense knowledge becomes at best some sort of mechanical action caused by God through His laws of motion. Man's affective life is completely neglected, and feeling becomes something like a confused idea.

The relationship of the body and the mind, separated so patently by Descartes, will be reasserted in more recent times. But the old balance which Descartes destroyed is never restored. Some philosophers and religious people will assert a dominance of mind over matter so naïvely and so simply that you believe in time that a strong enough wish can literally move a mountain. Or winning the hundred-yard dash is a matter of strong concentration. But most thinkers come to assert a deterministic influence of the body over the mind, so that in modern times bad thinking has come to be looked upon simply as the result of dispepsia or of glandular trouble. We know today that the mind does influence the body, and the body has influence on the mind. But Descartes obscured the problem of their mutual influence long ago, and he created all sorts of obfuscating conjectures that are only now being dissolved by observation and by common sense.

As Cartesian dualism does violence to man, so the criterion of truth Descartes set up, the clear and distinct idea, does violence to the world of nature. The world simply is not made up of neat little mosaics, each item clear and distinct, sharply separated from all the others and independent of them. But so Cartesianism would have it. Descartes is the sire of that modern type of mind which divides everything into sharply formed and clearly perceived and distinctly placed atoms. This is the mind which thinks things are true if they are clear and sharp and distinct. This is the mind which does violence to whatever is not clear and distinct, for it makes it so and thus compresses it into the already made molds of the mind.

Ultimately, Cartesian rationalism tended to be destructive of reason itself. It denied rational processes of obtaining knowledge and posited an intuitive process whereby man obtained his clear and distinct ideas by a kind of illumination. Descartes denied man his reason and gave him the spirit of an angel, a pure spirit unencumbered with a body, a mind that is pure thought and knows things immediately without taking those steps that men, as rational beings, must take. Descartes further limited the use of reason by denying it knowledge of anything but its own ideas. He denied that it could really know material things; it had to accept them on faith, as Catholics accept the mystery of the Trinity. And he went even further. He forbade man the use of his reason in studying theology. This, he said, was subject matter to be received submissively and passively and nonunderstandingly on faith. One was not even to try to understand it. Thus at the very beginning rationalism became a barren thing. The mind could only concentrate on itself, and it is no wonder that philosophers began to wonder whether there would be left anything at all to study.

Descartes, standing at the very threshold of modern philosophy, showed clearly how dangerous a thing philosophy could become when it took its sights off the mileposts of reality and began to wander it knew not where. He showed how absurd, and how far removed from common sense, philosophy could easily become. When a man can identify himself with his thought alone, when he can say "I, or my mind," it is time for him to quit philosophy and become a farmer or a bricklayer. Not enough philosophers in modern history have become farmers or bricklayers, and the result is that philosophy has earned a bad reputation for itself for saying things that the man-in-the-street, with a good sense of reality, readily condemns as nonsense. Thus philosophy, unfortunately for itself and for the man-in-the-street, unfortunately for all of us today, was itself discredited.

Descartes's failure is most consequential, for in most men's eyes his failure was the failure of reason itself. He is, indeed, more responsible than any single man in modern history for the discredit into which philosophy was to fall, for its withdrawing from reality and from the position of direction which it should exercise over society. Philosophers will tend through modern times to stay in their ivory towers and to leave the helm of modern society to be tended by scientists and, today at least, by psychiatrists and nuclear physicists. Descartes opened the door to all of this. Hume expressed the sad plight into which Descartes had plunged philosophers when he said, at the end of his *Treatise of Human Nature:* "I am affrighted and confounded with that forlorn solitude in which I am placed in my philosophy." Hume was intelligent enough to be "affrighted and confounded." Most modern philosophers were not.

V

LOCKE

JOHN LOCKE is the typical English thinker of modern times. There have been more profound and more consistent English philosophers, but none quite so English as Locke. Where Descartes was thoroughly French and did much to fix the French way of thinking, Locke appealed to the Englishman's common sense as the ultimate authority in philosophy and in action. Descartes's standard of truth was the clear and distinct idea, but Locke, feeling that clear and distinct ideas can be false, asks for things to be "consistent with common-sense." Descartes required the certitude of *évidence* and tried to resolve everything into mathematical formulas; Locke looked only for probability as his guide in all things. Descartes had tried to build an integrated system of philosophy which was to be consistent, complete, perfect. Locke tried only to solve individual, practical problems as they arose by dissolving them in the solvent of common sense, and he apparently never bothered whether one solution neutralized or contradicted another.

Except for their importance, Descartes and Locke seem to have had only one thing in common — they were both bachelors throughout life. But — symbolically — they were bachelors for different reasons. Descartes found woman's beauty dim beside that of truth. Locke was too concerned with himself, and especially his health, to consider marriage. "My health," he wrote from Paris to a friend in England, "is the only mistress I have a long time courted, and is so coy a one that I think it will take up the remainder of my days to obtain her good graces and keep her in good humor." It did. For seventy-two years. Of the two, Locke was undoubtedly the more humane, the more friendly and likable. On Descartes's side is nobleness, integrity, high pride; on Locke's side is affableness, adaptability, a measure of humility.

Descartes and Locke both made significant contributions to the development of the modern mind, and herein lies their largest common denominator. Locke, were he here now, would be genuinely surprised to find himself so important; Descartes, on the other hand, would be jealous and only grudgingly would he inch over to make room for the Englishman. And Locke would rightly be surprised, for, as one of his biographers aptly remarks, his importance "seems in excess of the author's speculative depth and subtlety, or grandeur of character." But, through accidents of time and circumstance over which he had no control, Locke — who really was not a philosopher at all — became one of the "Big Three" in the history of modern philosophy. George Santayana does not overstate the case when he observes of Locke: "Father of psychology, father of the criticism of knowledge, father of theoretical liberalism, godfather at least of the American political system, of Voltaire and the Encyclopedia, at home he was the ancestor of that whole school of polite moderate opinion which can unite liberal Christianity with mechanical science and with psychological idealism."

Locke is important for having rescued philosophy from the ivory-towered retreats where Descartes and his successors had imprisoned her. Locke brought her back into the parlor, the countinghouse, and the pub. The third Earl of Shaftesbury, whom

Locke tutored, appreciated this point. "It may well qualify," he says of his tutor's *Essay Concerning Human Understanding,* "for business and the world as for the sciences and a university. No one has done more towards the recalling of philosophy from barbarity into use and practice of the world, and into the company of the better and politer sort, who might well be ashamed of it in its other dress. No one has opened a better or clearer way to reasoning."

The man who rescued philosophy "from barbarity" and led her back into the market place was no philosopher. He was a man of the street, a man of the people, who clothed the maiden of philosophy in the raiment of common sense and smuggled her into the world so dressed that Englishmen would not be ashamed to be caught courting her. The Englishman of Locke's day, indeed, would not have been seen wooing philosophy unless she had been dressed like a fashionable English lady. Locke performed this service for his contemporaries. In dressing philosophy anew and teaching her a fresh idiom he made her presentable to Englishmen, but in putting new clothes on her back and new speech in her mouth Locke handled the delicate maiden of philosophy roughly — and she never recovered from the effects of this transformation.

Locke made her a popular lady. For he said clearly, with apparent wisdom and authority, what lay unexpressed deep in the hearts and minds of his contemporaries. People were tired of extremes in religion, in politics, in philosophy — and Locke was moderation itself in all fields. People were tired of philosophic bickering — and Locke's deceptive simplicity appealed to both their common sense and their intellectual slothfulness. Locke summed up all those forces which had been struggling through the seventeenth century; he justified them and enthroned them and, *ex post facto,* he showed the people of England how moderate, how reasonable, how tolerant they had been in their century of fratricidal struggle. He sounded notes that struck up sympathetic vibrations everywhere. Everything he said seemed so reasonable, so sensible, so fair. Because this is what the Whig victors of the Glorious Revolution thought themselves to be, Locke became their spokesman in all fields — and their children became his disciples.

Locke is important, then, for having justified the Whig revolution, a nice bloodless coup of which Locke could be proud. But he justified — without ever knowing it — other and bloodier revolutions to come in France and in America. In reacting reasonably against the arbitrary rule of the Stuart kings, Locke preached an individualism in politics, in religion, and in education that would be pushed through the following centuries into an extreme *laissez-faire* in politics, indifferentism in religion, and chaos in education which he would certainly condemn. Locke reasonably showed that men are not born with innate ideas, that knowledge is acquired through the senses; but doing this clumsily, he unknowingly opened the way to an environmental determinism which reduced men to the status of passive reeds bending before the breezes of nature. And Locke pushed God farther back into His heaven, thus preparing the way for eighteenth-century deism.

His moderate empiricism, his modified utilitarianism, and his hypothetical materialism were safe enough in his hands and in the hands of the average common-sense Englishman. But that was because they were not philosophers. They were content to stop short of the logical conclusions toward which their common-sense compromises pointed. Consistent philosophers were to come along, however, to push various Lockean theories to logical conclusions — just the sort of thing that is un-Lockean and un-English.

Thus Locke came to stand at the head of divergent streams of modern philosophy — all of which, in some way, stem back to him and are colored by his distinctive personality. Berkeley and Hume could follow him in one direction and get rid of everything except a stream of consciousness, thus ending in full skepticism. Empiricists, positivists, and utilitarians could follow him in another direction and end up denying the validity of speculation, but not of "facts." Voltaire could use Locke as a weapon against established institutions in France and thus make him the godfather of the French Enlightenment and of the French Revolution. This is very much for a mild-mannered bachelor to have accomplished. It seems almost unbelievable that John Locke, who was neither particularly profound, nor especially dynamic, could have stamped himself so strongly on the modern mind.

1

But he did. Or perhaps it is truer to say that he was stamped on the modern mind. For it was not so much Locke who made himself great, but rather the times in which he lived and causes for which he wrote that made him famous. Locke lived in troubled times; and it is only by keeping England's troubles in mind that we can understand his various writings, for Locke always addressed himself to practical problems. He never tried to create a systematic philosophy; his only interest was to solve problems bothering himself and other Englishmen.

John Locke was born in 1632, the fourth year of Charles I's "eleven-year tyranny," when Descartes was in Holland pondering his "marvelous discovery" and writing his *Traité du monde,* when parliamentarians and puritans were murmuring in England, and restlessness was in the air. Locke's parents were typical mid-seventeenth-century puritans — severe, pious, unmerciful, hard. When the civil war began in 1640, Locke's father joined the parliamentary forces against the king, and when Charles was beheaded nine years later young Locke was at Westminister school.

During the harsh days of Cromwell's commonwealth, Locke was a student at Oxford where Charles had established his headquarters a decade before. Here he came under diverse influences. The newly appointed dean, John Owen, was a puritan; but he and most of the Oxford faculty were Independent rather than Presbyterian, and they therefore favored rather wide toleration in religion. Locke's favorite professor, however, was Edward Pococke, the most prominent and most outspoken royalist on the faculty. It is certain, from what Locke says in later life, that he found Oxford a dilapidated palace of learning in these hectic times. He complained that logic, rhetoric, and "scholastic" metaphysics were badly taught, that it was absurd to use Latin as the medium of speech in the classroom. Against these things and against the strict, tedious religious services he was obliged to attend, he strongly reacted in later life.

In the days when General Monck was negotiating with Charles II for the Restoration, Locke was appointed lecturer in

Greek at the university, and a little later he was offered a lecturership in rhetoric. In 1661, he was given the censorship of moral philosophy at Oxford, a position usually reserved for those preparing for the Anglican ministry. During the next six years, however, he was drawn more and more into physical experiments, especially into the study of chemistry and medicine.

In 1668, he was made a Fellow of the Royal Society, no mean honor for a young master of thirty-six in the first heyday of mathematical and scientific discovery. Somewhere along the line Locke sidestepped ordination into the Anglican ministry, but by royal dispensation he managed to keep his studentship, ordinarily held by those in the ministry. Locke seems to have determined to become a physician instead, but when he first left the academic life of Oxford he had not yet received his degree in medicine.

His first visit to the continent of Europe was in 1665, when he went to Berlin as secretary to Sir Walter Vane, English ambassador to the Elector of Brandenburg. Locke's work as secretary to the ambassador enabled him to accomplish two things: first of all, he made connections with men important in English politics; second, he learned much of the world in which he now moved for the first time. His letters back home show he was particularly impressed with the religious tolerance practiced in Brandenburg-Prussia. "The distance in their churches," he wrote of the Prussian people to Robert Boyle, "gets not into their homes. They quietly permit one another to choose their way to heaven; for I cannot observe any quarrels or animosities amongst them upon the account of religion." Locke undoubtedly contrasted this latitudinarianism with England's strict sectarianism.

Upon his return home he was offered a secretaryship with the ambassador to Spain. But Locke refused the job. He had made the acquaintance of Lord Ashley, the future Shaftesbury, who was a prominent member of the famous "Cabal" ministry, and his destiny was intimately bound up with the Whig leader's affairs for the next twenty years. He became the Ashley family's physician, and the story runs that once he saved Ashley's life by operating on him. He tutored his son, and was later given the task of hunting him up a suitable wife. He assisted at the birth of this couple's son, the third Earl of Shaftesbury, whom, in turn, he tutored.

Meanwhile he served as handy man in furthering Shaftesbury's various enterprises. One of these was the administration of Carolina, granted to Shaftesbury and seven other "lord proprietors" in 1663. Locke became a sort of general secretary and home manager of the colony; he took an important part in drawing up its constitution, into which he worked his views on religious toleration. When Shaftesbury was made Lord High Chancellor, Locke dispensed the Chancellor's ecclesiastical patronage; and when Shaftesbury made his famous speech for war against the Dutch, Locke stood at his side, manuscript in hand, to prompt him if his memory faltered.

In 1673, Locke — then forty-two — was made secretary of the Board of Trade, an important position carrying the then handsome remuneration of £500 a year. His work on the board shows him methodical in administration and attentive to matters of detail. But shifts of political fortune, plus concern for his fragile health, caused Locke to give up his work for travel in Europe. For almost four years he lived in France, dividing his sojourn between Montpellier and Paris. Here he spent his time in the company of scientists and physicians, whom he preferred over the philosophers with whom he could have associated.

He arrived back in London in 1679, characteristically after Shaftesbury, who had been imprisoned in the Tower for a year, was released and made president of the newly formed Council. At this point political events in England take on a cloak-and-dagger mystery coloring. Shaftesbury was arrested for high treason on July 2, 1681, but he was released on bail. In the summer of 1682 he planned a Whig insurrection, but when the plot was discovered Shaftesbury escaped to Holland, where he died of gout early in 1683.

Locke's role was mysterious and obscure. At any rate, he stayed just out of harm's way. It is not unjust to state that Locke cleverly played both ends against the middle: his part was obscure enough that if the insurrection failed, as it did, he would not be implicated; but if it succeeded he would come in for preferment as Shaftesbury's trusted man. There was no evidence legally to implicate Locke, but he was suspected on all sides. His "mysterious and highly secret business" in these two years undoubtedly had something to do with the plot.

Prideaux wrote on March 14, 1682: "John Locke lives a very cunning and unintelligible life here, being two days in town and three out; and no one knows where he goes, or when he goes, or when he returns. Certainly there is some Whig intrigue a managing; but here not a word of politics comes from him, nothing of news or anything else concerning our present affairs, as if he were not at all concerned." When Locke stayed on at Oxford after Shaftesbury's escape to Holland, opponents tried to catch him off guard, but the dean of Christ Church tells how unsuccessful they were. "Although very frequently discourses have been purposely introduced to the disparagement of his master the Earl of Shaftesbury, his party and designs, he could never be provoked to take any notice or discover in word or look the least concern; so that I believe there is not in the world such a master of taciturnity and passion."

Nonetheless, in 1683, Locke, now fifty-one, decided his health would be better in Holland. There he retreated, and there he remained until the "climate" in England had grown healthier for Whigs through the deposition of James II and the installation of William III in the "Glorious Revolution" of 1688. In Holland, Locke lived carefully, even hiding under an assumed name for a while. Here he associated with literary and scientific leaders of the continent, among whom his closest associate was Philip van Limborch, a leader of the undogmatic, tolerant group of Calvinists in Holland. When he was fifty-four, the age at which Descartes died, Locke published his first article, a contribution to LeClerc's *Bibliotheque Universelle* in which he condensed the message he was to give the world four years later in his famous *Essay Concerning Human Understanding*.

In 1689, after William had safely established himself on the English throne, Locke returned to his native land — in the same convoy that brought Princess Mary to England. Back at home, Locke enjoyed political preferment. He was a member of the party that had managed the revolution, and he was personally acquainted with both the king and the queen. But he turned down the first several jobs offered to him. He refused to be ambassador to the Elector of Brandenburg because he had "reason to apprehend the cold air of the country," and because of "their warm drinking." Locke knew that the Berliners were hearty drinkers, he thought heavy drinking bad for his health, and he had the good sense to see this as a business handicap. "The knowing what others are doing would be at least one half of my business; and I know no such rack in the world to draw out men's thoughts as a well-managed bottle."

Locke became instead Commissioner of Appeals, a job involving little work and paying £200 a year. He held this position, along with other varying ones, for life. Locke is now to be found in and out of various government positions, sometimes administrative and sometimes advisory. It seems certain, for example, that he had a hand in framing the Toleration Bill of 1689, though its provisions, when passed, were less liberal than he wished. "But," he wrote to Limborch, revealing a characteristic Lockean attitude, "it is something to have got thus far." Two winters in London, combined with intense governmental work and literary activity, were too much for Locke's health. So in the spring of 1691 he went to live with the Mashams at their country home in Essex. Here he remained for the last fourteen years of his life, dividing time for the first ten years between London, where he did his government work, and Oates, where he did most of his literary work and enjoyed the companionship of the Masham family and their friends.

Upon his return to England, Locke, who had published only a single article in his lifetime, suddenly loosed upon the world a barrage of works in various fields of learning. In 1689 his first — the best — *Letter on Toleration* was published. Locke had written this letter to his Dutch friend, Limborch. It was published, apparently by Limborch, in Latin, in Holland, without acknowledgment of authorship. Nonetheless Locke was provoked, for he feared the censure and the opprobrium it might bring upon him. In the next year he published his two most famous and most influential works: the *Essay Concerning Human Understanding,* which he had labored on from time to time for many years; and the *Two Treatises of Government,* which he probably wrote during his last months in Holland.

In the same year of 1690, he published his second *Letter on Toleration,* followed two years later by a third. In 1691, he wrote a long essay on lowering the rate of interest; in 1693, his *Thoughts Concerning Education* was published; two years later appeared his last important work, *The Reasonableness of Christianity*. Posthumously published works show how wide were his interests — and how good was his self-judgment in withholding these pieces from the world. Among these works are such varied things as commentary on some of St. Paul's epistles, a discourse on miracles, observations on the culture of vines and olives, and the constitutions of Carolina.

But Locke was not primarily an author. He wrote only to solve a practical problem, such as that of toleration, or to justify a certain line of action, such as that of the Whig party in the "Glorious Revolution." His main work was political. And it always turned out to be both patriotic and at the same time remunerative to Locke. In 1694, for example, he became one of the original proprietors of the Bank of England, which was pushed through Parliament by the Whigs as a privileged company. Locke subscribed £500, a large sum in those days, on which he made good profit — as Whigs almost always managed to do.

In 1696, when the Whigs revived the Council of Trade and Plantations, Locke was made one of the commissioners — at £1000 a year — and until his resignation four years later he was the council's presiding genius. His work on that council is typical of Locke's philosophy of life. In 1697, when the commission faced the problems of discouraging Irish competition in the woolen industry, it was Locke's scheme which was adopted and which turned Ireland into a nation of flax spinners instead of wool makers. Locke's report was also the one accepted by the commission for dealing with the problem of keeping the poor off relief and at work for starvation wages. Each parish was to force its poor to work; anyone caught begging outside his parish was to be sentenced to three years on the ships or at hard labor in a house of correction.

Locke retired from public life in 1700 to spend his last four years with the Mashams, where he seems to have been a sort of beloved great-uncle as much at home as anyone in the family. He was a cheerful member of the family circle who insisted on paying his way, who was ready with practical advice for younger people, who was especially interested in little children and in young persons he wished to start through life on the right path. He delighted in the company of young men and women, but such a person as the sick old Bishop Fowler only annoyed him, for, he complained, "I find two groaning people make but an uncomfortable concert."

Careful as he was of his "coy mistress," Locke was not a groaner. He was, from all reports of the Mashams, cheerful to the end. He spent the greater part of his literary activity in writing on St. Paul's epistles and on miracles; biblical exegesis was the subject of many of his conversations in these years. Locke, who always led a virtuous life, was a genuinely religious man in these last four years. In his last hours of illness, which he seems to have borne without complaint, he talked much with the Mashams of their eternal concerns. "I heard him say, the night before he died," Esther Masham wrote to a mutual acquaintance, "that he heartily thanked God for all His goodness and mercies to him, but above all for His redemption of him by Jesus Christ." He who nursed his health so carefully for seventy-two years finally died sitting in a chair on October 28, 1704 — peacefully, quietly, without struggle or protest. Locke died as he lived. Posterity and circumstance assigned him a greatness he would never have given himself. It is to Locke's credit that he was nearer right than posterity.

2

Descartes, we have seen, always observed men in detached fashion; he was more concerned with philosophy than philosophers. Not so Locke. He studied people endlessly, he came to know them, and he liked them. Locke was especially fond of children, whom he watched at play by the hour, whom he understood, whom he studied as a physician, psychologist, and educator. Whereas Descartes had withdrawn from the world to contemplate truth, then, Locke stayed in the world to study man. He was well equipped temperamentally to make such a study, for certainly he felt what Pope so pithily expressed:

> Know then thyself, presume not God to scan,
> The proper study of mankind is Man.

Locke was a constant, acute observer of this man he proposed to study. His letters from the continent to friends in England show how carefully he studied manners and customs among the French, the Hollanders, and the Germans. His descriptions of church services in France, for example, are photographic — even to noting how the cardinal archbishop of Narbonne was "talking every now and then, and laughing with the bishops next him." Back in England he watched girls play "dibstones" by the hour — and figured out painless ways of turning this game into an educational device. He listened to babies cry, and soon he could discourse as learnedly on the meaning of various cries as the superintendent of a nursery can today.

His observation was not that of an idly curious person. It was always for a purpose. He used it to give him the factual data from which he could arrive at conclusions in law, in philosophy, in education, or in any of the other social sciences. His travels in France, for example, convinced him that men are moved more by the desire for good repute and fear of disgrace than by anything else. "He therefore that would govern the world well," Locke concludes, "had need consider rather what fashions he makes than what laws; and to bring anything into use he need only give it reputation." This sounds like the observation of a successful advertising executive. Descartes could never have made it. Locke alone, of our eleven makers of the modern mind, thought such thoughts and said such things.

As Locke was uniquely observant for a "thinker," so was he philosophically practical. He never tried to do the impossible or the dangerous — or even the difficult. Practicality, indeed, was a guiding norm for his reforms. When he could not get the right answer, he was content to get something nearly right. He favored tolerance, for example, because "it is impracticable to punish dissenters." He opposed a scheme to fix the rate of interest at 4 per cent, again, because he thought that interest could not be fixed by law, and any attempt to do so would only throw the money market into a state of confusion. He suggested that all gentlemen learn to keep accounts and that they learn one or more trades — all for practical reasons. It can indeed be said of Locke that he pushed practicality so far as always to take the easy way out of any difficulty, whether it was the right way or not. He always managed to find the easy, practical solution.

When various proposals were made in 1700 for bringing the

English calendar, then eleven days behind the continental calendar, up to date, Locke proposed "an easy way" that would gradually slide the English calendar into the Gregorian in forty-four years. Again, he insisted that learning should never be a burden; it should rather be an easy, painless affair accomplished with the least possible effort. Locke was concerned, he tells us, with "that way of training up youth, with regard to their several conditions, which is the easiest, shortest, and likeliest to produce virtuous, useful, and able men." He developed means whereby "children may be cozened into a knowledge of the letters," and he always insisted that "contrivances might be made to teach children to read, whilst they thought they were only playing."

Observant, practical, prudent to the point of timidity, Locke was a thoroughly likable man — unless, like Carlyle, one prefers a world filled with dynamic heroes. He was a kindly man who seems to have preferred playful banter with children to serious discussion with his equals. He was an amiable conversationalist who, from all accounts, had a full stock of humorous stories which he recounted with finesse. Locke is often called the most English of English philosophers. But he can well be pictured as a typical nineteenth-century American living in seventeenth-century England. He was free of mental worries, as well as we can tell, eminently sociable and, for a philosopher, remarkably even-tempered. And in many little ways he was typically American: his ordinary drink was water, to which he accounted his long survival and his good eyesight; he was assiduous in taking exercise, especially riding, walking, and gardening; to him, indeed, the development of English athletics as gentlemanly arts is largely due. He thought exercise rather good for gentlemen, and he made it pretty much a class affair.

Locke's opinion of himself is worth noting both because it is quite accurate and because it reveals something of his mind. He calls himself, at the height of his fame, "a bookish man." But he does not by any means believe that he ranks with Robert Boyle or "the incomparable Mr. Newton" or any of the great architects of the palace of human knowledge who built in his day. " 'Tis ambition enough," he decided, "to be employed as an under-labourer in clearing ground a little, and removing some of the rubbish that lies in the way to knowledge." After he retired and began to reflect upon his life, Locke came to place an even lower estimate upon his own worth. He was, he decided, "a poor ignorant man, and if I have anything to boast of, it is that I sincerely love and seek truth." On this point he remained firm, almost vehement for Locke — that he was a sincere seeker after truth, "the seed-plot of all other virtues." But as death came near Locke became convinced that, hard as he had tried, he had discovered only little snatches of that elusive entity. He summed up an old man's view of himself and of life when, toward the end, he wrote to Anthony Collins: "This life is a scene of vanity that soon passes away, and affords no solid satisfaction but in the consciousness of doing well and in the hope of another life. This is what I say on experience, and what you will find to be true when you come to take up the account."

3

Such is the man who was always concerned about immediate, practical problems. Even when he turned occasionally to writing, as we have seen, he had in mind an immediate solution to a pressing problem. But each of his works was fundamental enough to live on after the circumstances which evoked it had dissolved in the stream of history. Each was, in its way, a classic. Each struck up sympathetic vibrations with elements so fundamental in modern history that it survived for two or more centuries. Each of Locke's works, then, became a classic because the problem it was to solve remained a classic problem throughout modern history: the place of the individual in political society; the relationship of the world of knowledge to the individual; the role of organized religion in securing salvation for the individual.

His two most important works, of course, are his *Essay Concerning Human Understanding*, which is a two-volume book rather than an essay, and his *Two Treatises of Government*, of which only the second is worth more than passing mention. Although *Thoughts Concerning Education* is Locke's most typical book and reveals him at his best, it is of only secondary importance in the history of educational theory. So, too, his *Letters Concerning Toleration* and his *Reasonableness of Christianity* are as good as his better-known works, but because their influence was unnecessary for winning the attitudes they advocated they were never given a place of prime importance among Locke's writings.

Locke was not a deep thinker, and nothing he wrote has the slightest claim to profundity. Because he never thought his way back to first principles, he took much for granted on inadequate analysis and ended up combining contradictory propositions which just a little reflection would have showed him were incompatible. But Locke always had good sense, and he never allowed either his philosophy or his lack of logic to carry him far astray. Common sense told him that, irrefutable as it seemed, the Cartesian system did not square with the facts of life. Children are not born murmuring that things equal to the same thing are equal to each other; right and wrong are learned on parental authority and by repeated spankings, not by reflection on innate ideas; it is silly to identify the soul with thought, for a man who falls off his horse does not lose his soul until he regains consciousness; it is nonsense to identify matter with extension, for anyone bumping into a door in the dark can plainly tell you that the door is very different from the air through which he had been passing — but both have extension. Locke's common sense kept him close to the matter-of-fact things of life. But it did not help him get beyond them, for common sense, by itself, does not make for profundity. It has indeed been said of Locke that he was at his best when he was not philosophizing and at his worst when he was. Because he never philosophized for too long he never thought too wrongly — but at the same time he never thought very deeply.

Locke is generally considered a rationalist. And with justification, if it be remembered that Locke was never extreme in anything, even in being rational. He meant to be rationalist, of course, and he insisted that reason "must be our last judge and guide in everything." Christianity is to be accepted because it is reasonable; sound education assumes that children are rational, that "they love to be treated as rational creatures." This reason to which Locke appeals, however, is not the reason of Descartes, of Malebranche, or even of Voltaire. It is a mixture of human attitudes and emotions so compounded that no one passion, no one attitude can get out of hand — not even reason. The strongest element in the mixture is reason, of course, but it becomes the sweet reasonableness of the littérateur rather than the cold reason of the philosopher. Reason, with Locke, is common sense.

His method of reasoning, he tells us, is "plain historical," which apparently means what today we call inductive. In some respects Locke did for philosophy what Newton did for science by perfecting a new method of inquiry. He started with observable facts, from which he generalized, and from these generalizations he decided how other phenomena would act. This was not as revolutionary as Locke believed, but it was certainly a departure from the Cartesian method of pure deduction from innate ideas. Where Descartes had started with his *"Je pense, donc je suis,"* Locke stated that in finding the origin of ideas he would "appeal to everyone's own observation and experience."

His reflections on education are based on experience and observation, but much of his most important work is more Cartesian than Lockean — if we are to take Locke seriously when he tells us that his method is to appeal to experience and observation. For Locke did not always use the "plain historical" method. His entire philosophy of government is based upon gratuitous assumptions from which he deduces all sorts of conclusions. Just as Locke is not consistently a rationalist, so too he fails consistently to use any one method of reasoning — and it probably is a good thing he did.

But Locke is not to be too severely judged for his inconsistency. Unlike Descartes, he had no intention of building a systematic philosophy — or even of being a philosopher. He addressed himself to different problems at different times, and it was only natural for him to adopt what seemed the best method for the purpose in hand. While it is true that the empiricism of his *Essay* automatically eliminates the natural rights, the state of nature and the social contract of his *Two Treatises on Government,* it should be remembered that in the latter work Locke simply assumed as true what was generally admitted at the time. Locke never strove for consistency between his various works; it is enough to require consistency within each of his pieces. He wrote in an age that was empirical in science and rationalist in philosophy, and Locke, who was as much a scientist as a philosopher, used both methods without harmonizing them.

His style is lucid, especially when compared to most of his predecessors. But it is annoyingly wordy. Locke seems to have taken pen in hand and written away without ever having planned where his pen would take him or by what paths it would lead him to his conclusions. His repetitions are unnecessarily frequent; his digressions and his exemplifying instances tiresome. What he confesses in the "Epistle to the Reader" of the *Essay*, the meatiest of his writings, should be written before each of his works: "When I put pen to paper, I thought all I should have to say on this matter, would have been contained in one sheet of paper, but the farther I went, the larger the prospect I had. . . . I will not deny, but possibly it might be reduced to a narrower compass than it is. . . . But to confess the truth, I am now too lazy, or too busy to make it shorter." He should have. Rambling prose, however, was in style in Locke's day.

Like Descartes, Locke tried to write in the popular idiom. He disregarded philosophical phrases and resorted to the language of the average Englishman. But this involved him in a difficulty — of which he may never have been aware — for philosophy, like every other science, necessarily has its own terminology which Locke frequently violated in an effort to use the popular idiom. He tells the reader of the *Essay*, for example, that he will use the term *idea* "to express whatever is meant by phantasm, notion, species, or whatever it is which the mind can be employed about in thinking." And thus he tends from the very beginning to confuse intellection with sense perception, two factors which must be kept distinct if one is to trace clearly the origin of ideas. He complains that his meaning is often mistaken, that he did not have "the good luck to be everywhere rightly understood." But he should have expected this.

Locke's desire to popularize philosophy and to rescue her from the professional philosophers, however, had some good effects. He reacted healthily, for example, against the verbalism into which philosophers seem always to be falling. He complains that vague, high-sounding words had long passed "for mysteries of science," and he promises to substitute for such obscurantisms words that everyone can understand — a good thing for any philosopher to do. He also reacted to his age's formalism in education, to making children learn rules by heart and memorize "great parcels of the authors which are taught them."

His whole approach was fresh. It freed him from the stuffiness and the formalism and the obscurantism of his predecessors, but at the same time it demanded of him a fuller learning and a greater precision of thought than he could give his work. As a result, while he popularized philosophy by introducing her to a nonphilosophical reading public, he caricatured her somewhat in the process, and the lady to whom his readers were introduced was not the mistress of the philosophers. Locke was — if we may suddenly change the figure of speech — a bull in the philosophical china shop. He handled ideas clumsily, though popularly. He walked into the china shop of philosophy without previously having learned how to handle the philosophers' fragile wares. He therefore broke many pieces.

But his venture was popular. It was popular because it brought philosophy down to the level of the ordinary Englishman and expressed it in words which rested easily on his tongue. Sabine remarks that "the enormous vogue which he enjoyed during the earlier part of the eighteenth century was probably due precisely to the deceptive simplicity of his thought." In the same vein Santayana asserts: "Had Locke's mind been more profound, it might have been less influential. He was in sympathy with the coming age, and was able to guide it; an age that confided in easy, eloquent reasoning, and proposed to be saved, in this world and the next, with as little philosophy and as little religion as possible." Because Locke always took the easy way out he was popular with an age looking for easy solutions.

4

The most important of Locke's writings is his *Essay Concerning Human Understanding*, the only work which he did not compose to solve some practical problem facing his generation. This, indeed, is unique among Locke's works in more ways than one: it is the only one in which he seems genuinely to seek truth, the only one in which he has no ax to grind; it is a work which was composed over the years, a little at a time, and Locke seems not to realize that his frequent shifts of position make him at times contradict himself.

Locke wrote his *Essay* to refute Cartesian innate ideas, which he does rather convincingly in the first book. But he further wanted to account for the origin of ideas, a point which he and his friends had decided should be settled before they could proceed logically to other philosophical problems. He proposed to settle the problem by using a new method, "the plain historical," which apparently means the empirical method as contrasted to Cartesian deductive rationalism. Although Locke tells the reader that he will "appeal to every one's own observation and experience," it is really his own mind that Locke examines. This introspective method, which looms large in philosophy from Locke's day forward, is new and revolutionary; it introduces a strong strain of subjectivism into philosophy and at the same time renders philosophy more and more into psychology. Locke's inductive method was not as new as he thought it was, for Aristotelians had long used it. But it was revolutionary in his day, and in Locke's hands it did not possess the same objective independence of the philosopher's mind it had enjoyed with the scholastics.

In other ways, too, Locke reverted to Aristotle. He accounts for the origin of ideas much as Aristotle had done two thousand years before, but in oversimplified fashion which, in more logical followers' hands, will practically write off the mind as an unnecessary quantity. The scholastics had long maintained that knowledge comes through the senses; *nihil in intellectu nisi quod prius quomodo in sensu* their maxim ran. Locke looked into his own mind and saw how, as contrasted with the facile Cartesian explanation of the origin of ideas, this scholastic explanation squared with facts. But, not being a trained philosopher, Locke saw no harm in dropping their *quomodo* — "in some fashion." He was content to say that all ideas come from sensation or reflection, that the mind is passive in receiving simple ideas, out of which all knowledge is compounded. Thus the mind is left pretty much an empty compartment in which ideas are stored; it becomes less an active agent than a passive receptacle. It will not be hard for Locke's followers, in pushing this principle to an extreme conclusion, to render the intellect — and man himself — completely passive. Thus he opened the door to environmental determinism and inadvertently left man absolutely passive putty in the educator's hands.

Locke, not being a philosopher, offered a clumsy philosophical explanation for a series of facts that he had observed — and thus he opened the door to another bad strain in subsequent philosophy, subjectivism. Now Locke had observed that a warm rock feels hot to a cold hand, but it feels cool when transferred to a heated hand. He saw that cloth seemed of one color in the sunlight, of another in the shade, and of still another by lamplight. But obviously the rock cannot be both hot and cool, and the cloth cannot be two colors. How account for these contradictory ideas?

Locke thought he could with the following line of reasoning: All bodies have certain "primary qualities" which are "utterly inseparable from the body." These are the qualities of solidity, extension, figure, motion or rest, and number; they are qualities which really inhere in the bodies, as they appear to. Bodies also have "secondary qualities," such as color, taste, and sound. These are the qualities which seem to differ when the object is seen or felt under varying conditions — such as heat in the rock or color in the cloth. Locke therefore concluded that these "secondary qualities" are no more in the object "than sickness or pain is in manna." They exist in the mind and are falsely attributed by it to the object.

This distinction between primary and secondary qualities is typical of Locke. He put all his chips on sensation and then decided that it was not thoroughly trustworthy, for our mind deceives us in attributing secondary qualities to objects, where they do not really exist. But he still had faith in the mind properly to report primary qualities of the same objects. He thus made knowledge partly subjective, but he insisted on leaving it largely objective. More logical men came after Locke to insist that the mind attributes primary as well as secondary qualities to objects outside itself; they therefore soon came to say that the whole world of knowledge is projected by the mind and has no real existence outside of it. From there it is an easy step to deny everything but the mind — and Hume will go on to deny the mind itself.

Whether he realized it or not, Locke accepted many points of Cartesianism uncritically — whenever they seemed "consistent with common-sense." One such point is that "the mind, in all its thoughts and reasonings, hath no other immediate object but its own ideas." The mind, therefore, "knows not things immediately, but only by the intervention of the ideas it has of them." Locke considered himself a realist who, by denying innate ideas and supplanting the Cartesian deductive method with empiricism, had rescued philosophy and put it in touch with the world again. But he failed, logically, to get the mind outside itself to grasp reality. He left it locked up inside itself.

John Sergeant appreciated this point at once. He criticized Locke as an "ideist" in 1697 and maintained logically that he had forced the mind to retreat upon itself. "Those who have in their minds only *similitudes* or *ideas,* and only discourse of them, which ideas are not the thing, do build their discoveries upon nothing. They have no solid knowledge." Sergeant was consistent. But Locke was not. And herein lay his merit. Illogically, but sanely and rightly, Locke declared that he was a realist and that he could know with certainty the world outside his mind. But he had opened the door to skepticism, as Sergeant logically complained, and it only remained for Hume to reduce Locke's "ideism" to its logical conclusions.

There was a great amount of solid common sense in Locke's *Essay.* As long as he remained the English man-in-the-street criticizing philosophical meanderings for losing touch with reality, he was acutely sensible. His observations on the tyranny of words, for example, are sane and solid. But whenever he put on the toga of the philosopher to propound his own theories he seems to have gone astray. His theory on the origin of ideas left the mind too passive and thus it opened the door to later positivism and environmental determinism. His assertion that secondary qualities do not inhere in objects outside the mind, but are instead attributed to objects by the mind, opened the door to later subjectivism, to the belief that the mind creates the world rather than embraces it. His insistence that we know only our own ideas closed the door to the common-sense realism Locke thought he championed, and it led logically to the idealism of Bishop Berkeley. Because philosophers followed Locke and because they were not satisfied with his saving inconsistencies, he stands at the source of almost every subsequent school of philosophy. And he would have been horrified by every one of them — for none was consistent with his common sense. None stopped short, illogically, as Locke had done.

5

Locke's political philosophy maintained respectability longer than did his epistemology. His *Two Treatises of Government* were written, he tells the reader, "to establish the throne of our great restorer, our present king William; to make good his title in the consent of the people; which being the only one of lawful governments, he has more fully than any other prince in Christendom; and to justify to the world the people of England, whose love of their just and natural rights, with their resolution to preserve them, saved the nation when it was on the brink of slavery and ruin." That is a rather large order. So the reader is not to look for a completely objective political philosophy built upon incontrovertible first principles.

Nor does he find it. Locke was willing to use any material generally acceptable in his day to build his defense of the Glorious Revolution. He wrote for men of substance who were literally afraid of losing their heads. For all through Locke's lifetime it seemed that the Stuart pretender might win back the throne — with support from abroad, as well as from the Tories and from the disinherited in England. So Locke wrote his apologia hurriedly, but with apparent tranquillity and with Whiggish sweet reasonableness.

Locke combines two current, but contradictory theories in his justification of the Glorious Revolution: (1) the contract theory of government, whereby government is created by the people, like a piece of machinery, to perform certain assigned tasks; (2) a modernized theory of natural law, from which men derive their inalienable rights and by which the functions of government are limited. Locke ends up having the government both artificial and natural; he ends up having the individual supreme in one place and subject to society in another. But this does not seem to bother him.

Always more or less conventional, Locke begins his political theorizing in the state of nature. Here men live happily in a condition of "peace, good will, mutual assistance and preservation." Everyone enjoys the right to life, liberty, and property in this state of nature. But trouble arises. Because there is no judge to decide how far each person's right to liberty or property extends and because the human mind is fallible, there arise conflicting claims among men. And because in the state of nature each man enforces his rights with his own blackjack there arise conflicts among men. So peace disappears, life is in jeopardy, good will degenerates into hatred, and mutual assistance into mutual obstructionism. Locke's state of nature deteriorates into something pretty close to Hobbes's *bellum omnium contra omnes,* where life is "solitary, poor, nasty, brutish and short."

People (so Locke's theory runs) see the need of an objectively stated, clearly known interpretation of natural law to supplant each individual's own interpretation. They likewise see the need of a single, equitable enforcer of the law. So, Locke tells us, they agree to set up a state and give it the power of interpreting the law of nature (legislation) and of enforcing it (administration). Thus government is entrusted with strictly defined powers to accomplish a narrowly limited purpose — the preservation of life, liberty, and property.

It is hard to see the state, in Locke's eyes, as anything more than a collection of egoistic individuals pursuing divergent, selfish policies. Locke, indeed, says, "The commonwealth seems to me to be a society of men constituted only for the procuring, the preserving, and the advancing of their own civil interests." So men create the state and endow government with limited powers for purely selfish purposes. Probably with Locke, and certainly with his followers, the principal end of government is to protect men in the property they have amassed. Property, indeed, seems insensibly to take on a sacredness denied even to the human person. There is something sacramental about it.

Locke's second significant contribution to political thought is his doctrine of separation of powers. Government, he says, naturally divides itself into legislative functions, executive tasks, and the handling of foreign affairs (the judicial branch of government he considered a division of the executive). Of these the legislature is supreme; the executive is to enforce the legislature's will and is therefore subordinate to it. But even the legislature is subordinate to the people. Care must be taken not to allow power to make the law and power to enforce it to fall into the same man's or the same group's hands. For this means tyranny, from which the only escape is revolution.

Locke therefore justifies revolution whenever the government exceeds its powers or when the natural separation of powers has been destroyed. But even here Locke is moderate — for he had no intention of justifying a revolution against the Whigs. He hastened to reassure his readers that "such revolutions happen not upon every little mismanagement in public affairs." Then he went on, in words that have a familiar ring to every American schoolboy, to tell when revolution will occur. "If a long train of abuses, prevarications, and artifices, all tending the same way, make the design visible to the people, and they cannot but feel what they lie under . . ." — then revolution will come, as it had come in 1688.

Thus John Locke put together a political philosophy which seemed to justify the Whig rebellion without running into the danger of justifying another such rebellion each generation. But there were other countries — France and America — where men still felt the yoke of strong government on their necks. And they turned to Locke for justification and inspiration, for intellectual leadership in revolutions whose bloodletting would certainly have sickened the gentle old bachelor reading St. Paul at Oates.

6

Locke thought about religion too. For religion was as critical a problem as faced Englishmen of his day. Upon its solution, he could well believe, depended the future peace of his England. Locke, we must remember, lived through times when men plotted in the name of religion, when they heaped corpses high to promote God's glory on earth, when each sect thought that it had a divine commission to enforce its own brand of religion upon the unenlightened remainder of humanity. Locke lived through the days of the Civil War when Presbyterians vied with Independents and when all eventually came under Cromwell's iron hand. He traveled on the continent in those same days and saw how in Brandenburg men of various beliefs could live peacefully side by side, how in the Netherlands the better sort favored a wider toleration than the strictly orthodox Reformed Church allowed.

Locke therefore wanted to reduce all religions to their least common denominator, to erase differences between the various groups and find a broad basis upon which all could agree. He managed, as a result, to conclude that the truths of religion were few and simple. "All that is necessary for all to believe about God," he insisted, "must be easily understood. There be many truths in the Bible which a good Christian may be wholly ignorant of, and so not believe; which perhaps some lay great stress on, and call fundamental articles, because they are the distinguishing points of their sect or communion."

Religion should consist rather in good living and brotherly love than in a definite creed. Only two things, he believed, were necessary for salvation: (1) belief that Jesus is the Messiah; (2) a good life. "These two, faith and repentance, that is, believing Jesus to be the Messiah, and a good life, are the indispensable conditions of the new covenant to be performed by all those who obtain eternal life." Locke had no use for theological inquiry. "The true notion of God," he maintained, was that "of the independent Supreme Being, Author and Maker of all things, from whom we receive all our good, who loves us, and gives us all things. . . . I think it would be better, if men generally rested in such an idea of God, without being too curious in their notions about a Being, which all must acknowledge incomprehensible."

Locke remained basically Christian. Although he had no respect for church dogmas, he never doubted mankind's redemption by Christ, or the reality of miracles, the infallibility of Scriptures or the goodness of God. But his was a weak dilution of Christianity, and, from the point of view of his philosophic position, as Santayana points out, "his Christianity almost disappears."

Locke accepted his own watered-down version of Christianity because it seemed consistent with common sense, because it seemed reasonable. This is the message of his *Reasonableness of Christianity*. With him reason remains supreme, and whatever elements of Christianity seem consistent with it will be accepted. The rest will not. Christianity is therefore rendered by the lamp of reason into a natural, rational religion. "There is little need or use of revelation," Locke maintained, "God having furnished us with natural and surer means to arrive at a knowledge of them [religious truths]. For whatsoever truth we come to a clearer discovery of from the knowledge and contemplation of our own ideas, will always be certainer to us than those which are conveyed to us by traditional revelation." Locke's reason could accept the basic points of Christianity, but his followers rejected as contrary to reason whatever could not be established by it and thus they denied miracles and everything based on revelation. That is why Wright can observe that, "Locke was an unintentional forerunner of Voltaire and other sceptics and materialists of the eighteenth century."

Latitudinarianism and toleration go hand in hand. It is not surprising, therefore, to find Locke an early advocate of religious toleration. He reacted as a young man to the bitter religious divisions in Civil War England, and there is good reason for believing that the first letter on toleration was his earliest work. Characteristically, Locke's advocacy of toleration is based on expediency. He finds no theological, no metaphysical or logical reason for toleration. But he finds that religious intolerance simply does not work socially or politically. It deprives the state of useful citizens if religious dissenters flee abroad, as happened in Louis XIV's France; it drives political discontent underground and creates conspirators if they stay at home, as happened in Charles I's England. Therefore, he concludes, "it is impracticable to punish dissenters."

But Locke was never an extremist — even in toleration. He refused — as we still do today — to tolerate religious opinions "contrary to human society, or to those moral rules which are necessary to the preservation of civil society." He refused, moreover, to tolerate Catholics or atheists. Catholics, he understood, held that "faith is not to be kept with heretics"; they could not therefore be good members of society with whom property-conscious Whigs could conduct business in security. Neither would Locke tolerate atheists, because "promises, covenants, and oaths, which are the bonds of human society, can have no hold upon an atheist." Locke's toleration, then, was well advanced for his day, but it can hardly be called toleration by principle. It was based on expediency, and if the winds of political fortune should change, so too, on Locke's theory of toleration, would any group's right to be tolerated.

7

Locke's reputation would be higher today if his *Thoughts Concerning Education* were more widely read. For this work reveals him at his best. It consists of reflections on a subject he knew well — and Locke is always at his best when he is making an observation, when he is not trying to be profound. His work on education is, of all his works, the least in need of adaptation to the twentieth century. The reader can almost imagine most of this book written by a retired headmaster of Eton or Groton, a genial, white-haired gentleman who has seen three generations of pranksters and still has not lost faith in adolescent human nature, a liberally educated gentleman who has never let his learning tyrannize over his humaneness and who realizes that book learning is but a small part of education.

In these pages Locke reveals himself to the reader as a seventeenth-century Angelo Patri. He is modern, as educators use the word; he is progressive, as one school of educators use the word. Like them all, he considers education terrifically important. "Nine parts of ten are what they are, good or evil, useful or not, by their education." "The little, or almost insensible, impressions on our tender infancies, have very important and lasting consequences." Education, then, makes the man. Here Locke sounds like the keynote speaker at any modern educational conference. "I imagine the minds of children, as easily turned, this or that way, as water itself." It is all rather flattering for the educator; but Locke was one himself, and so he looks upon tutors as Svengalis and children as little Trilbies. Here he is quite modern. The educator ends up more important than the student.

His educational psychology is also quite modern. The important thing is not what information you pump into the student's head but what habits you settle in him. Habits are not settled by lecture, he insists, but by repetition, by practice, and **more** practice. Not by rules are children to be taught, but by example and by practice. Children's minds are not to be too much curbed, nor their spirits abashed, for then they will "lose all their vigor and industry." Education is to be made as easy as possible; through properly developed techniques the instructor will find various ways to turn learning into play — and suddenly the child will be educated without ever knowing it. Education might be a pill, but Locke insists it be a sugar-coated pill.

Like modern educators, Locke insists that the *mens sana* be situated in a *corpore sano.* Physician that he was, he prescribed a regimen of food and sleep and exercise that reads like a modern pediatrician's schedule sheet. The child is not to be over-dressed; he is to spend much time in the open air; his diet is to be "plain and simple," and "whatever he eats that is solid, make him chew it well."

Locke may have thought himself a "bookish man," but he did not stress book learning in his scheme of education. Learning, indeed, occupies last place among the four objects of education. Virtue he places first; wisdom, defined pragmatically as "a man's managing his business ably and with foresight in this world," is second; good breeding is third; and learning is fourth. Locke proceeds to draw up a complete curriculum in which he gets down to such details as asserting that the "Italian way of holding pen is best." Book learning is rounded out with such things as dancing, fencing, and riding, for Locke's gentleman was to be a well-rounded man. "The great business of all," however, "is virtue and wisdom."

8

Such was the man who said what the middle-class people of England wanted to hear. They were a practical people who prized common sense and were anxious to rationalize it into a philosophy. Locke seemed to do this. They were a selfish people who wanted to justify their revolution and their way of governing in their own interest. Locke did this for them. They wanted a system of education that would be practical and easy, but would still make gentlemen of them. Locke propounded such an education. They were the great compromisers who had no desire to see their revolutionary theories turned against themselves now that they were in power. And Locke always stopped short of logical conclusions to which his premises could be reduced. He was the typical middle-class thinker of modern times. Because the middle class remained long in power, Locke was long influential.

Because the middle class was in power in England, Locke was at home a conservative force in politics. That was an accident of circumstances. So was his influence everywhere. In France the middle class was struggling to obtain political power; they were soon to manage a preliminary revolution in men's hearts and minds, the intellectual revolution of the "Enlightenment," and they found Locke a respectable authority. Voltaire therefore popularized him in France, Helvetius and Holbach admired "the profound Locke," Diderot eulogized him, and Saint-Lambert referred to him as "the wisest and most enlightened of all the teachers of the human race." Condillac, "the French Locke," reduced Lockean sensism to a logical conclusion and completely got rid of the human mind. Helvetius developed Lockean notions on education and came forth with a closed system of environmental determinism which left the student mere putty in the hands of educators. "Man is nothing more than the product of his education," Helvetius concluded, and therefore "to be happy and powerful nothing more is requisite than to perfect the science of education."

Locke gathered together the various strands of seventeenth-century thought and handed them on to eighteenth-century thinkers. There is therefore truth in Fowler's observation that Locke "rang the bell to call the other wits together." At meetings of these wits through the eighteenth century will run certain notes that Locke had sounded faintly in his various writings: a rationalism in religion, in philosophy, and even in education; a new method, the empirical, in philosophy and in the social sciences; a strong individualism in every field of human speculation.

Locke was theoretically a full intellectualist individualist. "I can no more know anything by another man's understanding," he insisted, "than I can see by another man's eyes. The knowledge which one man possesses cannot be lent to another." But he did not logically set men off into hermetically sealed compartments between which there can be no communication. In political theory Locke was equally individualistic. His state consisted of a collection of self-seeking persons whose individual rights were apparently supreme, who had nothing in common except the desire each had for self-aggrandizement and for protection of already made gains.

John Locke was a more important man than he knew. Although he thought he was only "clearing the ground a little" for master architects like his friend, Newton, posterity accorded him a role almost as great as the one which it assigned to "the incomparable Mr. Newton." These two acquaintances worked out the modern inductive method, which did battle in men's minds with Cartesianism until it eventually triumphed. In the social sciences, in history, in almost all fields of thought today we use Locke's "plain historical method."

More important than his method, however, was Locke's attitude toward learning and life. Common sense and compromise have remained at the heart of British and American thought and institutions since Locke's day. His practical approach to all questions, including those of philosophical and religious truth, is still pretty much our approach. It has saved the modern world much bitterness and bloodshed. Though it may have dulled men's minds to sharp distinctions, it has preserved society from sharp words and bloody battles over questions of belief. For purely practical reasons, Locke did much to make religious toleration possible in the modern world. For the same reasons he furthered the cause of democracy, and he helped make the world a place where you can disagree with your neighbor and still live peacefully next door to him.

VI
NEWTON

ISAAC NEWTON was a curious man. Because he was undoubtedly a genius and because he was an English genius, his English biographers put divine intelligence into his head and a halo around his crown. They either overlook his peculiarities or treat them as additional proof that he was a heaven-sent genius. For geniuses are rare birds in England, and they are not considered quite human. They are "strange," "peculiar." So Newton was dehumanized for a worshiping England. Robbed of his human qualities and wrapped in a tinsel-like brilliance, he was put upon a pedestal by his disciples for the adulation of their children. There he remained for two hundred years, until Darwin suggested an alternative to the Newtonian world-machine and later Einstein showed its inadequacy. Then it was safe for biographers to take Newton off his pedestal for closer scrutiny, to discover what sort of man he was and what the secrets of his mind were.

Critical biographers have not denied that Newton was a

curious man. Nor have they robbed him of his title to being a genius of the first order, a title to which he has clearer claim than any other maker of the modern mind. Like Descartes and Locke, Newton was a bachelor. Like Descartes's, his intellect was both strong and brilliant. But unlike Descartes's, Newton's mental accomplishments were such as to make legends pale beside them. We cannot understand how his mind worked; we must simply accept the historical fact that twice he solved problems in an evening which eminent mathematicians had fumbled with for a year, that at the age of twenty-three he had made all his important discoveries, that in astoundingly short time he dashed off the *Principia* — no mean task for a brilliant scholar to accomplish in a lifetime.

Newton is a curious genius because he excelled at something he did not consider important. Where Descartes thought that he would be the modern Aristotle and was convinced that philosophy was of terrific importance, Newton described himself with these words: "a boy playing on the seashore, and diverting myself in now and then finding a smoother pebble or a prettier shell than ordinary, whilst the great ocean of truth lay all undiscovered before me."

Newton, moreover, was an example of a man whose genius was not the fruit of hard labor. For he was offhand about mathematics, and he could never understand why all mathematicians did not see relationships with the same penetrating insight that he did. And, strangely, his accomplishments were meager in those subjects he considered most important and in which he worked the hardest: alchemy, theology, and biblical chronology. Unlike Descartes, too, Newton accomplished nothing worthy of mention in the last forty years of his life. His genius matured early; in time he came actually to resent its encroachment on the hours he reserved for more congenial work; and after the publication of the *Principia* he refused to be dragged into mathematics again.

Like Descartes, Newton was rather unsocial, but unlike the French rationalist, he wanted desperately to mingle with the aristocracy and royalty, with the politicians and the merchant princes of England, to make good socially and politically. This was the life he longed for, and he used his scientific reputation as a lever for advancement in the political and social circles of

London. Descartes sacrificed society to scholarship; Newton deserted scholarship for society. Where Descartes voluntarily held aloof from men in a proud, austere way, Newton seemed simply unable to develop real friendships. He could never understand his fellow men. Even Locke, who was one of his closest associates, wrote to his cousin of Newton: "I have several reasons to think him truly my friend, but he is a nice [reserved, punctilious, shy, demanding] man to deal with, and a little too apt to raise in himself suspicions where there is no ground." Newton was, in fact, frequently petulant, ill-tempered, suspicious.

He had done his work when he was forty-two. Dissatisfied with the studious life of Cambridge, he spent the last decade there in restless, fitful work until influential friends had him commissioned warden of the Mint. For the next thirty years Newton spent a day a week at the Mint and the rest of his time in biblical and chemical studies. But his mathematical genius never deserted him — for several times when he thought his honor at stake he proved to the world that there was but one Newton, and Newton had no equal.

Before he left Cambridge, however, he had created the "Newtonian system," which was to go unchallenged in the Western World for two centuries. As "Legislator of the Universe" he had applied mathematics to the physical sciences and had thus realized Descartes's dream of a universal knowledge informed by mathematics. In creating his system, Newton had brought to conclusion and harmonized the disjointed efforts of his predecessors, that long list of scientific geniuses who cause the seventeenth to be known as "the century of genius" — men like Galileo, Kepler, Pascal, Toricelli, and Descartes. He had, in John H. Randall's words, "effected so successful a synthesis of the mathematical principles of nature that he stamped the mathematical ideal of science, and the identification of the natural with the rational, upon the entire field of thought. . . . This meant, on the one hand, that the secrets of the whole world could be investigated by man's experiments on this planet; and on the other, that the world was one huge, related, and uniform machine, the fundamental principles of whose action were known."

Pope, in his pithy way, showed how Newton soon came to be

not a man but a synonym for scientific truth. Newton was science, and science was *the* thing.

> Nature and Nature's laws lay hid in night;
> God said, "Let Newton be!" and all was Light.

Newton's quasidivine authority, the sway he held over men's minds for two centuries, is illustrated in the opening paragraph of N. W. Chittenden's biography of him:

"From the thick darkness of the middle ages man's struggling spirit emerged as in new birth; breaking out of the iron control of that period; growing strong and confident in the tug and din of succeeding conflict and revolution, it bounded forwards and upwards with resistless vigour to the investigation of physical and moral truth; ascending height after height; sweeping afar over the earth, penetrating afar up into the heavens; increasing in endeavour, enlarging in endowment; every where boldly, earnestly out-stretching, till, in the AUTHOR OF THE PRIN-CIPIA, one arose, who, grasping the master-key of the universe and treading its celestial paths, opened up to the human intellect the stupendous realities of the material world, and, in the unrolling of its harmonies, gave to the human heart a new song to the goodness, wisdom, and majesty of the all-creating, all-sustaining, all-perfect God."

This was written quite seriously in 1846. For what seems naïvely eulogistic today was taken literally and seriously for two centuries. No one thought of questioning Pope's couplet; no one thought of charging Chittenden with lyrical overstatement on Newton's greatness. All seemed to agree with the often-quoted line by which Newton's student and associate, Edmund Halley, placed him highest among men: *Nec fas est proprius mortali attingere Divos.* ("No mortal may be more like the gods.")

1

Newton was not a proud man. He realized he had accomplished a scientific revolution, but he knew the credit was not all his. In a letter to the scientist, Hooke, he confessed that "if I have seen farther, it is by standing on the shoulders of giants."

These "giants" had been at work for half a century when Newton came upon the scene; men like Galileo, Descartes, and Kepler had delved into the mysteries of science and the problems of mathematics, and they had come forth with answers that constituted the scientific revolution of the seventeenth century. They had discarded ancient authorities and they had learned by observation and experiment.

Galileo had popularized the heliocentric concept of the universe, discovered the law of falling bodies, enunciated the principle of the pendulum. Kepler had formulated three fundamental laws of planetary motion, and Descartes had applied mathematics to geometry. There were lesser figures, too, on whose shoulders Newton also stood, men like Borelli, who tried to account for the paths of the planets in terms of two forces, or Bulliadus, who discovered that the force of the sun diminished as the square of the distance to the object attracted to it. But none of these men, nor all of them together, equaled a Newton. They had discovered facts by experiment and they had speculated about conclusions, but they had not organized their knowledge into a system. Nor had they seen the ultimate consequences of their various discoveries.

Newton stood on the shoulders of giants, but he alone had the vision to perceive the full import of what these giants were doing. The problem of planetary motion could be solved only by a mathematical genius of first rank. Indeed, by 1674 Hooke had come as close to a solution of planetary motion as one could come through experiment. He had discovered that every heavenly body attracts every other to its center, that every body moves in a straight line until deflected therefrom by some force, that the attraction between two bodies is stronger when they are closer together. But Hooke was not mathematician enough to formulate the law of gravity. Someone was needed who had tremendous penetrating power as a mathematician, someone who possessed that mysterious quality known as "scientific insight." Such a man was Newton. Because he had these necessary qualities, not possessed by his contemporaries, it was he who put the copestone on the work of his predecessors and revealed what they had been feeling for in the dark.

Newton was born an unpromising baby on Christmas Day of

1642, the year that Galileo died. His father, described by neighbors as "a wild, extravagant, and weak man," was several months in his grave when Isaac was born. The infant, moreover, was premature and weak, so weak that its neck was supported for some time by a holster. Newton's mother often told him that he was so small at birth that he could have slept in a quart mug, that two women who went for medical aid after his birth never expected to see him alive when they returned. On neither side was Newton's family distinguished; nor is anything known of the three children his mother had by a later marriage. Of this family, then, Newton alone was of any account.

Young Isaac went to day schools near home until he was twelve. Then he spent four years at the King's School at Grantham, from which he was recalled in 1658 by his mother, a widow now for the second time, so that he could manage her estate. The only event to stand out in Newton's early schooling is a typical schoolboy fight. The lad immediately above him in class standing — Newton was next to last — had been bullying him incessantly. Young Newton finally gave him a terrific beating, and then, after having batted his enemy's head against the wall, he studied diligently to surpass him in class as well. This fight indicates how Newton needed an external stimulus to put him to work; and it further illustrates his dogged determination to pursue a quarrel to its final conclusion — in this case till his opponent had been battered and overcome physically and intellectually.

Outside the classroom, young Newton exhibited certain characteristics which were to remain with him throughout life. He proved, even as a youth, to be expert with tools and to be interested in practical things. He made kites with lanterns to scare the villagers at night, a mill worked by a mouse, a wooden clock that kept time, sundials, workboxes and toys for his girl friends. He seems not to have played much with other boys, but to have been always making something. Miss Storey, the girl he almost married, said of him many years later that he "was always a sober, silent, thinking lad, and was never known scarce to play with the boys abroad, at their silly amusements."

Even as a youth, Newton exhibited that unusual secretiveness of mind which troubles his biographers so much. He appears always to be guarding jealously the sanctuary of his mind; no one knew what was going on there until he finally divulged the results of many years of cogitation. Even as a youth, moreover, Newton showed that ability to enter a state of trancelike concentration which, in a weaker mind, is simple absent-mindedness. The story is told, for example, of how when he was about sixteen he led a horse up a hill by the bridle. When he got to the top, he turned to mount the horse — only to find that nothing was attached to the bridle. Again, Dr. Stukeley tells how he found a hot dinner waiting in Newton's apartments when he went to call on him one day. Newton arrived later — after Stukeley had eaten the dinner. Newton is supposed to have lifted the cover, looked at the empty plates, and remarked: "Dear me, I thought I had not dined, but I see I have." And to the conversation he turned.

Newton's mother saw that her son's mind was not on her estate during the two years he tried to manage it. He read under hedges while servants tended to the work; he read in the apothecary's attic while they transacted his business in town. So his mother sent him back to Crantham for a year's preparatory work, and, on June 5, 1661, he entered Trinity College at Cambridge as a subsizar. At Cambridge, one of his recent biographers puts it, "he drifted unerringly into the scholarly and celibate life." There is good reason to believe that he went to college with the idea of entering Anglican orders and returning to a rural pastorate. But he stayed at Cambridge forty years, and, when he left, it was the social life of London that called him rather than a rural retreat.

Up to this point — about his twentieth birthday — Newton was apparently a rather ordinary young man. He had exhibited talent for making practical gadgets and for drawing. He seemed good undergraduate timber, but nothing more. Within three years, however, his genius was fully awakened. He said later that he had arrived at his principal ideas on "fluxions," or calculus, when he was a junior in college. In the plague years of 1665 and 1666 Newton returned to his mother's estate. There, as a youth of twenty-three, he made the three discoveries that cause him to be ranked one of the foremost scientific minds of all time. For it was in these two years of uninterrupted contemplation that he invented the method of fluxions, discovered the law of universal gravitation, and proved experimentally that white light is composed of the light of all colors. The rest of his scientific life was devoted chiefly to developing these three discoveries. "All this," Newton tells us, speaking of them, "was in the two plague years of 1665 and 1666, for in those days I was in the prime of my age for invention and minded Mathematics and Philosophy [natural science] more than at any time since."

When the plague was over, Newton returned to Cambridge to finish his studies. In 1668, he received his master's degree and was made a fellow in the university. A year later he was appointed Lucasian professor of mathematics, a position of great distinction turned over to him by his instructor, Barrow. This position fitted Newton's needs nicely, for it gave him an income of £100 which, added to the income from his estates and his fellowship, enabled him to live comfortably. More important, his duties were not demanding. He lectured once a week every other term. He was apparently free to choose almost any course, for he lectured on such various subjects as geography, optics, and astronomy. He was free to devote the rest of his week to meditation on mathematics, experiments in alchemy, or research in biblical chronology.

Even in these early years Newton considered mathematics dry and barren. If we can judge from the mass of notes and data he gathered, he must have divided the greater part of his time between experiments in chemistry, a large proportion of which were on alchemy and magic, and research into religious questions. Such work, of course, was more congenial to Newton's temperament — for here there was mystery which challenged him. Alchemy, magic, and the mystery of the Trinity annoyed him, and he therefore kept working in these subjects because they did not readily yield clear answers to his inquiring mind. Mathematical and physical problems, on the other hand, he seems to have exhausted in a single act of concentrated, penetrating meditation. As early as 1679 he wrote to Hooke: "But yet my affection to philosophy being worn out, so that I am almost as little concerned about it as one tradesman used to be about another man's trade or a countryman about learning, I must acknowledge myself averse from spending that time in writing about it which I think

I can spend otherwise more to my own content and the good of others."

Had not one of his disciples, Edmund Halley, skillfully urged him to save his honor and reputation, and had not controversies with the annoying Hooke driven him to it, Newton would likely never have written his *Principia*. But he was finally driven to it in the last weeks of 1684. Seventeen months later he delivered the finished manuscript to the Royal Society in London. His latest biographer tells us that through this time "he behaves like a man dominated by an irresistible force. And it did not relax its grip until it had pushed him on to the accomplishment of the greatest intellectual feat in the history of science."

When Newton had finished the work he was through with it. He took no pride in it and showed no interest in its fate. He always referred to it, in fact, as "Halley's book." Although he was only forty-two when he finished the *Principia* and was to remain in full possession of his faculties for another forty years, he never again took up scientific investigation seriously. He turned instead to what he considered important things. It is for this reason that the mathematician, Bell, writes ruefully: "Mathematics, dynamics, and celestial mechanics were in fact — we may as well admit it — secondary interests with Newton. His heart was in his alchemy, his researches in chronology, and his theological studies." In those seventeen months, nevertheless, he had done work enough to be called "the greatest scientific genius the world has ever seen."

2

Newton divided the next ten years between alchemy, worry, religion, and occasional involuntary excursions into lunar speculation. He grew restive in these years at Cambridge. The routine of college life palled him, and he assiduously cultivated such distinguished men outside his college circle as Boyle and Locke, Pepys, Bentley, and Henry More. Through these men, who circulated in the society to which Newton was irresistibly drawn, the Cambridge don sought contacts which would take him out of his dry, academic seclusion. As well as we can tell, Newton never was active in college affairs, never associated with his fellow professors. He probably found them quite dull, and Newton could not tolerate dullness.

It was his prominence in a political dispute at Cambridge, however, that started him off to London. In 1687, King James II ordered the officials at Cambridge to grant the master's degree to a certain Catholic priest, a Benedictine monk named Father Alban Francis. The candidate, James instructed the vice-chancellor, was to receive his degree without taking the required oaths in support of the Anglican faith. Newton opposed the king's request. His Whiggish views on the limits of kingly power made him insist that "the vice-chancellor cannot by law admit one to that degree, unless he take the oaths of supremacy and allegiance which are enjoined by three or four statutes." The king, he was saying, could not dispense individuals from obeying the law.

His conduct in this affair made him a popular political figure at Cambridge, for he was one of the two representatives chosen from the university to sit in the Convention Parliament of 1688–1689 to bestow the crown upon William and Mary and consolidate the "Glorious Revolution" in legal form. His taste of "real life" at London in this year is taken by his biographers to be the turning point of his life. Bell writes sorrowfully that it "proved his scientific undoing." Louis T. More concludes more objectively in his excellent study: "His whole outlook on life seems to have changed; he met, and was courted by, those who were prominent in the affairs of the state and the church; he mingled in society and lost all desire for the academic life and for scientific work." Newton had long before lost all taste for academic work, but now his taste for the "real life" of London was whetted.

Hereafter, Newton's life centered at London. But he remained seven more years at Cambridge while friends were trying to find him a suitable position in politics. He served a second term in Parliament, but remained safely silent through all debate. It was reported by a contemporary wag that Newton spoke only once in Parliament — when he asked an usher to close a window. He may have worked in committee or in the cloakrooms, but there is no record of his having said a word from the floor.

A strange interlude occurs in Newton's life after his return to Cambridge from the Convention Parliament. Through 1692 and 1693 he was despondent, and for a short time in the latter year he apparently lost his mind. The first news of Newton's derangement came from the gossipy Pepys; soon scholars both on the continent and in England were inquiring about the mathematician's "condition." Rumor had deprived him of his mind and even of his life. Rumor, too, had assigned all sorts of causes for his malady — from the accidental loss of a manuscript in a fire to overwork in composing the *Principia*.

Whatever the cause, Newton's temporary loss of sanity was exposed pathetically in letters to Locke and to Pepys. A note to Locke tells how he had accused the philosopher of "embroiling me with women" and how he had publicly wished that Locke were dead. For this he begs Locke's forgiveness and implies that their friendship must now come to an end. Locke, of course, was bewildered. So too was Pepys when he received a letter from Newton telling the diarist that "I never designed to get anything by your interest, nor by King James' favour, but am now sensible that I must withdraw from your acquaintance, and see neither you nor the rest of my friends any more, if I may but leave them quietly." A month later Newton wrote to Locke, explaining that he had been ill for some time, that he had gone as long as five days without sleep, but that he was then on the mend. We hear no more of this trouble, and whatever had happened to Newton seems to have left no serious permanent effects.

In 1696, when he was fifty-three, Newton at last received his long sought-for appointment in London. On March 19 of that year, Montague wrote him that the king would appoint him warden of the Mint, an office "most proper for you, [that] has not too much business to require more attendance than you may spare." For a few years, however, the job took most of Newton's time. He had to manage the recoinage of English money, a procedure made necessary by the debasement of money through counterfeiting, adulteration of coins, and the clipping of their unmilled edges. Newton did the job efficiently and honestly, again proving his ability at practical tasks. He increased the weekly coinage of silver tenfold, and in three years he finished the job.

In 1699, Newton was made Master of the Mint, a position he held until his death twenty-eight years later. The various emoluments from this position amounted to more than £2000 a year. So, in 1701, Newton felt himself financially able to resign his connections with Cambridge and to cut his last ties with the academic world. As Master of the Mint, Newton was required to drop into his establishment only once a week; the rest of the time was his for research in theology and chemistry, and occasionally, when his honor was at stake, for excursions into mathematics or physics.

That his scientific genius was not dimmed in the least in these later years was demonstrated particularly on two occasions when difficult problems were submitted to him in such fashion that he had to solve them to prove his mastery in mathematics. Although Newton was irritated by his friends' attempts to drag him into scientific discussion, when his honor was at stake he took up the challenge in spirited fashion. In 1696, John Bernoulli proposed two problems to mathematicians of the world. He allowed six months for their solution, but when Leibniz, who had solved the first problem, asked for an extension of time, Bernoulli allowed another year. Newton received the problems one evening, and he brought the answers to the president of the Royal Society the next morning. Again, in 1716, Leibniz proposed a similar problem "for the purpose," he said, "of feeling the pulse of the English analysts." Newton realized it was a challenge directed at him personally, so — at the age of seventy-three — he solved the problem the same evening he received it.

But these were only occasional excursions into the field of his genius. The rest of the time he devoted to London society and to making money. And in both pursuits he was more than moderately successful. Newton is, indeed, one of the few real geniuses in history to have become wealthy, popular, and honored in his lifetime, for he received honors, money, and adulation sufficient for anyone. He was knighted by Queen Anne, and he was admitted to court almost from his first day in London. He was elected president of the Royal Society in 1703 and was annually re-elected until he died in 1727, even though toward the end, so it is reported, he frequently slept through the meetings. He was made one of the first eight foreign associates of the

French Academy of Sciences in 1699. It must have piqued his sensitive sense of pride, though, to learn that he was the seventh named, whereas his great rival, Leibniz, was first. He was courted in social circles in London and worshiped at a respectful distance by younger English scientists. And finally, he was buried with royal honors in Westminster Abbey when he died in his eighty-fifth year.

Newton's later life was not completely happy, however, because he never felt secure in his justly acquired fame. He was, after all, a country boy who had made good first in the academic world and then in London. As a country boy, he felt an urge continually to assert himself, to climb socially, to be ever pushing. There is no other way to explain why he searched so diligently — and futilely — through his family connections to establish his status as an English gentleman. There is no other way to explain his many quarrels with fellow scientists who, he believed, were depriving him of his justly earned honors.

There were three principal quarrels which he pursued relentlessly through his later life. One was with the cantankerous Hooke, whom Newton rightfully judged an inferior scientist trying to be his equal. A second was with Flamsteed, who simply was not capable of furnishing Newton with the data he demanded on the movements of the moon, and who therefore found himself involved in censorious bickering with this demanding genius who lost his temper whenever that "litigious Lady" of science was involved.

But Newton's third quarrel was with Gottfried Leibniz, a worthy rival who surpassed Newton in almost everything. Newton was a mathematical genius without equal; Leibniz was a universal genius who excelled ordinary men in almost everything he touched. Both these men had discovered calculus independently — not a surprising thing, for calculus was very much in the air in the seventeenth century. Newton, however, did nothing to publish his work on "fluxions"; he was anxious only to preserve for himself the title of discoverer. So when Leibniz wrote to Newton about ten years later explaining his system fully, Newton answered with a letter designed to prove that he had already discovered the system. But he concealed his ideas in a double-talk sentence so that his secret would remain safe.

Newton acknowledged this much when he published his *Principia* in 1687. So far there was nothing like a quarrel. The same thing had been discovered by two men working independently in two different places; neither had denied the other's independent discovery. Newton never let his secret out, but Leibniz, whose spirit was both more generous and more genuinely that of a scholar, published articles on the subject. Both Newton's and Leibniz' followers, young and zealous men, were anxious to exalt their respective idol's reputation by attributing to him exclusively the discovery of calculus. Both sets of followers therefore accused the rival master of plagiarism.

Newton took no active part in the controversy until an anonymous review of his *Optics* in 1704 contained an unmistakable charge of plagiarism against him. Then Newton threw himself into the fray with the same pertinacity, the same implacable, driving heartlessness that he showed in his schoolboy fight. As the controversy wore on Newton came to believe really unbelievable things about Leibniz, and even after the latter died Newton carried on his relentless attacks. Bitterness ate into his soul, and he spent hour after hour drawing up vindications of himself and proofs that Leibniz was a plagiarist. The quarrel, which was unfortunate in every way, clearly reveals certain of Newton's character traits. He loved quiet and repose. He was calm and tranquil until he was disturbed. But when once he began a quarrel he entered upon it as a mathematician undertakes the solution of a problem — in objective, unsympathetic, relentless fashion. Newton was in this way cold, nonhuman. He never made allowance for human weakness or human folly. This quarrel with Leibniz also reveals how concerned Newton was about his reputation and his honor — as though he was not quite secure, as though he expected he might some day be sent back to the country a disgraceful failure. There seems no other way to explain his doing some rather dishonorable things in this quarrel — all to save "honor," all to prove that he was not a plagiarist.

3

Newton is most difficult to know. He seems consciously to have kept jealous guard over his mind, and biographers therefore find it almost impossible to discover what went on there. In the days when he did his great work at Cambridge contemporaries did not think him worth describing, and the word-pictures made after his death are tinted strongly by age and free fancy. There is no doubt, however, that Newton was no ordinary mixture of mind and matter. He was as close to pure mind as man can come. His body seems never to have been a drag on his spirit; never did it seem to make imperious demands; never did it cry for satisfaction. This helps account for his amazing accomplishments, for Newton could ignore bodily needs when he absorbed himself in trancelike contemplation. He had the body, as well as the mind, of an intellectual genius.

Throughout life, whether he was deep in mathematical contemplation or immersed in London society, Newton was largely exempt from those passions and emotions that play so dominant a part in most men's lives. Love, patriotism, religious exaltation are experiences he never had. His most human emotion seems to have been a filial love for his mother — but this was never the sort of attachment to upset him or interfere with his intellectual activity. He never came really to know or to understand those other men who inhabited this world whose workings he so clearly perceived. All through life, Newton shows complete lack of tact in dealing with friend and acquaintance.

Newton, then, was a powerful mind inhabiting an unobtrusive body. His health, in fact, was phenomenally good. He had only two sick spells in his life, and when he died at the age of eighty-four he had a full head of silvery hair and all his teeth but one. This health he enjoyed without perpetual self-doctoring, as was the case of Locke. When he was absorbed in chemical experiments or in the writing of his *Principia*, he slept only four or five hours a night and he took out only a few minutes a day to bolt down some food — often eating in a standing position to save time. He could ignore his body for long stretches of time, and he could put himself into an almost mystic state of contemplation when he struggled with a mathematical problem. Just how he did this no biographer can tell us; we simply know that it was done, and we have to accept it as a fact.

One of the few descriptions of Newton at work is the one given by his assistant from 1685 till 1690, a certain Humphrey

Newton (no relative): "I cannot say I ever saw him laugh but once. . . . I never knew him to take any recreation or pastime either in riding out to take the air, walking, bowling, or any other exercise whatever, thinking all hours lost that were not spent in his studies. . . . He ate very sparingly, nay, ofttimes he has forgot to eat at all. . . . He very rarely went to bed till two or three of the clock, sometimes not until five or six, lying about four or five hours. . . . I believe he grudged the short time he spent in eating and sleeping." This description, of course, is of the Newton who was immersed in writing the *Principia,* the Newton who, Sullivan puts it, "behaves like a man dominated by an irresistible force." He did not always work so furiously, but in the days of his great achievements he was capable of so working — which accounts for his being so remarkable a genius in a subject to which he devoted so small a part of his time.

The fact that Newton thought mathematics and science of secondary importance does not detract from his unusual ability in these subjects. On the contrary, it makes him all the more unusual. For he is unique in excelling in something he thought relatively unimportant. Yet despite his competence in science, his attitude toward the subject was hardly "scientific," as we understand that term today. He viewed it much more as a lawyer or a professional baseball player might look at it. He had absolutely no interest in promoting it; he never wanted to pass his discoveries on to others, or even to publish them for the profit of fellow scientists. He would never have worked on an atomic bomb project, or even on the application of atomic energy to practical peaceful purposes. He would never have done cooperative work, for he was interested only in solving problems, in finding answers that had never been found before. When he found the answer, he was content.

Newton, furthermore, never thought of science serving utilitarian purposes. He never considered science man's handmaiden who, when properly trained, could be put to cleaning kitchens or seasoning meat. If mathematics and science were to serve an ulterior purpose with Newton, they were to lead to a firmer belief in God's existence and to a surer knowledge of His nature. For he always looked upon science as subordinate to theology and as legitimately connected with it. "To discourse of [God] from the appearance of things," he insists, "does certainly belong to Natural Philosophy." On various occasions he commented that the chief value of his scientific work lay in the support it gave to revealed religion; the *Principia* and the *Optics* he considered useful chiefly for making manifest God's laws and partly revealing His nature.

Such an attitude toward science was normal for Newton's age. But because Newton soon became science incarnate, this point must be emphasized for a proper understanding of Newton the man. When Richard Bentley proposed using the *Principia* for his series of lectures on "the defense of religion against infidels," Newton wrote three letters to him on the connection of science and religion. In the first of them he observed: "When I wrote my treatise about our system, I had an eye upon such principles as might work with considering men, for the belief of a Deity; and nothing can rejoice me more than to find it useful for that purpose."

Newton was seriously offended when Leibniz — a much more competent philosopher and theologian than he — wrote to Princess Caroline that the *Principia* undermined religion. So when Newton prepared a second edition of this famous work, he added a general scholium in which he advanced his belief in God's existence and tried to show, with a flourish, how "this most beautiful system of the sun, planets, and comets, could only proceed from the counsel and dominion of an intelligent and powerful Being." When he finally published his lectures on *Optics* in 1704 he devoted several pages to showing how the machinelike design of the universe argues back to the existence of an intelligent Designer. Then he went on to show how a fuller knowledge of science will enlighten mankind ethically and theologically. "If natural philosophy in all its parts . . . shall at length be perfected, the bounds of moral philosophy will be also enlarged. For so far as we can know by natural philosophy what is the first cause, what power he has over us, and what benefits we receive from him, so far our duty towards him, as well as that towards one another, will appear to us by the light of nature."

Science, then, was to serve the ulterior purpose of revealing God to us. But in itself, Newton thought, it was a dry subject.

Even in his most fertile periods he looked upon science as an irksome taskmaster, and frequently during his lifetime he threatened to abandon it for keeps. As early as 1674 he wrote to Oldenburg, secretary of the Royal Society; "I have long since determined to concern myself no further about the promotion of philosophy [natural science]. And for the same reason I must desire to be excused from engaging to exhibit yearly philosophic discourses." He had been annoyed, as he was to be all his life, at the obtuseness of scientists who could not understand what he said. They threw up absurd objections and demanded that he disprove various hypotheses. "I see," he therefore concluded, "a man must either resolve to put out nothing new, or become a slave to defend it."

He could therefore write to Halley, when the young astronomer was urging him to publish, that "philosophy is such an impertinently litigious Lady, that a man had as good be engaged to lawsuits, as to have to do with her." When Hooke endeavored to engage him in scientific correspondence again, Newton answered rather petulantly: "I had for some years last been endeavouring to bend myself from philosophy to other studies in so much that I have long grutched the time spent in that study unless it be perhaps at idle hours sometimes for diversion."

But fortunately for science Newton was skillfully handled by his young associates. Halley talked him into writing the *Principia,* and young Roger Cotes urged him to prepare a second edition. The *Optics* would never have appeared, Newton tells his readers, "had not the importunity of friends prevailed upon me." His minor papers were prepared in connection with his work at Cambridge or as contributions to the proceedings of the Royal Society. So even though Newton considered science a barren subject, "an impertinently litigious Lady," he nevertheless contributed more to its development than any single predecessor in history.

4

We have seen that Newton devoted the greater part of his time to nonscientific studies, that in mere quantity of note taking and authorship his work in these subjects far surpassed his labors in the scientific field. What he produced in these subjects is worthless today — and even in his own day it was of little value. Newton was a genius in only one field, but a genius cannot be adequately known if he is observed only in the field of his precocity. We must therefore see what he tried to do in his chemical experiments and in his researches into the Bible.

Newton surprises his biographer with his vast erudition in nonscientific studies, and he disappoints him with his almost paralytic inability to put that erudition to use. His learning in history was immense — for his age — and his knowledge of geography perhaps as great as that of any Englishman of his day. He edited Varenius' *Geography*, the outstanding treatise of the time, and he lectured on geography from the Lucasian chair at Cambridge.

Experiments in chemistry perhaps occupied more hours of his life than study in any other field. Even in the heat of composing his *Principia* Newton did not neglect his chemical experiments. His interest was devoted chiefly to that rather bizarre pseudo-chemistry which so gripped the best thinkers of his day; alchemy, the philosopher's stone, and the elixir of life were the elusive subjects which he pursued year after year. He seems, indeed, to be less of a scientist in the field of chemistry than a mystic. But here he was only following the other great minds of his day, men like Boyle, Locke, and Hooke. "There is nothing surprising in Newton being an alchemist," Sullivan says. "What is surprising, considering the time and thought he devoted to the matter, is that he should have done so little in the way of genuine scientific discovery. In this region he seems to show none of that power of isolating the essentials of a problem which is so characteristic of his other scientific work."

Robert Boyle believed that he had discovered the secret of making gold by treating a certain kind of red dirt with mercury. He still had not made gold when he died, but he left his recipe and some red dirt to Locke and Newton. The latter believed that such a transmutation as Boyle envisaged was possible, but he grew skeptical about the latter's process when he found that others had worked so long and so fruitlessly at the task. He seems to have remained skeptical of the actual transmutation being accomplished in his day, but he never doubted that gold could be made from baser material.

Newton's work in religion shows him absorbed in two main problems. First of all, good Whig that he was, he sought to expose the false pretensions of the Roman Catholic Church and establish the Bible as the sole rule of faith; second, he took the view — exceedingly radical in his day, making him liable to severe punishment — that the traditional Christian teaching on the Trinity was false. His arguments against the claims of the Catholic Church interest us chiefly for showing how much he knew, rightly or wrongly, about Church history, the early councils, the ancient heresies, the Roman and Greek Fathers of the Church.

The Apocalypse and the books of Daniel particularly interested him, partly because he believed they furnished him with ammunition against the papists, and partly because of their mystical prophecies — and Newton was ever drawn irresistibly toward the mystical. He interpreted the prophecies of Daniel as a warning against the pope and the Catholic Church, which he identified with the little horn of the fourth beast. Newton concluded from his study of the prophets that the Catholic Church would fall about A.D. 2000. His arguments against the Trinity were more cautiously advanced and were published posthumously, for Newton was not one to risk his position at the Mint and his honors for anything. His line of argument was that belief in the Trinity rested mainly on two scriptural passages, and these were corruptions introduced by St. Jerome in his Latin translation of the original text.

Newton's faith in the Bible itself remained unshaken. "The authority of emperors, kings, and princes," he wrote, "is human. The authority of the prophets is divine, . . . and if an angel from heaven preach any other gospel, than what they have delivered, let him be accursed." Newton evidently believed that scriptural scholarship could determine for once and for all what the prophets had said, and what they meant by what they said. His own scriptural scholarship is curious for the way he sought to verify the prophets' statements by intricate chronological tables and to support their theology by mathematical analysis. But when Bentley accused him of expounding prophecies as he demonstrated mathematical propositions, Newton was evidently annoyed at what he thought unfair criticism.

His idea of God is given tersely in the general scholium at the end of the second edition of the *Principia*. Newton's is a personal God, but imperceptibly He becomes the God of deism, the all-knowing, all-good Creator who, after making the best possible universe and giving it ironclad rules of operation, withdrew into His heavens to watch His perfect piece of machinery tick away with beautiful precision. This God, he tells us, "is a Being eternal, infinite, absolutely perfect." His wisdom, His power, and His dominion we can know from His handiwork, but we can learn nothing of His nature. "We have ideas of his attributes," Newton concludes, but we have absolutely no "idea of the substance of God."

Newton's religious views were one thing, his scientific another. He apparently did not think them incompatible, however, for when his system of the world, as laid down in the *Principia,* was attacked by continental philosophers as subversive of religion, Newton was genuinely hurt. But Leibniz and his associates were right in insisting that Nature became divine in Newton's world machine, that both God and man took minor roles. Newton's religious beliefs, nevertheless, were not in conformity with his rigorous laws of mechanics. He was a confessing member of the Church of England whose only heretical view was his skeptical attitude toward the Trinity.

5

Newton's big contribution toward the making of the modern mind lies in his scientific thought and in his methodology. The Newtonian method came to be *the* method, not only for scientific investigation, but for everything. His friend, Locke, for example, hoped to construct a system of ethics which would follow the line of reasoning and the system of demonstration used in the *Principia.* The Newtonian method became, by the time of his death, the method of investigation in economics and politics, in physics and chemistry, in all social and physical sciences.

"I frame no hypotheses," Newton said time and again. And in this statement he summed up his radical departure from the method of his predecessors and his contemporaries. In his day the Cartesian method, which based science on metaphysics, was still the vogue. Factual data were still compressed into an hypothesis obtained from philosophy. Cartesians believed that if one started with correct theories, experiment was unnecessary; to come to the right conclusion one had only to reason rightly.

To Newton, on the contrary, the physical universe was an unknown. There were no axioms or theories that had to be substantiated. As far as Newton was concerned, anything could happen: rivers could run uphill, or fire could freeze. He was interested in discovering what did occur, and he was free to admit whatever he discovered by observation or by experiment. His refusal to lay down *a priori* conditions which the phenomena were to fulfill was so novel that Newton simply was not comprehended by his contemporaries. Even so competent a scientist as Huygens did not understand the Englishman's point of view. Newton repeatedly insisted that he was not writing about hypotheses, that he was only describing experiments and from them drawing conclusions — but all in vain. That is why he was bewildered and annoyed by objections that he had not confirmed or rejected this or that hypothesis.

His inductive study of phenomena, however, was only the first step for Newton. And, as far as his eighteenth-century followers are concerned, it was the least important step. By analysis of his observed facts he arrived at a fundamental principle; then he proceeded to deduce the mathematical consequences of this principle, and finally to check his conclusions with further observation. In his first published paper Newton explains his method thus: "For the best and safest method of philosophising seems to be, first to enquire diligently into the properties of things, and of establishing those properties by experiments, and then to proceed more slowly to hypotheses for the explanation of them. For hypotheses should be subservient only in explaining the properties of things, but not assumed in determining them."

He explained this method more fully in the *Principia:* "Whatever is not deduced from the phaenomena is to be called an hypothesis; and hypotheses, whether metaphysical or physical, whether of occult qualities or mechanical, have no place in experimental philosophy. In this philosophy particular propositions are inferred from the phaenomena, and afterwards rendered general by induction. Thus it was that the impenetrability, the mobility, and the impulsive force of bodies, and the laws of motion and of gravitation, were discovered. And to us it is enough that gravity does really exist, and act according to the laws which we have explained, and abundantly serves to account for all the motions of the celestial bodies, and of our sea."

Science, Newton held, was concerned only with descriptive work. Its task was merely to discover how things worked, not why. He therefore insisted that it was not the province of science to discover ultimate causes or to investigate the essence of things. "To tell us that every Species of Things is endow'd with an occult specifick Quality by which it acts and produces manifest Effects, is to tell us nothing: But to derive two or three general Principles of Motion from Phaenomena, and afterwards to tell us how the Properties and Actions of all corporal Things follow from those manifest Principles, would be a very great step in Philosophy, though the Causes of those Principles were not yet discover'd." Here again he was misunderstood by his contemporaries, for they were not content with a descriptive law of gravity. They demanded a theory which would show not only how gravity worked, but why it worked as it did. They demanded to know whether Descartes's hypothesis of vortices, for example, was right or wrong. Before long, however, the Newtonian method of investigation and the Newtonian concept of science as a descriptive subject came to be universally accepted.

Newton's discoveries in mathematics and physics are so well known that every college student is acquainted with them. They are so much a part of our common knowledge that little more is required here than to catalogue them and credit them to their author. His first important discovery was calculus, but because he guarded it so successfully and because he did not develop a system of notation for it, his contribution to mathematical knowledge in this respect is negligible. Leibniz' system of notation is the one that came to be adopted, and calculus would be the same subject it is today had Newton never lived.

But his famous law of gravitation is quite another thing. Others had floundered toward a law of gravitation; but they had never been able to apply mathematics to their experimentally obtained knowledge and thus to arrive at a general law. Newton himself was held up for about twenty years by a mathematical difficulty.

But when he saw that bodies were attracted to each other as though each had its mass concentrated in a single point at its center, he was able to state his famous law that "any two particles of matter in the universe attract one another with a force which is directly proportional to the product of their masses and inversely proportional to the square of the distance between them." In this way he was able to explain the motion of the earth and the stars and the moon. In this way even comets were shown to follow regular paths and to behave according to physical laws.

Newton's work on light reveals him at his experimental best. For he even ground his own lenses and prepared his own special equipment for these experiments. By patiently studying the reflection, refraction, and diffraction of light under varying conditions he discovered that various colors have different constant refrangibilities. From this discovery he was able to show that white light is made up of the light of all the colors. All this he did before he was twenty-five. His later work on light did not yield such remarkable discoveries, for Newton never settled on any one theory of light, and it is typical of his scientific bent of mind that his last words on light are in the form of queries. He seems to have favored the emission over the undulation theory, but his final conclusions are a mixture of the two theories, which physicists today say is close to their conclusions. His successors, however, wholeheartedly adopted the emission theory — they thought on Newton's authority.

Newton's *Principia* is his great accomplishment, both by reason of its contents and because of the amazingly short time in which he drew up, proved, and wrote out the propositions and problems making up this work. There are three books in the *Principia* containing one hundred and fifty propositions; almost every one of these involves the presentation of corollaries and scholia, as well as the principal problem, all of which involves a tremendous amount of calculation, illustration, and explanation. It is for this reason that commentators on the *Principia* use such adjectives as "incomparable" and "incomprehensible" when they tell how Newton accomplished the task in seventeen months.

The book is written in what Sullivan calls "a style of glacial remoteness which makes no concessions to the reader," a style that Newton purposely adopted, he said, "to avoid being baited by little smatterers in mathematics." The particular propositions he proved in the *Principia* need not concern us here. It is sufficient to note that in it Newton applies mathematics to an explanation of the motion of the universe, that his dynamics informs the entire work, that in it he shows how the sun's mass can be calculated, how the mass of any planet having a satellite can be determined, how the moon is attracted by the sun as well as by the earth, how "lawless comets" are brought under the universal law of gravitation as members of the sun's system.

And, most important, the *Principia* contained Newton's law of gravitation, the law which so beautifully unified and systematized the mass of natural phenomena that had till then apparently been without sense or system. It is no wonder that Newton came to be hailed the discoverer of nature's laws, the man who showed that all matter acted according to uniform, intelligible law. Because he enabled men to reduce the movements of the universe to laws they could write out and understand, Newton made the world a thoroughly intelligible place for the first time in history. And men worshiped him for his accomplishment.

For almost two hundred years his system remained intact. Nothing in it was disproved, and very little was improved. Not until Darwin's work suggested evolution and development in the universe was any serious addition made to the Newtonian concept of a stable world-machine which had always run according to the same laws, with the same speed and force through the same space. Not until Einstein's work in relativity early in this century was there any reason for believing that perhaps Newton's laws were not as universally valid as men had unquestioningly believed for so long.

Newton had subjected the phenomena of nature to the laws of mathematics. He had discovered nature to be a wonderful machine whose movements could be explained mechanically. For him, space and time were two absolutes existing independently of each other. Time, as a matter of fact, plays no part in the Newtonian machine; for practical purposes it is ignored. Newton looked upon matter as a third independent entity, something thrust into time and space. The interdependence of these three elements never occurred to Newton. He was content that matter existed in time and space and that it obeyed certain mechanical laws which man was able to discover. And this, for his day, was a great accomplishment.

6

So great was it, indeed, and so completely did it offer a rational explanation of the universe that until a century ago no one dared question the Cambridge professor's conclusions in the field of science. Newton was science, and science was intellectual king of the modern world. To disagree with Newton was intellectual treason for which only a madman could be excused. All that is changed now. Newton explained the universe, but today his explanation is considered both inadequate and partly incorrect. His fundamental assumptions of space, time, and matter have changed so that Newton would never recognize them now; his work on mass, force, gravitation, and light has been superseded by developments from the discovery of electricity and of the atomic composition of matter. Scientists today look upon Newton as a seventeenth-century genius who completed the scientific revolution of his age and passed on its accomplishments, packaged nicely, to the eighteenth century. Although he remains a big name in the history of science, he is no longer science incarnate.

If only scientists and mathematicians had been affected by Newton, he would not be a maker of the modern mind. His influence, however, was felt in every field of thought. The "Newtonian mind" infused the bodies of all "thinking men" in the eighteenth century; one who had not adopted this Newtonian mind was simply an intellectual fuddy-duddy. Such popularization was accomplished because men who had never read a word Newton wrote still thought they knew him. Voltaire, himself no expert in science, complained that "very few people read Newton, because it is necessary to be learned to understand him. But everybody talks about him." So Voltaire told Frenchmen all about Newton in his *Elemens de la philosophie de Neuton* — published twenty-one years before anyone bothered to translate the *Principia* into French.

Newton was popularized more suddenly and more widely than

any thinker before him in history. Before the outbreak of the French Revolution in 1789 there were at least forty books about the *Principia* alone in English, seventeen in French, eleven in Latin, and a few in German, Italian, Spanish, and Portuguese. But this was only part of the campaign to sell Newton's system of the world to its inhabitants. Typical of the medium through which Newton passed on to ordinary people is the work published in 1751 by the popular lecturer, Benjamin Martin: "A Plain and Familiar Introduction to the Newtonian Philosophy in Six Lectures. Illustrated by Six Copper Plates. Designed for the use of such Gentlemen and Ladies as would acquire a competent Knowledge of this Science without Mathematical Learning; and more especially those who have or may attend the Author's Course of Six Lectures and Experiments on these subjects."

Newton had written with icy remoteness to avoid being bothered by amateur scientists, but his popularizers went to extremes in melting him down for easy consumption by lazy minds. In 1756, James Ferguson, for example, published his *Astronomy Explained upon Newton's Principles, and made easy to those who have studied mathematics,* a work which went through seven editions in seventeen years. In 1737, Count Alogrotti published *Il Newtonianismo per le dame,* which went through several editions in Italian and several more in its French translations. "Newtonianism" was not confined to popularized science. Even during Newton's lifetime, as we have seen, Bentley used the *Principia* to prove God's existence. And Colin Maclaurin, a young professor of mathematics at Edinburgh in Newton's old age, wrote *An Account of Sir Isaac Newton's Philosophical Discoveries,* in which he dogmatically expounded a general philosophy of the universe, including God, nature, and man — all based on his oracle, Newton. "To inquire into the whole constitution of the universe," he claimed, "is the business of Natural Philosophy . . . which is chiefly to be valued as it lays a sure foundation for Natural Religion and Moral Philosophy; by leading us, in a satisfactory manner, to the knowledge of the Author and Governor of the Universe."

These broader uses of Newton's thought gave him a popularity and an importance far beyond that of a scientific genius kept in his laboratory. The late Carl Becker put it well when he concluded: "His name became a symbol which called up, in the mind of the reading and thinking public, a generalized conception of the universe, a kind of philosophical premise of the most general type, one of those uncriticized preconceptions which so largely determined the social and political as well as the strictly scientific thinking of the age."

In this respect, Newton's importance in the eyes of the public lay largely in his seeming to have banished mystery from the world. "Philosophy," the designation he always gave to his scientific work, took on the clarity of mathematics and the easy method of patient observation. Where Descartes had failed in his ambition to make philosophy, and with it the world, a thoroughly intelligible place, Newton seemed to have succeeded. Everything moved according to law, and man could, by patient observation, careful experiment, and mathematical speculation, lay bare these laws. All the universe seemed so reasonable, so understandable. Indirectly, but powerfully nonetheless, Newton contributed to the optimism which flooded like warm sunshine across the eighteenth-century mind. Pope, the rhyming mirror of that mind, showed Newton's powerful influence when, in an age of wars and plague and famine, he happily sang:

> All are but parts of one stupendous whole,
> Whose body Nature is, and God the soul: . . .
> All Nature is but Art, unknown to thee;
> All chance, direction which thou canst not see;
> All discord, harmony not understood;
> All partial evil, universal good.

Newton discovered the world was a single, vast machine. Like a clock it had wheels and springs which moved according to discoverable mechanical rules. These rules came to be identified in the eighteenth century with natural law. Thus the laws of nature replaced the natural law of philosophers of days gone by. The old natural law was normative; it told men, through their conscience, what they should and should not do. But after Newton natural law is identified popularly with physical law. It becomes deterministic rather than normative, and when it is transferred into such fields as economics and politics it becomes the physical law of supply and demand, or the deterministic law of oligarchy, that is natural law in the social sciences. Newton is at least remotely connected with Representative Roe's profession of faith made in Congress in 1946: "I believe the law of supply and demand is a natural, divine, God-given law that cannot be set aside by man any more than we can stop the sun from shining or the tide from ebbing and flowing." A perfect example, in one sentence, of the new concept of natural law which Newton unwittingly created and others witlessly transferred into other fields than the scientific.

The Newtonian method, as well as Newtonian conclusions, held the field for two centuries in scientific thought. Newton combined with his friend, Locke, to replace the Cartesian deductive system of reasoning from fundamental axioms with the new empirical method. For this Newton can be given no large share of credit; but the new way of discovering truth was identified with him as well as with Locke, and where it battled Cartesianism it had the support of his august authority. Because Hume's skepticism made Newton's position philosophically untenable within fifty years, Kant will find it necessary to defend the Newtonian Universe and method against Hume's thoroughgoing skepticism. So Newton's system was soon under attack philosophically — but scientifically it was not questioned for two hundred years.

The author of the *Principia* affected religion in curious and ironic fashion. His religious heterodoxy, which his associates so much feared, had no influence at all. But his scientific work, which both he and his followers thought such a strong prop for belief in God, undermined that very belief. Newton had, whether he realized it or not, deified nature and depersonalized God. Nature was made absolute. God and man shrank beside her. God was allowed to be the Great Mechanic, the Master Architect, the Final Force, or some such thing called upon to account for the world-machine's existence. After His act of creation, however, He was pushed off to His heaven and told to stay there.

And before long Newton's scientific system was used as ammunition against the God of the Bible, whom he thought he was revealing through His works. Leon Block, for example, tells the readers of his *La philosophie de Newton:* "Henceforth it will be possible for natural science, that is to say physics, not only to struggle against theology, but to supplant it. The contradictory gods of the revealed religions will be replaced by a new idea, that of a being who is known to us through his works, and to whom we can attain only through science. The universal order, symbolized henceforth by the law of gravitation, takes on a clear and positive meaning."

There is a last sour little note to be added about Newton's influence on the modern mind — and this was hardly his fault. Englishmen, following their great scientist blindly — with stupid loyalty to him and with a strong nationalist antipathy toward non-British scientists — cut themselves off from communication with the rest of European thought. They stuck not only to Newton's ideas but also to his difficult methods of solving problems and to his clumsy notation. They went into intellectual isolation, and they fell a century behind the continent in mathematics and the allied sciences. All this came from the silly quarrel between Newton and Leibniz, and, as a result, in Bell's words, "the obstinate British practically rotted mathematically for all of a century after Newton's death."

VII

ROUSSEAU

DESCARTES was a rationalist. His followers, of course, never questioned the kingship of the mind over the heart, nor did they put any limits to the worlds which it could embrace. Even Locke and Newton, parents of empiricism, kept reason king over all. In 1750, when Descartes was a century in his grave, rationalism was still the vogue among European thinkers. It remained the fashion to appeal to reason, although its vigor had for some time been spent. But men still tried to measure all things by reason; they limited the universe by the compass of their minds.

The age of rationalism had become an artificial age. Gardens were geometric, clothes were stilted, things were "proper." Onto this scene of geometric propriety stumbled, by accident, an uncouth figure. Jean-Jacques Rousseau was nature's ragged urchin who, because of his grotesqueness, was welcomed by the principal actors onto their perfectly arranged rationalist scene — to serve as comic relief. Rousseau was a buffoon, and in rationalist *salon*

162

circles he did furnish the much needed comic relief. But he was more than a mere buffoon. He was eloquent. He was sincere. So people listened when he spoke his lines against the shallowness and the foppery of the scene onto which he stumbled. Rousseau commanded attention because he spoke from the heart, because he meant what he said, because he crystallized human emotions that thousands of other men felt but dared not utter. Therefore he was soon the central figure on the scene, and the remaining rationalists retired to the darkness of the wings — and to oblivion.

1

Men like Voltaire, who professed to worship Locke and Newton, were annoyed by this bad boy of Nature. Voltaire, for example, bitingly thanked Rousseau for a gift copy of his second discourse by observing that, "one longs in reading your book to walk on all fours." That was clever, but it was no answer to Rousseau's appeal for man to be natural. Again, Voltaire turned his favorite weapon of ridicule on Rousseau, calling him such things as "charlatan savage," "hoot-owl," and "enemy of the human race." But because men were tired of Voltaire's barbed witticisms, they joined their wives to listen raptly to Rousseau's eloquent plea for natural living and they looked on good-naturedly as their women fought for souvenirs of Nature's oracle.

People have listened raptly ever since. From Rousseau, indeed, have stemmed most of the currents of thought that have eddied for control of the modern mind since his day. From him the extremist democrats, who insist that nothing can stand in the way of the infallible, the good, the godlike majority of the people, draw their inspiration. From him the rugged individualists get their theories of an anarchically organized state with practically no social controls over the individual. From him stems modern romanticism with its insistence that "the heart has reasons which the reason knows not." From him comes modern anticlassical, anti-intellectual education. From him detractors of all "artificial" institutions — which might be religion or art or marriage or urban life — obtain their ammunition.

From him, too, stems the modern form of totalitarian absolutism compounded of voluntarism and a mystical identification of the government and the people. From him, in part, come our saner forms of humanitarianism, our respect for man as a human being, our faith in representative institutions. These are, of course, mutually exclusive and mutually antagonistic bodies of thought. But Rousseau was pre-eminently inconsistent. His famous *Contrat social,* for example, can be used to nullify everything in his discourses on nature; and his constitutions prepared for Poland and for Corsica can be used to answer everything in the *Contrat social.* Rousseau can always be used to refute Rousseau. He is that sort of person.

Rousseau could never have been important except in the mid-eighteenth century. At no other time in modern history would women have followed him back to nature by dressing up as peasant girls and watering artificial flowers set in pavement gardens. But they did in his day. For the eighteenth century was highly artificial in its mode of thought, in its way of life, in its social intercourse, in its government, in its very heart. People saw nothing ridiculous then in playing "back to nature" on paved patios. Men's very souls, following Newton and Descartes, were constrained by mechanical "natural laws"; men's bodies were pieces of machinery moving in deterministic fashion. Holbach was only saying the generally accepted thing when he stated pontifically: "All bodies act according to laws inherent in their peculiar essence, without the capability to swerve, even for a single instant, from those according to which Nature herself acts. . . . Nature does not make man either good or wicked; she combines machines more or less active, mobile, and energetic. . . . The same necessity which regulates the physical, also regulates the moral world, in which everything is in consequence submitted to fatality." Diderot spoke for "enlightened" men when he observed that he liked Holbach for being "clear, definite, and frank." But Goethe spoke for a greater number when he said of the *Système de la nature* that it was "so gray, so Cimmerian, so corpse-like, that we could hardly endure its presence; we shuddered before it as if it had been a spectre." It is against the "enlightened" rationalism, typified by Holbach, that Rousseau preaches.

Compared with his rationalist contemporaries, Rousseau is refreshing. His was an age, for example, that was unnaturally irreligious. In a day when Voltaire poked sly fun at Joan of Arc, Rousseau created at least a saint of nature in Julie, the heroine of his *Nouvelle Heloise*. In a day when Voltaire said that Christ was "a well-meaning fanatic," and Jean Meslier called Him "a vile and wretched good-for-nothing, low-born, ignorant, untalented and awkward," it is refreshing to find Rousseau courageous enough to assert: "If the life and death of Socrates are those of a philosopher, the life and death of Christ are those of a God." It must have been like a breeze from the Atlantic to the middle-class people of France to hear Rousseau's command: "Dare to confess God before the *philosophes;* dare to preach humanity to the intolerant."

Rousseau's was a barren age in every way. Reason, so glorified by the rationalists, had cut itself adrift from living reality; it had withered and dried, until only a crackling pod was left. The atmosphere was cold, arrogant, haughty, smugly selfish; there was a spiritual vacuum in men's hearts. And Rousseau rushed in where abbés feared to tread. He preached a secularized religion, it is true, but at least it was religion. People drank deeply of it, and for a while they thought they were satisfied. Rousseau fed their hearts and he appealed to their consciences. Compared to the shallow witticisms of Voltaire or the weak, tiresome *bons mots* of his less gifted associates, Rousseau seemed to probe deep. For he touched the heart. The elder Mirabeau spoke the mind of many when he wrote to Rousseau: "I know no morality that goes deeper than yours; it strikes like a thunderbolt."

2

"I am not like anyone else I have been acquainted with, perhaps like no one in existence." Thus did Rousseau begin his *Confessions.* Because he was right we must study this unique man whose mold was broken after his birth. Otherwise we cannot hope to understand his works, for they all are intensely personal writings in which Rousseau bares his soul. He was a pitifully weak person whose every undertaking was a failure, until suddenly his protests against society struck a sympathetic note throughout France — and the queer Genevan had become an oracle in Paris. Since his protests can be fully understood only in the light of his early failures, however, it is necessary to follow Rousseau's vagrant wanderings from his abnormal youth to his mad old age.

As far back as we can trace the Rousseaus we find them fleeing from difficulties. In the first days of the Protestant Revolt, Rousseau's ancestors adopted Protestantism and fled to Geneva, a city which still maintained rigid doctrine and severe morality when Jean-Jacques was born in 1712. His mother died in giving him birth, and for some time it was feared the baby would die too. But Jean-Jacques lived, carrying with him, he tells us, "seeds of a disorder that has gathered strength with years." His father was a dissolute figure in the midst of this puritanical austerity. He seems to have loved his son, in his peculiar way, and Rousseau tells us how his father introduced him to the Muse by reading pornographic literature to him through the night.

His father fled from Geneva when Rousseau was still a small boy. Characteristically, he left Jean-Jacques behind. The boy came under the control of severe relatives, and for the first time he felt restraint. And he rebelled. He tells us, for example, of being falsely accused by his guardians of breaking teeth out of a comb. Despite his protests of innocence he was spanked, and from that moment, he claims, he never knew perfect happiness. His relation of the comb incident reveals his unnatural sensitiveness, his persecution complex, and his propensity to hold a grudge forever. Forty-five years later, as he recalls the incident, he confesses: "Even while I write this I feel my pulse quicken, and should I live a 100,000 years, the agitation of that moment would still be fresh in my memory." You cannot expect normal thinking from such a person.

Rousseau's boyhood in Geneva was unhappy. His were the trials of a lad who could stand no restraint, who would assume no responsibility, who believed all Geneva was conspiring against him. He was fired from his first job for incompetency, and then he was apprenticed to an engraver. He tells us frankly how he stole from him, but forty-five years later he still believes there was nothing wrong with his stealing or his lying. One evening in 1728 he returned from a hike to find the gates of the city locked for the night. Twice before he had been locked out, and he therefore knew he would be whipped for his delinquency. So he fled.

This boy of sixteen who ventured forth from Geneva had done nothing to impress the citizens of that town. They knew him as a lad who showed no ability, a boy who lied as readily as he told the truth, who feared physical punishment with abnormal fear, who was socially a misfit. He could not play well with his fellows, and he had a phobia against any kind of restraint or authority. "I love liberty," he writes of this period, "and I loathe constraint, dependence, and all their kindred annoyances."

A Catholic priest in the neighborhood saw in the wandering youth a possible convert to his religion. So he took him in and fed him well and argued against Genevan Calvinism. And Rousseau seemed to agree with the priest. "His Frangi wine, which I thought delicious, argued so powerfully on his side, that I should have blushed at silencing so kind a host. I therefore yielded him the victory, or rather reclined the contest. Anyone who had observed my precaution would certainly have pronounced me a dissembler, though in fact I was only courteous." Abbé Pontverre sent Rousseau to a Madame de Warrens, herself a convert to Catholicism, who lived in Savoy.

This strange lady did more, perhaps, to raise Rousseau than anyone. Her religious beliefs were, to put it mildly, unorthodox. She believed only such Catholic doctrines as appealed to her. Her morality was Quietist, which in Madame de Warrens meant amoral. With her nothing was bad. She was a warmly sentimental person who took in bums of every sort. Impulse moved her at all times — and sometimes her impulses were not so good. But she impressed the young Genevan. And she made him a Catholic, her own peculiar kind of Catholic. Rousseau observes that "her taste was rather Protestant." But it certainly was not Genevan. "A religion preached by such missionaries [as she]," the lad thought, "must lead to paradise!"

Rousseau made her home his headquarters for the next thirteen years. From it he frequently wandered, but to it he always returned when he was discouraged, tired, and dirty. He wanted to be with "mama" again. It was during these thirteen years that Rousseau matured and developed what we can call Rousseauvian attitudes. Madame de Warrens tried to place her charge in the world. She talked him into studying for the priesthood, but he failed his preliminary subjects miserably. He was then subjected to dancing lessons, to fencing, to music, to arithmetic, and to various other studies. Only music pleased him. The other studies demanded too much physical skill or too much concentration. "Nature never meant me for study," he confesses, "since attentive application fatigues me so much, that I find it impossible to employ myself half an hour together intently on one subject."

Rousseau's wanderings in these years reveal how completely he surrendered to himself, how he can hardly be considered a morally responsible person any time throughout his life. He once traveled with a local musician, for example, and when Le Maître took an epileptic fit in the street Rousseau ran away leaving him to his fate in a strange town. "As to my desertion of Le Maître," he later observes, "I did not find it so very culpable."

It is hard not to believe that Rousseau was living in his own dream world at this early age. He tells, for example, how he decided to pick up some money teaching music, "which I did not understand, and say I came from Paris, where I had never been." When he boasted of his composing skill and was asked to write a piece for local performance, he actually wrote something and tried to direct the musicians through it. And he could not recognize a note of music! Later, when he was traveling in a coach, he pretended to be an Englishman — and he knew not a word of English. But when people suspected him of not being English or accused him of being a bad musician, he complained that they persecuted him. Rousseau seems actually to have fooled himself in these assumed roles. His dream world was real, and the real world was not. Rousseau rages whenever he is forced to face reality. "The more I have seen of the world," he truly says, "the less I have been able to adopt its manners." So he fled from the world and lived in one of his own creation. This was his real world. But Rousseau was sincere in fooling himself. He was indeed his own first dupe.

Another point to be observed about Rousseau's travels in those days is that he went on foot, without luggage, whenever he could. He could not bring luggage because he felt it pinned him down. He wanted no responsibility, no impedimenta as he wandered aimlessly but freely through life. So it was with his

attempts to settle down. Madame de Warrens got him a job
with a group making a survey of the neighborhood, but after
two long years of this work he quit to teach music — of which
he had meanwhile acquired a meager knowledge. He loved his
music, "the only inclination I have constantly adhered to," but
he could not stand the constraint of teaching. "I was fond of
teaching," he explains, "but could not bear the idea of being
obliged to attend at a particular hour; constraint and subjection
in every shape are to me insupportable, and alone sufficient to
make me hate even pleasure itself."

When Madame de Warrens' house manager died, Rousseau
was given the job of handling finances. It was too much for him.
Whenever he got into a financial fix he fled and stayed away
until he was confident the crisis had passed. Meanwhile, he
frankly tells us, he embezzled his mistress' funds. But he excused
himself with a typical Rousseauism. "Being persuaded that what
I might refuse myself would be distributed among a set of
interested villains, I took advantage of her easiness to partake
with them, and, like the dog returning from the shambles, carried
off a portion of that morsel which I could not protect." Here is
Rousseau complacently surrendering to his inability to manage
finances and then to his peculation.

These were undoubtedly the happiest years of Rousseau's life.
He was not yet famous, and he was not yet ambitious. And
nature had never made him for either fame or success. He tells
us how he enjoyed Madame de Warrens' retreat at Les Char-
mettes, how living in solitude with her he was happy, blissfully
happy. "I rose with the sun, and was happy; I walked, and was
happy; I saw Madame de Warrens, and was happy; I quitted her,
and still was happy! Whether I rambled through the woods, over
the hills, or strolled along the valley, read, was idle, worked
in the garden, or gathered fruits, happiness continually accompanied me; it was fixed on no particular object, it was within
me, nor could I depart from it a single moment."

This was a period when Rousseau read much, but his mind
was passive. And he was therefore happy. For thinking always
disagreed with him. He tells us many times how hard it was for
him to reason consecutively, or even to follow another's line of
thought. Studies of any kind were too much for him; chess he

could never learn, and his attempts to memorize opera parts always ended in humiliating failure when his mind went blank. We should remember that Rousseau was never in completely good health. He thought much of his physical disabilities, so much so that even he admits that "my disorder was in great measure hypochondriacal." He believed himself to have every disease he read about, and he thought the doctors liars when they told him he was not desperately ill.

Rousseau returned from one of his trips in 1741 to find a stranger occupying his place of favor with Madame de Warrens. She assured him there was room in her house and in her heart for both, but he could not bear to share place with another. So he left for Paris to make a fortune with a novel system of music notation he had devised. In Paris, Rousseau found his discovery unappreciated, but it brought him in contact with such reformist thinkers as Condillac, Fontenelle, and Mably, and it gave him entree into such *salons* as Madame Dupin's and Madame de Broglie's. The latter secured him a position as secretary to the French ambassador at Venice, where the future father of democracy showed himself to be a horrible snob ever insistent on keeping servants in place and maintaining his own proper dignity. Rousseau had difficulties with the ambassador, so he left for Paris "to give an account of my conduct and complain of that of a madman."

In Paris again, Rousseau tried to be a true Parisian, a good *philosophe*. But he did not have the heart to be a true Parisian nor the head to be a good *philosophe*. He eked out a meager, precarious existence by copying music — which he always did very badly. Meanwhile, however, he met such associates as Grimm and Diderot — and he met his Theresa. His relationship with Theresa de la Vasseur is typical of his entire life. She was an ignorant serving girl who seems to have been the butt of customers' endless crudities. Rousseau saw in her a simple girl who needed protection. She appreciated his kindness, and he became attached to her for the rather singular reason that she was so simple, so stupid, and so docile. Soon they were living together, and Rousseau found Theresa the only woman, except Madame de Warrens, whose company he could endure in moments of silence without profound embarrassment.

But life with Theresa was no paradise. Rousseau tried, he said, "to improve her mind." She could never learn to tell time, however, to count money, or to tell off the twelve months of the year. Moreover, she had a mother who was less simple than she, and who therefore was a constant source of uneasiness to Rousseau. Finally, he had trouble with Theresa about marriage and about their children. Years later he seems to have satisfied her by going through a homemade ceremony in which he pledged his troth to her. She bore him five children whom, much against Theresa's desire, he put into foundling homes. The author of the classic on education, *Emile*, was himself unable to raise his own offspring. Rousseau apparently was not bothered by abandoning his children. "I said to myself," he tells us, " 'Since it is the custom of the country, they who live here may adopt it.' This is the expedient for which I sought. . . . I thought I acted like an honest citizen and a good father, and considered myself as a member of the republic of Plato."

On one of his walks to the jail at Vincennes in 1749, where he was visiting Diderot, Rousseau saw the announcement of an essay contest on the subject: What have the arts and sciences done for civilization? He decided to compete — and his decision was a fatal one for himself, for the French Revolution, and for Western civilization. "All the rest of my misfortunes," he will complain, "were the inevitable effect of this moment of error." Certainly his fame resulted from this decision, for had not Rousseau competed in the Dijon contest he would most likely have lived obscurely, gone mad unnoticed, and died unknown.

But he entered the contest, and he won it with an essay that was to electrify the France of the rationalists. For Rousseau dared to be different — and Frenchmen, tired of barren rationalism, welcomed his daring attack upon reason and upon civilization. Rousseau tells us that "of all the works I ever wrote, this is the weakest in reasoning"; but he also observes, and truly, that it was "full of force and fire." In this essay he makes an eloquent attack on the artificialities of civilization, an attack that came from the heart of a man who hated the civilization of his day because he could not shine in it. Strangely enough, Rousseau appreciated the cause of his eloquence. "In the first work I wrote," he tells us, "I introduced the peevishness and ill-humor which were the cause of my undertaking them. . . . I became sour and a cynic from shame, and affected to despise the politeness which I knew not how to practice."

This first essay caused a literary and a social furor in Paris when established men of letters attacked it with such concert and with such vehemence that Rousseau believed "they had agreed with each other to do it." But those who were not securely established in rationalist circles hailed it as a clarion call to a better, a more natural life. They played at being "natural." This essay brought Rousseau both fame and annoyance, for it denied him the solitude which he henceforth vainly sought till death. It pushed him into literary circles in France — and literary people are always a jealous, faultfinding group. Henceforth Rousseau could not live alone, and he could not get along with his associates. He became more and more a misanthrope; more and more he was Mother Nature's bad boy.

He decided about this time to retire from the world, to live a Spartan life, and to earn his living by copying music. But he found himself the butt of the *philosophes*' barbed wit. He was convinced that "it was less my literary fame than my personal reformation, that drew upon me their jealousy. They perhaps might have pardoned me for having distinguished myself in the art of writing; but they could never forgive my setting them, by my conduct, an example which, in their eyes, seemed to reflect on themselves." Rousseau simply was unable to defend his position in *salon* circles. He seems, moreover, to have become an annoying self-appointed father confessor who meddled in the intimate affairs of all those with whom he came in contact.

His life for the next six years or so was unhappy. He wrote a second essay, the *Discourse on the Origin of Inequality,* which was not well received. Typically, he blamed its poor reception on the cabal formed against him and on the part Diderot played in helping him compose it. He never thought that it could in any way be his fault. He thought of settling in Geneva, but even though he had been readmitted to the Calvinist church there and had been restored to full citizenship he found that his second discourse caused such a furor in Geneva that life would not be placid there. So he returned to Paris and thence to his country retreat which Madame d'Epinay had prepared for him.

Here he enjoyed six years of comparative happiness. "I felt a natural inclination to retirement and the country," he observes, "it was impossible for me to live happily elsewhere." The seclusion of Montmorency gave him peace of mind so that he could concentrate on his writings; and in a period of four years he produced his most widely known works: the *Nouvelle Heloise, Emile,* and the *Contrat social,* as well as his better minor pieces. Rousseau is almost unique among men in the accurate insight he has into his own being. He knows his weaknesses and he excuses them all — but at least he knows them. His observation on this period, which is the sanest and the most productive in his life, is therefore deserving of attention.

"I was really transformed," he writes; "my friends scarcely knew me. I was no longer that timid and rather bashful than modest man who neither dared to present himself nor utter a word, whom a single pleasantry disconcerted, and whose face was covered with a blush the moment his eyes met those of a woman. I became bold, haughty, intrepid, with a confidence the more firm as it was simple, which resided in my soul rather than in my manner. The contempt with which my profound mediations had inspired me for the manners, maxims, and prejudices of the age in which I lived rendered me proof against the raillery of those by whom they were possessed, and I crushed their little pleasantries with a sentence, as I would have crushed an insect with my fingers."

This is a short period in Rousseau's life when he is free from the annoyances of men — whom he could never tolerate, for he was antisocial — and from the harassing annoyances of his own weak body. It is a short period when his genius is released for great accomplishments. Until that time Rousseau had been a failure. His sole success had been due not so much to his genius as to his peevishness, and to France's desire for novelty. And after he fled from Montmorency, Rousseau was never really sane. His persecution complex and his unrestrained imagination kept him in a world of devilish conspirators. His *Confessions* were written when he was partly mad, his *Reveries* when he was completely insane. But in the four years, from 1758 till 1762, he produced three works which were to cause a revolution in literature, in morality, in social relationships, in education, in politics. For

Rousseau rose to unsurpassed heights of his genius in those few years.

The story of his remaining life is pitiful. But because it had no influence on his previous writings, there is no need to watch his mind deteriorate as he flees about Europe and finally decays in Paris, nor need we follow up his wild charges against those who sought to befriend him. The opening remarks of the seventh book of his *Confessions* are perhaps enough to show his state of mind: "At present my head and memory are become so weak as to render me almost incapable of every kind of application: my present undertaking is the result of constraint, and a heart full of sorrow. I have nothing to treat of but misfortunes, treacheries, perfidies, and circumstances equally afflicting. . . . The ceiling under which I write has eyes; the walls of my chamber have ears. Surrounded by spies and by vigilant and malevolent inspectors, disturbed, and my attention diverted, I hastily commit to paper a few broken sentences, which I have scarcely time to read, and still less to correct. I know that, notwithstanding the barriers which are multiplied around me, my enemies are afraid truth should escape by some little opening."

3

But it is not the mad Rousseau in whom we are interested. What can we conclude of the genius Rousseau who lived at Montmorency in those years when he produced his remarkable works? We know that he was always ill at ease, that until his retreat from Paris he tried desperately to be a social success, to please all persons he met. He was a miserable failure, and because he knew how ridiculous he appeared in society he came to hate it with hot, irrational hatred. Through all his main works except the *Contrat social* runs an intense antisocial strain. This is Rousseau speaking from the depths of his heart, for he had so unreservedly accepted himself that he had to hate society. He is happy only in his solitude.

In solitude, he believes, men can be natural. There they can grow as Nature meant them to grow, unfettered, unrestrained, straight and tall like the tree that is not crimped or pruned by the gardener's knife. There men will be free from the conspiracies, the plots, and counterplots of jealous rivals. (We must remember that Rousseau had developed a strong persecution complex which was to influence his every writing.) The natural man, he believes, is a good man. And Rousseau thought himself to be natural. For this was the way he distinguished himself from a Voltaire or a Grimm or a Hume.

So he accepted himself exactly as he was. He was in his own eyes a perfect creature. He admitted defects, but in his twisted reasoning he came to accept them and even to glory in them and to see them as part of his perfection. "I doubt," he says, "whether mortal ever said better and more sincerely to God: Thy Will be done." Again, "Let the trumpet of the last judgment sound when it will, I shall come to appear before the sovereign judge with this book in hand. I shall say boldly: This is what I have done, what I thought, what I was. . . . I have shown myself just as I was: contemptible and vile, when I was so; good and generous and sublime, when I was so; I have revealed my heart as it was in Your eyes, eternal Being. Gather round me the countless multitude of my fellow creatures; let them hear my confessions, let them lament my infamies, let them blush for my meannesses. Let each of them in his turn disclose his heart at the foot of Your throne with the same sincerity, and then let but one of them say, if he dare, I was better than that man." Rousseau meant every word of it when he wrote, "I am convinced that of all the men I have known in my life none was better than I." If he had defects, it was God's fault. It could not have been Rousseau's.

It is hard to understand how Rousseau could know his weaknesses so acutely and still accept them so complacently. But we must simply reconcile ourselves to this twisted personality and accept the fact that he was fully reconciled to himself. This is what Seillière calls his immaculate conception. For in his own eyes Rousseau was without defect, without inclination to evil. He had created an angelic counterfeit self in his imagination — and accepted it for the real thing. So it was with the world. Rousseau escaped from the world of other men into one of his own creation. At Montmorency, for example, he created his own set of creatures as he worked on the *Nouvelle Heloise,* and he was furious when anyone interrupted his reveries in the woods around his retreat. That dream world was real to him, its creatures more alive than even his Theresa. Throughout life he fled from the world. And he fled into a world of his imagination, which became, to him, his only real world.

We should remember that, like Martin Luther before him, Rousseau is hostile to reason. Reason corrupts and perverts man, he insists; it leads him astray from the path of virtue to which his heart inclines him. He disliked reason on the same basis that he disliked society: he failed to get along with either. He tried at first to be a rationalist, but he found he could not think facilely or profoundly. "My disposition is extremely ardent," he tells us, "my passions lively and impetuous, yet my ideas are produced slowly, with great embarrassment and after much afterthought. It might be said that my heart and understanding do not belong to the same individual. . . . When I write, my ideas are arranged with the utmost difficulty. They glance on my imagination and ferment till they discompose, heat, and bring on a palpitation; during this state of agitation I see nothing properly, cannot write a single word, and must wait till it is over."

So it was only natural for Rousseau, who always surrendered to himself, to decide that "reasoning, far from enlightening us, blinds us; it does not raise our soul, it enervates and corrupts the judgment, which it should perfect." With him feeling is the infallible guide to truth. He asks only that his reader *feel* his arguments are right; he denounces the *philosophes*, he admits, because he *feels* they are lying. *Feeling* replaces *knowing*. Rousseau's feeling, moreover, was particularly sensitive. Hume, a most acute English observer, saw this point. "He has only *felt* during the whole course of his life, and in this respect his sensibility [feeling] rises to a pitch beyond what I have seen any example of; but it still gives him a more acute feeling of pain than of pleasure. He is like a man who was stripped not only of his clothes, but of his skin, and turned out in that situation to combat with the rude and boisterous elements."

But Rousseau was more than merely emotion run riot. He was more than a mad fool. The emotions which he voiced were emotions which had been stifled through long generations of rationalism. They had been suppressed, but because they were essential human emotions they had not been killed. Rousseau sounded them, and people readily responded. More than that, this man who contemns reason, this man who is never consistent, says many wise things, many sound, shrewd, many magnificent things. He utters much nonsense, it is true, but he also touches on deep truths that men of his age ached to hear. That is why Maritain can call him a "corrupter of hallowed truths." "He perceived great Christian truths which his age had forgotten, and his strength lay in recalling them; but he perverted them."

Certainly this is the secret of Rousseau's striking success. When abbés tried, not too successfully, to offer rational arguments against Voltaire's strictures on their God, Rousseau demolished Voltaire with the observation that, "while he appeared to believe in God, he never really believed in anything but the devil." Voltaire had no answer to such an attack. When home life had dried up into a round of social engagements for wealthy Frenchmen, when children were turned over at birth to wet nurses and seen by their parents only on formal occasions, when ennui ate at their hearts, Rousseau's sentimental passages moved his jaded readers.

For there was something sound in them. "The charms of home," he says, for example, "are the best antidote to vice. The noisy play of children, which we thought so trying, becomes a delight; mother and father rely more on each other and grow dearer to one another; the marriage tie is strengthened. In the cheerful home life the mother finds her sweetest duties and the father his pleasantest recreation. The real nurse is the mother and the real teacher is the father." Thus did Rousseau appeal to his age. He appealed to the heart, and in his day the heart thirsted sorely for what it was denied by Voltaire and his fellows.

4

The basic point running through Rousseau's writings is that man and society must be "natural." He insists that whatever is natural is good, what is opposed to nature is bad. But it is impossible to decide exactly what Rousseau meant by natural. He did not, it would seem, mean simply primitive, let alone apelike. Ultimately, the norm for determining what is natural is Rousseau's own unreasoned approval or disapproval. What he likes is labeled natural; what he dislikes he condemns as unnatural. Rousseau's conscience is to be our infallible guide. There is nothing for us to do, in following his line of argument, but to surrender to his conscience and let it guide us through the maze of his illogical polemics.

Rousseau, then, wants man to be natural. He wants him to live in a natural society under a natural government, to practice a natural religion. Now all of this is to be accomplished by subjecting man to a natural education. Rousseau was first and foremost an educationist. He agreed with Locke's successors that man is an unformed lump of humanity at birth, that whatever he becomes will be the result of his education. To Rousseau, however, man was fundamentally a good lump of flesh who had been made vicious by bad education and by bad social institutions. Make these natural and man will enjoy his paradise here on earth.

It is important that since man is born good he be raised rightly, that he be preserved from vice. Rousseau therefore insisted that *Emile* "was the best as well as the most important of all the works I produced." This is the story of a youngster's education from the time of his birth until his marriage. Emile is subjected to no restraints whatsoever, for Rousseau believed restraint of any kind unnatural. "Instead of keeping him mewed up in a stuffy room," Rousseau advises us, "take him out into a meadow every day; let him run about, let him struggle and fall again and again, the oftener the better; he will learn all the sooner to pick himself up. The delights of liberty will make up for many bruises. My pupil will hurt himself oftener than yours, but he will always be merry; your pupils may receive fewer injuries, but they are always thwarted, constrained, sad." Rousseau wanted no one thwarted or constrained — as he somehow felt he had been.

Emile is not to be reasoned with, for that is unnatural. Emile is to learn from experience. He is, in truth, to teach himself everything he learns; his tutor is only to arrange the props so that, as a matter of survival, Emile must learn. Instinct and emotion are to be cultivated rather than reasoning power. "Small minds have a mania for reasoning. Strong souls speak a very different language; and it is by this language that men are persuaded and driven to action." Emile is to be a strong soul who acts instinctively and strongly. He is to feel rather than think. And because reason is the source of all error, Emile will always be both right and happy.

Voltaire observed of *Emile* that it was a stupid romance, but that it contained fifty pages worth binding in morocco. These fifty pages were the Savoyard Vicar's profession of faith, fifty pages that stirred all France. They are fifty powerful, but curious pages. For in them Rousseau presents, in the mouth of his Savoyard vicar, his own religious beliefs; he presents them in a chain of reasoning worthy of any rationalist, but blended with the rationalist arguments is Rousseau's strong sentimentalism. Compounded from the two is Rousseau's religion, which annoyed the skeptics and angered the devout people of France.

Rousseau attacks the *philosophes* for their skepticism, which he claims is gratuitous. He goes on to decide, reversing the Cartesian procedure, that he must accept all that he cannot honestly refuse to believe. He rejects all organized religions, however, because he insists that no religious sect offers anything to him that God has not already placed in his heart. And he wants no one to come between himself and God. Revelation is unnecessary, for God has communicated directly with Rousseau; His law is written in Jean-Jacques's heart. Moreover, no one religion can be true, for that would be unjust to all other men. If one religion were right and the others wrong, he argues, a man would have to spend a lifetime in the study of comparative religion. "So," he has his Savoyard vicar say, "I closed up all my books. There is one book which is open to every one — the book of nature. In this good and great volume I learn to serve and adore its Author."

From this book of nature Rousseau thought he could prove the existence of a personal, benevolent God. The existence of the universe argues for a Creator, he insists; the design of the universe and the movement of the planets argue for an intelligent Creator. "Let Newton show us the hand that launched the planets in the tangent of their orbits." This supreme will, this supreme intelligence, Rousseau tells us, is what he means by God. "I know full well that he exists, and that he exists of himself alone; I know that my existence depends on his, and that everything I know depends upon him also. I see God everywhere in his works; I feel him within myself; I behold him all around me; but if I try to ponder him himself, if I try to find out where he is, what he is, what is his substance, he escapes me and my troubled spirit finds nothing."

So he leaves theological speculation to examine himself. He finds that he is a creature who has a material body and an immaterial spirit, a soul. Rousseau arrives at this conclusion in typical Rousseauvian fashion. "In vain do you argue this point with me," he says; "I feel it, and it is this feeling which speaks to me more forcibly than the reason which disputes it." So he accepts it. He also feels that he has free will. And it is in the abuse of this freedom that he discovers the cause of all evil, all suffering, all misery in the world. Where Voltaire threw the blame for evil on God, Rousseau places it squarely on mankind. "O man! seek no further for the author of evil; thou art he. There is no evil but the evil you do or the evil you suffer, and both come from yourself."

After having posited an omnipotent God and a man with free will, Rousseau has his vicar search for principles of conduct. "I find them," he has him tell Emile, "in the depths of my heart, traced by nature in characters which nothing can efface. I need only consult myself with regard to what I wish to do; what I feel to be right is right, what I feel to be wrong is wrong." One does not, therefore, reason to the goodness or the badness of an act. He *feels* it. Conscience is exalted as "divine instinct, immortal voice from heaven, sure guide for a creature ignorant and finite." But conscience has nothing to do with reason. "The decrees of conscience are not judgments but feelings." The goodness or badness of an act, then, depends on how you happen to feel about it. Thus is Rousseau resigned to himself, to his inconsistent, emotional, highly sensitive self. He accepts the unreasoned urgings of his animal nature as infallibly deciding what is right and wrong. What he feels is right, is right. There is no arguing about it.

Rousseau's views on social institutions permeate all of his works. They are of a piece, except for the *Contrat social*, for they consist of one long polemic against civilization and against all man-made institutions. His most direct and his bitterest attacks are found in his *Discourse on the Arts and Sciences* and his *Discourse on the Origin of Inequality.* The basic theme is stated in the opening words of *Emile:* "God makes all things good; man meddles with them and they become evil." Again: "Men are naturally good and it is through institutions that they become bad."

Man, then, is good. He is naturally free and independent, naturally good to his fellow man, naturally honest with himself. But the arts and sciences, Rousseau tells us in his first discourse, "stifle in men's breasts that sense of original liberty, for which they seem to have been born; cause them to love their own slavery, and so make of them what is called a civilized people." Men come to live under constant constraint; they live a herdlike existence, each one seeking to abide by the socially accepted pattern. They become evil and corrupt in proportion as they are civilized. Thus "sincere friendship, real esteem, and perfect confidence are banished from among men. Jealousy, suspicion, fear, coldness, reserve, hate and fraud lie constantly concealed under that uniform and deceitful veil of politeness."

Men's virtues, Rousseau holds, are all natural. His natural actions are instinctive, passionate. But man is equipped with the power to reason — and this is his Achilles' heel. It is the instrument he uses for plotting against his fellows, for aggrandizing himself in "unnatural fashion," for creating social institutions, for developing the arts and sciences. These, indeed, are born of man's vices. "Astronomy was born of superstition, eloquence of ambition, hatred, falsehood and flattery; geometry of avarice; physics of an idle curiosity; and even moral philosophy of human pride." The intellect and its products, the arts and the sciences, are unnatural. They are therefore bad.

Men are naturally equal, Rousseau always insists, and they are naturally good. Now since the arts and sciences have corrupted men and since inequality did exist in his day, it would seem incumbent upon Rousseau to show how the change came about. This he tried to do four years later in his *Discourse on the Origin of Inequality.* The purpose of the work, he wrote, was "to mark, in the progress of things, the moment at which right took the place of violence and nature became subject to law, and to explain by what sequence of miracles the strong came to submit to serve the weak, and the people to purchase imaginary repose at the expense of real felicity."

Like Locke, Rousseau starts this essay in the state of nature, a state, he tells us "which no longer exists, perhaps never did exist, and probably never will exist." But this state of nature is like natural man: it is society as it should be. With Rousseau "natural" always means good. Thus the state of nature is the norm whereby existing society is judged. Man in this state is only an animal with free will. "The only goods he recognizes in the universe are food, a female, and sleep: the only evils he fears are pain and hunger." Man in the state of nature, therefore, is amoral. "He cannot be either good or bad, virtuous or vicious." But unfortunately he has the power of reason and a sense of compassion. Reason corrupts him — "a thinking man is a depraved animal" — and his sense of compassion leads him to form social relationships.

Society, however, results directly from private property. "The first man who, having enclosed a piece of ground, bethought himself of saying 'This is mine,' and found people simple enough to believe him, was the real founder of civil society." With society formed and with a sense of mine and thine comes morality. With property and morality come crimes, with crimes the necessity of protection. So men set up government by means of a social compact — as Locke had them do. "Such was, or may well have been," Rousseau concludes, "the origin of society and law, which bound new fetters on the poor, and gave new powers to the rich; which irretrievably destroyed natural liberty, eternally fixed the law of property and inequality, converted clever usurpation into unalterable right, and, for the advantage of a few ambitious individuals, subjected all mankind to perpetual labor, slavery and wretchedness."

Such a contract, he insists heatedly, could never have been entered into freely. No one could have voluntarily set up a tyranny — and Rousseau believes that all government is tyranny. For this is "degrading our very nature, reducing ourselves to the level of brutes, . . . and even an affront to the Author of our being, to renounce without reserve the most precious of all his gifts, and to bow to the necessity of committing all the crimes he has forbidden." No state, therefore, can be justified. Man must live a natural life, which is anarchical life. "A really happy man is a hermit."

Rousseau could never have been the prophet of a new age, however, if he only condemned civilization with its artificial accouterments. Mere detractors soon wear thin. Nor do they inspire men to martyrdom. Rousseau has lasted and he has inspired men to heroic action because he appealed to their sense of virtue. He condemned the *philosophes* because "they smile contemptuously at such old names as patriotism and religion, and consecrate their talents and philosophy to the destruction and defamation of all that men hold sacred. . . . The question is no longer whether a man is honest, but whether he is clever. . . There are thousands of prizes for fine discourses, and none for good actions." Against these attitudes Rousseau defended what men had formerly held sacred. He extolled honesty, self-sacrifice, patriotism, justice, charity. Thus he moved men as the rationalists had never moved them.

In the Seven Years' War men like Voltaire openly supported their hero and France's enemy, Frederick the Great. But Rousseau would have no part of such treasonable cynicism. Instead, he penned an encomium of that patriotism which "produces so many immortal actions, the glory of which dazzles our feeble eyes; and so many great men, whose old-world virtues pass for fables now that patriotism is made mock of. . . . The love of one's country, which is a hundred times more lively and delightful than the love of a mistress, cannot be conceived except by experiencing it." People who read Rousseau wanted to experience this lost feeling.

Rousseau moved people when he told them to be virtuous. "Oh! let us first be good and then we shall be happy. Let us not claim the prize before we have won it, nor demand our wages before we have finished our work." Or when he told them to be charitable. "Be just, human, kindly. Do not give alms alone, give charity: works of mercy do more than money for the relief of suffering; love others and they will love you; serve them and they will serve you; be their brother and they will be your children." He moves men when he appeals to them in this fashion, and when he tells them to live fully, zestfully, keenly. Men should learn, he tells his readers, "to live rather than to avoid death: life is not breath, but action, the use of our senses, our mind, our faculties, every part of ourselves which makes us conscious of our being. Life consists less in length of days than in the keen sense of living." And people, jaded by the long, dry reign of the *philosophes,* grasped at Rousseau's urgings to live the full, natural life.

5

Rousseau is important for having delivered the decisive stroke in the romantic, voluntaristic revolution of the latter eighteenth century. But historically he is more important still for a little work neither he nor his contemporaries valued highly — his *Contrat social.* He dashed it off at Montmorency to get a little more money with which to retire from the world. It attracted scant attention in his day, and Rousseau himself never thought it particularly important. Before the French Revolution it was a little noticed piece; for every reference to the *Contrat social* in those days there were at least ten to *Emile* or *Nouvelle Heloise.* Mornet describes it rather well as "merely a mental exercise, an effort at organization of ideas."

It is a puzzling piece, this *Contrat social,* and in many ways it is unlike Rousseau's other writings. Everywhere else he extols feeling while inveighing against reason; but in the *Contrat social* everything is reason. Rousseau writes here as though he were a distracted rationalist; even his language differs from his usual moving style. And the message is completely different. In his other works liberty is the pearl of great price; here it is cast off by mankind for a security which Rousseau had contemned in his previous writings. Here he justifies the state with all its pomp and power; elsewhere he failed to make a single kind remark for the state. The *Contrat social* simply cannot be reconciled with Rousseau's other writings, either with his earlier works or his later pieces. Whereas it sets up a totalitarian arrangement, the discourses had been thoroughly anarchistic. The constitutions he prepared for Poland and Corsica, as well as the remarks he appended to his edition of Saint-Pierre's *Paix perpetuelle,* are a full refutation of the *Contrat.*

But because men have taken this work seriously from the days of the French Revolution till today, we too must surrender ourselves to it, contradictions and all, and see what Rousseau has to say in this confusing essay. "Man is born free; and everywhere he is in chains," he tells us at the beginning. "How did this change come about? I do not know. What can make it legitimate? That question I think I can answer." The *Contrat social* is therefore an attempt to show how free man has legitimately been put in chains.

Rousseau quickly dismisses others' explanations of how man became a political animal. He insists that man cannot be justly enslaved or conquered, for might does not make right. Neither can he simply give up his liberty, for "to renounce liberty is to renounce being a man, to surrender the rights of humanity and even its duties." And no man can do that. There is no possible explanation except that of a social compact. Now Hobbes, Locke, and many others had tried to justify the state on this ground, but Rousseau asserts that no one has yet succeeded. For they all have man surrender his full freedom and at least some control over his property. No one, therefore, has yet justified the state.

But Rousseau has the solution up his sleeve. Before pulling it out, however, he states the problem in its most difficult form. "The problem is to find a form of association which will defend and protect with the whole common force the person and goods of each associate, and in which each, while uniting himself with all, may still obey himself alone, and remain free as before. This is the fundamental problem of which the *Contrat social* provides the solution." All Rousseau need do is invent a contract with terms to fit the problem of man's creating a state to which he surrenders everything without giving anything up.

This he does by some mental gymnastics which, whether they were sincerely meant by Rousseau or not, have been taken seriously by a very serious posterity. In the first place, Rousseau tells us, everyone surrenders himself and all he possesses absolutely and irretrievably — which gives men equality, the equality of zeroes. But — and here is the magic — Rousseau has arranged it so that no one really loses anything. "Each man, in giving himself to all, gives himself to nobody; and as there is no associate over whom he does not acquire the same right as he yields others over himself, he gains an equivalent for everything he loses, and an increase of force for the preservation of what he has."

What has happened is that men agree with each other to subject themselves totally to the state. By this act they have created the famous Rousseauvian *volunté générale,* which is practically the same thing as the state. This general will is supreme and infallible. It is the collective people. Rousseau has thus made the people collectively supreme, while he has left the individual person absolutely a cipher. Man as a single person must bow before the dictate of collective mankind, the general will. Against it he has no rights, from it he has no recourse. "Whoever refuses to obey the general will shall be compelled to do so by the whole body. This means nothing less than he will be forced to be free." So a man who disagrees with the general will — which for practical purposes is the will of the majority — is really disagreeing with his better self. By coercion he is "forced to be free" — a truly terrible device created by Rousseau to solve the problem of reconciling freedom with authority.

Again, he tells men that the sovereign created by their contract cannot harm them. "The Sovereign, being formed wholly of the individuals who compose it, neither has nor can have any interest contrary to theirs; and consequently the sovereign power need give no guarantee to its subjects, because it is impossible for the body to wish to hurt all its members. We shall also see later on that it cannot hurt any in particular. The Sovereign, merely by virtue of what it is, is always what it should be." The State, then, is perfect; it "is always what it should be." And the State is the people assembled, the people who are deified, who are given all the attributes mankind had formerly reserved for God, who are incorruptible, who are omnicompetent and omnipotent. This was a sophistry surpassing any *philosophe's,* and Rousseau breathed into it intense vitality such as no *philosophe* could do.

As the Christians had allowed their God to be limited only by His own nature — he could not, for example, be unjust — so Rousseau limited the general will only by its very nature. If one looks to the first part of the *Contrat social* he finds Rousseau advocating a totalitarian despotism of the general will; if he looks to the latter part, where Rousseau limits the general will, he finds him so paralyzing his Sovereign as to end up an anarchist. In the first place, the general will must apply to all equally, it must be literally general. An act of the general will, Rousseau tells us comfortingly, is "but a convention between the body and each of its members. . . . So long as the subjects have to submit only to conventions of this sort, they obey no one but their own will; and to ask how far the respective rights of the Sovereign and the citizens extend, is to ask up to what point the latter can enter into undertakings with themselves, each with all, and all with each." So it is only a case of Doe the citizen agreeing with Doe the subject.

Rousseau also nullifies the general will by making it inalienable. "The Sovereign cannot act save when the people is assembled." How to get the people of France assembled? Rousseau answers that that is not his problem. It has been done in the past, in Athens at least, and "it is good logic to reason from the actual to the possible." So unless the people of France gather on a single field to express themselves, the general will cannot express itself. For it cannot be represented. "Sovereignty, for the same reason as makes it inalienable, cannot be represented. . . . The deputies of the people, therefore, are not and cannot be its representatives: they are merely its stewards, and can carry through no definitive acts. Every law the people has not ratified in person is null and void — is, in fact, not a law." Here Rousseau is saying that he has justified an arrangement which must result in anarchy. And he has expressly stated that his is the only justification for the state.

The government he would set up is decreed by the general will, is, indeed, merely to serve as its agent. This government need not be of any particular kind. For, as regards government, Rousseau was far from a democrat. "Were there a people of gods," he writes, "their government would be democratic. So perfect a government is not for men." He sees advantages in democracy, aristocracy, and monarchy, and he comes to the rather evasive conclusion that "it is the best and most natural arrangement that the wisest should govern the many." But whatever government is set up is subject to the general will. When the people are assembled the government, by the very nature of things, dissolves and a new government must be reconstituted by the assembled people. Rousseau has in this fashion justified perpetual revolution, for the people may dissolve their government without cause. Not liking it is cause enough for Rousseau. Revolution is only a matter of the people getting together.

Jean-Jacques may actually have believed that he had resolved the age-old dilemma of creating authority without sacrificing liberty. He pretended to believe that he had justified man's being in chains by having shown that the chains were of his own forging, that they could be unlocked whenever the people collectively wished to unlock them, that meanwhile man really wanted to be in chains if only he had sense enough to know it. And if he did not, then he must "be forced to be free."

It is small wonder that the rationalists of his day paid scant attention to his *Contrat social*. They had taken his discourses seriously, for those seemed to be powerful frontal attacks upon the civilization of their time. But the *Contrat social* could have appeared as nothing but mental gymnastics in which Rousseau was exercising his unbalanced reason. Conundrum as it was, it was clearly a Janus-faced essay, one view of which was totalitarian, the other anarchistic. And it has been so used ever since Rousseau's day — to justify either the new kind of "democracy" which came to Italy, Germany, and Russia this century, or to justify the Mazzini type of bourgeois democracy of the past century. Rousseau caused men to put faith in the common man — and this seems to be his only contribution to the democracy of England and America, a democracy derived more directly from John Locke, political experience, a frontier, and an individualistic outlook than from Rousseau.

6

The unsettled Genevan's influence on modern history, and on the modern mind, is tremendous. The rationalist experiment begun by Descartes and modified by Locke and Newton had ended in the skepticism of Hume, the negations of Voltaire, the futility of Condorcet. The world looked for a substitute, and Rousseau offered it — a pulsating, throbbing, sobbing substitute for the barren, cold, and now discredited rationalism of the eighteenth century. Life had left the corpse of rationalism; Rousseau's thought quivered with life. Rousseau is the father of the

nineteenth- and twentieth-century romantic, voluntaristic movements in literature, philosophy, education, politics, and sociology.
He is, many scholars maintain, "Father of the Modern World."

Rousseau lived to see his gospel eagerly preached in France —
and even shallowly practiced. His *Nouvelle Heloise* was read
avidly; it was loaned out, as a matter of fact, at ten sous an hour.
Women of distinction became so engrossed with it that they
forgot to attend dances and even court functions. It is said that
the only time Kant missed his afternoon walk was when he
became so absorbed in *Emile* that he could not put it down.
Rousseau made people abandon reasoning to cultivate feeling.
He made them shed big and copious tears, for he was the most
successful proponent of the great moral and social benefits of
weeping on one another's shoulders. "Nothing so cordially at-
taches two persons as the satisfaction of weeping together."

But Rousseau really came into his own during the French
Revolution. His *Contrat social* became the book of vindication,
as well as inspiration, for the Reign of Terror; his moral preach-
ments were the guide for the Republic of Virtue. And the revolutionists used Rousseau knowingly. He was read in chorus at
Jacobin meetings, he was quoted reverently and authoritatively
in national assemblies. Rousseau was indeed the polar star of the
French Revolution. Moreover, his sentimentalism was incorporated even into the Catholic revival in Napoleon's time; for
Chateaubriand, the incarnation of this Catholic resurgence, was
little more than a Catholic Rousseau.

Nor is Rousseau's influence merely a thing of the past. He
still moves men, not so much any longer to maudlin weeping
as to wishful thinking about the good, pure people in whom
should reside unlimited power of life and death, in whom is to
be found all wisdom and all virtue. The naïve belief that the
simple farmer or bricklayer, just because he is simple, is better
morally and wiser politically than the professor or politician
stems directly from Rousseau. G. D. H. Cole, for example, goes
so far as to insist that "the *Social Contract* . . . is still by far the
best of all text-books of political philosophy." Edwin Mims, Jr.,
in *The Majority of the People*, claims that we in America have
followed the Lockean concept of democracy rather than the
Rousseauvian brand, which would leave the majority despotically

supreme. Mims believes that if we are going to have real democracy we must abolish minority rights protected by the supreme court so as to put no barrier in the way of the general will. He wants Rousseau taken literally. Although Rousseau is close to right in many respects, although his name has been used to further good democratic causes, to take him this way is to push tyranny rather than sound democracy. Locke was a truer democrat by far than was Rousseau.

Rousseau is important, then, for having brought the little people of the world onto the stage of history. With him, the people become the nation; they discard their passive role in history for the active role of soldiers, voters, revolutionists. The people become the directors of governments, an element to be reckoned with. They can no longer be ignored. The nation-in-arms of the French Revolution is a Rousseauvian creation, and an armed nation cannot be treated by its government as if the soldiers were plowing fields or spinning cotton. And a nation in arms is a nation of patriots — which is again peculiarly a Rous-seauvian creation. For Rousseau's was a voice ringing in the wilderness of rationalist cosmopolitanism when he preached his doctrine of patriotism. Love of one's country, he cried, should transcend one's self-love; it is the basis of all virtue and is there-fore part of Rousseau's new morality. "Do we wish men to be virtuous?" he asks. "Then let us begin by making them love their country."

The people whom Rousseau gave an active role in history had long been ruled badly. They had every right in the world to assert themselves. But unfortunately they were not equipped to rule themselves even as well as the benevolent despot had ruled before. What made the Rousseauvian democratic revolution a dangerous thing — as John Adams saw from Boston and John Stuart Mill later on from London — was that where even the tyrant was limited in many ways, there was no limit upon the people. Rousseau made the people, the general will, irresistible, infallible. These little people would have come onto the stage of history even had there been no Rousseau. What he did was to clothe them in white garments of unimpeachable purity and invest them with infallibility.

For the people, with Rousseau, took the place of God. They

become the source of all power, of all morality, of all justice. From the general will there is no appeal, for there is no right and wrong save in the general will, which is, in fact, the source of all right and wrong. Rousseau, then, supplants the despotism of the king by the despotism of the people. But where the despotic king could be hauled to the block by a revolting people, the despotism of the people is uncontrollable. It is like a torrent of water rushing down a mountain canyon after the dam has burst. It is absolutely irresistible. Rousseau would have it so. For he is convinced that the people are both infallible and good. "Man," he wrote, "is naturally good, as I believe and have the happiness to feel."

To feel — that is the thing with Rousseau, and that is the heritage he bequeathed to the world. The English moral sentimentalists had reasoned about a moral sense and about feeling; they had by rational criticism showed that reason was not everything. Rousseau is different. He is all feeling. He peels off man's skin to leave his nerves raw. Reason is vicious, but feeling is good; thinking is antihuman, but impulses are "natural." "Let us lay it down as an incontrovertible rule," he insists, "that the first impulses of nature are always right; there is no original sin in the human heart." Rousseau appealed to feeling as no one before him had done, and that is why Morley sums this point up by observing that "this was not merely a new doctrine . . .; it was a battle cry."

Rousseau creates his new morality on feeling, and for this reason he is termed by Kant the "Newton of the moral order." His morality is fresh, indeed, but it is built on the shifting foundation of impulsive feeling, so that right and wrong change as rapidly with him as does his impulse. Right and wrong, after Rousseau, are more closely connected with good or bad digestion than ever before in history. Objective right and wrong give way to your emotional impulses. What you feel is right, according to Rousseau, is right simply because you feel it so.

Finally, Rousseau gave great impetus to the romantic movement, then sweeping over Europe. This romanticism swept into literature with men like Burns and Wordsworth, it slipped into international politics with men like Byron, it revived a dried-out Christianity with men like Chateaubriand, it invaded the field of history with men like Scott. Romanticism and sentimentalism had a terrible effect on man's concept of man as it degenerated into a sickly humanitarianism and was finally perverted into humane societies. On the basis of Rousseauvian voluntarism, Be-Kind-To-Kitty clubs, the Ku Klux Klan, and the Nazis are equally right — as long as they all feel equally strongly about cats, "niggers," and Jews. There is little difference between Rousseau's feeling and a Nazi's thinking with his blood, or the Klansman's unreasoned advocacy of white supremacy. They are all of the same breed, and they can all be pushed back historically to the half-mad Genevan who revolted against the decadent rationalism of the *philosophes* because he could not make good in the Parisian *salon* of his day.

VIII
KANT

"AFTER Newton and Rousseau, the ways of God are justified."
Thus spoke Immanuel Kant. Newton, he thought, had penetrated
God's design in the universe to discover how all things ran according to immutable law. Rousseau had discovered the dignity
of man, whose worth was independent of his social position or the
opinion of his fellow men. Newton's work constituted a scientific
revolution, Rousseau's a moral and social revolution. Kant
summed up his opinion of their work when he observed:
"Newton saw for the first time order and regularity combined
with simplicity, where before him disorder and scattered diversity were discoverable, and since then the comets move in
geometrical paths; Rousseau discovered for the first time, under
the diversity of the forms assumed by humanity, the deeply
hidden nature of man."

So the ways of God were justified — or almost. For Kant was
acute enough to see that Newton's world-machine disallowed

human freedom by making each man merely a nut or a bolt in the vast universal machine. It was all so logical; there seemed no escape from Newtonian laws of nature, which were God's laws. Rousseau, on the other hand, had asserted man's freedom and dignity, concepts which put man outside the Newtonian machine and apparently left him a law unto himself. Worse than this apparent contradiction between Newtonian science and Rousseauvian morality was the fact that both stood like naked, defenseless giants before the relentless, sapping attacks of the two current systems of philosophy, German rationalism and English empiricism. Rationalism denied the validity both of Newton's empirically acquired knowledge and of Rousseau's finding truth in his heart. Hume's empiricism robbed science and morality of all philosophical foundation by asserting that causality is an invention of the mind, that man can objectively assert only that things happen in sequence.

Kant therefore had a complicated problem on his hands. Fundamentally, it was the problem of reconciling the claims of rationalism and empiricism, taking what was good in each system and from them creating a new philosophy which would offer a foundation for Newton's science and Rousseau's morality — both of which Kant felt to be true and therefore demanding preservation. The Wolffian brand of rationalist philosophy dominant at the time in the Germanies stood firm on the fundamental Cartesian position that all true knowledge is at bottom speculative or analytical, that by working up the contents of your mind you obtain all valid knowledge. It therefore invalidated Newton's position of starting with a blank mind and admitting all "the phenomena" of nature, and it committed science to going around in useless circles, inasmuch as there could never be anything really new in knowledge.

The rationalist experiment in England had gone around the circle to skepticism again. The experiment begun by Descartes to end all uncertainty had ended in Hume's skeptical empiricism, and the empirical philosophers found themselves in the same position in 1770 that the skeptics had occupied in Descartes's boyhood. Hume had simply replaced Montaigne. And Hume's skepticism sapped the philosophical foundations of Newtonian science as thoroughly as did rationalism. For Hume claimed that causality is a product of the mind rather than a certain, objective fact. He had made experience, the raw material of any science, a blurred sensation of some sort of something the mind could never comprehend or control, and he had dissolved the mind itself into nothing but a stream of impressions. The scientist was therefore unscientific, according to Hume, when he presumed to talk of causal relationships or of empirically established laws.

So Kant's problem was to rescue the new science and the new morality from attacks by either Wolffian rationalism or Humean empiricism. He saw, too, that he must properly limit the philosopher's domain and create, within proper limits, a new philosophy which would be impervious to the attacks of such skeptics as Hume and which would give philosophical foundation to all the sciences. His work, he therefore believed, would constitute a revolution in philosophy, because he proposed to prove that the methods of philosophy thereto used were false and then to show mankind for all time to come both the proper domain and the correct method of philosophical thinking. That is why he considered himself the "Copernicus" of philosophy and looked upon his three *Critiques* as the starting place for all future philosophers.

Kant's estimate of himself was historically not far amiss. He is without doubt the most influential of modern philosophers. One author voices the consensus of opinion when he observes: "In our time a thinking person, who has not talked things over with Kant, cannot claim the title of philosopher." And one of the outstanding contemporary Kantian scholars tells us: "To write an adequate account of the influence of Kant would be to write the history of post-Kantian philosophy. In him, as truly as in Descartes, philosophy made a new beginning."

It is not only, or perhaps even mainly, in philosophy that Kant has been influential. For it is the gloomy dean of Königsberg more than anyone else who gave the Western World its severe, formalistic morality which has disintegrated only in the past generation. According to Kant religion becomes a doctrineless affair equated with morality — a horribly forbidding morality that saw sin in every pleasure and virtue in acidosis and biliousness. Kant cut Calvinistic virtues away from their assumed theological justification and passed on to mankind an empty duty-for-duty's-sake mentality that made goodness such an old-maidish thing in modern times and looked on pleasure as down-right devilish. Largely because of Kant lively minds in the past century and a half see better prospects of fun in hell than in heaven.

This self-assured, little East Prussian is important, then, both in the history of philosophy and in the making of the modern mind. His influence, of course, has not been as direct as that of Rousseau or Marx or Darwin. Because none but philosophers and Protestant theologians presume to read him, his influence on the modern mind is indirect. But it is nonetheless real and potent, because Protestant teachers and preachers — or their teachers — read Kant and were influenced by him. Their whole movement of philosophy and of religion throughout the nine-teenth and twentieth centuries has taken its direction from Kant, and his influence has therefore seeped down from the univer-sities and pulpits of Europe and America to the multitudes. So the vast masses have been affected by the thoughts that fer-mented for long years in the head of the Sage of Königsberg and finally found their way into print in the decade of the 1780's.

Kant is particularly important because of the central position he occupies in the history of human thought. Like Descartes, he found philosophy a disintegrating corpse. Through an over-dose of skepticism it had committed logical suicide in England, while in Germany it simply failed to square with the undeniable facts of life. Either it had to be buried or it had to be given new life. And Kant gave the old corpse of philosophy new life. He preserved what he wanted of both decadent rationalism and the new empiricism, and he organized this debris into his new critical system, which in turn became the springboard for nineteenth-century philosophers. In the same way, when faith in religious doctrines was weakening, Kant rescued morality from theology and passed on to subsequent generations Calvin's forbidding precepts without their logical basis in a severe God's arbitrary will. Thus Kant acts, historically, like the waistline of an hourglass. Everything salvaged from this eighteenth-century philosophy and religion passes through him; whatever the nine-teenth century possesses in this regard it gets from him. Perhaps one can be a good philosopher without knowing Kant, but one cannot understand how the modern mind came to be what it is without knowing this engineer of philosophy's last great revolution, from which stem all subsequent little philosophical uprisings.

1

"It is a difficult matter," says the German romanticist, Heinrich Heine, "to write the life history of Immanuel Kant, for he had neither life nor history. He lived a mechanically ordered, abstract, old bachelor kind of existence in a quiet, retired alley in Königsberg, an old town in the north-east corner of Germany." If we grant Heine the license with which poets — especially of the romantic school — handle historical facts, we can agree to the truth in his statement — but it does not draw an accurate picture of Kant.

True, Kant's life was undramatic. He was born in Königsberg in 1724, when Newton was at the height of his fame and Rousseau was still an unknown apprentice in Geneva, and he died in the same city in 1804, the year in which Napoleon was crowned emperor. In those eighty years, when scholars normally traveled extensively, he never set foot outside East Prussia; and though for many years he regularly drove into the country for recreation, in later life he denied himself even this break in his rigorous schedule of duty-imposed labor. Like Descartes, Newton, and Locke, he lived out his days a bachelor. He is reported to have considered proposing twice, but each time he was so long mooting the step and calculating his finances that when he came to a decision he found the object of his choice had already married. No wonder Heine thought he had "neither life nor history!"

Kant came from self-consciously respectable, middle-class people. His father was a saddler by trade, a severely moral rather than a really religious man. His mother is remembered as a deeply religious woman whom Kant describes thus: "My mother was a sweet-tempered, affectionate, pious and upright woman and a tender mother, who led her children to the fear of God by pious teaching and virtuous example." Both Kant's parents, in fact, were warm adherents of the pietistic movement then so strong in the Germanies. From them young Immanuel seems to have received a strong sense of independence, a respect for education, and a schooling in pietism, which was one strong current of the eighteenth-century German *Aufklärung,* or Enlightenment. Of this religious movement Kant said in old age: "People may say of Pietism what they will. Those in whom it was sincere were worthy of honor. They possessed the highest thing that man can have — the quiet, the content, the inner peace, which no suffering can disturb. No need, no persecution could disturb them; no quarreller could move them to anger or hate."

In 1732, Immanuel entered the Collegium Fridericianum, where for eight years he received a solid training in Latin and a thorough soaking in pietistic principles. Here he was appalled by the insincerity of most of the students, who were compelled frequently to utter highly emotional prayers and always to wear the forbidding countenance of a good pietist — while scheming and pranking as normal boys have always done. In 1740, Kant matriculated at the University of Königsberg, where he received whatever formal education he obtained, and where he met the second strong influence of the *Aufklärung* — rationalism. For although the university was hardly an institution of higher learning in those days, it seems that in it Kant became acquainted with the Wolffian brand of rationalism then popular in the German universities, and with Newtonian science. His most capable teacher, Martin Knutzen, must have considered him an unusual student, for he gave him free run of his private library and encouraged him to work in the popular field of the natural sciences. Very little is known of Kant's student days, but we can surmise that he was an able student and that he was strongly enough attracted to university life to make teaching his career.

For some years after graduation Kant served as a tutor in various East Prussian households, then a menial position which he apparently filled with only mediocre success. He tells us of his tutorial work that no one's theory was better than his, and no one's practice worse. In 1755, Kant returned to the University of Königsberg as a private lecturer. He was allowed to give courses at the university, but he was paid no salary except what he collected in fees from the students. For fifteen years he held this position, during which time he gained reputation as an excellent lecturer not only among the students, but also with the general public. In these years he lectured on such diverse subjects as logic and geography, mineralogy and mathematics, natural law and pedagogics.

Twice, when there were vacancies on the staff, Kant applied for a professorship, but the only official position he obtained before 1770 was that of assistant librarian. In 1770, however, when he was forty-six, he was given the professorship in logic and metaphysics, a position he held for the rest of his life. From this time on Kant's life moved — as Heine described it — like a clock. Daily he rose at five, studied till either seven or eight in the morning (depending on whether it was the summer or winter semester), lectured for two hours, and then studied the rest of the morning. He dined at one, prolonged the meal two or three hours with conversation, walked for an hour, and then spent the rest of the day in reading and meditation till ten in the evening, when he retired.

For over a decade Kant wrestled with the new philosophy that was taking shape in his head. At length, in 1781, fearful that he might die before he could put his revolutionary ideas on paper, he hurriedly wrote his *Critique of Pure Reason*. Ten amazing years of production followed, during which time Kant published his *Critique of Practical Reason*, his *Critique of Judgment*, and such less important works as *Prolegomena to any Future Metaphysic*, *Fundamental Principles of the Metaphysic of Morals*, and *Metaphysical First Principles of Natural Science*. Thus Kant published all the works on which his fame and importance rest after his fifty-fifth birthday, at which age Descartes was a year in his grave.

Through the last decade of the eighteenth century Kant steadily declined in health and in mental vigor. In 1795, he restricted himself to his daily public lecture, and two years later, after forty-two years of lecturing at the University of Königsberg, he retired from the platform altogether. His health grew progressively worse in the last five years of his life, a fact which he characteristically blamed on the excessive amount of electricity in the air. His mental activity was so impaired in these last years that his younger associates had to care for him like a child. Finally, in 1804, shortly before he finished his eightieth year, he died within a few blocks of his birthplace. Fittingly, he was buried in the professors' vault of the university to which he had given the repute of his name.

2

Kant was a "typical" professor, an ideal figure to caricature. And Heine, as we have seen, drew a caricature of the Prussian philosopher that has passed for an accurate portrait this past century. "Getting up," he tells us of Kant, "drinking coffee, lecturing, eating, going for a walk, everything had its fixed time; and the neighbors knew that it must be exactly half-past four when Immanuel Kant, in his gray frock-coat, with his Spanish cane in hand, stepped from his door and walked towards the little lime-tree avenue, which is called after him the Philosopher's Walk."

Such a picture, again, is misleading. Kant came to live with clocklike regularity only through long, tedious discipline. He trained himself to regularity of physical and mental living so as to make the most efficient use of the hours measured out to him. Even his style of writing seems to have been so pruned, for whereas his earlier works show some degree of literary skill and facility of expression, his later writings are studiedly arid and repellingly technical. Kant, like Newton, schooled himself to write so that the phrase never dressed up the idea. Like Newton, too, he apparently wanted to repell all but really serious readers.

Originally he was quite a social light in Königsberg. He played billiards and cards — at both of which he excelled, and at both of which he regularly won money. He was a lively conversationalist, a celebrated storyteller, a popular guest at any social gathering in Königsberg. He clearly had social talents of a high order — even for the cosmopolitan eighteenth century. His friends in Königsberg were many, from members of the nobility to officers of both the Prussian and Russian armies. But his closest associates came from the merchant classes of the city, men whose thinking was more progressive and apparently more congenial to Kant, men whose regularity of life he approved, whose knowledge of foreign lands he wished to acquire.

He was, in his early days, anything but the dry, turgid lecturer that a "typical" professor is supposed to be. He was popular as a teacher, both with the students and with the public who were admitted to many of the university professors' lectures. He lectured to officers of the Prussian garrison stationed in Königsberg, and even to Russian officers occupying the city during the Seven Years' War. Herder, who attended his classes in the sixties, speaks of the "joyous courage" Kant exhibited on the platform, and of the "cheerfulness and joy" which he infused into his work. "He had at his service," Herder goes on, "jest, witticism, and humorous fancy, and his lectures were at once instructive and most entertaining. With the same spirit in which he criticized Leibniz, Wolff, Baumgarten, Crusius, and Hume, he investigated the natural laws of Newton, Kepler, and the physicists."

Kant was not content to be entertaining and witty and popular. He had a great mission in life — to be the Copernicus of philosophy — and he must dedicate his every moment to fulfilling that mission. He came, then, rigorously to regulate every act of his life by principles he laid down for himself. Everything was brought under a severe regimen — physically, morally, economically, even dietetically. The late Ernst Cassirer, an outstanding Kantian scholar, tells us that "in Kant rule and method constituted the animating and inspiring principles. . . . Order and law, coherence and consistency, are the guiding stars of Kant's being." All this self-discipline was for what he deemed to be his duty. Kant's life, indeed, was one long ode to Duty.

Like most bachelors, Kant was much concerned with the health of a never robust body, which nevertheless he managed to keep in action for almost eighty years. Wisely, he refused to have anything to do with eighteenth-century doctors; he devised instead his own set of rules for keeping fit. To these he adhered rigidly; about them he was always glad to discourse when he could find a listener. His daily life became, from outward appearances at least, absolutely mechanical. Everything was done according to the clock throughout his later life, from the time he was called at 4:55 in the morning until he retired at 10 in the evening. And his thinking was as systematic, as regular as his daily routine. Kant is one of history's most methodical thinkers, a man who rejoiced in definitions, distinctions, and deductions, whose treatises often seem more the work of a lawyer than a philosopher.

But for all this emphasis on order and system, Kant did not delimit his horizon to the narrow alley of later German *Wissenschaft*. He read everything he could lay his hands on, especially travel literature, works on natural science, and newspapers — then a novelty. He was the walking library of Königsberg, a fund of information to all citizens of the town. When the earthquake of 1755 rocked Lisbon, causing consternation all over Europe, it was Kant who explained the phenomenon to his fellow townsmen. Although he had never set foot outside East Prussia and had never seen a mountain, or probably even the sea, Kant's wide reading enabled him to teach physical geography at the university — the first academic teacher of this subject. An English visitor who heard him describe Westminster Bridge could not be made to believe that Kant had not seen it with his own eyes!

Kant was a thoroughly respectable middle-class Prussian, then, who strictly regulated the social side of his nature to devote himself exclusively to his double mission of teaching at the University of Königsberg and of founding his new philosophy. His life was directed by principle, and so far as we know he never wandered from the path of duty as he saw it. Respectable as Kant was, he does not seem to have elicited love or admiration. Like many teachers, he grew to be a bad listener. "I must give myself up to the movement of my own thoughts," he tells us, "which for some years have followed a kind of beaten track." So he came to have patience for little but his own thoughts and his own voice. In the days of his fame, he was annoyingly dogmatic. Although he never completely cut himself off from the thinking of other men, as tradition has it, nor did he remain completely unmoved by criticism of his views, nevertheless he tended to look upon those who differed with him in later life as false friends and bad philosophers.

The little Prussian philosopher of Königsberg has often been likened to Socrates. Kant was not the man, however, to drink hemlock for his principles; his was not a strong, forceful nature. For although he was resolute in following his thoughts to their logical conclusions, he was not forthright in stating them publicly. While he never said what he knew was untrue, he sometimes avoided stating the truth. He admitted that, "I think many things with the clearest conviction and to my great satisfaction, which

I never have the courage to say; but I will never say anything which I do not think."

He submitted without struggle in the one instance when his writings offended the government, because he thought it was his duty to do so. In 1794, the Prussian cabinet issued a "cease and desist" order when it thought that the new critical principles in Kant's *Religion Within the Bounds of Pure Reason* undermined the foundations of religion. Kant believed the government wrong, but he was not made of martyr's or of hero's stuff. Moreover, he had by this time convinced himself of the absolute duty of obedience that he, as a subject, owed to his sovereign. So he submitted to the order and consoled himself by reflecting: "Recantation and denial of one's inner convictions is base, but silence in a case like the present is a subject's duty. And if all that one says must be true, it does not follow that it is one's duty to tell publicly everything which is true." When the pious Frederick William II died three years later, Kant considered himself absolved from the prohibition, so he prepared a second edition of the work.

3

Kantian students divide their master's life into two periods: the precritical till 1770, and the period after 1770 when his thought reached maturity. Except for the light they throw upon his mental development, his earlier writings are of no account. Through the 1750's he wrote on such scientific subjects as earthquakes, the theory of the heavens, and whether the west wind in Europe is moist because it has crossed the Atlantic Ocean. In the next decade he turned toward metaphysical and ethical problems. Through both these decades Kant groped for principles by which he could explain science and morality and philosophically establish their claims to be accounted branches of valid knowledge.

By 1770, when he received his appointment as professor at the University of Königsberg, he had arrived at the threshold of his critical system. The road had been long and hard for Kant because he had seen the difficulties besetting philosophy in the eighteenth century and he had not sidestepped them. He had

seen the claims both of rationalism and empiricism; he had seen
the conflict between rationalism and Rousseau's sentimental
morality, between Newtonian science and Hume's indifferentism.
These were conflicts which Kant had to show to be apparent
rather than real — or else it would be necessary for him to give
up either the new science or the new morality.

Although he had been teaching the Wolffian brand of rationalism for two decades, Kant was both open-minded enough and
acute enough to see its inadequacy. He saw how it made knowledge essentially a closed system, with philosophers condemned to
nothing but analysis and deduction, more deduction and more
analysis. By its denial of empirically acquired knowledge, Kant
saw, rationalism sentenced itself to a smothering death. Hume's
criticisms awoke him, he tells us, from his "dogmatic slumbers,"
for he saw that rationalists had no answers to the difficulties
raised by the Scotch skeptic. He saw truth, moreover, in Hume's
claim that knowledge is acquired empirically, that it is *a posteriori* rather than *a priori*.

But at the same time Kant did not like Hume's skepticism,
because it denied the validity not only of philosophy but also of
science. Nor did he think Hume right in getting rid of the mind
altogether by reducing it to a succession of experiences. Kant
felt, therefore, that he must make a new start. The philosophy
of the rationalists, he decided, had become "a dark ocean without
shores or lighthouses." "There reign in philosophy," he wrote
in the preface to the *Critique of Pure Reason,* "weariness and
complete indifferentism, the mother of chaos and night in all
science." Skepticism is one answer to such a state of affairs — but
it did not satisfy Kant. He was not one to surrender without a
battle, as skeptics do.

He therefore decided to take stock of man's intellectual accomplishments, to rescue what was valid from rationalism and to
reconcile it with what he could find valid in English empiricism
— for Kant was realistic enough to see that knowledge is neither
independent of experience, as the rationalists held, nor a mere
succession of experiences, as the empiricists held. Neither was
completely right to the exclusion of the other, because both were
partly right. From all these elements he would therefore build
a system which would stand proof against the new skepticism —

as Descartes had decided to do a century and a half earlier. Where Descartes had adopted the deductive reasoning of the mathematician for his new philosophical system, however, Kant turned to the physicist's empirical approach as the surest and safest method of building a body of knowledge. In this way Kant hoped to construct an unassailable body of principles; his new philosophy, like the new science, would be cautious in accepting only empirically verifiable truths. It would, in short, be the critical philosophy. And through the sieve of his critical method Kant was sure he would sift only the sands of truth. All else would be rejected.

It was natural for Kant, in taking stock of man's intellectual accomplishments, to contrast Wolffian rationalism with Newtonian science. Philosophy was in no better condition than it had been two centuries before; it was worse, in fact, for while philosophers bickered and got nowhere, philosophy had fallen into deserved discredit. Science, on the other hand, had progressed steadily, as Bacon and Descartes had observed long before. It accepted as true only what could be demonstrated and proved by controlled experiment. Therefore it was respected both for its progress and for its modesty, since it made no extravagant claims. Moreover, it not only found new truths, but on the basis of what it had established empirically it predicted additional discoveries. As its hypotheses became theories, and its theories laws, science enlarged the domain of human knowledge steadily and surely until it promised, by this method, to stretch out the horizons of man's mind to unimaginable limits.

Kant therefore asked himself how science differed from philosophy. He found, in the first place, that it subjected itself to self-criticism, where philosophy did not. "Our age is, in every sense of the word," he concluded, "the age of criticism, and everything must submit to it." His Copernican revolution in philosophy must therefore make this subject self-critical. In the next place, Kant decided, philosophy must change methods. Since Descartes's time, rationalists had relied on the mathematical method of deductive reasoning. But this method, valid for a subject which begins with definitions and proceeds to build an edifice constructed *a priori* by the mind, is not valid for philosophy. There, Kant held, "we have to do with a reality which we do not construct; we cannot begin with definitions; we must begin with experience. We shall, therefore, profit most if we study the method of physics."

Kant will proceed with philosophy, then, as Newton had proceeded with physics. "The true method of metaphysics is fundamentally the same as that which Newton has introduced into natural science, and which has there yielded such fruitful results." He therefore commits himself to a denial of all knowledge that transcends experience. All valid knowledge is *a posteriori*. To this extent his reaction to rationalism was much the same as Locke's. Kant insists on the empirical element in all knowledge; nothing which does not enter through the senses, or is implicit in sense knowledge, is to be accredited as authentic. But at this point, as we shall see later, Kant breaks with Locke. For he insists that all sense knowledge has *a priori* as well as empirical elements in it, that knowledge must, by its very nature, be affected by the knowing subject.

But Kantian philosophy is more than Newtonian science applied to metaphysics. There was something else which Kant wanted to salvage from the eighteenth century, and this was the Rousseauvian concept of man's worth, and dignity, and freedom. There is no doubt that Kant, who was the opposite of Rousseau in almost every way, was nevertheless strongly impressed by the unruly Genevan. Kant was one of the first Germans to see good in Rousseau's passionate essays; he was undoubtedly the first to appreciate their fundamental importance. It is, however, not so much specific points of Rousseauvian doctrine as the latter's general attitude that Kant incorporated into his own work. Herder tells us how, in his lectures in the 1760's, Kant "took up the writings of Rousseau, then just appearing, his *Emile* and his *Heloise* . . . appraised them and returned again and again to an unaffected insight into the nature and the moral worth of man."

Kant frequently mentions his debt to Rousseau. "I am myself by inclination a seeker after truth," he summed it up. "I feel a consuming thirst for knowledge and a restless passion to advance in it, as well as satisfaction in every forward step. There was a time when I thought that this alone could constitute the honor of mankind, and I despised the common man who knows nothing. Rousseau set me right. This blind prejudice vanished; I learned to respect human nature." Kant appreciated Rousseau for his fearlessness, for the independence of his thought and feeling, for his insistence on the primacy of morality over dogma, of action over theory. And he prized him for extolling man as man.

Thus Kant began to construct his new critical philosophy out of two elements: Newtonian science and Rousseauvian morality. His new philosophy had to reconcile these elements and at the same time keep from future conflicts by confining them to distinct realms of thought. Well could the epitaph Kant wrote for his own tombstone be placed on the title page of his collected works:

> The starry heavens above me,
> The moral law within me.

It is therefore not surprising to find that, as Descartes's philosophy became a kind of mathematicism, so Kant's was a combined physicism and moralism.

4

In building his new system Kant saw himself faced at the outset with Descartes's problem of answering the skeptics. Can we know things? If so, what can we know, and under what conditions is knowledge authentic? His answer seemed to be so very reasonable — but it was an ingenious answer which has done philosophy an injury from which it still suffers. Kant began by distinguishing the world as we know it from the world as it is. The world we know consists of phenomena, of things as they appear to us. We look at the world through a magic looking glass, as it were, and we see wonderful things. But we can never know to what extent they correspond to the real world. We can know what is in the looking glass, but we cannot be sure it gives us a true reflection of things outside.

This distinction of Kant's between phenomena and noumena — things-in-themselves — is frequently misunderstood. Kant never denied the existence of things-in-themselves, or of raw facts. He only insisted that they cannot be known. To ask what they are is to ask what they would be if we did not know them. The very knowing of a thing makes it no longer a thing-in-itself, or raw fact, but a thing known, a phenomenon, because in the act of knowing an object man contributes to the raw fact certain subjective elements. Whatever we know, therefore, is a secondhand fact. Knowledge consists of man-handled facts, so to speak. Behind the known secondhand fact, of course, is the raw fact, or noumenon, which we simply cannot know. Thus, against Hume, Kant denies the possibility of pure empirical knowledge. Everything we see is seen in the looking glass.

How does the looking glass differ from the world beyond it? Everything is known in time and space, Kant points out. Now time and space do not exist as independent entities, according to Kant, but only as the media in which things are known. Thus time and space are the equipment of the knower and cannot be attributed to things-in-themselves. In this way, then, time and space are posited only of the phenomenal world, which comes, for all practical purposes, to be the world of the mind's making. So the world we perceive is not the world as it exists independently of us; it is rather the world our knowing powers create for us out of things as they exist. Things-in-themselves are the raw material of knowledge; knowledge is this raw material molded by our knowing powers. Because he believed the human mind essentially the same in all men, Kant never asserted that each man made a world all his own. The man-made phenomenal world, he insisted, is the same for all men.

This sounds, nevertheless, like thoroughgoing idealism, and the *Critique of Pure Reason* was so taken by many readers. But Kant was no more a transcendental idealist, in his own mind, than he was an empirical realist. His desire was to steer a middle course between what he considered the Scylla of idealism and the Charybdis of realism — so that he might be a transcendental realist. He therefore wrote a new chapter for the second edition of the *Critique,* entitling it a "Confutation of Idealism," in which he pointed out that the mind was not free to transcend experience; that, even though the phenomenal world was not the world as it exists independently of the mind, still all men share in a common knowledge of this phenomenal world; and that the subjective elements of knowledge do not differ from man to man, but are the same for all. Kant is distinguished from true idealists by his confining knowledge within the limits of experience, by his refusal to cut knowledge loose from its moorings in empirical fact and to assert that the idea is the ultimate reality.

As sense knowledge is affected by the knower, according to Kant, so too is thinking. The empirical method of science, as he analyzed it, is not the mere obtaining of one fact after another, as Hume would have it. That, perhaps, is the way babies or idiots would amass information. But the scientist applies *a priori,* rational principles to his empirical investigation. These principles are independent of experience, and their use is what makes the scientist's subject truly a science. In the preface to the second edition of the *Critique,* Kant uses this simile to state his position: "Reason, holding in one hand its principles, according to which alone concordant phenomena can be admitted as laws of nature, and in the other the experiment which it has devised according to those principles, must approach nature in order to be taught by it, but not in the character of a pupil who agrees to everything the master likes, but as an appointed judge, who compels the witnesses to answer the questions which he himself proposes."

Transcendental reason, therefore, imposes its rules on matter. And matter must conform to these rules — it must answer the questions reason asks. Thus, while Kant limits knowledge to the matter of experience, he has the human mind control experience. It is no longer the passive receptacle Locke had made it. Where the realist insists that the mind must conform itself to outside reality, Kant has the mind mold this reality, according to reason's own rules, out of empirical facts. All knowledge for Kant is therefore partly objective and partly subjective, or, more properly, at the same time both thoroughly objective and thoroughly subjective. These rules by which the mind operates are the famous Kantian categories, which are not derived from experience but rather make it. The mind is not a pupil who learns whatever experience would teach it, but a judge who tells experience what questions it wants answered. Experience determines the answers, but the nature of the human mind determines the questions. In this way, then, empirical knowledge is partly independent of the knower and still partly affected by him.

Kant has, indeed, destroyed the age-old distinction between object and subject by making all knowledge at once subjective and objective. The very knowing of a thing destroys its objectivity, in the older sense of the word. So although Kant insisted he was not a subjectivist, he would have to admit that he was not an objective realist, as Aristotle or St. Thomas claimed to be. Kant has, in fact, pushed the tyranny of the mind over matter even further than Descartes had done. Descartes had simply made the idea independent of objective reality and had left it up to a good God to guarantee conformity of thing and idea. Kant goes further by making phenomenal reality conform to the idea the human mind has of it. Knowledge is limited by experience, it is true, but the mind molds this raw material of experience as a sculptor molds his raw rock. The finished idea, like the finished statue, depends more on the maker than on the raw material.

5

What, then, has become of metaphysics with Kant? As a valid science, he assumes, it is impossible, for by its very nature it is an inquiry into objects which transcend the bounds of experience. Therefore, since Kant limits knowledge to experience, for him metaphysics cannot possibly be a valid science. So he has made physical science in a way a subjective thing and metaphysics definitely an impossible thing. Nevertheless, he argues, metaphysics is a natural disposition of the human mind, and metaphysical questions arise inevitably from the very nature of man's reason; but inasmuch as these questions cannot be answered, he concludes, we are left in the unsatisfactory position of having to raise problems we cannot solve. For him, then, the task of philosophy is simply to show why they cannot be answered, to limit the mind to what he considers its proper subjects of inquiry, and mark "out of bounds" around the field of metaphysical inquiry. In his attempt to salvage the elements of rationalism and reconcile them with the claims of empiricism, Kant has thrown up the sponge as far as metaphysics is concerned. Philosophy has become what it is in modern times — critical philosophy, with emphasis on epistemology, or the problem of knowledge.

"Metaphysics," Kant tells us, "has as the proper object of its inquiries three ideas only: God, freedom [of the will], and immortality — so related that the second concept when combined with the first, should lead to the third as a necessary conclusion. Any other matters with which this science may deal serve merely as a means of arriving at these ideas and of establishing their reality." Now none of these three objects stands the test of Kant's new critical method; none, he holds, can properly be the object of knowledge, for each transcends experience. Kant insists, indeed, on the existence of God, but he also insists that it cannot be demonstrated philosophically. So it is with freedom and the existence of an immortal soul. In these things Kant believes most firmly, but he is also convinced that all metaphysical proofs for their existence are worthless, that by the very nature of things they can never be established by any argument advanced by pure reason.

Kant was particularly thorough in seeking to demolish the metaphysical proofs for God's existence, because he was convinced that these arguments had to be exposed as bad in order to make room for faith. Since he further believed that all metaphysical proofs eventually rested on the ontological argument, he made his attack on this proof especially devastating. This is, of course, Descartes's famous proof based on the following line of deductive, analytic argument: I have a concept of an *ens realissimum*, a Being of perfect reality; but existence is a note of perfect reality; therefore, such a Being exists. To demolish such an argument, as we have seen, is no great accomplishment. Here Kant rather is endeavoring to demonstrate that all metaphysical proofs for God's existence eventually resolve themselves into the ontological proof. So he rejects them all.

He treats the teleological argument — which goes from purpose in the universe to a Creator — least roughly of all metaphysical proofs. It "always deserves to be mentioned with respect," he wrote. "It is the oldest, the clearest, and the best suited to ordinary human reason." But it is not valid to jump mentally from apparent purpose in the universe, Kant insisted, to a creating God. So he rejected this proof as invalid too. God, Kant therefore concludes, cannot be an object of knowledge, nor can He be arrived at by pure reason. He must remain an object of belief rather than knowledge; His existence must be proved by practical rather than theoretical reason. Kant always insisted, of course, that though man cannot demonstrate through pure reason that there is a God, human nature demands that he live as though he could. This is the beginning of the *als ob* — the "as if" — philosophy of modern times. Man denies rational certainty of the noumenal world, it holds, but he must live as though he knew a great deal about it. We could thus never be sure of what lies beyond the looking glass, but we are simply to live as though we could.

Because his admirers believed he had so thoroughly demolished the rationalist's proofs for God's existence, Kant was called *der Allzermalmende* — the all-destroyer. This was not quite fair to the Sage of Königsberg, because he always insisted, "I have destroyed reason to make room for faith." He was convinced that it was his duty to get rid of these arguments for God's existence, for the immortality of the soul, and for freedom of the will because they had been shown incompatible with the new critical philosophy he was creating. But by getting rid of these proofs he did not mean to get rid of God or freedom of the will or immortality. By getting rid of these proofs, on the contrary, Kant believed he had cleared the way for the really valid method of positing God's existence, the immortality of the soul, and freedom — on the basis of moral law. His conclusion was that "the only theology of reason which is possible is that which is based upon moral laws or seeks guidance from them." Kant wanted to prove God's existence from moral law so as to get a moral God — and with Kant morality was more important than God.

What Kant does, therefore, is to postulate God's existence as the necessary consequence of justice and morality. The basic thing here is man's sense of moral obligation. Obligation requires freedom for man; otherwise it is meaningless. So Kant postulates a freedom which tends to cut man loose from all influences and to make him autonomous in every sense of the word. This free man, of course, is transcendental man, for Kant had divided man into the phenomenal man who fitted into the deterministic phenomenal world like a bolt into a machine, and the transcendental man who was free in every way. Now obligation also requires justice, without which it would be meaningless, and from the existence of justice Kant believes he can postulate, as necessary consequences, both God's existence and the immortality of the soul. For justice would be impossible without a God and a future life. Therefore, Kant concludes, man can be assured by his practical reason, or faith, that God surely exists. It is all arrived at deductively from that sense of moral obligation which man

spontaneously experiences. It is, necessarily with Kant, a purely
rationalistic argument cut cleanly away from experience. This
is why many Kantian critics complain there was more of the old
rationalism in the Sage of Königsberg than he realized.

6

Kant based his morality on practical reason, as distinguished
from pure or speculative reason. This practical reason, upon
analysis, seems to approach Rousseau's intuition or innate feeling.
It is man's spontaneous feeling of respect for moral law, an
innate sense of *ought*. Kant puts it this way: "There is a practical
knowledge, which though it is based entirely on reason and needs
no historical learning, yet lies as near to every one, even the
simplest, as though it were written in letters on the heart. It
is a law which has only to be named, and every one at once
understands what it is they are asked to consider. It brings with
it in every man's consciousness unconditional obligation. This is
the moral law. What is still more, either this knowledge leads by
itself to faith in God, or at least it determines the conception of
God as a moral law-giver, and so it leads to a pure religious faith
which every man finds not only conceivable but worthy of the
highest honor. It does this so naturally that if the attempt is
made, it will be found in the case of every man, though he has
been taught nothing about it, that it can be elicited from him
by questioning." How like Rousseau's Vicar of Savoy!

Kant gives a philosophical analysis of what Rousseau was
content to accept on intuition. Moreover, there is nothing of the
heart, nothing sentimental in Kant's practical reason. It is an
intellectual faculty used for different purposes than the theoretical reason, and it operates on rationalistic deductive lines
rather than according to the critical schemata. It is, primarily,
the faculty by which man arrives at moral laws, and it is therefore
more directly in contact with reality than is speculative reason.
It knows things immediately. No time or space intervenes, as is
the case when the senses acquire empirical knowledge; no categories are imposed on the objects of practical reason, as is the
case when the understanding acts upon the data of the senses.
Kant's morality is thoroughly rationalistic, deductive, analytical;

he insists that moral truths are *a priori*, that they do not depend in any way upon experience. The empirical method, he tells us, "is incapable of explaining the nature of obligation, the distinction between what is and what ought to be, between right and wrong, good and bad." All these things are known *a priori*. Each moral decision, of course, requires the active use of practical reason, but such reasoning is deductive and analytical, based upon *a priori* principles and independent of experience.

In building his system of morals, Kant was particularly anxious to preserve man's freedom and dignity. Therefore, because rigorous determinism makes liberty impossible in the phenomenal world, Kant must discover his moral principles *a priori* outside experience. Kant makes each man autonomous, an end in himself, because he thought this was the only way to preserve man's independence and his high worth as a free being. Only in this way could he be saved from becoming a link in the chain of causality. In this respect, again, Kant sounds like a scholarly echo of Rousseau. "The man who stands in dependence on another," he writes, "is no longer a man, he has lost his standing, he is nothing but the possession of another man." This is only another way of expressing Rousseau's dictum that "man is too noble a being to serve simply as the instrument for others." Kant insists that morality is possible only when "a reasonable being can be an end in himself, because only through morality is it possible to be an autonomous member of the realm of ends." This is asserting philosophically and ethically as extreme a doctrine of individualism as the mind of man can conceive. By making man absolutely autonomous and absolutely free Kant has placed on him a weighty moral responsibility which admits of no extenuating circumstances — physical, mental, or moral.

When Kant speaks of human dignity and worth, he means the worth of every man as a man, regardless of social position or intellectual accomplishments. In good Rousseauvian fashion he puts his faith in human nature, which is essentially the same for all men everywhere. And apparently for that reason he hailed the successful rebellion of George III's subjects in America; for that same reason he looked upon the French Revolution as the dawn of a new and glorious era in the history of mankind. On his faith in man's goodness he placed his expectation of peace among nations, a hope voiced in his little *Essay on Everlasting Peace,* which was sanguinely republished as a guide to the peacemakers at Versailles in 1919.

Kant put his faith in man, as man, because he believed that moral principles could be known, with just a little reflection, by every member of the human race — a rationalistic belief common enough in the eighteenth century. But he demanded of the common man a severity with one's self which few have shown in Kant's day, or any time in mankind's history. His ethical principles were relatively simple — but as severely demanding as one would expect of a Prussian pietist. They are Calvin's ethical principles cut off from Calvinistic theology. They are severe for severity's sake rather than for God's sake.

The moral law, as Kant saw it, can be said to possess four characteristics. First, as distinguished from scientific law, it defines what ought to be rather than what is. It is a command of duty, not a statement of fact. And duty's commands, as we shall see, are absolute. Second, the moral law is dictated to man by his practical reason, since man as a moral agent is autonomous and his reason is therefore self-legislative. The good man therefore obeys God's laws not because they are God's laws but because his practical reason commands him to. Third, the moral law is universally and necessarily binding on all rational creatures alike. Although man is autonomous and free as a moral agent, he does not enjoy the license to create whatever law he likes. He is free only to act according to the dictates of his moral reason, which is the same as every other man's. Fourth, the moral law cannot be derived from experience; it is known *a priori.*

Kant's ethical principles center around his concept of the "categorical imperative." He claims that all previous attempts to establish principles of morality failed because they were conditioned upon the object or reward that the individual had in view. *If* you want to live peacefully in society, then do not commit murder; *if* you wish to be trusted, then do not steal. Now this conditional imperative is not of the subject's own making; it is imposed on him by custom or by some external authority. Aristotle had said, *if* you want to be happy, then be virtuous; Catholic moralists had said, *if* you want to go to heaven, then be good. Kant's imperative, on the other hand, will be imposed on man by himself, for, he insists, man "is only bound to act in conformity with his own will." The Kantian imperative, moreover, will be limited by no condition. It is therefore categorical; there is no *if* about it, because it is a command of the will that one's action conform to a universal law. One lays down for himself the simple categorical command: do not commit murder, do not steal. Be good simply because one ought! This is a spontaneous command human nature imposes on man — to be good for goodness' sake.

Kant therefore concludes that "there remains nothing but the general statement that the maxim should conform to a universal law, and it is this conformity alone that the imperative properly represents as necessary. There is, therefore, but one categorical imperative, namely this: Act only on that maxim whereby you can at the same time will that it should become a universal law." Kant reformulated this principle in two other ways. The first he put in these words: "So act as to treat humanity, whether in your own person or in that of any other, in every case as an end as well, and never as a means only." And finally: "Hence follows the third practical principle of the will . . .: the idea of the will of every rational being as a universally legislative will. On this principle all maxims are rejected which are inconsistent with the will being itself universal legislator. Thus the will is not subject simply to the law, but so subject that it must be regarded as itself giving the law."

One obeys the categorical imperative simply because it is an irresistible command of practical reason. It is one's duty. And the virtuous man never reasons why. He simply does his duty. Duty for duty's sake never had a stronger champion than Immanuel Kant. "Duty!" he exclaims rapturously. "Thou sublime and mighty name that dost embrace nothing charming or insinuating, but requirest submission, and yet seekest not to move the will by threatening aught that would arouse natural aversion or terror, but merely holdest forth a law which of itself finds entrance into the mind." This is the terrible formalism that has plagued the Western World since Kant's day. This is the morality without content that has made goodness synonymous with sternness, hardness, sobriety, downright discomfort. This is the morality which made pleasure practically synonymous with sin and virtue the same thing as sorrow and gloom. This is the morality which is essentially negative, making virtue consist in the following of a thousand prohibitory commands. This is the morality that made prohibition seem a noble experiment.

Kant reduced religion to mere morality, to his formalistic, empty morality. He did this of necessity, for his critical philosophy had ruled theology and all religious doctrine out of bounds for speculative reason. And he based his practical reason on the moral sense. As a result, whatever one could ascribe to religion depended ultimately upon what his practical reason could deduce from the innate sense of duty found in all men. Kant's phenomenal system, moreover, had to rule out a God, for there is no reason in the deterministic phenomenal world for such things as creation in time, providence, miracles, prophecy, or the intrusion by God in any way into the phenomenal world. After Kant, therefore, religion became a thing without dogma, a thing that dealt exclusively with conduct — and it came, in time, to consist in believing and doing as one felt.

7

Heine calls Kant "a petty tradesman" whom nature intended "to weigh out tea and sugar." But Kant perversely crossed nature and became a philosopher instead of a grocer, and, Heine claims, his thought was "subversive, world-bruising." This evaluation of a mighty thinker by a great poet is, in some respects, both apt and penetrating. Like a petty tradesman weighing out tea and sugar, Kant delighted in weighing out ideas, sifting them, making fine distinctions, dividing up ideas or reality into various mental cubicles, mixing them all up to make his new critical system. Like Descartes before him, Kant is a watershed figure in the history of human thought. Secular philosophy truly divides itself into pre-Kantian and post-Kantian, with every important development in the history of that philosophy down to the present time ultimately traceable to Immanuel Kant.

Like Descartes, moreover, Kant was a great divider. His first sharp division, found in the *Critique of Pure Reason,* is between man's perception and his understanding. Kant separates these two sources of knowledge and makes them heterogenous, yet he leaves them located working together as independent entities in the same mind. How they work together so well he never explained, although he did admit that they may have a common source more fundamental than the distinction he had made between them. This concession, however, his followers soon forgot, and they looked on perception and understanding as two different faculties completely independent of each other.

In the next place, Kant made a sharp distinction between man living in the world of nature and man living in the world of morals. This is a nice and easy way of preserving liberty for man and at the same time satisfying the deterministic demands of science. But it seems an uneconomical solution made rather to fit into Kant's division of things into the phenomenal and noumenal worlds than into the reality of human experience. Man's freedom is limited in both worlds. He is neither as free in the moral world as Kant made him, nor as determined in the physical world as the Prussian philosopher would have him.

Kant's most important distinction was that which he made between the phenomenal world and the noumenal. The world we know is only part of the universe of reality, Kant insists, and he maintains a balance between the known and unknown worlds by never giving up the reality beyond knowledge, never making phenomena independent of unknown raw facts, but never allowing us to know the facts as they exist outside of us. Although Kant denied man access to raw fact and did not allow him to know God or freedom by speculative reason, still he allowed him to reach these things by faith and thus to believe in them with practical truth. Followers of Kant, however, emphasized one or the other aspects of this duality; few, if any, maintained Kant's nice balance between them. Fichte, for example, went to complete idealism. He and Hegel made reality simply a product of the mind. With them the idea is the ultimate reality, and many philosophers claim that Hegel is only Kant being consistent with himself. Others, notably Comte, could deny the reality of Kant's noumena and make his phenomena the sole reality. And thus they slid quite naturally into positivism, a system denying everything but the natural phenomena or properties of knowable things.

Kant divided other things that do not admit of such sharp

division without suffering irreparable injury. He cut faith loose from theoretical reason, which he thought a poor prop for belief in God or immorality, and he made faith and religion and morality rest upon practical reason instead. Thus he gave a philosophical impetus to the modern religion of wishful thinking, wherein doctrinal truth is a matter of indifference, because he destroyed the apologetic value of theoretical reason and he denied God or freedom a place in the phenomenal world. Kant also cut action away from theoretical knowledge, but not practical reason, of course, a position which many have pressed to its conclusion in modern times by holding theoretically to one set of ideas but acting as though they have no validity outside the covers of their philosophy books. Few philosophers act as though automobiles are mental products, and none acts as though food were not a reality outside the eater's mind — but many hold to such theories.

The *Critique of Pure Reason* is important, too, for having destroyed metaphysics. Ironically, Kant set out to create a system of knowledge that would stand the test of Hume's skepticism and would incorporate the truth of rationalism — but he ended up by dealing a deathblow to metaphysics. He merely allows the ghost of metaphysics to hover around as a "natural disposition" asking questions which man can never answer. And it is only within the past twenty-five years that philosophers are beginning to tire of this metaphysical agnosticism and to look for certainty again. Even H. G. Wells — no philosopher himself — was keen enough to comment shortly before his death that what the world needs is a metaphysics. Men are tired of the *als ob* philosophy. They want certain answers. They want to know that this is so, and this is not. But Kant could allow men only to act *as if* such and such were so, while insisting they could never know by speculative reason whether it was or not. If men must live by faith, they at least want that faith to be based on the credentials of speculatively ascertainable knowledge.

Though not a subjectivist himself, strictly speaking, Kant bequeathed to philosophy the legacy of subjectivism, for his *Critique of Pure Reason* denied the possibility of our knowing reality in the raw. For him the phenomenal world which we come to know is in some measure the world of our own making; the objects we know are objects in space and time, and both space and time are subjective elements. Just as sense knowledge is subjective with Kant, so too are the objects of understanding. With Kant, as we have seen, the mind does not conform, like a pupil, to reality. Instead, it molds and shapes reality to its own pattern. In this way he reversed what ordinary people think the proper procedure of judging truth and error. Objects for him must conform to knowledge to be true, not knowledge to objective reality. Thus we can know nothing in the raw, so to speak, but only man-handled material. For the phenomenal world is the product of our own thinking. This note of subjectivism — to which farmers or bricklayers or railroad switchmen have fortunately never quite conformed in their working hours — has vitiated the world of knowledge ever since the publication of the *Critique of Pure Reason*. This is perhaps Kant's chief legacy to the modern world — the destruction of the old line of demarkation between subject and object.

Though Kant himself was anything but an individualist as regards speculative reason, nevertheless his new critical philosophy opened the gate to individualism in philosophy as well as in morality. It was easy for philosophers, in time, to have each man create his own phenomenal world by the action of his individual knowing powers on the raw material of reality. Thus it came to pass that the known world was different to each knower. It was no longer mankind's common possession, as Kant had considered it, but a different possession for each man. Individualism developed even more markedly, after Kant, in the field of morality. Man was bound to obey his conscience alone, Kant had held, and it turned out quite naturally that the dictates of practical reason differed from man to man. Kant had left each man absolutely autonomous in morals. It is therefore not surprising to find various individuals turning up with various and widely differing codes of morality — the one as good as the other, since each man is a self-legislative creature.

Kant left us quite another heritage in his *Critique of Practical Reason*. If the first of the *Critiques* left reason impotent in the field of speculation, the second certainly leaves it sovereign in the sphere of action. This practical reason, which Kant leaves supreme, gives way in the nineteenth century to will, especially with Schopenhauer and Nietzsche. Good, with Kant, depended on practical reason, an intuitive thing, rather than on speculative reason; with later Kantians, however, the good man is a man of good will. This emphasis upon will rather than intellect is another note which reverberates noisily from shortly after Kant till today. Through the nineteenth century and the first part of the twentieth the will tends more and more to replace the intellect; it becomes with many philosophers the measure not only of goodness but of truth, and with some it becomes the ultimate reality. Though Schopenhauer and Nietzsche are the best-known exponents of voluntarism, they are by no means alone in their stress on will rather than reason. Kant was by no means a voluntarist himself, but his critical philosophy served as the point of departure from which stemmed streams of thought that ended up logically enough in voluntarism.

Kant's influence on religion has been pervasive and strong, so much so that one Protestant minister could write recently "that there are two kinds of theologians, those before, and those after, Kant." The Sage of Königsberg gave philosophical impetus to the doctrineless kind of Protestantism known today as modernism. He has thus been influential on all Protestants except the ever-diminishing number of Fundamentalists. Following Kant, it becomes possible to have a religion without a creed or a cult. Only a moral code is necessary.

Morality is the thing with Kant. It is probably not too much to say that he saved puritanical morality from the doctrinal shipwreck of the eighteenth century and passed it on to posterity. Because of Kant, Calvinistic ethics survived independently of Calvin's theology for another century. Kant's ethic was one without content. It was a formalistic ethic of duty for duty's sake, a bundle of severe prohibitions that made the negative man the good man. And it took the place of religion. When a poet like Nietzsche rebelled against Kantian ethics, then, he seemed to rebel against religion. In most men's minds, therefore, the collapse of Kant's formalistic ethics — a wonderful thing to transpire — also seemed a collapse of religion — a sad thing, we are learning today.

If Kant were to do a critical commentary on the couplet he chose for his tombstone, he would have to say that the first line —

The starry heavens above me — might not be true, for astronomy tells us only of phenomena, and we can never be sure that the stars are really in their heavens as they seem to be. He could, however, be logically sure of the second line — *The moral law within me* — but this is a law of man's own making. It binds him categorically, but it is only man binding himself. Thus Kant leaves us certain we see the stars in the heaven, but intellectually uncertain whether they are there, or even that there are heavens for them to be in; and he preserves moral law for us, but he leaves man to a law of his own making. After Kant, therefore, comes intellectual agnosticism and moral subjectivism.

IX
BENTHAM

THE HUMAN CALCULATING MACHINE

JEREMY BENTHAM was the leader of a curious group of Englishmen known in their day as "Radicals." And for early nineteenth-century England they were radical: they demanded universal manhood suffrage, a secret ballot, free trade, universal education, reform of the judicial system, a humane code of laws, and a hundred other "drastic" reforms. These Utilitarians, as they came to be known from their key doctrine, were a group of young men who lived in the nineteenth century but possessed eighteenth-century minds. These were men who followed the rationalism of Voltaire and Helvetius, who never understood what Rousseau or Shelley and Keats or Kant and Fichte were getting at. Feeling and passion they could never quite comprehend; sentiment they looked upon as a feminine weakness to be confined to the boudoir and kept out of the countinghouse and the market place.

These were men who put all their chips on cold, calculating

reason. They looked upon bricklayers and dock hands as men who settled down with Helvetius or Hume in the evening to arrive at the rational foundation of Parliament's latest bill. They were therefore certain that society could be run perfectly, automatically in fact, when all these human calculating machines had their mental mechanism properly adjusted. They needed only the right kind of education, and then, as rational automata, they would all grind out the same answers to the same problems. For man, to the Utilitarians, had no free will, no will of any kind. He was pure reason. His mistakes were the result of ignorance, since his mental machinery worked according to the law of association of ideas, and he responded automatically to the drives of pleasure and pain. Consequently, it seemed so easy to overhaul society in order to provide the right environment for these human calculating machines — and then all would be well forever more.

The leader of this group was a very nice old man, Jeremy Bentham, who had been an extraordinarily precocious child. But unfortunately, Bentham never matured. He remained a precocious child ignorant of the ways of the world and the workings of men's minds till the day of his death — in his eighty-fifth year. Bentham reasoned much about men in the abstract, but he never really knew a single flesh-and-blood human being. He was admired by his associates for his integrity and his zeal, and as an outstanding champion of reform he attracted younger men into his circle — men who were in many ways their master's better. They looked to him as a lovable old master whose eccentricities only enhanced his unique value in their eyes. Thus Bentham could write to Brougham as "My dearest Best Boy," or "Dear sweet Little Poppet," and Brougham would dutifully answer with a "Dear Grandpapa." This is about as sticky as two rationalists can get.

The close-knit little group that gathered around the elderly Bentham in the first two decades of the nineteenth century included some of the best, the sharpest minds of the time. The most important of his followers was James Mill. This dour Scotsman served as liaison man between the master and his disciples; he sold Bentham to the vigorous minds of his day, and he headed the group that agitated for Parliamentary reform along Benthamite lines. Mill's most important personal contribution to the group's theory was his development of the associationist psychology, which had been implicit in all of Bentham's work. Mill introduced David Ricardo into the Utilitarian group, and soon the brilliant economist's iron laws of rent, value, and wages were part of the Utilitarian creed. Malthus, too, was brought into the sacred circle by Mill, and his population theory was made a test of Utilitarian orthodoxy.

Mill was the driving force of the Utilitarian group, the man who encouraged Grote, Romilly, Burdett, Brougham, Place, and others to work for Utilitarian reforms in Parliament. And the "Radicals" put their print upon England, down through the nineteenth century and on into the twentieth. Their reforms appealed to reason, and in the nineteenth century — in England at least — rational arguments convinced men and eventually moved them to action. Almost everything the Utilitarians advocated was eventually written into English law because, as Bertrand Russell observes, "in the Victorian era, this victory of reason surprised no one; in our more lunatic period, it reads like the myth of a Golden Age." Bentham failed to realize his desire of becoming the "Newton of the moral order," but he did become the guiding star of nineteenth-century legal and political reform movements.

1

Jeremy Bentham was born in 1748, when Voltaire reigned as king of the rationalist universe, and the English reformer never outlived the intellectual climate of his birth. Rousseau attained fame in Bentham's youth, Kant started philosophy on its new path in his early manhood, romanticism swept across the Channel to capture young hearts and minds in his middle age — but Bentham's mind remained in the world of its origin, the world ruled by Voltaire, Diderot, Helvetius. Jeremy was a peculiar, dwarfish child whose precocity was his father's delight. The boy studied Latin grammar at four; and, his gratified father noted, he wrote a scrap of Latin phraseology at the age of five years, nine months, and nineteen days.

Jeremy's father was ambitious — but Mr. Bentham's ambition centered around his promising son. At home, Jeremy was made to read widely and deeply. At school, meanwhile, he suffered untold agonies preparing to become the lawyer his father had decided he should be. Classes made him wretched, for the instruction he found poor and the young "barbarians" he was thrown among insufferable. The usual father-son relationship on the subject of school was reversed with the Benthams: the father plied his son with money and encouraged him in frivolous pleasures — wisely, it would seem, in this one case — but Jeremy retreated into his books. He preferred reading to play; he loved flowers and animals all his life, but could never quite bring himself to love human beings. Bentham tells us, for example, how he "became once very intimate with a colony of mice. They used to run up my legs, and eat crumbs from my lap. I love everything that has four legs." He did — more than twice as much as the two-legged animal, whom he never understood as sympathetically as he did his mice.

At the age of eighteen this bright young man had his master's degree from Oxford. He went on in law, finished his courses, and began a very short and very disappointing career as a barrister. All this was done, apparently, to satisfy his ambitious father. Meanwhile, young Bentham had been reading Locke and Hume, Montesquieu, Helvetius, and Beccaria. He was in correspondence with D'Alembert and Morellet, he was a worshipful follower of Voltaire. On his own, then, he had caught up with the most progressive thinkers of the day. He was better informed than his father knew.

Young Bentham grew to manhood a naïve, childlike person. He had the simplicity and the good humor of a healthy child; he was never seriously ill, he never knew deep sorrow or high excitement, his life flowed on simply and placidly. Nevertheless, Bentham did not melt into his surroundings. He was a learned eccentric who would attract attention today even in Hollywood or in the country's largest university. The daring of this man who loved flowers and feared the dark must have occasioned many good stories in London. Once for example, he wrote to the formidable Wellington — who was too much for Napoleon — reprimanding the duke for his duel with Lord Winchelsea. The letter began with the salutation: "Ill-advised Man!" and it concluded: "Now, then, if to personal and physical, you add moral courage, I will tell you what to do. Go to the House of Lords. Stand up there in your place, confess your error, declare your repentance; say you have violated your duty to your sovereign and your country; and promise, that on no future occasion whatsoever, under no provocation whatsoever, in either character — that of *giver* or that of *accepter* of a challenge, will you repeat the offense."

Bentham's arithmetic precision of speech sometimes perplexed his disciples — but they loved it. He called his walks before breakfast and after dinner, for example, his "ante-jentacular and post-prandial circumambulations." Again, he bid young Robert Owen good-by by saying: "God bless you, if there be such a being, and at all events, my young friend, take care of yourself." Bentham never understood the connotation of words or phrases; the rational denotation was all he saw. That is what he meant by his "substantive-preferring principle." A verb, he felt, "slips through your fingers like an eel." On the other hand, nouns are solid. So, the ideal language for Bentham would be algebraic, the nouns, like numbers, connected by relationship signs.

So it was with literature, which Bentham simply could not appreciate. "Prose," he wrote, "is when all the lines except the last go on to the margin. Poetry is when some of them fall short of it." Bentham seems to have been a mind trotting around amiably on two legs with his stick Dapple. He had neither sentiment nor passion nor imagination. He was a lovable mind on legs, however, who had a series of pet cats, a beautiful pig at one estate, and a pet donkey at another. And wherever he resided in later life, he was surrounded by eager disciples.

Bentham lived and wrote with monotonous regularity. Every day he filled ten to fifteen folio pages in manuscript, which he filed away for his disciples and for posterity. He published only two things himself: his *Fragment of Government* in 1776, an anonymous work which attracted much favorable attention; and an *Introduction to the Principles of Morals and Legislation* in 1789. His other works were published by such followers as Dumont or Mill from the mass of nearly undecipherable manuscript he ground out so regularly. As a matter of fact, much of

Bentham's writings remain unpublished today, deposited in boxes at the University of London. Posterity has not prized them as highly as he thought it would.

The success of the *Fragment on Government*, combined with Bentham's hatred of law as a profession, made him a reformer for life. He was keenly interested in practical reform of any kind, and he worked for years on such various projects as his *Panopticon*, a prison guaranteed "to grind rogues honest and idle men industrious," and his *frigidarium*, an 1800 model food locker. He spent two and one-half years cogitating a scheme for interest-bearing notes, he tells us, and again he was completely absorbed with an improved system of patents. He worked on methods for improving the metropolitan police of London, and then he worked on a system of limited liability companies. With Bentham's support, his disciples took the lead in establishing London University, where, more or less symbolically, Bentham's skeleton today sits in its chair, his face covered by a wax mask, his bones clad in his accustomed dress. His body was dissected in the interests of anatomy, as Bentham willed, and the remains given a chair at London University.

His most precious reform measure was his *Panopticon*. This was a star-shaped prison which he was certain would make criminals both honest and industrious. The keeper was to be seated in the middle of the prison, the inmates arranged in rows of cells radiating out from the center toward the points. By means of mirrors and blinds the keeper was to see every prisoner in his cell, but no prisoner was to see the keeper. For thirteen years or more, Bentham pressed Parliament to legislate him one thousand prisoners and sufficient money to put his plan into effect. Parliament delayed from year to year, however, until finally in 1811 a committee reported against the proposal. The committee noticed one point Bentham had not stressed in his application: he and his brother, Samuel, were to make a good profit from the convicts' labor.

Parliament's delay in acting on his request, topped by its final refusal, made Bentham, the reformer, a Radical in politics. Till that time he had been a Tory, firmly believing that all he had to do was show the rationale of his reforms to the party in power — then the Tories — and his proposals would be both graciously received and enthusiastically executed. But now he saw that government cannot be entrusted to such opponents of reform as George III and the Duke of Wellington. So Bentham became a democrat. The people, he reasoned, must favor reform, because they are bound to follow their enlightened self-interest. He therefore proposed the "bettering of this wicked world by covering it over with Republics."

At the age of fifty-five, then, when most men are settling down to enlightened conservatism, Bentham turned radical and advocated such practical changes in England's government as universal manhood suffrage, annual parliaments, vote by ballot, equalization of electoral districts, abolition of the monarchy and of the House of Lords. There was never anything halfhearted about Bentham's reform when once he took a project up. The rest of his bachelor life — he never married, although he proposed by letter when he was almost sixty to Caroline Fox, whom he had not seen for sixteen years — he devoted to reforming governments and drawing up constitutions. He was willing to prepare a constitution for any nation, to codify the laws of any country. He asked Madison for permission to draw up a complete body of laws for the young United States; he planned to go to Mexico to write that country's laws, then he planned visiting Venezuela instead; meanwhile he dabbled in the affairs of such diverse countries as Spain and Portugal, Tripoli and Greece, Russia and Argentina. Finally, in 1822, he made an offer at large to draw up a code of laws for any nation in the world needing a skilled legislator.

2

Except for his *Introduction to the Principles of Morals and Legislation,* Bentham wrote almost nothing that directly influenced the world. But he kept alive the spirit of social, political, and legal reform. This spirit, together with his greatest-happiness principle, he passed on to a group of capable, energetic younger men who, in turn, scattered his ideas abroad in England and, on the second bounce, to other countries such as France and the United States. The most important of these followers was James Mill, who proved just the man to serve as program chairman for the group offering Bentham's ideas to England. Mill had the unquestioning faith of a true disciple in everything Bentham held, and at the same time he had the driving energy, the stamina, and the forcefulness to stand at Bentham's right hand and to keep the other disciples in line.

James Mill was a Scottish Presbyterian minister who had turned sour on religion after coming to London in 1802. Throughout life he possessed both the good and bad qualities of a Scottish puritan. He was harsh with himself and others; even his son, generous John Stuart, admitted that he was disagreeable and that his children did not love him. He abominated the slightest sign of softness. He was dogmatically sure of himself and sharply critical of everyone else. Bentham remarked that his closest disciple "is a character. He expects to subdue everybody by his positiveness. His manner of speaking is oppressive and over-bearing." George Grote believed that Mill was truly "a very profound thinking man." He went on to observe, however: "His mind has, indeed, all the cynicism and asperity which belong to the Bentham school, and what I chiefly dislike in him is, the readiness and seeming preference with which he dwells on the *faults and defects* of others — even of the greatest men." Mrs. Grote adds that Mill had "a scorn and hatred of the ruling classes which amounted to a positive fanaticism."

Most of all, James Mill had absolute confidence in human reason, especially in the reason of James Mill. He never doubted how perfectly right he was in his every opinion, nor was he able to see how anyone else could be even a little right if his reasoning did not coincide perfectly with Mill's. He looked briefly at some of Kant's major works once, for example, and then commented characteristically: "I see clearly enough what poor Kant is about." Neither Mill nor any of his associates could ever have fathomed what "poor Kant," or any other German philosopher of their day, was about.

As a sergeant is important in the army, then, so Mill was important in the Utilitarian group. He put together several of Bentham's works, arranging his master's voluminous jottings topically, working them into cohesiveness, and finally getting them into print. He also brought into the circle such writers as

Ricardo, Malthus, and Austin, and he converted such men of action as Francis Place, Sir Francis Burdett, Joseph Hume, and George Grote, men who tried to get Benthamite reforms adopted by Parliament. But most important, perhaps, James Mill furnished the group with a guinea pig, his eldest son, John Stuart. This pathetic test case was raised on a rigid rationalist regimen: he studied at least nine hours a day, read Aristotle at four, discoursed on the relative merits of Marlborough and Wellington at five, began to write the history of Rome at six, wrote letters in Latin to his sister at fourteen. Meanwhile, he tutored his younger brothers and sisters and read his father's books in the manuscript stage. But the raising of this child prodigy seems only to have proved that an Englishman can receive a good education without going to school — for there is no doubt that John Stuart was widely read and well educated.

David Ricardo and Thomas Malthus are the other two principal contributors to Utilitarian thought. Ricardo, the son of a Dutch Jew, received little formal education; instead, he worked in his father's business from early childhood. Clever speculation during Britain's long war with Napoleon brought him a large fortune, so about 1814 he bought a large estate, retired from business, became a member of Parliament, and began to associate with "thinking men." James Mill was so impressed with Ricardo's sharp mind and his grasp of economic theory that he finally prevailed upon him to write his *Principles of Political Economy and Taxation,* which became the economic bible not only of the Utilitarian school but also of almost all English classical economists. Malthus, on the other hand, was not, strictly speaking, an associate of the Benthamite group. Nevertheless, this amiable Anglican clergyman's dismal views on population problems, expressed in his *Essay on Population,* were accepted by the entire school. This was the key point, in fact, which separated the Utilitarians from such other "Radical" groups as the Owenites and the followers of William Cobbett.

Bentham's followers held closely together on all essential points of doctrine. The pleasure-pain principle enunciated by the master himself, the associationist psychology of Mill, the iron laws of rent, value, and wages stated by Ricardo, the law of population formulated by Malthus — all became common property of the school. It is quite proper, therefore, to treat them all together and to label them "Benthamite" or "Utilitarian."

3

Bentham and his followers were, for their day, naïvely simple rationalists. They were thoroughly rational creatures themselves, of course, and because they never bothered meeting other men they concluded that everyone was moved by the force of unadorned reason. Mill spoke for the group when he observed: "Every man possessed of reason [and for the Utilitarians all but lunatics are possessed of reason] is accustomed to weigh evidence, and to be guided and determined by its preponderance. When various conclusions are, with their evidence, presented with equal care and with equal skill, there is moral certainty, though some few may be misguided, that the greater number will judge right, and that the greatest force of evidence, wherever it is, will produce the greatest impression."

How much more orderly — and how much duller — the world would be if Mill were right! But the simple fact is that men are not so moved, as even the Utilitarians could have discovered of themselves by a little profounder introspection. Because they saw man as a simple thinking machine, they oversimplified all human relations, all social problems. Their conclusions were nice, neat, methodical, schematic — but not correct.

They generalized about all men from what they knew of themselves, and thus they created an "Average Man," father of the next generation's "Economic Man" and grandfather of Marx's Proletarian. Mr. Average Man was moved by cold reason, by machinelike calculation, by prudent selfishness. Bentham's willingness to legislate for Hindustan, Russia, Morocco, or Mexico as readily as for London shows rather pathetically how he thought his Average Man lived and moved, a real person everywhere the same. There is justification, therefore, for Marx's remark on Bentham: "With the driest naïveté he takes the modern shopkeeper, especially the English shopkeeper, as the normal man." Coupled with Bentham's belief in the Average Man was his typically rationalist propensity of not distinguishing between paper constitutions and workable reform. The problem of getting

men to do what seemed rational never occurred to the Utilitarians, for they never experienced that practical difficulty of
trying to change a group's ways of acting. They worked on paper,
not on human skin. If the reform was rational, they believed,
and was so explained to men, then the problem was solved. For
they were convinced that man could not act irrationally, that his
every error was due to ignorance alone.

The fact was, however, that in 1800 — as at any time in history
— men were sentimental, possessed of passion and of strong
feeling. Such emotions, the Utilitarians explained, were a hang-
over from primitive society. As such they were inveighed against;
as such they must disappear like morning mist in the strong sun
of reason. This is why Bentham condemned poetry so strongly.
It proved nothing; it was full of "sentimentalism" and "vague
generalities"; it did not appeal to reason. It was, he said, the
"production of a rude age," the silly jingling that might satisfy
savage ears but could make no impression on a mature mankind.
It was to slide into oblivion, then, with the religion and mythology and superstition which it expressed. Rational men used
simple language, he always maintained, to state barren, unadorned facts.

The Utilitarians expected education to remake the world. "If
education does not perform everything," James Mill wrote,
"there is hardly anything which it does not perform." Their faith
in the power of education, indeed, was such as could be produced only by the combination of rationalism in philosophy,
associationism in psychology, and democracy in politics. Bentham's views on education are embodied in his *Chrestomathia*
— the study of things useful — in which he revolted against
classical education in favor of practical training. The Utilitarians
wanted all children sent to school: the poor so that they could
at least learn a trade and therefore not become a burden on the
taxpayer; the middle class so that they could learn to think and
thus take their proper place as leaders both of the poor of purse,
the workers, and the poor of mind, the aristocrats.

To suggest that the working classes be taught to read and
write, to reason, and to work at a trade seems a niggardly proposal today. In Bentham's age, however, it was dangerously
radical. When a bill to provide elementary schools for all was

introduced in Parliament, for example, the president of the Royal Society voiced the pervailing view in these words: "However specious in theory the project might be, of giving education to the laboring classes of the poor, it would in effect be found to be prejudicial to their morals and happiness; it would teach them to despise their lot in life, instead of making them good servants in agriculture, and other laborious employments to which their rank in society had destined them; instead of teaching them subordination, it would render them fractious and refractory, as was evident in the manufacturing counties; it would enable them to read seditious pamphlets, vicious books, and publications against Christianity."

Against this mentality Bentham and his associates vainly but untiringly urged universal education. Not until late in the next generation were educational steps, suggested by the Utilitarians, taken by the English government. The Benthamite faith in education has by now been proved naïve, it would seem, for education has not made all men saintly as well as wise. But at the same time it has also been proved not nearly so radical as its opponents feared it to be early in the nineteenth century. Benthamite arguments in favor of education helped wear down the opposition, and the Utilitarians deserve no small share of the credit for selling universal education to the English people.

Although the Utilitarians were rationalists, they insisted that they were not philosophers. To them "philosopher" was a term of disparagement, for philosophy was concerned with vaporous theory, with fuzzy thinking, with fantastic meanderings of the uncontrolled imagination. The very language of philosophy drove Bentham to desperation. "The *summum bonum* — the sovereign good —," he asks, "what is it? . . . It is this thing, and that thing, and the other thing — it is anything but pleasure — it is the Irishman's apple-pie made of nothing but quinces. . . . While Xenophon was writing history, and Euclid giving instruction in geometry, Socrates and Plato were talking nonsense under pretense of teaching wisdom and morality. . . . 'Moral sense,' 'common sense,' 'understanding,' 'reason,' 'right reason,' 'nature,' 'nature's law,' 'natural justice,' 'natural equity,' 'good order,' 'truth' — all are but the dogmas of men who insist on implicit obedience to their decrees."

Ethicians especially annoyed this father of Utilitarianism, because their precepts stood in the way of his becoming "the
Newton of the moral order." Natural rights, he declared, were
"simple nonsense: natural and imprescriptible rights, rhetorical
nonsense — nonsense on stilts." He hated to hear ethicians speak
of duties even more than of rights, for "the word itself has in it
something disagreeable and repulsive." The very concept of
duty, he preached, was the unnatural invention of priest-thinkers.
"A man, a moralist, gets into an elbow-chair, and pours forth
pompous dogmatisms about *duty* — and *duties*. Why is he not
listened to? Because every man is thinking of *interests*."

Bentham wanted to start his morality, as Newton had apparently started his physics, with concrete reality. This he found in
pleasure and pain alone. "Take away pleasures and pains," he
tells us, "not only happiness but justice and duty and obligation
and virtue — all of which have been so elaborately held up to
view as independent of them — are so many empty sounds." So
Bentham was going to start morality from a new basis — self-
interest, which consists of enjoying pleasure and avoiding pain.
He was going "to prove that the immoral action is a miscalculation of self-interest, to show how erroneous an estimate the
vicious man makes of pains and pleasures."

Thus he arrived at one of his basic principles. But there was
another, for Bentham saw the necessity of making man's reason
move him in deterministic fashion. He could not allow his
Average Man freedom to see the truth and still reject it. He
summed up these two basic points of his Utilitarian system on
a scrap of paper thus: "*Association Principle.* Hartley. The bond
of connection between ideas and language; and between ideas
and ideas. *Greatest Happiness Principle.* Priestley. Applied to
every branch of morals in detail, by Bentham; a part of the way
previously by Helvetius."

4

The "association principle" was an essential element of the
Utilitarian system, because Bentham and his associates were
going to make men automatically good and happy. It is implicit
in all Bentham's writing, but the psychologist of the group who

worked out the principle of association to explain all mental activity was James Mill. His *Analysis of the Phenomena of the Human Mind,* published in 1829, was not widely read at first, but it convinced all Utilitarians, so much so that the next generation of the school republished the work in 1868. It remained the ultimate explanation of mental activity for Englishmen and Americans until the experiments of Pavlov and Watson substituted a biological for a mental causation.

Mill attacks his problem of explaining how the mind works in characteristic rationalist fashion. The problems of philosophy, he explains, are all very simple if they are attacked scientifically. So he makes use of the newly developed science of chemistry to explain the origin of ideas. Davidson aptly labels the doctrine of association "mental chemistry." "The explanation of the mind to him [Mill] was just the exposition of the mode of combination and coalescence among its varied states, and what transformations this process could effect." Ideas are atoms; psychology is the study of laws under which they combine into mental molecules.

All ideas, Mill explains in Humean fashion, are "copies of sensations." All knowledge results from the association of these transformed sensations, associations which are made in time and place. Mill uses the example of thunder following lightning so regularly that we come to associate the two of them in causal relationship; in the same way the word "man" comes to arouse in us the idea of a human being simply because the word and the idea have always been so closely associated in the mind. Mill therefore concludes: "The fundamental law of association is that when two things have been frequently found together, we never perceive or think of the one without thinking of the other." This is good — as an explanation of some mental activity. But Mill concludes that he has hereby explained everything the mind does. His psychology is as naïvely simple as that.

The *Analysis* is thoroughly nominalistic. Mill insists that names, such as "man" or "duck," are nothing more than tickets or labels placed upon objects that can conveniently be put into the same pigeonhole. Classification is simply a process of naming, and predication is merely the substitution of one name for another. The predicate is always implied in the subject. Thus when you say that man is a rational animal, you are really not saying anything of man; you are only saying that these are two names which you have attached to a certain class of creatures. Leslie Stephen can therefore conclude in his study of Mill that, "his 'Analysis of the mind' seems to get rid of the mind itself." It is not much more than a mechanical grain grader, which automatically separates the kernels of grain into various compartments.

But more important from the Utilitarian point of view, Mill gets rid of free will as a bit of absurd nonsense concocted by moralists in days gone by and accepted by people who did not understand the chemistry of their own minds. The human mechanism of the mind — a rather simple calculating machine for Mill and his associates — explains all knowledge, all decisions, all muscular activity. The law of association controls the working of this human machine. The only points of entry for bettering the world, therefore, are two: first, each man's mental mechanism, which must be perfectly adjusted so that it operates with automatic precision on the transformed sensations fed into the mind; second, the outside world, from which sensations derive, which must be changed so that the matter entering the mind is sifted, winnowed raw material. The Utilitarians therefore believed that in a world of flowers and trees, birds and bees, happiness would not only be possible — it would be inescapable when men's minds operated properly. So for them happiness is at hand.

But what is happiness? The answer to this question served as the second basic principle of the Benthamite school — and it earned them the then derogatory tag of "Utilitarian." Bentham had an easy, simple answer for the question: happiness is pleasure, pain is its negation. "Every act," he tells us, "by which pleasure is reaped, without any result of pain, is pure gain to happiness; every act whose results of pain are less than the results of pleasure, is good, to the extent of the balance in favor of happiness." Pleasure equals happiness, and happiness equals good. "Every act whereby pleasure is reaped is, all consequences apart, good." Ethics, Bentham therefore concludes, is the science of pleasure and pain, the study of means to achieve happiness, the showing how virtue and felicity are interchangeable terms.

Bentham thought that this business of morality was as simple as elementary mathematics or physics. As Newton had worked out formulas with matter and motion, so Bentham thought that he could work out formulas with pain and pleasure. Most of his work on this subject is summed up in his *Deontology*, the province of which, he tells the reader, "is to teach him a proper arithmetic, to lay before him a proper estimate of pain and pleasure — a budget of receipt and disbursement, out of every operation of which he is to draw a balance of good." He goes on: "Vice may be defined to be a miscalculation of chances: a mistake in estimating the value of pleasures and pains. It is a false moral arithmetic; and there is the consolation of knowing that, by application of a right standard, there are few moral questions which may be not resolved with an accuracy and a certainty not far removed from mathematical demonstration."

So Bentham worked out a table of pleasures and pains — much like a logarithmic table in the back of an elementary trigonometry book. He drew up a list of fourteen simple pleasures (of sense, wealth, amity, skill, and power, for example) and twelve simple pains (such as privation, enmity, and memory), lists certainly not devised on any scientific, logical plan. These pleasures and pains, he goes on to show, are all of the same quality; they differ only in duration, intensity, certainty, proximity, extent, purity, and fecundity. Such an analysis of pleasure and pain shows how little Bentham knew of human nature. The table might appeal to a mathematician, but it would appall anyone who had even the slightest knowledge of men. Underlying this "felicific calculus" is Bentham's narrow view of man as a robot equipped with a mechanical mind, powered by love of pleasure and fear of pain. Bentham never knew how noble, nor how mean, man can be. That is why Nietzsche thrust viciously at Bentham by observing: "Man does not desire happiness, only the Englishman does."

Legislation is therefore an easy science for the Utilitarians, the science which they took most seriously and which they considered a sure means of bringing utopia to this miserable world. The simple problem of the legislator is to apply proper legal sanctions to certain acts so as to put an equal sign between private happiness and general welfare — which consists of the happiness of all people. All the legislator need do is keep Bentham's table of sanctions in one hand and his felicific calculus in the other. Then he is to attach to all those acts which are criminal — and these are found to be criminal by the fact that they cause more pain in the community than happiness — such sanctions that the happiness the potential criminal would receive from committing the crime is overbalanced by the punishment attached to it. Stealing, for example, must be so punished that the thief's enjoyment of the stolen goods is nullified by the pain of punishment he receives under the law.

All the legislator need do, then, is analyze the extent, duration, intensity, and such of the pain caused in the community by stealing; against this he must balance the pleasure the thief receives. If the pain suffered by the community outweighs the pleasure enjoyed by the thief, then stealing is immoral and a physical sanction must be attached to it by law so that the potential thief will suffer more pain than he will gain pleasure from the act. Bentham firmly believes that this will end all stealing — as soon as men's minds are adjusted to work the right way. It will always be possible, of course, for the potential thief to miscalculate his pleasure and pain and thus to become a criminal. But education will reduce such miscalculations to a negligible factor.

English law was in such a chaotic condition in Bentham's day, there was so much need for reform, and Bentham had done so much work on codification of the law that his name became almost synonymous with legal reform in his country. His disciples soon pushed the matter so vigorously in Parliament that they began to drive wedges in the antiquated bulwark of English criminal and civil law. And they did so under Bentham's coaching. In 1828, Brougham opened up the campaign in Parliament with a six-hour speech, which he had prepared in consultation with Bentham. Ten years later he claimed that fifty-five of the sixty reforms he had advocated in 1828 were adopted. In that first speech he declared that Bentham was the world's "first legal philosopher," that "the age of law reform and the age of Jeremy Bentham" were interchangeable terms. Certainly it is true that Bentham was the guiding light of the law-reform group in Parliament in those days, that the reform was salutary, that much humanitarian legislation in England received its impetus from this rather inhuman group of Utilitarians.

Bentham's work on penology took up as much of his time and interest as did his law reform. Here he gained attention for spreading the ideas of Montesquieu and Beccaria through the English-speaking world, but Bentham dresses them up in his own terminology and arranges them in his peculiar tables. Punishment, he insists, should not be vindictive. Its aim is not to make the criminal pay for his crime but rather to use him as an example in order to discourage future potential criminals. Punishment is preventative, then, rather than vindictive. To serve this purpose it must therefore be administered publicly, it must be certain and impartial, it must be proportioned to the crime, and it must outweigh the pleasure that the crime promises. Jails, he concludes, are for the rehabilitation of criminals, not for their confinement and suffering. Criminals are imprisoned in order to be "ground honest" and taught a trade, and thus to be sent out into the world useful citizens, units of productive labor.

Typical of Bentham's mentality is his view on condemning men to hard labor in prison. "The policy of thus giving a bad name to industry, the parent of wealth and population, and setting it up as a scarecrow to frighten criminals with, is what I must confess I cannot enter into the spirit of. I can see no use of making it either odious or infamous. . . . To me it would seem but so much the better, if a man could be taught to love labor, instead of being taught to loathe it. Occupation, instead of the prisoner's scourge, should be called, and should be made as much as possible, a cordial to him. It is in itself a sweet, in comparison with forced idleness; and the produce of it will give a double savour. . . . Industry is a blessing; why paint it as a curse?" He opposed hard labor in prison, then, not for man's sake but for hard labor's sake. He loved work more than he did the workingman.

5

Economics was a big thing with the Utilitarians, for through this science were revealed vistas of a better world. They were not alone, of course, in looking so hopefully at the new science of economics, since theirs were exciting times economically. The Industrial Revolution was getting well under way, and England was leading the world in the new race for wealth. Yeomen had long been flocking into the cities, where they worked the new machines to turn out all sorts of finished products, making their employers ever richer and themselves ever more miserable. Much wealth was being produced, but there were still famine and hunger, poverty and cold, misery and want resulting from an absolute shortage of goods. The problem of production had by no means been licked in 1800.

Here was a subject, this business of producing and distributing wealth, to which the Utilitarians could turn their organizing, systematizing, codifying minds. And they did — with a gusto and a sureness which today seem amazing. They plunged into this business to find the same kind of laws Newton had found in the physical world and Mill had found in the world of the mind. The first such law they found was Malthus' law of population, first published in 1798 and republished with strong supporting evidence in 1803. This was an ideal law for the Utilitarians. It was so conclusive, since it was stated in arithmetic and geometric ratios — then all the rage; it was so imposing because of the mass of evidence accumulated to support it; it was so comforting and consoling, since it assured the Benthamites that neither they nor anyone else was responsible for the misery and suffering they saw everywhere about them.

The key thesis of Malthus' *Essay on Population* can be stated simply: population increases, unless it is checked somehow, at a geometric ratio, whereas the means of subsistence increase at an arithmetic ratio. The results are frightening. In one century, Malthus pointed out, the population would be 32 times what it was then; in two centuries it would be 1024 times greater; in three centuries 32,768 times greater. After that, it would seem, there just isn't room for men to sit down on this earth. Meanwhile, food increases so slowly. In the year 2003, Malthus pointed out, 256 people would have to live on what was consumed by nine in 1803.

But it was an inescapable fact that such a formidable increase of population had not occurred in the past. This is true, Malthus claims, because of checks nature has imposed on mankind's fruitfulness: poverty, vice, disease, famine, war, and so on. "The vices of mankind," he explains, "are active and able ministers of depopulation. They are the precursors in the great army of destruction, and often finish the work themselves. But should they fail in the war of extermination, sickly seasons, epidemics, pestilence, and plague advance in terrific array and sweep off their thousands and ten thousands. Should success still be incomplete, gigantic inevitable famine stalks in the rear, and at one mighty blow levels the population with the food of the world." Mankind, therefore, is condemned to live on a minimum essential diet. For when there is extra food, more babies will survive until the food is leveled off to the population; when there are extra babies, then some must starve till the population is leveled off to the food supply.

This is a rather disturbing situation. Is there no way of improving man's lot here on this earth of limited food supply? Malthus has one, and only one solution — his famous "moral check." Men can limit their offspring by marrying late in life, by not marrying at all if they do not have good prospects of supporting a family, or, if they must marry, by limiting the size of their families. The only solution, Malthus therefore concludes, "is the exercise on the part of the poor of prudence in marriage, and of economy both before and after it." In this way Malthus sweeps away all attempts to tackle the problem of poverty unless through limiting the population. "I see no way," he writes, "which man can escape from the weight of this law which pervades all animated nature. . . . Were I to propose a palliative, and palliatives are all that the nature of the case will admit, it should be a total abolition of all the present [forms of relief]." This "law," then, is more than a scientifically established fact. It is a moral argument justifying poverty and suffering, for which, indeed, neither the government nor the employer is at all responsible.

The conclusions to which the law of population mathematically led the Benthamites were inescapable. The state has no choice but to adopt a social *laissez-faire* policy. By trying to relieve poverty it would only increase the population and thus level more people down to the margin of subsistence. By letting the poor alone and by allowing them to starve themselves out of their miserable existence, it would teach them to help themselves — or to perish, which they must eventually do anyway, relief or no relief. The poor, therefore, must be satisfied with their hard lot. Their only chance to obtain a few luxuries is to remain unmarried, or, if they must marry prudently to trim their families to their income.

What Malthus did for the problem of population and poverty, Ricardo did for the more technical phases of economics. Everything in business, he showed with mathematical certainty, follows inescapable laws involving men, money, machines, and raw material. All these factors, man included, move through Ricardo's pages as the planets move through Newton's *Principia*. As matter blindly obeys the law of gravity and is attracted to other matter in proportion to their weight, so man is blindly attracted to profit in proportion to the number of dollars involved and in reverse ratio to the risk he runs. This Economic Man of Ricardo is Bentham's human calculating machine who seems to have put one equal sign between pleasure and profit and another between pain and loss. This Economic Man is a rationalist robot that coldly calculates all factors involved in a problem, weighs alternatives, and then automatically selects the choice which is most profitable.

The material with which the Economic Man works are nice, clear-cut blocks labeled capital, labor, value, utility, rent, wages, profit, and so on. Each one of these items is seen, in rationalistic fashion, as a clear and distinct entity with an independent existence. It enters into relationships with the other items according to certain easily found and clearly defined laws. This economic science, therefore, becomes exceedingly abstract and mathematically exact, so that the reader of Utilitarian economic textbooks begins to wonder whether it is a science created arbitrarily in the Utilitarian mind, with definitions, rules, and all imposed by the mind, or whether it is supposed to have some relation to the mass of men sweating in the coal mines of Wales or toiling in the factories of Manchester. Its scientific appearance, however, did not hide the fact that the arguments were also moral and reformist: moral, because they justified individualistic capitalism and its abuses; reformist, because they advocated sweeping away the remnants of English mercantilism and protectionism.

Apparently the new economics was supposed to explain what real men were doing in the factories and mines — and why they were doing it. The explanation was best given, all Benthamites agreed, by David Ricardo in his *Principles of Political Economy and Taxation,* which Mill finally got him to publish in 1817. This work became the economic Bible of the Utilitarians, a Bible which was put in simple form by James Mill in a *Schoolbook of Political Economy* and was revised some decades later by John Stuart Mill. The most famous of Ricardo's "laws," certainly the one most closely associated with his name and with Utilitarians generally, was his "iron law of wages." "The natural price of labor," it runs, "is that price which is necessary to enable the laborers, one with another, to subsist and perpetuate their race without either increase or diminution."

This, coupled with Malthus' law of population, put the poor man forever in his place. For if higher wages are paid, workers will have larger families. If the supply of workers increases, the employer will be able to bargain advantageously — because the supply of labor will be above the demand — and thus pay lower wages. Then some workers will starve — until the employers find they are running short of labor. Whereupon they will pay higher wages until the supply and demand level off again. So it goes on endlessly — with the worker always ending up just where he started, that is, barely keeping alive and barely perpetuating himself.

Logically and inevitably the Benthamites arrived at a *laissez-faire* stand on the state's role in society. They got there, as a matter of fact, by two different lines of reasoning, either of which was conclusive enough for them. Bentham believed that state interference with business was bad because "pain is the general concomitant of the sense of such restraint." The others rejected state control of private enterprise on the grounds that it was both useless and pernicious: useless because it was a vain attempt to interfere with physically determined laws, like supply and demand, the setting of wages or rent, and so on — as vain as the attempt to change the law of gravity; pernicious because such attempts always interfered with the proper working out of these laws by throwing up obstacles in their path.

"All government," Bentham solemnly proclaimed, "is in itself one vast evil." He therefore insisted that best results were obtained in society when men agree that "the general rule is that nothing ought to be done or attempted by the government." He argues for a policeman state, in which the government is only to preserve order, guarantee property rights, make sure that men do not murder one other. "Security and freedom are all that industry requires," he tells us. "The request which agriculture, manufactures, and commerce present to governments, is modest and reasonable as that which Diogenes made to Alexander: 'Stand out of my sunshine.'" This comparison was meant literally. When Parliament was debating a bill to prohibit children from working more than ten hours a day, the *Economist*, presenting the Utilitarians' viewpoint, ran the headline: "The lords leagued with the Commons to prohibit Industry."

6

Unswerving faith in democracy came to be an article in the Utilitarian creed in rather curious fashion. Bentham, as we have seen, had long been a Tory; his only interest was to see the greatest possible number of mankind receive the greatest possible measure of pleasure and suffer the minimum amount of pain. For many years he thought that he could accomplish this by showing the ruling classes how to promote the people's happiness. But when he found himself whistling in the wind, when he discovered Tories and Whigs were not so benevolent as he had thought, he concluded that democracy was a prerequisite to his grand reform projects. Bentham himself never worked out a theoretical defense of popular government; it was implied, however, in his later work on law reform and in specific changes he advocated in the government.

It remained for James Mill to work out the Utilitarian theory of government. This he presented in an article on "Government," which appeared in the 1820 edition of the *Encyclopaedia Britannica*. This article was for Utilitarian political theory what Ricardo's book was for their economics. It was gospel truth from which no orthodox Benthamite dared deviate; so inviolable did they hold its truths, indeed, that Macaulay taunted them for holding it "perfect and unanswerable." Fifty years later John Stuart could still call his father's article "a masterpiece of political wisdom," although he had himself written incomparably more wisely on the same subject.

Mill begins his article by asserting that the end of government is the increase of human happiness; it is essentially an association into which men enter for the protection of their lives and their property. The big problem presented by the existence of governments, therefore, is to prevent them, once they are given the power to protect us, from plundering us instead. Power must be given to the government to protect, and the danger always exists of that power being turned against the people from whom it came. This dilemma of government, Mill tells his readers, has been solved by the "grand discovery of modern times" — representative government. For the community at large cannot, following the Utilitarian principle of selfishness, have any interest opposed to its own happiness. So the only problem is to obtain a government truly representative of the people, because such a government is prevented by the very nature of things from making the people unhappy. Politics was as simple to Mill as psychology — and both were as simple as elementary arithmetic.

Proper mechanical devices are to achieve true representation. First, the vote should be extended as widely as possible, because, in Bentham's words, "every person is not only the best, but the only proper judge of what, with reference to himself is pleasure, and what pain." Each man must therefore have the right to vote for one who can most accurately represent him in Parliament. Second, the representatives should be elected frequently — annually, Bentham held — so as to be held closely accountable for their work in Parliament. Bentham and his followers added some features to Mill's proposals: abolition of the House of Lords, since it is not truly representative of the people; secret ballot, to ensure free voting and thus more accurate representation; redistricting, to afford people actual rather than virtual representation in Commons.

For rather poor reasons, the Utilitarians were for good government. The democracy they advocated came in time to be adopted in England, and though it was a distinct improvement on the government by a privileged few of days gone by, it never realized Utilitarian expectations. The majority has proved, it, too, can err, it can be as tyrannical and selfish as an aristocratic minority. The Benthamites concluded logically from their deterministic view of man that good machinery of government will make men good and happy simply by operating automatically according to the laws of its — and man's — nature. Stephen can therefore conclude of Mill's essay on government that "he is not less certain that a good constitution will make men virtuous, than was Bentham that he could grind rogues honest by Panopticon." John Stuart Mill offered much better arguments for democracy than either his father or Bentham, but by then (1871) the victory of democracy was already assured.

Religion was one subject on which the Utilitarians felt strongly but dared not talk freely. Suspected for their social and political radicalism, they could not risk their cause by a direct attack on religion. Instead they "contented themselves," as Stephen puts it, "with sapping the fort instead of risking an assault." To avoid scandalizing the servants, they employed code words for religious terms in their discussions at home, using "Juggernaut," for example, to mean "Christianity." Their views on religion were strong. It was, they held, nothing but a sedative to keep people submissive. They insisted that the Established Church of England was a means whereby the sinister interests controlling the government kept people diverted from obtaining happiness on earth by hanging huge slices of pie high in the sky for their rapt contemplation.

Their one direct attack on religion was a little book written by "Philip Beauchamp," a combination of Jeremy Bentham and George Grote. This work, John Stuart Mill points out correctly in his *Autobiography*, "was an examination not of the truth, but of the usefulness of religious belief." Nevertheless, the conclusion was that if religious belief was not useful it must be false. On the Utilitarian standard of pleasure and pain Beauchamp undertakes a devastating rationalistic analysis of the worth of religion. By religion, he tells his reader, he means a belief in the existence of "an Almighty Being, by whom pains and pleasures will be dispensed to mankind during an infinite and future state of existence." Such a belief is purely gratuitous, he insists, since no one can have experienced this afterlife — and there is no other way of knowing about it. Religious belief is good or bad, consequently, according to the amount of pleasure or pain it brings to believers in this life. If it orders men to do what is good and useful, Beauchamp's argument runs, it is unnecessary, for then it merely coincides with human reason and with rational legisla-

tion. It does not even offer additional assurance that these useful
precepts will be obeyed, for its sanction is too remote and too
uncertain to be effective. One who will murder in the face of
the hangman's knot will not flinch before far-off and not very
probable hell fire. If, on the other hand, religion orders men to
do what is not useful, it is on that account vicious. So at best
it is useless; at worst it is vicious.

Beauchamp then proceeds to show that religion causes mankind more pain than pleasure on this earth. The consolations it
offers an afflicted heart are meager, but the dread of eternal
suffering it stirs up in their minds truly causes misery. The picture
of hell is more vivid than the picture of heaven; no one can
really enjoy the prospect of heaven, but the fear of hell can
cause men a lifetime of frightful anguish. The Christian concept
of God is repulsively vicious, Beauchamp argues, for the God of
the Christians is a capricious tyrant who makes all men suffer,
who slays the innocent and rewards the wicked, who makes man
weak and then places him amidst unavoidable pitfalls. Christianity therefore produces all sorts of evils which Beauchamp
catalogues something like this: it demands useless, painful practices, such as fasting, celibacy, self-torture; it suggests terrors
which drive many persons to the verge of insanity; it denies men
the enjoyment of many innocent pleasures; it divides men against
men, condemns innocent persons to social banishment, perverts
morality by substituting capricious standards for the true one
of utility, and finally it arrests intellectual progress.

These strictures against religion are as close as the Utilitarians
ever come to passionate argument, but even here there is the
appearance of vigorous, unflinching reasoning rather than emotional rhetoric. The God against whom they argued was not, as
they seem to have thought, the God of the Established Anglican
Church; it was rather the God of Calvin and Knox to whom James
Mill had been introduced in his studies for the ministry in
Scotland. It was the God whom extremist dissenters called down
upon the Utilitarians for their hedonism; it was therefore the
God this agnostic group could most easily observe as the almighty
Sovereign of English believers.

7

The Utilitarians were a small, unpopular sect in their day. On all sides they were shunned, because of their personalities and because of their doctrines. They were a cold, self-righteous group utterly contemptuous of any benighted fool who differed from their systematically worked out theories. And their ideas were stated bluntly, coldly, unflinchingly. No attempt was made to "sell" them to the English public; they were simply propounded as absolute truth, and anyone who did not take them up was scorned. They were indeed a strange combination of rationalist and puritan. They threw philosophy overboard, but they kept the philosopher's faith in reason; they threw the puritan's God overboard, but they kept the puritan's social virtues. They eulogized labor and the industrial system, they exalted prudence, frugality, and sharp dealing with one's neighbor. And all the while they held to that hedonistic morality which only the aristocrats they despised knew how to practice. They were intellectually convinced that pleasure was the sole good in life, but they were temperamentally incapable of experiencing any pleasure but that of being right.

Utilitarian ideas were even less popular than Utilitarians. For they were dangerous, and dangerous ideas are never popular. They advocated republicanism, which in 1800 was almost as radical as communism was a century later; they held rigidly to such iron-clad economic principles as Malthus' law of population and Ricardo's iron law of wages, and for this they were scouted by aristocrats, Whigs, and socialists alike; they were suspected of atheism, and for this they were feared by all respectable Christians — which included almost everyone else in England. Unpopular as their ideas were, they nevertheless made headway throughout the nineteenth century, partly because of the Utilitarians themselves and partly because of the march of events over which they had no control.

Their influence in the next two generations, Bertrand Russell maintains, was "astonishingly great, considering their complete absence of emotional appeal." It is certainly true that they were prime movers in pushing many a good cause which other parties, notably the Whigs, later took up. Bentham and his associates did more than any other group to convince the Englishman that his laws needed codifying and his penal system overhauling. And all through the nineteenth century, Whig vied with Tory in bringing about these sorely needed reforms. The Benthamites pushed such radical proposals as universal manhood suffrage, vote by ballot, frequent elections, and equable representation — all of which came to be accepted when they were no longer "radical." On the other hand they pushed a *laissez-faire* attitude on the part of the government toward industry and commerce — and in time this too was realized, though with such non-Benthamite compromises as legal limitation of child labor.

More important in the long run than these practical reforms, perhaps, were the attitudes and theories which they helped generate. They played an important role in breaking the English-speaking world away from its philosophical past and putting it on the road of frank pragmatism. The Anglo-Saxon temperament was pragmatically inclined for centuries, it is true, but the Benthamites worked out an intellectual defense for this way of life as the only good way. They were themselves Utilitarian rather than pragmatic, but it is only a short step from the former to the latter. Their Utilitarian case was rested upon man's being inveterately selfish, and thus they furthered that individualism which becomes more and more prominent through each decade of the past century and a half.

Unfortunately, at the very time when the Benthamites were pushing individualism they were freeing the individual of human responsibility for his acts. As rationalists, they insisted that all wrong is the result of intellectual misapprehension, that such things as murder or bank robbery are caused by some human calculating machine getting out of gear and coming out with a wrong answer in its felicific calculus. As environmental determinists, they fell victim to that modern disease of "institutionali-tis" which is still so strongly with us. Good government, good business, good family relationships, good living can be achieved, institutionalists believe, simply and solely by getting the right kind of machinery. No room is left in their minds for the men who operate the machine; it is the machine alone that counts. The blind trust in co-operatives, proportional representation, unicameral legislatures, or the right curriculum in college is a faith that one finds logically held by Utilitarians. And they denied man any faculty not possessed by the machinery of which he was a cog. He was, to them, a mechanism that they had taken apart and studied so expertly that they knew exactly what made him tick.

The Utilitarians were the world's last influential group of rationalists. It is unfortunate that they were so naïve in their trust in reason that they left no proper place for emotion or caprice, for heroism or villany, because their barren brand of rationalism tended to discredit man's very reason. The mechanical robot they thought man to be was an unlovable machine: he was utterly selfish, his wheels were turned by love of pleasure and fear or pain alone. He was an unromantic machine indeed. A world reformed along Benthamite lines and run according to Bentham's standards would be a dreary, dismal place. It would be a loan shark's world, or at best a world where everyone was his own bookie, calculating the odds on every choice and making his every move in perfect accordance with what the odds dictated. Men would move like the planets through the universe — except that by figuring out their own laws of motion they would be self-steering bodies.

James Mill's eldest son, honest John Stuart, saw how barren and unsavory — and incorrect — Jeremy Bentham's naïve rationalism was. He tried to wed it to the feeling he found deep inside of man by substituting a "higher utility" for Bentham's and his father's simple utilitarianism. He tried to modify Benthamite psychology, morality, political science, and economics — but his attempt was vain. The flood of German voluntarism and subjectivism engendered by Kant, Fichte, Hegel, and their associates engulfed poor John Stuart and cut short his strong influence in England. Even more ironic and more pathetic, from the younger Mill's point of view, was the rise of two movements that came logically from his father's own doctrines — movements usually associated with the names of Charles Darwin and Karl Marx.

Socialism was an infant when Utilitarianism was putting on long pants for the first time. But the baby dared to ask for his share of the pie which he thought his big brother was unjustly keeping all to himself. William Thompson of Cork, for example, argued against the Benthamites that if Ricardo's theory of value were true, laborers were being cheated of their just wages. And Thomas Hodgskin answered Ricardo's famous work with *Labour Defended Against the Claims of Capital,* in which he argued logically that if labor creates all value, then all the returns of production should go to the workingman, that what the landowner and entrepreneur and capitalist withhold is robbery.

Darwinism, like socialism, derives logically from Utilitarian doctrine. As a matter of historic fact, Darwin's theory on the survival of the fittest by natural selection was suggested to the famous biologist from his accidental reading of Malthus' *Essay on Population.* If population is always pressing against the food supply, it follows that people are constantly struggling with each other for food and for survival. What are the laws determining who will get the food and survive? Darwin proposed to discover why and how some survive while others do not. And Darwin's followers worked out a theory of individual and class competition that was the Utilitarian theory of business competition with no holds barred. The Benthamites are therefore important as makers of the modern mind, both for their own contributions to modern mentality and for occupying a transitional position, giving way logically to socialism on the one hand and Darwinism on the other.

X

DARWIN

STRUGGLE FOR SURVIVAL

THE direct influence of the Benthamites was cut short by changes in the temper and the tempo of Western life, changes which they ignored. Life quickened in the nineteenth century as steam and electricity were applied to industry, and within a few years the face of civilization was changed as it had not been changed before within centuries. Anyone with even a short memory could see how change was the only constant factor in life, how man was progressing year by year, growing wealthier, healthier, and more powerful as he conquered nature for the first time since he emerged from the cave. Benthamites did not take this newly intensified element of change into consideration. Their thought was posited of a static world where institutions and customs would remain as unchanged as man himself. Because there was no room in their theories for radical alterations in society, or man's way of thinking, their thought was soon discarded — as boy's clothes are thrown aside when the gangling fourteen-year-old suddenly sprouts up.

Rapid change is taken for granted today, with last year's model in hats or automobiles, bombs or airplanes considered antique. It was not so in the middle of the nineteenth century. Things were changing more rapidly year by year, it is true, but habits of thought changed almost as slowly as ever. Bach's restrained music of the eighteenth century, for example, had given way to Beethoven's somewhat looser compositions of the early nineteenth; and Beethoven in turn gave way to noisy Wagner in the middle of the century. Only a small group of thinkers in Europe, however, had formulated their thought in terms of change. Hegel was the chief of these, and his dialectic, whereby everything was conceived in terms of movement, was a philosophical explanation of an older idea man had long cherished: that he was progressing toward a better life, that each generation was further advanced than its predecessor. Hegel explained all history in terms of the Divine Idea unfolding itself through history in accordance with certain laws of movement Hegel had discovered.

Such a philosophy suited the changing temper of the times, but it was abstruse, even for philosophy, and only the small group known as the Young Hegelians — mostly Germans — took to it at first. Englishmen who were told that Napoleon was the Divine Idea on horseback, as Hegel claimed, understandably shrugged their shoulders and turned to find another use for the steam engine. Not even Frenchmen could take to the dialectic. They too would wag their heads when told that Prussia was the most perfect self-realization of God on earth in Hegel's day. So although Hegel had the right tune for the time, he failed to hit the right key. It remained for Charles Darwin to strike the note that awakened immediate response in all minds later in the nineteenth century.

Darwin's importance is therefore out of all proportion to his ability, his profundity, or his originality. He is like the new organ which, by playing a certain note, broke all the windows in the church and in the neighborhood by starting sympathetic vibrations in them. For Darwin was neither a great mind nor a powerful writer. Nor does he even stand among the ten or twenty greatest scientists of the world. He simply happened to say what the age wanted to hear, and he said it in terms that pleased the age's ear. Darwin spoke of struggle for existence, survival of the fittest, competition for world resources, rapid increase of population, and all those other things the nineteenth century believed in so firmly. He mirrored the age's mentality perfectly, saying what was already believed, but putting it all together in a single pattern under a Master Idea — survival of the fittest through natural selection. This is the secret of Darwin's popularity. This is why he became a maker of the modern mind when many greater thinkers failed.

Hegel was a philosopher who claimed that the ultimate reality in history is the Idea. The nineteenth century, however, was indifferent to philosophy of any kind, and it was positively hostile to a philosophy that tried to resolve dollars and wheat, factories and ships into an Idea, whether it be labeled divine or not. Darwin, on the other hand, spoke in scientific language about things one could see and touch — and in that age who dared to doubt Science? Who dared argue with a man who told you, in effect, to go out into your garden or your barn to do as he had done, and see if his results would not be yours? Darwin backed up what he had to say about the struggle for existence with an amazing array of facts, showing how vegetables, bugs, little animals and big, all fought for the limited supply of food. He went further and, in the same scientific language and with the same mass of evidence, sought to show how lowly animals varied from time to time, how these variations accumulated until varieties melted into species, and how out of it all came new forms of life — until finally he included man himself. Moreover, he argued, if man had come so far by means of struggle and survival of the fittest, how much higher on the ladder of progress could he not climb? There seemed no limit, according to Darwin's theory, and this was just what these people of the nineteenth century wanted to hear. Darwin had apparently proved their fundamental assumptions correct, and apparently had shown that their wildest dreams for the future were scientifically established great expectations.

Jacques Barzun therefore claims that "Darwin may be said with a slight exaggeration to have found the right wrong idea for cementing together in the minds of his contemporaries the elements of doctrine which had repeatedly been proposed along separate lines of thought." This is why Darwin's contemporaries looked upon him as another Newton, England's second gift to the scientific world. Alfred Wallace, who discovered the key idea of the theory of natural selection independently of Darwin, called him "the Newton of Natural History." Darwin's "bulldog," Thomas Huxley, drove this idea home by comparing the men personally, by putting the *Origin of Species* alongside the *Principia* in importance and in grandeur. The English people prided themselves on Darwin as they had on Newton. They rewarded him, like Newton, in his own lifetime: they made him a Fellow of the Royal Society and an honorary member of the Royal Society of Edinburgh; they bestowed the Copley Medal on him in 1864; they buried him in Westminster Abbey with England's most distinguished gentlemen looking on.

Like Newton, Darwin was significant for one book, *The Origin of Species,* although he wrote many other things. In this one book Darwin did for the biological sciences what Newton had done for physics in the *Principia* — though with less originality and far less brilliance. He arranged in a systematic pattern what hundreds of predecessors had discovered, and it all made new sense in the light of a Master Idea: survival of the fittest in the struggle for existence because of the process of natural selection. This prompted Huxley to assert that from Aristotle's time to his own "there is nothing comparable to the *Origin of Species,* as a connected survey of the phenomena of life permeated and vivified by a central idea."

Finally, Darwin's key idea was seized upon, as Newton's had been, and applied to every field of thought. Darwin's name was used to justify war as a natural form of struggle for survival among nations. It was used to justify the Marxian idea of class struggle as the inevitable, natural relationship between economic groups. It was used to justify the most ruthless kind of capitalistic competition as good for mankind, since the fittest producers survive for the benefit of all. It was used to justify the persecution of some races by others, the refusal of poor relief to the less aggressive members of society, the rule of the weak by the strong few. All these things were excused in Darwin's name because he had struck the note which appealed to all from his day till our own. This has been an age of struggle and of competition — which is the basic theme running through Darwin's thought.

1

In 1819, when Charles Darwin was ten years old, or even in 1830, when he was twenty-one, Lloyds of London would have given any betting Englishman long odds that Dr. Robert Darwin's second son would never amount to anything. For throughout his boyhood and his youth Charles gave promise of being only an insignificant member of a fairly prominent English family. His grandfather, Dr. Erasmus Darwin, had made a name for himself as a physician, a naturalist, and an author. His father was Shrewsbury's leading doctor, an imposing man who was respected by his neighbors and was influential in his community.

For a long time young Charles remained in the shadow of his grandfather, who had been a genius in a mild way, of his domineering father, and finally of his brilliant brother, Erasmus. Charles never met his grandfather, but the latter's fame lingered on, and Charles tried to be a loyal Darwin by reading the doctor's *Zoonomia* — he should have found out about evolution as expressed in that work. Charles's father, on the other hand, was very much in evidence throughout his son's youth and into his early manhood. Doctor Robert was called "the Tide" by his children, because when he rolled his giant frame into the living room he drowned out the conversation and even the unvoiced opinions of everyone present. The doctor expected Erasmus to carry on the family profession and to distinguish himself as his namesake had done. But of Charles not much was expected, for his father complained that he "cared for nothing but shooting, dogs, and rat-catching." Robert tried nevertheless to make a physician of his second son, and, when that failed, to educate him for the ministry.

Inconspicuous and unpromising a lad though he was, Charles did not find his home life at all unhappy. Born on the same day as Abraham Lincoln, Charles Darwin grew up in entirely different circumstances from the great American's. His family occupied one of the best, most spacious homes in the community. Whatever money could buy — food and books, clothing and domestic help — was provided in abundance. Here the six Darwin children grew up in an intimate, closely knit family. Charles tells us in pre-Freudian fashion that the first three years of a person's life are the most important, for then he possesses "a virgin brain adapted to receive impressions." But he cannot tell us much of his early impressions; he remembered even his mother only vaguely, though he was eight years old when she died.

His relatives and acquaintances considered Charles a rather sluggish boy. He had the imagination of an average child, however, if we can judge by the fictions he invented to attract attention to himself. Biographers note only one thing about him which might seem unusual: his bug-collecting habits. But even this is not so unusual as his biographers have made it. He lived in a bug-collecting age, and he came from a bug-collecting family. They all did it. So Charles did it too. This is the secret of understanding Charles Darwin. He grew up doing what others did, believing what others believed, conforming to the accepted pattern without criticism, almost without thinking.

He was therefore a commonplace lad at home. At school he was the same. He attended classes at the Shrewsbury Grammar School from his tenth year until his eighteenth. Headmaster Samuel Butler thought him a little fool and repeatedly told him so. The boy simply remained indifferent to the classical curriculum then followed. He was bad at spelling, weak in languages (as he remained till the end of his life), poor at composition, terrible at versifying. But Charles was not a simpleton. Even as a boy he showed that when his interest could be aroused he was far from stupid. In this sense should we understand his statement in later life that his best early education was participating in his brother's experiments in the tool shed.

The simple fact is that both Charles's father and Butler lacked understanding. Because the boy did not do well in school they thought him stupid. By the time Charles was eighteen, his father was sure that he would grow up to disgrace the family. So Charles was taken out of the local school and sent off to Edinburgh with his brother, Erasmus. There he was to study medicine, his father had decided, and because Charles was essentially an accepter he entered upon his medical studies without protest. He tells us how he found the lectures "intolerably dull," and how he had no stomach for the dissecting room. Medical studies simply failed to interest Charles's intellect or appeal to his temperament.

At Edinburgh, as at school in Shrewsbury, Charles completely wasted his time, if we can believe what he tells us in his *Life and Letters.* He made certain acquaintances, however, who apparently influenced his interests at this time. One of these was Robert Edmund Grant, a young zoologist who praised Lamarck's evolutionary views in conversations with Darwin in 1826. It was Grant who invited him to join the Plinian Society, where he heard the eccentric Audubon tell all about the American turkey-buzzard.

Two years at Edinburgh convinced Darwin that he was not meant to be a doctor. As a matter of fact, at this time he apparently did not want to be anything in particular. So his father again made a decision. Charles was to become a clergyman. Without protest, he therefore went to Cambridge in 1828 to begin his theological studies. The three years he spent there, he states, were "wasted, as far as the academical studies were concerned, as completely as at Edinburgh and at school"; but he goes on to admit that they were "the most joyful in my happy life, for I was then in excellent health, and almost always in high spirits." This was just what his father feared, for Charles had fallen in with the sporting set at Cambridge to lead an aimless life of hunting and of gathering in fellows' rooms.

Darwin's set was much given to bug hunting, and Darwin was soon seized with the popular undergraduate mania of collecting beetles. There was nothing scientific to this hobby, however, for all the undergraduates cared about in their bug-hunting competition were number and variety of specimens. At Cambridge, Darwin came under the influence of the personable young John Henslow, who, although he lectured in botany, tried to interest Charles in geology. He put Sir Charles Lyell's recently published *Principles of Geology* in his hands and introduced him to Adam Sedgwick, the professor of geology at Cambridge. Darwin liked both the man and the subject, for it aroused his curiosity about the unknown — one of the basic traits of Darwin's mind. About this time he wrote to a friend: "It strikes me that all our knowledge about the structure of our earth is very much like what an old hen would know of a hundred-acre field, in a corner of which she is scratching." Darwin was curious to know what the whole field was like, and he was willing to scratch to find out.

But his father had decided he was to become a clergyman. So he worked without interest at his theological classes until the beginning of 1831, when he passed his examinations for the degree. At this point in his life, when Charles Darwin was twenty-two, it seemed that he was destined to be a parson in some inconspicuous rural parish. It seemed, too, that he would be the typical nineteenth-century English clergyman whose hobby took up more time and interest than his official duties as minister. It seemed, finally, that he would continue to putter around with rocks and bugs, go on walking trips to hunt new specimens, write occasionally to men like Henslow and Sedgwick, read their books as they appeared, and spend his vacations at scientific meetings.

A letter from Henslow, however, changed the whole course of Darwin's life. In the summer of 1831, Henslow wrote to tell him that Captain Fitzroy wanted a young naturalist to accompany him on an expedition into the southern seas. Henslow went on to say that he would recommend Charles for the position if he were willing to take the two-year trip. Charles was told by his father to refuse the offer. So he did. But the next day his Uncle Jos talked Robert into changing his mind, and young Darwin scribbled off a second letter informing Henslow that he would apply for the position after all.

Once or twice in the next few days Charles decided to abandon his quest for the position, but at Henslow's insistence he finally arrived in London for an interview with the formidable Captain Fitzroy. Charles liked the captain at once, but Fitzroy, who was an amateur physiognomist, did not like Darwin's nose, nor did he think his face revealed sufficient energy and determination for the job. He tried to discourage the young naturalist, but in successive interviews when Charles persisted in his desire to sail on the *Beagle* Fitzroy decided to accept him for the position. So in the last month of 1831 Charles Darwin prepared for a two-year voyage that was to stretch out to five years and profoundly affect his remaining life.

Sailing on the *Beagle* was the making of Charles Darwin. He sailed a bug collector and he returned a naturalist. For his five years of scientific work on the *Beagle* made him not only collect specimens but also study them and classify them. Five years on board ship, moreover, was just what Darwin needed to develop self-reliance and the ability to make his own decisions. It is not too much to say that the trip changed this father's son into a mature man.

2

More legends have collected in sixty years around Darwin than around any other maker of the modern mind. One of them pictures Darwin as the ideal man of science, the humble, patient student who followed the trail of factual evidence to its inescapable conclusion, and then resolutely and fearlessly announced his findings to a hostile world. This picture is largely the creation of Thomas Huxley, who devoted the greater part of an energetic, vociferous lifetime to popularizing Darwin's ideas. "The more one knew of him," Huxley claims, "the more he seemed the incorporated ideal of a man of science."

It is true that Darwin was an able scientist. Especially is it true that he had real devotion for the work. Darwin states the bald truth when he says, "my chief enjoyment and sole employment throughout life has been scientific work." Equally important with his love for science was Darwin's intellectual curiosity. He always felt the need to understand natural phenomena which others took for granted, to establish order over a whole field of facts by formulating a law to explain them all and establish their interrelations. To this curiosity was added the power to stay with a subject patiently and persistently until it seemed thoroughly explored. Darwin possessed one more quality making for a scientific bent of mind: he was an acute observer who managed to see what others overlooked. This, again, was a quality he appreciated in himself, for he admits that he was "superior to the common run of men in noticing things which easily escape attention."

These are qualities necessary for a man of science. But by themselves they do not make for genius. To them must be added scientific imagination and a speculative ability always under tight control. Imagination and speculative ability Darwin possessed in too full a measure. He was conscious both of possessing this ability and of its vital importance in the making of a scientist.

"I am a firm believer," he wrote late in life, "that without speculation there is no good and original observation. . . . I can have no
doubt that speculative men, with a curb on, make far the best
observers." Darwin knew that the scientist cannot give free reign
to his imagination, as the poet can, and he realized that on this
point he was constantly tempted to violate the sacred canons of
science. Because, he confesses, "a number of isolated facts soon
become uninteresting, the habit of comparison leads to generalization. . . . Hence arises, as I have found to my cost, a constant
tendency to fill up the wide gaps of knowledge by inaccurate and
superficial hypotheses."

Darwin's tendency to generalize drove him to conclusions not
warranted by his factual evidence. There is no doubt that when
once he arrived at his conclusion he amassed such facts as supported the conclusion and looked on everything not supporting
it as an "obstacle" to be overcome. His theory of natural selection,
as we shall see, was essentially completed by 1838; for the next
twenty years Darwin collected facts to prove it. This tendency
led him to adopt some wildly erroneous theories, such as his idea
of "pangenesis," which he considered second in importance to
natural selection itself. It is more the idea of a poet than of a
scientist, that "every unit or cell of the body throws off gemmules
or undeveloped atoms, which are transmitted to the offspring of
both sexes, and are multiplied by self-division," which no one
takes seriously today. Darwin was a great scientist, but his
tendency toward hasty generalization denies him the appelation,
"Ideal Man of Science," given to him by Huxley — as Darwin
himself would have had the good sense to admit.

Huxley was not content with making Darwin merely an ideal
scientist. He went on to tell readers that, "one could not converse
with Darwin without being reminded of Socrates." Such a
statement could never have come from Darwin, for though he
considered himself a competent scientist, he insisted strongly
that he "had not a metaphysical head." "I have no great quickness
of apprehension or wit," Darwin wrote of himself accurately.
"My power to follow a long and purely abstract train of thought
is very limited; and therefore I could never have succeeded
with metaphysics or mathematics." It is for this reason that
Darwin honestly confesses that, "my theology is a simple

muddle. . . . The more I think the more bewildered I become."

Huxley and his associates, then, used as much fiction as truth in weaving the legend of Darwin's mental powers. He was not a profound thinker; in the realm of abstract thought he simply lost himself in confusion. "Facts compel me," he says without excessive modesty, "to conclude that my brain was never formed for much thinking." His strength of mind lay not in reasoning power but in those more pedestrian qualities of accurate observation, patient reflection, industry in collecting massive quantities of evidence, and ability to arrange it all systematically so as to arrive at general conclusions. His weakness lay principally in his quickness to generalize, which, combined with the inability to reason abstractly, sometimes led him to absurd conclusions — and always left him absolutely helpless outside his chosen field of natural history.

That part of the Darwinian legend which has him a Galahad of the intellect, searching nobly for the truth and defending her against obscurantists, has recently come under fire — perhaps unfairly to Darwin. It is now commonly asserted that Darwin was downright dishonest in his treatment of predecessors and contemporaries who prepared the way for his famous theories, and certainly the way he dismisses those who had written on evolution before the publication of the *Origin* seems to justify the attack. There is no doubt, for example, that his grandfather had stated almost every theory found in the *Origin* before Charles was born, but the latter dismisses Erasmus with a curt complaint about "the proportion of speculation being so large to the facts given." In similar fashion he referred disdainfully to Lamarck and to the others whose writing made Darwin's world ready to acclaim the *Origin*. Contentious Samuel Butler demanded to know why Darwin had not credited his predecessors, and when no satisfactory explanation was offered the blunt old critic wrote his *Evolution Old and New* to take credit and honor from Darwin and to pass it back to such men as Buffon, Erasmus Darwin, and Lamarck, where Butler thought it belonged.

One need not consider Darwin dishonest, however, to account for the slighting way he treated his scientific predecessors. It is only necessary to appreciate this unusual contradiction in the man: although he was apparently isolated from his age, actually he soaked up its attitudes, its speculations, its very atmosphere without knowing it. Darwin was essentially spongelike, as we have seen, which accounts not only for his success but also for his not knowing the source of his ideas. It is a fact that he had read and reread his grandfather's *Zoonomia* only to lay it down believing he had got nothing from it. He had either read or heard of Lamarck's views, and he had discussed the alteration of species with scientist friends. Evolution was in the air, and Darwin soaked it in. He probably never realized how spongelike, how accepting he was, so he could have been honest with himself in believing that his ideas were original.

As a man, Darwin was lovable, gentle, simple. He was very much the family man, a fond father, a loving husband, solicitous for the welfare of each member of his family. In this respect, as in all others, he conformed perfectly to the accepted Victorian pattern of his age. He was properly modest in demeanor, thoroughly industrious in pursuing his work. His diversions were those of a simple man: walking, puttering in the garden, entertaining friends, going on vacations with the family, reading a great deal of light fiction. Lewis Carroll and Mark Twain delighted him, and he seems to have enjoyed any sentimental novel where virtue triumphed over vice and all characters eased gracefully off the last page made happy by the author. If he could have had his way, he proclaimed rather vehemently, he would have had a law passed requiring a happy ending for every novel. As his appetite for fiction suggests, Darwin was a timorous soul who lived in continual fear of some dreadful happening. For some time he feared that France and England would go to war, whereupon, he thought, Napoleon III would cross the Channel and march toward London by way of the Darwin home at Downe. The discovery of gold in California, again, threw him into panic because he thought that inflation resulting from an increase of the world's gold supply would make his fixed income worthless. These and other fears preyed upon Darwin while he was studying barnacles or conducting experiments with his pigeons.

Physically, Darwin was an imposing man. He was tall, broad, well built, and in his youth he exhibited a liking for and an ability at athletics. But after his return from the *Beagle* trip he developed a mysterious stomach disorder from which he suffered for the rest of his life, so that he complained he "never knew one day of the health of ordinary men." The cause of his trouble remains undiagnosed, but the fact that it hampered his activity in one way, while helping it another, must be remembered to understand Darwin's persistent, though procrastinating, accomplishments. There were long stretches of time when he could not work at all. Usually, however, he was able to work three or four hours a day. The rest of the time he lay around, rested or studied, or had his wife, Emma, read to him. Darwin could never have earned a living, but his illness did not prevent him from turning out an amazing quantity of writing.

Fortunately, Darwin never had to work for a living. The directory at Downe classified him as a "farmer" by profession, but the only farming he did was either experimenting with plants, or raising flowers and vegetables as a hobby. He lived from an income settled on him by his father, so his time was free entirely for his studies and his writing. He did not teach, nor did he lecture, as so many of his contemporaries did. He lived his life within his home, going away only occasionally for a change of scenery or, in his earlier years, to attend various scientific meetings. His life at home followed a clocklike routine. Every day he rose early, took a walk, ate breakfast alone, and worked from about eight till nine-thirty. Then he took an hour's rest, sometimes following this with another hour's work before he went for a second walk. After lunch he read the papers, had Emma read to him, took a nap, then walked again before supper. Sometimes, if he felt particularly well, he worked another hour before supper. After the evening meal he played backgammon with Emma, had her read a novel to him, or listened to her play the piano. Promptly at ten-thirty he went to bed.

This routine was modified slightly in Darwin's later years, as his health improved, to accommodate his many famous guests. Darwin's list of friends and acquaintances includes most of the famous names of nineteenth-century English history. As a student he had listened to Audubon and Sir Walter Scott; as a young man he had been helped by persons like Sedgwick and Lyell; as a famous naturalist he was host to such men as Gladstone, Morely, Lord Playfair, Carlyle, and Butler; at various times he associated with such persons as Ruskin and Mark Twain. His disciples included such prominent people as Spencer and Huxley, Weismann and Haekel, Asa Gray and Tyndall.

Darwin's unvarying routine, combined with his devotion to science alone, tended to dehumanize him, as he realized later in life. He had studied the classics and theology in preparation for taking orders in the Anglican Church. But he put off settling down to pastoral work, first for five years on the *Beagle,* then for a few months to classify his specimens and write up his *Journal,* a period which stretched into years. As other more immediate tasks presented themselves, Darwin never got around to becoming a clergyman. It is difficult to say just when and where he gave up the idea. Perhaps Darwin himself never knew.

As it was with his vocation, so it was with his faith. Disbelief in the Old Testament, then in the miracles of the New Testament, then in Christianity itself, crept over him so gradually that he accepted his eventual agnosticism without pain or protest, not knowing precisely when he had arrived at that position. So it was with his aesthetic tastes, as he gradually lost his appetite for poetry, music, and painting. His mind had become nothing, he admitted, but "a kind of machine for grinding general laws out of large collections of facts." He therefore concluded: "If I had to live my life again, I would have made a rule to read some poetry and listen to some music at least once every week; for perhaps the parts of my brain now atrophied would thus have been kept active through use. The loss of these tastes is a loss of happiness, and may possibly be injurious to the intellect, and more probably to the moral character, by enfeebling part of our nature." This passage is typical of Darwin. Its sentiment and its self-judgment are sound; its basic assumption, on the other hand, is a gratuitous materialistic belief that certain brain tissues atrophy from not recording music occasionally, that human shortcomings are basically mechanical defects in the organism.

3

Darwin is popularly, though mistakenly, thought of as inventor or discoverer of evolution. He neither discovered it nor proved it. As a matter of fact, he did not even use the word "evolution" in the first edition of the *Origin*. He did two things for evolution: first, he sought to amass evidence to support the general evolutionary theory, which had been propounded in various ways by any number of men before him; second, and most important, he offered a formula to show how evolution could have proceeded by centering his observations around the central fact of natural selection. Evolution sneaks into the *Origin* by the back door, for Darwin's concern was only to account for the origin of individual species by means of natural selection. That is why he originally planned to call the book *Natural Selection,* and only reluctantly did he allow the publisher to change the title.

By the time Darwin knew he wanted to write his Great Work, evolution was in the air — as much as gravity was in the air when Newton wrote the *Principia*. Barzun sums this point up well: "The spirit of evolution hovered over the cradle of the new century. So far it was not tied to any underlying philosophy. It followed its subject matter: mechanical action in astronomy and geology; unconscious will and purpose, or use and disuse in biology; climate and the conscious aims of men in the social progress revealed by history." Hegel had promoted an evolutionary mentality in philosophy and logic, Comte had furthered it with his historical and pseudoscientific theories of progress.

There were any number of works in the more specific field of organic evolution before Darwin started on the *Origin*. Bacon, Descartes, Leibniz, Kant, Lessing, Herder, Shelling had all looked at evolution as a possibility. Buffon, however, is the first great naturalist who can be classed among modern evolutionists. He seems to have glimpsed the importance of the struggle for existence in getting rid of the less fit, but his stress was on environment as the agent producing change in animal species. Strictly speaking, Lamarck and Erasmus Darwin were the first evolutionists to work out a scheme whereby all species evolved from a single origin through variation, the inheritance of acquired characteristics, and survival of some varieties in the struggle for existence.

Both Lamarck and the elder Darwin had stressed the role of environment in changing habit, and of altered habits in changing the creature. Lamarck therefore attributed an important place to the use or disuse of particular organs to account for their developing or disappearing from the species' bodily organization. Closer to Darwin in point of time were Englishmen who stressed the element of natural selection rather than use and disuse in causing variation in creatures. W. E. Wells had spoken of natural selection in a paper read to the Royal Society in 1813, and in 1831 Patrick Mathew had written of it. So the elements were all there. It remained for Darwin to play the role of Newton for the biological sciences, to put all the elements together, arrange them around a master idea, and thus bring light into the comparative darkness where men were groping toward what he was to say so clearly.

The evolution of the idea of evolution in Darwin's own mind is an interesting story. He had sailed on the *Beagle* a convinced creationist. Nor did he change his mind about evolution while aboard ship, though he later wrote that "vague doubts occasionally flitted across my mind" as he read Lyell's *Principles of Geology* or turned over new specimens. These vague doubts became stronger in the next few years as he studied his specimens and the notebooks which he had written aboard the *Beagle* and was now preparing for publication. As he arranged his collection of bones he observed how extinct species were similar to existing ones, while the writing of his *Journal* clarified his thought on the problems to be faced by either the evolutionist or the creationist. But his best biographer, Geoffrey West, shows that he approached no closer than this to the subject of evolution. "Clearly," West observes, "he was at this point picking at the problem rather than facing it."

He finished his *Journal* in the summer of 1837, however, and immediately started his first notebook on the transmutation of species. By the following February his notebook was full of pertinent observations, and Darwin had convinced himself that species evolved from a few parent forms of organic life. How to account for the changes that took place therefore became his task. By this time he had discovered his point of attack: variation among domestic creatures, through controlled breeding, was apparent enough. His immediate problem was to find an equivalent in nature for this human selection and preservation of the better varieties.

Darwin was convinced that he was on the threshold of a discovery comparable to Newton's. He conceived it as his life's work, his great contribution to the fund of human knowledge. But first he had some other things to get out of the way, chiefly his geological discoveries made while on the *Beagle*. Toward the end of 1838, however, he stumbled by pure chance upon the key to the whole problem of how species change. He was reading Malthus for diversion one day when he suddenly realized that here in the *Essay on Population* was the agent of natural selection he had been seeking. The necessary result of unrestrained multiplication among any species would obviously be competition for the means of existence. What Malthus had said of man was obviously true of plants and animals as well. The success of one competitor, among animals and plants as well as among men, meant the failure of others — and therefore their extinction. So by using Malthus he could show how species became extinct, but not how they originated. Darwin concluded, however, that the latter was only the reverse of the former, when variation is taken into account. "Under these circumstances [of struggle for existence]," he tells us, "favorable variations would tend to be preserved, and unfavorable ones to be destroyed. The result of this would be the formation of new species."

So by the end of 1838 Darwin had arrived at all his fundamental theories. Twenty years were to elapse, however, before they were published, twenty years which Darwin seemed to dawdle away, procrastinating for years over geological studies, then for years more over his work on barnacles. In these years, nevertheless, and from these apparently unrelated studies he gathered evidence to support his thesis of natural selection. In 1842 he completed his first draft of ideas for the *Origin*, a paper running slightly over thirty manuscript pages. In it were all the ideas to be found seventeen years later in the published work, and they were arranged on the same general plan. His first point was that variation occurs within species under domestication. Then he showed how similar variation occurs among wild species because of geological changes. Next he invoked Malthus to show a struggle for existence among creatures bringing about a "natural selection" more vigorous than man's in breeding animals. He therefore concluded: "Admit selection under subsistence pressure and change of environment, and — could we set a limit to variations?"

A second draft written in 1844 was extended to 189 pages, although it contained no new ideas. Darwin thought this draft important enough to make special arrangements for its publication in case he should die before finishing the Great Work. Two years later he proposed getting to work seriously on the subject, which he hoped to have ready for publication within five years. But for ten more years other matters, such as writing on volcanoes, occupied him. In 1855, Alfred Wallace wrote an article, "On the Law Which Has Regulated the Introduction of New Species," which was so similar to Darwin's own views that Lyell urged the latter to publish at least a sketch of his theory to protect his claim to priority. Darwin agreed to do so in "a very *thin* little volume."

He began writing this "little volume" in the summer of 1856, but he was so fully convinced that this was *the* book of his lifetime that he found himself marshaling more and more evidence to support his views. So again publication was put off. This sort of thing would probably have gone on interminably had Wallace not sent him the manuscript of an article, "On the Tendency of Varieties to Depart Indefinitely from the Original Type." With the manuscript Wallace sent a note explaining that he thought his idea was new, and that he hoped it would provide Darwin with the missing link in the work he was projecting. Darwin, terribly agitated, wrote to Lyell: "I never saw a more striking coincidence; if Wallace had my MSS. sketch written out in 1842, he could not have made a better short abstract."

By mutual agreement, Wallace's essay and Darwin's sketch of 1844 were read at a meeting of the Linnean Society by its secretary on July 1, 1858, and in this way the theory of natural selection was announced to the world. By October of 1858, Darwin's manuscript had grown into a small volume, and by the end of the year it had become a five hundred page book which was to be entitled *An Abstract of an Essay on the Origin of Species and Varieties through Natural Selection*. On Lyell's recommendation John Murray had agreed to publish Darwin's work sight unseen, but when the manuscript arrived its size and its argument aroused serious misgivings on Murray's part.

The publisher was sure the work was too long and uninteresting; he was convinced, moreover, that its central thesis was absurd. So he suggested that Darwin rewrite the manuscript, confining himself to his observations on pigeons, for "everybody is interested in pigeons." Darwin refused, of course, and Murray proceeded with the original manuscript. On November 24, 1859, the long delayed *Origin of Species* appeared; the entire edition of 1250 copies was sold at Murray's annual book sale — and Darwin was standing on the threshold of fame.

4

Significantly, its full title is *The Origin of Species by Means of Natural Selection, or the Preservation of Favored Races in the Struggle for Life*. "This whole volume," Darwin says in his concluding chapter, "is one long argument," a point overlooked by those who consider Darwin the ideal man of science. In it he amasses circumstantial evidence in favor of evolution, but he does not present any positive proof that the theory is true. It is a book which need not be read to be talked about. It need not even be read from cover to cover to be understood and appreciated, for the whole argument is presented in a masterful summary in the last chapter. One need only to read the first few chapters and the last, dipping occasionally into the others to see what kind of evidence Darwin adduces to support his general theories.

The first five chapters contain the fundamentals of Darwin's theory. The next four discuss possible objections in his theory; chapters ten to thirteen deal with geology, the geographic distribution of plants and animals, classification, morphology, and embryology in the light of the fundamental theories presented in the first five chapters; the fourteenth chapter is a recapitulation of the argument, where Darwin discards the boots of plodding science to put on poet's wings for a majestic, sweeping flight into the rarefied atmosphere of pure literature.

"It is interesting to contemplate a tangled bank," he concludes, "clothed with many plants of many kinds, with birds singing on the bushes, with various insects flitting about, and with worms crawling through the damp earth, and to reflect that these elaborately constructed forms, so different from each other, and dependent upon each other in so complex a manner, have all been produced by laws acting around us. These laws, taken in the largest sense, being Growth with Reproduction; Inheritance which is almost implied by reproduction; Variability from the indirect and direct action of the conditions of life, and from use and disuse: A Ratio of Increase so high as to lead to a Struggle for Life, and as a consequence to Natural Selection, entailing Divergence of Character and the Extinction of less-improved forms. Thus, from the war of nature, from famine and death, the most exalted object which we are capable of conceiving, namely, the production of the higher animals, directly follows. There is grandeur in this view of life, with its several powers, having been originally breathed by the Creator into a few forms or into one; and what, whilst this planet has gone cycling on according to the fixed law of gravity, from so simple a beginning endless forms most beautiful and most wonderful have been, and are being evolved."

The book is imposing. Its very size is enough to convince many readers. The fact that Darwin raised every possible objection, some of which he could not answer, convinces many others of his objectivity. The mass of evidence from the geological record, from domestic experiments, from geography and from embryology, bears down upon the average reader to crush his resistance as the weight of the sea crushes the life out of a man pulled to the floor of the ocean. But Darwin was right in saying that it is one long argument. It is an argument in favor of the thesis stated by the title, an argument supported by five hundred pages of detailed evidence Darwin had accumulated over the space of almost thirty years. The *Origin* was a powerful book because it was an abstract of a greater, more detailed work yet to come, because it seemed to be so objective, because it was Science speaking — and Science was infallible, was indeed divine in Darwin's day.

Darwin approaches the proof of his thesis logically, step by step, handling one point at a time. His first step is to prove that "under domestication we see much variability." He notes three principal points about variation under domestication: (1) it is large in amount; (2) it is inherited; (3) it is not caused by man.

Step two is to apply these conclusions to species in the state of nature. "There is no reason why the principles which have acted so efficiently under domestication should not have acted under nature," where, he therefore concludes, variation also occurs. This brings us to the third step: struggle for existence. "A struggle for existence inevitably follows from the high rate at which all organic beings tend to increase. . . . As more individuals are produced than can possibly survive, there must in every case be a struggle for existence, either one individual with another of the same species, or with the individuals of distinct species, or with the physical conditions of life. . . . There is no exception to the rule that every organic being naturally increases at so high a rate, that, if not destroyed, the earth would soon be covered by the progeny of a single pair."

From this comes the fourth and crucial step — Darwin's distinct contribution to the theory of evolution. In the struggle for existence, some survive and some fall by the wayside. What determines which will survive and which will not? Darwin answered this question by showing how alterations in the organism occur from time to time, and how some of these alterations enable the organism to adapt itself more perfectly to its environment. These can be called "favorable variations." A white rabbit, for example, will be better adapted for survival in snowy regions than his brown brother — so in time the brown rabbits will all be exterminated by predatory animals, whereas the white rabbits will have escaped detection and will go on living and reproducing. Or some parent animal of the present giraffe had a long-necked offspring one day who was better equipped to eat top leaves from the trees, so he survived drought years when his shorter-necked brethren perished. His progeny, of course, inherited this favorable variation, and so the giraffe survived as a long-necked animal. What caused the "favorable" variation — the white rabbit or the long neck — was purely a matter of chance.

Thus the fittest survive. And the agency determining their survival is called Natural Selection. In later editions of the *Origin* Darwin gave an increasingly large part to such other agencies as use and disuse, and the direct action of environment, but he always insisted that the dominant role was played by natural selection. These variations, each one slight in itself, add up until there is sufficient change to call the altered animal or plant a new species. Thus the origin of species is explained. And this was all Darwin sought to explain, for he did not deal with the origin of *life*, as is popularly believed, but rather with the origin and extinction of different *forms of life* called species.

5

Like Newton, Darwin is a man of one book, though like Newton he wrote many. None of his other works, except perhaps *The Descent of Man*, proved to be of general interest, for they were all scientific treatises on geological or biological problems, or else they were worthless speculation in fields where Darwin was incompetent to trod. He considered his *Origin* merely the abstract of his Great Work, which at this time he thought of as a three-volume opus organized on the same general plan as its abstract. It would differ only in its fuller development and in an exhaustive presentation of factual evidence supporting each theory. But each section he worked upon grew under his hand as the *Origin* had grown from an essay to a pamphlet to a small book to a big one, and Darwin's Great Work therefore remains in the land of unwritten masterpieces.

The first volume of the Great Work appeared in 1868 as an expansion of the first chapter of the *Origin*. Twice as long as the *Origin*, it was called *The Variation of Animals and Plants under Domestication*. It failed to arouse interest, save among naturalists, for whom it was a mine of information. The theory of pangenesis running through it, however, has since been discredited as a gratuitous assumption that warped Darwin's thinking on the subject.

Darwin's "other book" appeared in 1871, published reluctantly by the author and called *The Descent of Man*. Ever since 1859 he knew the book would have to be written, for he believed that the whole case for natural selection would be ruined if an exception were made for man, as many naturalists wished to do. He had avoided the subject in the *Origin*, because he was afraid that applying natural selection to man might prejudice his entire theory by stirring up unnecessary opposition. For some time after 1859 he looked to Lyell to present the Darwinian theory in the book he was doing on man, but when Lyell's *Antiquity of Man* appeared in 1863 Darwin was disappointed to find that natural selection was not given what he considered to be its proper place. In 1864, he pinned his hopes on Wallace, even offering him his accumulated notes on the subject. But Wallace's views eventually proved as unacceptable to Darwin as Lyell's, for Wallace wanted to put man in a class apart from the lower animals. So Darwin was driven to write the book himself.

As he worked on *The Descent of Man*, the book grew too large, so Darwin found himself postponing the section on Expression of the Emotions for a separate future volume. Despite the cutting, *The Descent of Man* was half again as long as the *Origin*. In it Darwin sought to explain "how far the general conclusions arrived at in my former works were applicable to man." "The sole object of this work is to consider, firstly, whether man, like every other species, is descended from some pre-existing form; secondly, the manner of his development; and thirdly, the value of the differences between the so-called races of man." In this work Darwin presented evidence purporting to show that the difference between man and beast is only one of degree, that such things as conscience and the moral instinct are the natural product of living together in society. No new ideas either on man or on evolution are to be found in its many pages. It is only an application of the *Origin's* theories to man's evolution from lower forms of life; it should therefore be called the Ascent rather than the Descent of Man.

The *Expression of the Emotions* came out as a lesser work, which is of little importance either for the theory of evolution or for an analysis of man. Darwin continued to write on various other subjects, his books all appearing as long, forbidding tomes, but none of them caused the stir that the *Origin* had. Darwin gradually gave up the idea of doing his Great Work. In 1872, he wrote to Wallace that he had "taken up old botanical work and . . . given up all theories." He continued to interest himself in evolution and natural selection till the end of his life, but he was certain by 1872 that his theories were firmly established and he was safe to putter around in his garden and entertain famous visitors. The Great Work was never written, so by default its abstract, the *Origin*, remains Darwin's great book.

6

Darwin's fame and his standing as a maker of the modern mind therefore rest upon the *Origin* alone. When one speaks of Darwin, he refers to the author of the *Origin;* when one discusses Darwinism, he talks of those theories which are either found in his masterpiece or the ideas that derive almost inevitably from it. Darwin had written a book that was more important than its contents, for behind it was the force of ideas generating throughout the earlier half of the century. The accumulated force of these ideas, each of which had remained more or less isolated before, was concentrated for the first time in a single work. The *Origin* was consequently an explosive thing in its power. Huxley observed without exaggeration that, "it is doubtful if any single book, except perhaps the *Principia* ever worked so great and so rapid a revolution in science, or made so deep an impression on the general mind."

So Darwin found himself suddenly famous. Bunbury noted in March of 1860 that "Darwin's book has made a greater *sensation* than any strictly scientific book that I remember. It is wonderful how much it is talked about by unscientific people." Natural selection was the topic of conversation at every informal gathering during the British Association's convention in 1860. Murray was surprised to find that he had a best seller on his hands, and he was hurried into one printing after another. When the sixth and final revision in English appeared in 1872, five German editions had been published, four French, three Russian, three American (besides early pirated editions), and at least one each in Dutch, Italian, and Swedish.

Darwin became the center around which a man-made tempest raged. He was a hero or a villain, a martyr for science or a villifier of the human race, depending on one's stand on the subject of evolution. He was seldom looked upon simply as a scientist whose work deserved serious examination, the acceptance or rejection of which should rest upon the scientific validity of the theories it contained. Instead, one accepted or rejected Darwin because of one's previous convictions, not because of the evidence he presented in the *Origin,* and Darwin's defenders were every bit as absurd and naïve as were his attackers. Huxley is typical of these younger materialists who found Darwin justifying their beliefs and their prejudices. He therefore promised to sharpen up his "claws and beak" for the coming fray, and from his pen poured forth such statements as this: "The publication of the *Origin of Species* marks the Hegira of Science from the idolatries of special creation to the purer faith of Evolution." Huxley did the review in the London *Times*, wrote essays on the *Origin* in *Macmillan's Magazine* and *Westminster Review*, lectured at the Royal Institute on the new ideas — and Darwin was famous throughout England.

Huxley summed up Darwin's role in the "great monkey battle" thus: "He found a great truth trodden underfoot, reviled by bigots, and ridiculed by all the world; he lived long enough to see it, chiefly by his own efforts, irrefragably established in science, inseparably incorporated with the common thoughts of men, and only hated and feared by those who would revile, but dare not." It is difficult to gather more inaccuracies into one complex sentence than Huxley had done in the above statement. There was no simple line-up of honest scientists against bigots, as Huxley maintains. There were bigots on both sides, and there were more capable, honest scientists opposed to Darwin's views than there were in favor of them. As a matter of fact, only a minority of naturalists, the younger generation to whom Darwin appealed, accepted the *Origin's* central thesis.

Scientifically, the problem was how large a role natural selection was to play in causing variations. Many scientists were willing to allow it an important role, but they insisted that other factors played some part in the evolution of species. Some insisted that use and disuse had been neglected, as Darwin's emendations in later editions tacitly admitted. Others, like the American, Asa Gray, wanted to substitute a supernatural selection for Darwin's rather inadequate natural selection. Still others, like Lyell, were willing to admit natural selection's dominant role in causing the origin of new animal species, but they refused to merge man into the evolutionary process — a point on which Darwin remained adamant till his death. Others, like Mivart in the *Tablet*, considered Darwin's explanation satisfactory if one would admit a special act of creation by God for man.

There were still others who were willing to concede almost

everything Darwin had said, as long as it was not assumed that his theory was not only true but was also the whole truth. Carlyle summed up this view by remarking caustically: "That the weak and incompetent pass away, while the strong and adequate prevail and continue, appears true enough in animal and human history; but there are mysteries in human life, and in the universe, not explained by that discovery." Darwin's former professor, Adam Sedgwick, saw the crux of the problem when he accused Darwin of absolute materialism and of falling before the temptation of becoming philosopher and theologian as well as scientist, of jumping unscientifically at conclusions unwarranted by empirically ascertained evidence.

"We all admit development as a fact of history," he wrote to Darwin, "but how came it about? Here, in language, and still more in logic, we are point-blank at issue. There is a moral or metaphysical part of nature as well as a physical. A man who denies this is deep in the mire of folly. 'Tis the crown and glory of organic science that it *does,* through *final cause,* link material and moral; and yet *does not* allow us to mingle them in our first conception of laws, and our classification of such laws, whether we consider one side of nature or the other. You have ignored this link; and, if I do not mistake your meaning, you have done your best in one or two pregnant cases to break it. Were it possible (which, thank God, it is not) to break it, humanity, in my mind, would suffer a damage that might brutalize it, and sink the human race into a lower grade of degradation than any into which it has fallen since its written records tell us of its history." Sedgwick was a grimly accurate prophet, as two world wars have testified, but Darwin could not understand what his professor was saying.

John Stuart Mill — as objective a seeker after truth as England ever knew — summed up the *Origin's* rightful place in the history of ideas by his comment that although Darwin could not "be said to have proved the truth of his doctrine, he does seem to have proved that it *may* be true, which I take to be as great a triumph as knowledge and ingenuity could possibly achieve on such a question." That seems to be the status of the question today. No progress has been made by naturalists since Darwin's day in discovering the mechanism whereby evolution works.

The evidence in favor of natural selection remains negative rather than positive. It still may be true, as Mill observed, but it has not been proved true, despite Huxley's naïve assertions to the contrary. Later biologists have illuminated the problem, but at the same time they have complicated it. There is no aspect of evolution which is not honestly held in question by contemporary biologists, from natural selection and sexual selection to the causes of variation, the inheritance of acquired characteristics, and the influence of environment.

It was popularly believed that Darwin had set out to prove evolution. Many reviews of the *Origin* either condemned it or applauded it in that light, and most scientific popularizers, like Huxley, talked about it and fought for it because of its support of the evolutionary theory — support which they changed from circumstantial to direct in the course of their popularization. When Darwin went to Cambridge to receive an honorary degree in 1877, for example, the undergraduates cheered him, jeered an unpopular proctor, dangled a monkey (supposed to be the missing link) on a string, and cried "mawnkey! mawnkey!" Thus from the beginning Darwin's name was associated with the theory of evolution. Those who supported the theory believed that Darwin had given it its biological, scientific credentials; those who opposed it saw that he was the man to be refuted or discredited.

Darwin had said that through the process of natural selection the fittest survive. But within a short time he was popularly understood to hold that the best survive — which was in perfect accord with the faith these people put in Progress. There was some basis in Darwin's writing for this piece of intellectual sleight of hand, for he believed deep in his heart that, by and large, the fittest were the best, that evolution was synonymous with Progress. In his notebook for 1837 he had observed: "From death, famine, rapine, and the concealed war of nature we can see that the highest good, which we can conceive, the creation of the highest animals has directly come." The same idea is expressed in almost the same words in the poetic last paragraph of the *Origin*. Darwin had said fittest, but he confused fittest with best in his own mind, and occasionally the confusion showed up in his writings.

Natural selection was therefore justifiably taken as the mechanism whereby this Progress, so evident to even the casual observer of the nineteenth century, actually took place. In the eighteenth century men thought that by intelligent effort they could achieve Progress; Darwin made it evident to the nineteenth century that Progress operated by mechanical laws over which men had no control, that it would continue independently of man through the operation of natural selection. It was comforting to think that the human race was driving inevitably to perfection, that the weaker, more corrupt members fell by the wayside, that the struggle for existence was a great screening process whereby the best specimens, physically and morally, were sifted by natural selection and allowed to propagate their kind. All this was done mechanically by self-sufficient laws of nature; a cosmic purpose had replaced a divine purpose, and, as Darwin's wife commented ruefully on her husband's work, it put God "further off."

That is why the *Origin* must be included among the world's important books even though contingent circumstances rather than its own merit made it of such great consequence. West sums up its impact on the Western mind thus: "The effect was truly tremendous. Almost by the mere statement of a new principle of approach, dynamic, not static, he revolutionized every department of study, from astronomy to history, from paleontology to psychology, from embryology to religion." Darwin seemed to redeem the nineteenth century from a chaos out of which earlier static thought could bring no order. He apparently explained the mystery of life and the process of Progress. His was the Master Idea of the century.

This Master Idea appealed to all kinds of people: it used the concept of matter and motion to explain life itself; in evolution it offered a method for tracing the origin of all things, and people thought that exhaustively tracing something to its origin completely explained it; it offered a pragmatic test of value, survival, which could be applied to insects or to human institutions; it made the highly competitive economic system of the time a natural thing following the eternal law of struggle for existence and survival of the fittest; it explained the "miracle of Progress," and it promised untold Progress in the future. It was an unconscious rationalization and justification by a respectable scientist of the temper of his age. Fighting was the order of the day, in business, in diplomacy, in war; and Darwin had explained scientifically how from struggle the highest good emerges, how, from struggle and through the survival of the fittest lowly animals, majestic man had originated. This was music to the nineteenth-century ear — the right tune played in the right key.

7

So the age snatched up Darwin's Master Idea and applied it to all fields of thought. It was used to give scientific credentials to what the age had been doing even before Darwin wrote his book, but there can be no doubt that Darwinism not only justified but also promoted these trends. The Master Idea that was applied so widely was a three-sided idea consisting of struggle for existence in which the fittest survive through the process of natural selection. This was taken to mean that morality was outmoded, that approval was given to any devices whereby a man or a class or a nation could overcome its enemies in the struggle for existence. A Manchester journalist observed, as soon as the *Origin* appeared, that "might is right and therefore Napoleon is right and every cheating tradesman is also right."

This popular application of Darwin's three-sided Master Idea was not always fair to Darwin, but it is true that he fathered the idea and could not logically deny his paternity of the popularized offspring that came to be known as Social Darwinism. In the last chapter of the *Origin* he suggested that his theories be applied to such subjects as geology and psychology, that by its application to social studies "much light will be thrown on the origin of man and his history."

The idea of struggle being a natural and a good thing permeated the book. Darwin approved of this struggle because of the beneficent results which came from it; it was for this reason, and not for any moral scruples, that he refused to contribute to the defense of Bradlaugh for circulating a book on birth control. He wrote in answer to the request for money that he "disagreed with preventive checks to population on the ground that over-multiplication was useful, since it caused a struggle for existence in which only the strongest and ablest survived." And the fittest, those who win the wars or make the most money, are hailed as the best. In the closing pages of the *Origin* Darwin observed: "As natural selection works solely by and for the good of each being, all corporeal and mental endowments will tend to progress towards perfection." It is for this reason that West concludes: "Popular Darwinism may be a crude but it is scarcely an unfair or inaccurate presentation of the broad effect of Darwin's basic writings."

Darwinism was used, then, to explain everything from language to war. Bishop Trench, an English language authority, showed how the fittest words survive and the less fit become obsolete. Sir Henry Main, an authority on government, wrote of the "beneficent private war which makes one man strive to climb on the shoulders of another and remain there through the law of the survival of fittest." Darwinism was used to justify competition with no holds barred as a natural struggle for existence among business firms. The fittest survived, and the world progressed as weak — or honest — firms went bankrupt.

So it was with human beings. Eugenists, like Sir Francis Galton, were convinced Darwinists, who consciously applied his theories to society to conclude that since men are not equal and since inequalities are inherited, social misfits should be allowed to perish and should be prevented from breeding additional inferior stock. Herbert Spencer invoked Darwin to show how, "under the natural order of things, society is constantly excreting its unhealthy, imbecile, slow, vacillating, faithless members."

The idea was applied to social groups by such men as Walter Bagehot and Ludwig Gumplowitz — and the path led straight from them to the ideologies of facism and nazism. Bagehot's famous work, *Physics and Politics,* should have been called "Biology and Politics," as is indicated by its subtitle, "Thoughts on the Application of the Principles of 'Natural Selection' and 'Inheritance' to Political Society." In this work Bagehot taught that "social progress took place only because the struggle for existence caused men to form strong, compact social groups having despotic control over the entire conduct of their members." History is the record of the struggle between groups, and in time between national groups. Those groups which are most tightly organized, most compact and homogeneous, are victorious. So Bagehot concludes: "What you want is a comprehensive rule binding men together, making them do much the same things ... fashioning them alike, and keeping them so."

Others picked up the Darwinian idea of struggle for existence and survival of the fittest to apply it to races. Thus Alfred Rosenberg follows the Darwin line in writing that history is the "dramatic battle of distinct races," that survival is the only test of value between races, that the struggle is inevitable and perpetual. In the same way Darwin's idea was used to justify war as a form of struggle between nations from which good is bound to come. Darwin himself believed that a short war benefits the world because it brings out good social qualities without killing off too many fit men. The Franco-Prussian War of 1870 was translated in Darwinian terms everywhere. Bagehot approved of war because "the hard impact of military virtues beats meanness out of the world," and Spencer insisted that "without war, the world would still have been inhabited only by men of feeble types sheltering in caves and living on wild food."

Struggle for survival was extended by Marx from the individual, where Spencer would have liked to keep it, to classes. Marx wrote of social evolution through class struggle, just as Darwin had written of natural evolution through struggle among individuals. Marx used that objective, material thing called the forces of production in the same way that Darwin had used natural selection.

Whether he fully realized it or not, Darwin had sanctified struggle as history's great selector and purifier which promised untold blessings in the future. Everyone picked up the Master Idea as a directive toward his own Utopia. Marx planned a Utopia that Darwin could never enjoy, but the English biologist had nonetheless furnished Marx with a road map which England's adopted son thought pointed the way to the utopian classless society.

XI

MARX

On St. Patrick's Day of 1883, when Karl Marx was buried in Highgate Cemetery near London, his name was hardly known outside Communist circles. So in the eulogy Friedrich Engels delivered at his friend's grave, he tried to show Marx important by coupling his name with Darwin's. "Just as Darwin discovered the law of evolution in organic nature," Engels told the small group at the grave, "so Marx discovered the law of evolution in human history." The comparison was happy, because Marx liked to think of himself as the Darwin of the social sciences and to believe that Darwin's theory of evolution supported his own class-struggle view of history. Marx was a typical nineteenth-century intellectual who thought that Darwin's theory was both

284

respectable and irrefutable, that any body of thought which could be linked to it would thereby become scientific and unanswerable.

For many years, indeed, Darwin and Marx lived within an hour's journey of each other. Although he never met Darwin, Marx regarded the famed naturalist as a great man, a great scientist, a great revolutionist. His son-in-law, Aveling, tells us how Marx studiously read each of Darwin's writings as it came off the press, how he wanted to dedicate *Das Kapital* to Darwin, how he sent an autographed copy of it to him, and how Darwin answered with a polite little "bourgeois" note in which he remarked: "Though our studies have been so different, I believe that we both earnestly desire the extension of knowledge; and this, in the long run, is sure to add to the happiness of mankind."

Marxists refuse to admit that their studies are "so different" as Darwin believed. They frequently point out how the one substantiates the other, how natural science is the solid foundation of both Darwinism and Marxism, how both are coldly scientific in all respects, how both are brilliant objective reports on inevitable trends. Most important, they believe, both are "dialectic" in orientation and are therefore opposed to the "formal logic" of bourgeois thinkers. They go on to indicate that the variations in the method of production brought about by new inventions are shown by Marx to correspond to the biological variations of Darwin. So compatible do Marxists consider Darwinian and Marxian thought that Russian followers of Karl Marx have made Darwinism part of the official teaching in all Russian schools.

It is true that Marxism and Darwinism possess certain similarities. Both offer a dynamic, evolutionary explanation of their respective phenomena in contrast to former static views. Both claim to be scientific; both are materialistic; and both constitute complete syntheses compiled by systematizers who try to provide the ultimate solution to all problems in their respective fields. Both rest their cases upon man's inescapable struggle for survival, and both therefore presume to be analytical in a hard, realistic way. Both are strongly flavored by their age; they smack of Cavour and Bismarck, of the "blood and iron" by which all things are done. They fit in nicely with the "realism" which the late nineteenth century exhibited in all fields of activity.

By the middle of the century a new self-conscious class had come into being in Europe — the proletariat, a propertyless class created by the factory system who were the disinherited of the earth. They were the men who sweated and toiled in the factories, who froze and starved in their tenements, who had no homes or gardens, no possession but their precarious jobs. They were a class who suffered mutely because they had no voice. They sorely needed a prophet. And Marx proposed, like his fathers of the Old Testament, to be their prophet. He must speak the language of the century, however, if he would be a successful prophet; if he wanted to be heard, he must use the magic words of science, he must be realistic and hard, he must consider struggle and violence as inevitable, he must be thoroughly materialistic. He must, in short, be the Darwin of the social sciences if he would command the respectful ear of Europe in Darwin's day.

But he must be more than a scientist. He must become a prophet who has vision in his eye and fire in his nostrils, who enkindles the hearts of his followers by offering them a glimpse of the promised land, and lashes out hotly at their oppressors. Marx was the man for the job — a man who was both scientist and prophet, erudite and demagogue, scholar and pamphleteer. He was a sentimentalist at heart, a man of deep passion and strong feeling who hated with a vindictive, unslakable hatred because his heart had been so torn by the sufferings of the wage earner. Marx was the Rousseau of the proletariat. Where Rousseau was the prophet of the bourgeoisie, Marx was the prophet of the masses; where Rousseau hated the privileges of the nobility with a raw hatred, Marx hated the bourgeoisie with red, vicious hatred. As Rousseau justified the covetousness of the bourgeoisie and made a moral issue of its being satisfied, so Marx gave the masses a religion — with a creed, a bible, a code, a mission, and a promised land — which justified their demand for a share in the spoils of the Industrial Revolution.

Marx was basically a prophet, much closer to Rousseau than to Darwin. Good prophets both, he and Rousseau held forth ideals which were not too critically examined because of the powerful protests each made. Each, like a good prophet, put together a doctrine which simply was not subject to refutation.

Where Rousseau found his truth through feeling rather than reason and could therefore not be answered, Marx found his truth through dialectical reasoning, and one who criticized him simply was not thinking "dialectically." So Marx had the soul of a Rousseau — which is necessary for the leader of a powerful protest movement at any time in history. But he wore the intellectual apparel of a Darwin — which was necessary for anyone who would win acceptance in the late nineteenth century. The secret of his success lies, then, in having Rousseau's passion and in using Darwin's language, in being a prophet who preached "scientifically."

Marx was more successful than his contemporaries could have imagined he would be. The Weimar Republic of postwar Germany is partly his child; and he is intellectual father of Soviet Russia. He made the European world conscious of the proletariat, and in this way he pushed governments everywhere to adopt various kinds of "socialist" or "paternalistic" legislation, such as old-age pensions, unemployment insurance, maximum-hour and minimum-wage laws, and safety regulations for industry. He is important because in his hands socialism acquired a philosophy and became a religion. Though his classless society is as far from realization today as it was in 1883, Marx has nevertheless made his imprint on Western civilization. Though Marx's conclusions in history and economics are now discredited, historians write as they do today because of Karl Marx, politicians devise the legislation they do in many countries because of him, class hatreds are as bitter as they are because of him. For better and for worse, Marx is still very much with us. What his ultimate effect on the Western World will be we still cannot say, for the children of Karl Marx are fighting today to make his dream of world revolution come true. But of his paramount importance we can have no doubt.

1

Karl Marx was born in 1818 in Trier, a cosmopolitan town in the Rhineland, German in speech but largely French in culture. His parents were Jewish, but when Karl was six they joined the National Evangelical Church, and the children were educated as Protestants in this overwhelmingly Catholic community. The oldest son of a respectable middle-class family, Karl found that great things were expected of him. His father had selected him as the son to be educated, the child chosen to make a place for himself in the world. This responsibility weighed heavily on him throughout his early years. Combined with a pressing consciousness of his Jewish origin, it apparently developed in him that feeling of inferiority which lies at the basis of his abnormal personality.

Although he had proved only a moderately successful student in his preparatory work, his father nevertheless sent him to the university at Bonn in 1835. There, in his daughter's words, "to please his father, he for a time studied law, and, to please himself he studied history and philosophy." At Bonn young Karl Marx showed tremendous but ill-directed strength. He wrote to his father, for example, telling how all at the same time he was writing three volumes of poetry to his fiancée, translating large sections of Tacitus and Ovid, writing a book on the philosophy of law, composing a play, learning Hegel from beginning to end, and meanwhile reading books on diverse subjects.

This was a time, of course, when there was intense intellectual activity in the German universities. Intellectually they were far ahead of the rest of Europe, but politically and economically they were still under Metternich's strong hand — and as a result the students were inclined toward revolution of any kind. Marx studied at two universities, Bonn and Berlin, and got his doctorate by mail from a third, Jena, then notorious for the laxness with which it granted degrees. By 1842, he was ready to return to Bonn as a lecturer in philosophy, but instead he became editor of the *Rheinische Zeitung* and thus began his career of revolutionary agitation.

The next seven years were a period of enforced wandering for the young journalist and his noble-born wife, Jenny Westphalen, whom he had married in 1842. The couple went to Paris in 1843 when Marx's paper was suppressed. There he met Friedrich Engels, who was finishing his study on the condition of the working class in England, and the two men began a forty-year friendship and a collaboration which was to prove most effective for the Communist movement. Engels was primarily a man of action and a pamphleteer; Marx was primarily a theorist and a library recluse. Engels was inclined to science, Marx to philosophy and history. Engels' father had money on which both he and Marx could live; Marx was socially a helpless individual who could never have survived had it not been for his friend's generosity.

The first fruit of their collaboration was *The Holy Family*, written in 1844 against Bruno Bauer and other "young Hegelians" then prominent in the German universities. In 1845, Marx was expelled from France by the Guizot government, so he went to Brussels. There he wrote such things as his *Essay on Free Trade* and his *Poverty of Philosophy*. More important for the Communist movement, however, he and Engels founded the German Workers' Association in 1846, which they associated with the Communist League in the next year. They were commissioned by the league to draw up a program of party principles, the formulation of which appeared in 1848 as the famous *Communist Manifesto*, written chiefly by Marx, it seems, but officially produced by their joint authorship.

In 1848, revolution broke out in Paris, and soon it was spreading all over Europe. When it threatened Brussels, Marx was asked to leave Belgium. He returned for a short time to Paris to witness events in that capital of revolution; from there he went to Cologne to establish the *Neue Rheinische Zeitung*, which was suppressed in the spring of the following year. Again Marx went to Paris, again he was asked to leave, and this time he went to London "for a few months." But the few months dragged on until his death in 1883. For the last thirty-four years of his life he enjoyed the comparatively tranquil life of a political refugee in that home of exiled revolutionists and deposed monarchs. He devoted the rest of his lifetime to a scholarly formulation of Communist theory, to planning a program of action, to stirring up workers to prepare themselves for the great day of revolution which lay ahead.

The year of 1848 is therefore the dividing point in Marx's life. Before then, and especially through that year of revolution, he lived in excited momentary expectation of revolution to put the proletariat in power throughout Europe. But the failure of revolutions everywhere, from street fighting in Vienna and Berlin and Paris to the Chartist fiasco in London, convinced him by the end of 1848 that careful planning was needed, that the proletariat had to be schooled in revolutionary technique, that the bourgeois state was not yet ripe and soft enough to fall. He therefore settled down to long-term planning and to the creation of a body of doctrine which would both instruct and inspire his followers, "the vanguard of the proletariat." Marx the agitator became Marx the scholar after 1848 — but he never fully quenched the agitator in his make-up.

At first Marx's life in London was dreary, miserable, wretched. His family lived in squalid poverty until the middle fifties — for which Marx's wife deserves more sympathy and earns more admiration than he. All but three of his children died in these years of disease, consequent upon their poverty, a fact which aroused fierce resentment and a sense of helpless despair in Marx's heart. His family lived in two rooms in Dean Street, Soho, where Marx devoted himself entirely to study and writing. He earned a pittance by sending articles to the *New York Tribune,* but his chief source of income consisted of remittances from Engels. These were never as much as Marx needed, because Engels' father was the tightfisted kind of capitalist whom Marx so furiously berates. So for several years Marx's life was a continual bout with hunger and bill collectors, with disease and dunners, cold and lawyers. After the middle fifties Marx was not so desperately poor, and after 1869, when Engels paid up his debts and settled a comfortable income on him, he had no difficulty living the life of a moderately well-fixed bourgeois pensioner.

Through disease and poverty and the noise of squalling children — maybe partly to escape them — Marx spent every day deep in research in the British Museum. There he amassed the information he was to put in *Das Kapital;* there he followed the Kant-like routine for which nineteenth-century German Ph.D.'s became notorious. Meanwhile, he turned his pen to pamphleteering whenever the occasion presented itself, essays which appear as bright red spots in the long gray stretch of his economic *Wissenschaft.* In 1859, he published his first notable piece of scholarship, the *Critique of Political Economy,* and, in 1867, the first volume of *Kapital* appeared. Some years later the second volume appeared, but the third was still a jumble of notes when he died; and Engels put them together to make the post-humous third volume.

Marx's life at London was not devoted to scholarship alone. He was also active in promoting Communist theory among the workingmen of London. This activity led to the establishment of the First International in 1864 when Marx attended a meeting at Saint Martin's Hall on behalf of Poles who were then revolting from Russian rule. A proposal was made at this meeting for the founding of an International Workingmen's Association which, as the First International, was the body through which Marx's spirit found expression. Although he was officially only corre-sponding secretary for Germany and Russia in the International, Marx was the leading spirit in all general councils, the author of almost all documents and addresses it issued, from the inaugural address of 1864 down to the dissolution of the International after the fall of the Paris Commune in 1871. Internal difficulties, chiefly with the anarchists led by Bakunin, combined with the odium cast upon the International by the extremism of the Paris insurrection of 1871, made advisable the suspension of the body's activity and the transferral of a skeleton organization to New York.

When Marx died in 1883, therefore, he was apparently a failure. The Communist revolution had not come, as he had prophesied it would, either in England or in Germany. The optimistic note, sounded in the *Communist Manifesto* and in subsequent addresses, must have mocked this prophet of the proletariat if he recalled those writings in his last days. But his followers, who were for a time few in number, had great faith in the movement — a faith which had been made possible by Marx's unique fusing of pseudoscientific scholarship with mis-sionary zeal, a faith which cannot be disassociated from Marx the man. For Communists have universally treated him with the respect reserved for a Messiah of the proletarian covenant, the prophet who, after the manner of Moses, provided his fol-lowers a glimpse of the promised land — and put a road map in their hands so that they could not lose their way. Marx has thus been made the symbol of a movement that is much bigger than either Marx or his theory.

2

It is important, then, to see what sort of person Karl Marx was. And it is as difficult as it is necessary. It is difficult, because Marx has been treated either as a diabolically inspired, bewhiskered Jew who plotted the downfall of civilization, or as a lovable saint who selflessly devoted himself to the betterment of the down-trodden. Marx was neither the one nor the other, though he sometimes seems to be both. It is necessary to know the man, because Marxian doctrine is made up of scattered sentences and paragraphs that the reader must cull from Marx's various volumi-nous writings (only half of which have ever been published), and the reader can cull more intelligently when he knows the man who is always saying more than he means.

Marx was one man to his family, another to the world. He spent Sunday with his wife and daughters, going to Hampstead Heath for a picnic or playing family games and entertaining close associates at home. He seems, from all descriptions, to have been a lovable, devoted father who could create a wondrous fairy tale at command, or be very serious playing such a game as "Confession" with his daughters, or be an omnibus for his favorite grandson, or an amateurish declaimer of Shakespeare on the walk home from Hampstead Heath. The Marx who was ridden as an omnibus is not the same man who wrote the *Communist Manifesto* or penned vitriolic calumny against Bakunin. There were two Marxes, in fact, and the family Marx was a lovable, rather helpless head of the family who was a lot of fun when he could be dragged out of his study. He was very much like an industrial tycoon playing with his grandson's elec-tric train under the family Christmas tree.

To the world Marx was quite a different man. Janus-like, he reveals two faces to the world: at one time he is a student deep in the archives of the British Museum analyzing contemporary capitalism; at other times he is an incendiary pamphleteer, a street-corner demagogue who glories in arousing the passion of his listeners. Paul Lafargue, his secretary and son-in-law, there-fore warns us that "we shall never understand him unless we contemplate him simultaneously as man of science and as socialist fighter." Marx did not keep these two personalities nicely

separated. Soapbox invective slips into his most learned disserta-
tions, and German *Wissenschaft* parades learnedly in his platform utterances and his call-to-action pamphlets.

Both as demagogue and as scholar, however, Marx was hostile
to all the world beyond the rim of his family circle. Karl Marx
had no real friends. He was at ease with his family, with faithful
'Lenchen the maid, and with such followers as were willing to
sit worshipfully at his feet burning their incense of adoration to
this superbrain. Even Engels was more a willing man Friday
than a real friend or equal. Carl Schurz voiced the opinion of
almost everyone who tried to meet Marx on a plane of equality
when he observes of him: "I have never seen a man whose bear-
ing was so provoking and intolerable. To no opinion which
differed from his own did he accord the honor of even conde-
scending consideration; every argument that he did not like he
answered either with biting scorn at the unfathomable ignorance
that prompted it, or opprobrious aspersions upon the motives of
him who had advanced it." Bakunin had personal reasons for
describing Marx as "immensely malicious, vain, quarrelsome, as
intolerant and autocratic as Jehovah, the god of his fathers, and
like him, insanely vindictive. There is no lie, no calumny, which
he is not capable of using against anyone who has incurred his
jealousy or his hatred; he will not stop at the basest intrigue if,
in his opinion, it will serve to increase his position, his influence,
and his power."

While Marx was reading in the British Museum, a young
physician in Vienna was making observations which today throw
some light on Marx's abnormal personality. Certainly he suffered
from a gnawing feeling of inferiority. There is no other way to
account for "Daddy Marx's" lovable dealing with children and
worshipful followers, whereas he was so irritable and quarrelsome
and aspersive with all rivals or opponents. This feeling of inferiority was doubtlessly intensified by constant reference to his
Jewish origin. His frequent diatribes against Judaism show his
shame of being Jewish and his unsuccessful attempt to disassociate himself from his race. His failure to achieve the early
striking success he knew his father expected of him probably
deepened this sense of inferiority.

Marx therefore matured a terribly self-centered personality

with a deep sense of inferiority which made him abnormally quarrelsome, unduly aggressive, unjustifiably suspicious, thoroughly ungrateful. He made much too much of his own sufferings; he found no thought processes but his own deserving of examination or discussion. His correspondence with Engels reveals how self-centered, how ungrateful he could be. Marx answered Engels' letter telling of his mistress' death, for example, by dismissing his friend's loss in a sentence and then filling the remainder of the letter with the usual list of lamentations: bills unpaid, threatened action at law by his creditors, sickness at home, bad weather, and on and on with all those griefs experienced by so many households. Marx seemed to think no one but he ever suffered. For he was incapable of thinking, except in the abstract, about anyone but Karl Marx.

Marx's aim in life after 1848 was to become the scientist of world revolution. Like Bentham and Ricardo, Marx believed that social relationships can be reduced to numbers and equations, to ratios and abstract quantities which are more real than men and machines. In the preface to his *Critique of Political Economy* he tells us that economic phenomena "can be watched and recorded with the precision proper to natural science." Engels tells us even more specifically how the Communist sociology is to be made an exact science. "With the same certainty with which from a given mathematical proposition a new one is deduced, with that same certainty can we deduce the social revolution from the existing social conditions and the principles of political economy." Marx and Engels frequently stated that a science — even their social science — was perfect only when it could be expressed in mathematical terms.

A purely scientific attack is therefore needed on those social and economic problems. And Marx thinks he is purely scientific. His repeated references to the work of the physicist, the chemist, the biologist, show how he looked upon himself as a Darwin who had scientifically arrived at the foundations of his new body of knowledge. He was great, he believed, and he differed from all other socialists because he had scientifically analyzed capitalist society and discovered its laws of operation. The other socialists had dreamed wishfully of pie in the sky, whereas he had examined society, as a mechanic examines an engine, to discover how the goal of socialism was to be realized out of the existing materials of capitalism.

But Marx never pretended to be objective — like a scientist working in his laboratory. Lenin is a good Marxist when he tells the reader that objectivity is "rather stupidly naïve," that "an impartial social science is impossible in a society founded on class struggle." Lenin is probably right in this latter claim, but he and other Marxists are wrong in claiming that Marx was both scientific and partial. Still Marx would have it so. He had arrived at the position, through his German philosophy, that knowledge cannot be objective, that knowing consists not merely in absorbing factual information but in altering it in the process. He could therefore logically maintain that he was both subjective and scientific, that what he said was "proletarian" truth, which at his moment in history was universal truth.

So Marx considered himself "scientific" in all his writings even though they are polemical rather than objective. Everything Marx wrote, as a matter of fact, was directed against some individual or some school; everything he wrote finds him overstating the point at issue, saying more than he means. The reader who would understand Marx must keep this point in mind. Otherwise, by taking each statement literally at face value, he will have Marx even a worse bundle of contradictions than he really is. He overstates his materialism, for example, against Bruno Bauer's idealism; he overstates his principle of reciprocity and activity against Feuerbach's passive materialism; he overemphasizes the principle of authority against the anarchists. Against the classical economists he insists on historical relationships; against the historical economists he insists on the analytical method; against the fatalists he insists that human beings make their own history; against the individualists he insists that everything is determined by the method of production. Emphasizing now one point, now another, Marx contradicts himself constantly. Sometimes he contradicts himself within two or three pages of a single pamphlet, and occasionally he reverses himself within a single paragraph. Consistency is not one of Marx's virtues.

For that reason it is difficult to evaluate either the man or his thought. He was at bottom a sentimentalist nursing an inferiority complex — which helps account for his being a loving father at home, "Daddy Marx" to the neighborhood children, a benevolent old man to worshipful young followers. It also accounts for the coarse abuse, the puerile sarcasm, the malevolent imputations of vice with which he treated all opponents. Sentimentalists love ardently and hate fiercely, because they feel intensely. Because Marx never gave up Hegel's method of "thinking in the dialectic" and because he approached economic questions from the evolutionary point of view, he could consistently be inconsistent. Marx could be all these contradictory things and, like Rousseau, be quite satisfied with himself.

He must be taken in one piece, as pseudoscientist and demagogue, as soft sentimentalist and vitriolic hater, as missioner who bitterly condemned force used by the bourgeois state but exulted in violence used by the proletariat. Marx was all these things at once. And because he was all these things he became the voice of the proletariat, a class that was easily moved, that at this time could not help having a social inferiority complex, and that under such circumstances could more readily be roused to bitter antagonism — but a class that, like Marx himself, accepted much more of nineteenth-century bourgeois attitudes and standards, beliefs and judgments, than it ever knew.

3

Analysts of Marxian theory almost always explain it as a blend of Hegelian philosophy and English economics. The Hegelians were collectivists, these critics argue, and their method was historical, whereas the English were individualists and their method was analytical. The combination of these two outlooks and these two methods, they conclude, made for scientific socialism. Marx, as the author of *Das Kapital,* can be explained on these grounds, but this explanation does not hold for Marx as the author of the *Communist Manifesto* and the leader of the Communist party.

Lenin adds a third source of Marxism to German philosophy and English economics. This is the radical French socialism which Marx came to view closely in the 1840's, which he saw fail, under Louis Blanc, to seize control of France in 1848. Lenin thus gives a fuller picture of Marxism, one which is better rounded and better shaded than if the French socialist element is left out. Even

Lenin's picture, however, is not complete enough to account for Marx's unique success in putting together a body of doctrine which somehow caught on when other similar attempts by equally intelligent socialists failed.

Marx was successful because he caught the temper of his time as no other socialist had done. Evolution, in one form or another, was in the air. It was propounded in Hegelian philosophy and in Darwinian science, as we have seen, and Marx was therefore in swing with the age when he used it to explain all human history and all social arrangements. It was a materialistic age, and Marx was only stating generally assumed but not yet loudly shouted beliefs when he propounded his dogmatic, thoroughgoing materialism. Realism was the pervading keynote of the age, a ruthless realism which preached to those who were physically and morally strong that they were duty bound to trample their competitors. In international affairs it was called *realpolitik,* in economics it was competition, in biology it was struggle for existence, in philosophy it was the will to survive and the will to power. And now in his explanation of man's social history, Marx explained it as class struggle, a term which nineteenth-century intellectuals were ready to accept without question. So Marx spoke the language of his time and accepted uncritically many assumptions of the age — a secret of wide reception at any time in history. He was much more a nineteenth-century bourgeois than he knew — or than Marxists will admit today.

The principal ingredients of his system, however, are undoubtedly Hegelian philosophy and British classical economics, to which he added the socialist conclusions of such predecessors as Owen and Fourier, Saint-Simon and Sismondi. From Hegel he obtained the dialectic, which is an explanation of the laws by which history operates. Hegel was an idealist, of course, who insisted that the ultimate realities moving through history are ideas, that material things are only a manifestation of basic reality — the Idea. Hegel differed from earlier idealists in holding that ideas are not static, that they are in a state of fluid, logical development. This, he held, was true both of particular ideas and of the great Idea whose struggle toward self-realization through the dialectical process is the essential cord of history. Hegel explained how progress was achieved by this law of logical development. Any idea, by the very nature of things, begets a negation of itself; the combination of the original idea, called the thesis, with its negation, called the antithesis, results in a synthesis — which, in turn, serves as the thesis when the process begins all over again. The law of movement is therefore to be found within the idea itself; ideas are, so to speak, self-debating entities that move through history according to laws of logical self-development. And they move in zigzag fashion from thesis to antithesis to synthesis.

Marx rejected Hegelian idealism before he was twenty-five, but he always adhered to the dialectic as giving the true evolutionary explanation of mankind's social development. It will only be necessary for him to stand Hegel on his feet, to use his own metaphor, and to show that it is not ideas but classes that move through history, that not ideas but things are the ultimate realities in the world, that the self-debating process is dependent upon economic relations and upon the method of production adopted by a given civilization at a given moment in history. Thus he will show "scientifically" and "conclusively," to the satisfaction of all his followers, that capitalism begets its own negation and brings about its own end because of "the inner laws of capitalistic development."

Whereas Hegel's contribution to Marxism was historical and stressed the collectivity of social groups, the English economists' contribution was analytical and stressed man's individuality. Whereas Hegel made Marx a system builder, Engels and England made him an analytic critic of the capitalist system. Until he met Engels, Marx had been too theoretical, but from that time on he amassed a world of facts on the working of the factory system, the stuff from which *Das Kapital* was to be made. But Marx got more than factual information from his English connections. He also accepted the "laws" propounded by Malthus, Ricardo, and Mill, laws which he was to modify as Hodgskin and Thompson had modified them a quarter of a century earlier.

From Malthus he obtained the notion of struggle for survival, which he converted from a struggle among individuals to a struggle between classes. From Ricardo he obtained the labor theory of value, from which he naturally deduced his surplus theory of value to justify "expropriating the expropriators." From the classical economists he obtained the practice of looking upon economic activity in highly abstract fashion to create scientific laws that allowed men no leeway to wander and err as human beings are wont to do.

Marx's Proletarian, in the last analysis, is nothing more than Ricardo's Economic Man with dirty hands. He is a wage earner who is determined by Marx to follow his selfish, materialistic interests as logically, as intelligently, and as ruthlessly as Ricardo's entrepreneur had followed his interests. Both the Economic Man of the classical economists and the Proletarian of Marx follow the irresistible urge to accumulate dollars as mechanically as a magnet collects iron filings. Neither Ricardo nor Marx will allow their respective heroes the right to be human beings, to exercise free will, or to make any mistake other than that of miscalculation. Marx differs from the English economists in only one important respect: he replaces their static world of the producers' paradise with his evolutionary, progressive world where everything is fluid, where everything turns into a negation of itself. This was the revolutionary effect of his combining the Hegelian dialectic with the English science of economics.

Marx lived in a world where the word *socialism* was already well known. It was associated, however, with the utopian schemes of such goodhearted men as Robert Owen in England, and Saint-Simon, Fourier, and Cabet in France. All these men had exposed the terrible social results of the Industrial Revolution: poverty and starvation for the workers, disease and cattlelike crowding in the cities, malnutrition and deformation of human cogs in the big machine of industry, hopeless misery and dark despair in all workers' hearts. These utopian socialists had proposed their remedies, remedies which differed somewhat with each author but which all depended on the benevolence of the employing class. Such schemes had been tried by 1848, and they had failed. Nevertheless, the fact remains that they had been proposed, that theoretically they did remedy the worst abuses of capitalism, that their failure seemed to be due chiefly to the method by which they were put into practice. In 1848, moreover, Marx witnessed what he thought was the momentary triumph of workers in almost every capital of Europe — and he witnessed their final failure.

By 1848, then, when Marx was thirty years old and when he had decided to become the scientist-prophet of the proletariat, he had obtained all the constituent elements of his doctrine. From Germany he had obtained Hegel's dialectic which he had "placed upon its feet" to serve his revolutionary ends. From the English he had obtained the abstract science of economics. From the French socialists and from personal observation of the revolution of 1848, he had obtained the notion of class struggle and the vision of a happy world where workers were producers enjoying the full fruit of their labor. From all three countries he had absorbed the atheism, the evolutionism, and the scientism which were in the air. By 1848, Marx had become a truly cosmopolitan figure who could read almost all the leading European languages and could write German, French, and English fluently. By reason of his background and his schooling, his travels and his experience, he was qualified to be the prophet of a revolution that professed to ignore national lines and to concentrate on class lines instead.

4

In his funeral eulogy Engels told his listeners that Marx made two most important discoveries: the law of historical materialism, and the surplus theory of value. The first epoch-making discovery Engels went on to describe thus: "He discovered the simple fact, heretofore hidden beneath ideological overgrowths, that human beings must have food and drink, clothing and shelter, first of all, before they can interest themselves in politics, science, art, religion, and the like. This implies that the production of the immediately requisite material means of subsistence, and therewith the extant economic developmental phase of a nation or an epoch, constitutes the foundation upon which the State institutions, the legal outlooks, the artistic and even the religious ideas, of those concerned, have been built up."

Marx evolved this theory of history described by Engels by combining two principal ideas: that the units moving through history are economic classes, and that these classes, with their outlooks and their institutions, depend ultimately upon the method of production. The first of these ideas is found succinctly stated as the first sentence of the *Communist Manifesto:* "The history of all hitherto existing society is the history of class struggles." Where Hegel made ideas the real units moving through history, Marx substitutes classes. And these classes move in dialectical fashion. They are, by the very nature of things, bound to be in conflict with each other. Each class begets its negation by the method of production it employs. The feudal class, for example, created a bourgeois class of money lenders and commercial people who, because they had no place in feudal society, worked for its overthrow. They were successful at length and they created their own capitalistic society. By their factory method of production the capitalists in turn produce a class of wage earners, the proletariat. And the proletarians are bound to work for the overthrow of the capitalists.

In their struggle for power these various classes adopt whatever ideas and practices, whatever social or political devices will serve as weapons against their antagonists. Religion, law, decent behavior, social etiquette, Marx insists, are all bourgeois inventions for keeping the proletarian in chains. That is why "law, morality, religion, are to him so many bourgeois prejudices, behind which lurk in ambush just as many bourgeois interests." So it is with the government, the army, the police. "Political Power," Marx explains, "is merely the organized power of one class for oppressing another."

Marx modestly admits that his predecessors had recognized that men are divided into economic classes which are necessarily in life-and-death struggle with each other. He claims credit, however, for discovering "that the existence of classes is bound up with certain phases of material production." His most specific statement on this point is to be found in the preface to the *Critique of Political Economy*. There Marx tells the reader: "I was led by my studies to the conclusion that legal relations and the forms of the state could neither be understood by themselves nor be explained by what was called the general progress of the human mind, but were rooted in the material conditions of life."

He then proceeds to explain this basis of class struggle in what is perhaps his most noted passage: "In the social production of their subsistence men enter into determined and necessary relations with each other which are independent of their wills — production-relations which correspond to a definite stage of development of their material productive forces. The sum of these production-relations forms the economic structure of society, the real basis upon which a juridical and political super-structure arises, and to which definite social forms of consciousness correspond. The mode of production of the material subsistence conditions the social, political and spiritual life-process in general. It is not the consciousness of men which determines their existence, but on the contrary it is their social existence which determines their consciousness."

Everything, then, is determined by the method of production used at a particular time in history. On it ultimately depend all ideals and all morality, all prejudices and all social groupings, all leisure activity and all cultural pursuits. "Men's conceptions, thoughts, spiritual intercourse, here still appear as the direct emanation of their material conduct." This is true, according to Marxian theory, because the method of production determines the relationship which is established between classes in this basic business of producing wealth. Upon this relationship will depend the class's attitude toward the whole of life. And since men, for Marx, are only automata who act blindly according to the class label they wear, then everything they do or think or say or dream will be determined by their class membership. The class, moreover, is determined by the method of production. So ultimately everyone's hopes and desires, pet peeves and idiosyncrasies are determined by the method of production — in our day, the factory system.

Engels sums up Marxian theory on this point succinctly: "It was seen that all past history, with the exception of its primitive stages, was the history of class struggles; that these warring classes of society are always the products of the modes of production and of exchange — in a word, of the economic conditions of their time; that the economic structure of society always furnishes the real basis, starting from which we can alone work out the ultimate explanation of the whole super-structure of juridical and political institutions as well as of the religious, philosophical, and other ideas of a given historical period."

This is the materialism for which Marx is so widely known — and almost as widely misunderstood. He frequently inveighed against contemporary "crass materialists" who denied the existence of anything but hard, substantial matter. Engels remarked, late in life, that the materialism commonly imputed to him and Marx was more extreme and simple than was justified; but, he added, it was probably their own fault because of the overstatements they continually made in their polemics against the Hegelian idealists and the utopian socialists. Marxian materialism does not deny the existence of nonmaterial things. But it does make them mere reflections of material realities. On this point, incidentally, Marx is neither consistent nor precise. Sometimes he calls ideals, religion, literature, and art "reflections" of material things; sometimes he calls them derivatives; again they are superstructures erected upon the economic foundation. Whatever they are, nevertheless, he always insists that they are "nothing else than the material world reflected by the human mind and translated into terms of thought."

Another point in Marxian historical materialism on which there is properly much confusion is man's role as a human being. There is confusion among both Marxists and their critics because there was confusion in Marx's own mind. Logically, his system was deterministic; everything flows inevitably and necessarily from the method of production according to the laws of the dialectic. Actually, Marx seems usually to have thought that history moved independently of men; he constantly uses such terms as "necessarily" and "determined." Occasionally, however, he leaves room for man's role as an undetermined human being who is only conditioned by his environment. In *The Eighteenth Brumaire* he writes: "Man makes his own history, but he does not make it out of whole cloth: he does not make it out of conditions chosen by himself, but out of such as he finds close at hand." Engels puts the same idea this way: "History proceeds in such a way that the end-result always issues from the conflict of many individual wills. . . . For that which each individual desires meets an opposition from every other, and the result is something which nobody desired."

Marx simply had to deny his logical determination if he were to stir the proletariat to action. Marx the scientist was deterministic, Marx the prophet was not. Marxists have tried to reconcile the two by insisting that everything that happens is necessarily going to happen when conditions are set, but individuals can hurry the process up by intelligent, ruthless action in the right direction. They do not say whether individuals can turn the dialectic in a different direction so that a completely different goal is eventually reached. It is better for Marxists not to enter upon this problem if they would keep their faith.

5

Marx applied his historical materialism, with the doctrine of the class struggle, to contemporary capitalist society in order to come forth with revolutionary conclusions. Whereas Malthus and Ricardo framed their laws as if they had always worked exactly as they did in 1800, Marx looked upon capitalism as a passing phenomenon in world history. The general thesis of *Kapital* is that capitalism was produced from the competition of many small owners of private property, because the survival of the fittest eliminated small producers and concentrated wealth in fewer men's hands, that there is a "contradiction" within capitalism that drives it in turn into socialism, because the factory system of production is a "socialized" system. Since it depends upon the factory method of production, therefore, capitalism by its very nature begets a negation of itself. This, of course, is socialism.

Here, briefly, is how it happens: competition resulting from private property reduces most workers to the status of wage earners employed by the few most ruthless employers who have survived and become capitalists. Now competition among these capitalists reduces their numbers, puts more and more wealth into fewer and fewer hands, increases the proletariat, and decreases the number of employers. Production, meanwhile, is becoming more and more socialized in larger and larger factories; at the same time "there occurs a corresponding increase in the mass of poverty, oppression, enslavement, degeneration, and exploitation; but at the same time there is a steady intensification of the wrath of the working class, a class which grows ever more numerous, and is disciplined, unified, and organized by the very mechanism of the capitalistic method of production." This continues to the point where the few remaining capitalists can no longer control the masses now constituting the proletariat.

Whereupon "the knell of capitalistic private property sounds. The expropriators are expropriated."

So the new society comes into being. About this new society Marx has very little to tell us. Here he resorts conveniently to his dialectical determinism, telling the proletarians that "they have no ideal to realize: they have only to free the elements of the new society." Marx's ideal society simply gets itself established by those "historic necessities" to which he turns in moments of difficulty. He makes no blueprint for the ideal society, for planners are utopian socialists and Marx is a scientific communist. He does tell us in *The Poverty of Philosophy* that it will be a society "which will exclude classes and their antagonism, and there will no longer be political power, properly speaking, since political power is simply the official form of the antagonism in civil society." In his *Criticism of the Gotha Program* he draws his most detailed picture of the future society. But here he only tells us that it will be a society without government by force, that it will be classless, that in it will be realized true freedom and true equality, that there will be common ownership of the means of production, that at last will be realized the ideal of "from each according to his abilities, to each according to his needs."

This ideal society cannot be reached at once, a point on which Marx waxed vehement against anarchists like Bakunin. It can be ushered in only by the famous dictatorship of the proletariat, which Marx says, "is but the transition to the abolition of all classes and to the creation of a society of the free and equal." This is a period which Marx does not describe at all, either as to duration, technique, successive stages, or anything else. All he says is that it lies between the downfall of capitalism and the beginning of the ideal Communist society. Russia has supposedly been in that state since Lenin's November revolution of 1917. What Russia should have accomplished in the past thirty odd years Marx never said. Conveniently for his followers, he left the immediate steps to be determined by time and circumstance — and the school of Marxian exegesis one subscribes to.

He seems equally undecided on how the revolution itself is to be accomplished. Most frequently he speaks of the revolution as though it were to be a violent upheaval led by the Communist party, "the vanguard of the proletariat," whenever capitalistic society is ripe for successful revolution. "It is to force that in due time the workers will have to appeal if the dominion of labor is at long last to be established." Occasionally, however, he speaks of winning "the battle of democracy," or getting control of the state by legal means, especially in England and the United States. He left the road open for his followers to go down the evolutionary road or to struggle up the revolutionary path. Social Democrats in Germany chose the evolutionary road — and they could find passages from Marx suggesting that they were true disciples in winning the battle of democracy? Bolsheviks in Russia chose revolution instead — and Lenin could resurrect "forgotten words" of Marx and Engels to show that they really approved of the revolutionary approach. Trotsky favored revolutionizing the world overnight; Stalin preferred to make Russia strong first. It is hard to believe that Marx cared much how the dictatorship of the proletariat was achieved — so long as it became a reality. If he did care, it is impossible to decide from his writing whether he favored evolution or revolution.

6

Engels always believed that Marx's most important discovery was his law of historical materialism. But he considered the second discovery — the surplus theory of value — a greater scientific triumph, the sort of thing that only a genius such as Marx could ever formulate. This surplus theory of value originally appeared absolutely essential to Marxism, "the cornerstone of Marx's whole scientific interpretation of society," Jacques Barzun calls it; it seemed that the class struggle rested upon the surplus theory, as did the ruthless competition that would wreck most capitalists and make it possible for the workers eventually to usher in their revolutionary dictatorship. Marx's scientific labors and erudition on this economic problem have been of no permanent avail, however, for his theory has been discredited both by analysis and by subsequent events. Even Marx himself practically undoes his surplus theory of value in the postmortem third volume of *Kapital* — and there is good reason for believing that his wrestling with this problem kept him from publishing this concluding work in his lifetime. Even though the theory has been discredited, Marxian faith has not suffered. It served its purpose in seeming to make Marx's system scientifically unassailable when it was first offered to the world. It overawed critics, and it dazzled enthusiasts as only scientific economic theories could do in the last half of the nineteenth century.

In propounding his theory of value Marx sets out like a typical classical economist. He works in abstractions which are much more the creation of his mind than flesh and blood employers and employees at work in the factory. He tells us in the preface of *Kapital*, in fact, that "individuals are dealt with only insofar as they are the personifications of particular class relations and class interests." Marx accepts Malthus' theory of population and Ricardo's iron law of wages, whereby under competitive conditions the worker will get a bare subsistence wage. He also accepts the Ricardian theory that the value of an article depends upon the amount of labor expended in making it. Then, in the tradition of classical abstract analysis, he combines these theories and turns them against the capitalist system which Malthus and Ricardo were defending.

The worker employed by the capitalist, Marx maintains, does enough labor within a part of the day — usually about half — to increase the value of the goods he produces to an amount equal to his wages. The rest of the time he works for nothing, for he is producing value for his employer for which he himself gets no return. The difference between his pay and the value he produces amounts to the profit expropriated from him by the capitalist. This is the "surplus value" for which Marx became so widely known. The worker is obviously treated unjustly, Marx claims, for he alone is not paid according to the value he gives in exchange. The capitalist pays for raw material according to its value; his activity as entrepreneur is rewarded according to the social value of his labor. The worker alone does not receive fair payment for the value of the labor he offers in exchange for his wages. Profit is the difference between what workers should receive and what they actually do receive. All profit in the capitalistic system is therefore stolen from the workers. Such a theory appears scientific — but its moving power is ethical: its insistence that workers are defrauded of their just wages.

Such an analysis suffers from the same defects as does Ricardo's. It is oversimplified, arithmetic, deductive — indicative of what went on in Marx's head rather than in the factories he spoke about. But it does seem to follow logically enough from the labor theory of value and the iron law of wages. If these theories were correct, Marx might be right. If Ricardo and Malthus were wrong, Marx had to be wrong, and for the same reasons. It does not matter much for the Marxian faith, however, whether he was right on this particular point.

7

Marx's theory of history was made into a faith whose motives of credibility were originally his scientific analysis of the capitalistic system with its method of defrauding the laborer of his wages. It was a faith that could live on, once it seemed credible, whether Marx's analysis was correct or not, because Marx's theories of history and value do not explain his greatness. They were merely the scientific aura with which he invested his mission, the credentials which his age accepted, credentials examined critically by none of his followers and by few of his critics. The Marx of history is the author not of *Kapital* but of the *Communist Manifesto*. Engels was right when, after telling of Marx's scientific discoveries, he concluded in his graveyard eulogy: "Before all else, Marx was a revolutionist."

As a revolutionist rather than a social scientist Marx has moved millions. His protest appeal has been potent because the Industrial Revolution created such vast wealth but kept it out of the wage earner's reach. Marx's protests against capitalism have been accepted as true by men whose stomachs were achingly empty, whose children's bellies bloated as their eyes took on a vacant stare before they died of starvation, whose wives suffered mental and physical anguish because they were denied the very things their husbands made in the factories. These men did not analyze Marxian theory. They did not distinguish the truth in Marxism from the error. They took it all on faith because it made so much sense when their stomachs were empty. They knew it was right because it expressed their mute hatreds and it turned their despair into bright hope. For these millions of disinherited souls Marx had to be right. He was their prophet, and his word was infallible truth.

To the Marxist masses, therefore, Marxism appeared a simple religion. It had its creed, which was accepted uncritically by the millions, but had its credentials of scientism for those who were critical minded. It had its code, which was the struggle-for-survival code of Darwin, Spencer, Gumplowitz, and other realistic thinkers of the late nineteenth century. It had its bible — the writings of Karl Marx and Engels. It had its mysteries — the hidden, inner law of the dialectic, which was made more hidden, more inner, and more mysterious in the hands of Marxist theorizers of the second generation. It had its promised land — the classless society. It had its chosen people — the proletariat. And the chosen people had received their religious mission — to usher in the promised land through revolution and the dictatorship of the proletariat. Marx is first of all a prophet, whose god is Inexorable Process. To Marx alone has the Process been revealed, his word alone is infallible.

As a prophet, Marx reveals to his followers a double message. In the first place, he foretells the doom of capitalism in words as ringing and terrible as Isaias'. "The centralization of the means of production and the socialization of labor," he tells us, "reach a point where they prove incompatible with their capitalist husk. This bursts asunder. The knell of capitalist private property sounds. The expropriators are expropriated. . . . With the inexorability of a law of nature, capitalist production begets its own negation." Second, the prophet Marx foretells the blissful life to come when the struggle is done. In this happy society there will be no force, no struggle. All will be absolutely free and absolutely equal, everyone will receive absolute justice, each will give according to his abilities and receive according to his needs. It is a land sweet with honey and full of the milk of human kindness. This is perfection indeed — and it is taken on faith from the prophet who alone among men has seen the vision revealed by Inexorable Process.

Marxists, therefore, enter into the fray hopefully as missioners who know they are fighting the good fight, as crusaders whose ultimate victory is assured. No blood is shed in vain, no suffering, no setback can dampen their hopes. Marx's religion therefore becomes a fighting religion of crusaders who are the compeers of the early Christian martyrs, of Savanarola, of Calvin's doughty Puritans. That is how Rosa Luxemburg understood it when she spoke of the proletariat marching "triumphantly forward with its head high . . . due to its tranquil understanding of the ordered objective historic development. . . . In this understanding the workers' movement sees the firm guarantee of its ultimate victory, and from this source it derives not only its zeal, but its patience, not only its strength for action, but also courageous restraint and endurance." That is what Lenin meant when he said, "Only the philosophic materialism of Marx has shown the proletariat a way out of that spiritual slavery in which up to now all oppressed classes have been sleeping." That is what Marx meant when he ended his *Communist Manifesto* with a crusading prophet's ringing words: "Let the ruling classes tremble at a Communist revolution. The proletarians have nothing to lose but their chains. They have a world to win. Working men of all countries, unite!"

The Marxian creed is not a body of dry statistics with demonstrable conclusions reached by scientific reasoning. It is a fighting philosophy at which Marx had arrived before he began his researches in the British Museum, a belief he felt in his heart and which he therefore backed up with whatever evidence he could find. It is essentially a religious belief, even with Marx himself, involving assumptions which he never investigated and which he never dared call into question. The one-time Marxist, Max Eastman, who rejects this religion precisely because it is in his eyes a religion rather than a science, comes to this conclusion: "Marx studied the world with a view to making himself believe that it is in process of change according to his plan. . . . But the belief is super-scientific, metaphysical — religious in the truest sense of the term. It is a scheme for reading the ideal purpose of the communists and their plan for achieving it into the objective facts, so that their account of the changing world and their plans for changing it become one and the same thing."

Rational criticism cannot shake a true Marxist's faith. For the dialectic is unassailable by human reason. By its very nature it does not admit of criticism. This is the great value of the dialectic to Marxists, for the dialectic makes not only history, but truth

itself fluid. It denies the principle of contradiction, asserting that
a thing can both be and not be at the same time, that nothing
is but everything is becoming. And everything becomes by the
process of self-realization through self-negation. So if it is pointed
out to the Marxist that the classless society is farther than ever
from realization in Russia, he answers by saying that the dialectic
process demands the state become more powerful before becoming less powerful. If it be shown that nationalism has increased
since Marx's day, when he said it was disappearing, the Marxist
answers by saying that this is all part of the dialectic and a time
will come when the very intensification of nationalism will cause
its utter negation. The dialectic gives the Marxist religious assurance that he is right, that it is in the very nature of things
for him to seem wrong — but this is additional assurance he is
right. So moves the Inexorable Process to its realization in the
classless society. The ways whereby it goes are not for man to
inquire. Marx has spoken the infallible truth, and one who
criticizes him is thinking "statically" rather than "dialectically."
In other words, he does not have the faith — and he who does
not have the faith cannot know it and therefore cannot criticize it.

Marxism, like every other religion, has its code — a code prepared by Malthus and Darwin, Bismarck and Palmerston, but
applied ruthlessly, honestly, without Victorian hypocrisy, by a
Marx who took seriously the struggle-for-survival view of his
respectable contemporaries. Marx repeatedly condemns the bourgeoisie for the use of force against the proletariat; he burns with
white-hot indignation when he writes of the massacre of Communists in the insurrection of the Paris Commune in 1871, but
he defends their murder of hostages as necessary and good.
Force used against the proletariat is wrong, he sincerely argues,
but force used by them is just. Marx was indeed a fierce hater
by intention as well as by disposition. He cultivated a hatred
of all opponents, and he condemned any Communist who
preached against the system of private property but did not
hate its owners. Marx's morality was simply the morality of the
Social Darwinists. Whatever benefited the proletariat in its struggle for power — murder, arson, rape, or fratricide — was good;
whatever hindered the chosen class was bad.

Marx's absolute condemnation of all other religions springs

from his having created his own religion. Any religion, if it is honest and consistent, must be jealous, for it cannot have strange gods beside it. Marx fought religion for other reasons too. In the first place, he was opposed to all organized religions because he believed they supported bourgeois society. They were class weapons for keeping the bourgeoisie in power, they reflected bourgeois ideals, they considered property more sacred than human life. Worst of all, they slyly preached a passive acceptance of one's lot in life by glorifying the virtues of resignation, meekness, and humility. They served, therefore, as the opium of the people. Here, of course, he was partly right; and he could always find concrete instances — especially in Tsarist Russia — on which to base his generalizations. "The social principles of Christianity," Marx writes, "preach cowardice, self-contempt, abasement, submission, humility . . . but the proletariat, which will not allow itself to be treated as canaille, regards its courage, self-confidence, independence, and sense of personal dignity as more necessary than its daily bread. . . . The social principles of Christianity are mealy-mouthed; those of the proletariat are revolutionary." Here, of course, he was largely wrong. Marx opposed religions for a second reason: they distracted the proletariat from his struggle for power by putting the classless utopia in heaven. They offered him happiness after death instead of bliss in this life, and paradise was greater competition for the classless society than Marx could stand.

8

No one can help seeing certain fundamental errors in Marx's thought. Even intelligent Marxists admit this. They therefore commonly distinguish the essential doctrine from articles of belief that they consider inconsequential. But even in essentials Marx made serious errors. His surplus theory of value — the cornerstone of Marxian economics — has been discredited. Its propaganda value, nevertheless, remains unimpaired. His diagnosis of the inevitable course that capitalism must follow in its development has been proved wrong by subsequent events. Misery, suffering, and poverty of the wage earners have not intensified since Marx's day, as he said they must. Their real wages reached a nadir in his lifetime. Labor unions have done much indeed to prove that Marx's Inexorable Process need not be nearly so inexorable as he thought. The revolution did not occur in England or Germany, where Marx thought it would, but in the Russia he despised, a country even today not ready for revolution on the Marxian pattern.

Marx erred grievously in underrating the strength of nationalism among workers. He wrongly identified nationalism with capitalism because he rightly saw a connection between them. In 1846, he wrote: "Only the proletarians can destroy nationality, the proletariat alone can allow the different nations to fraternize." Two years later he wrote that "national differences and antagonisms between peoples are daily more and more vanishing." But unfortunately they have not vanished — even in Russia. They have intensified instead. History has not heeded Marx's declaration that national loyalties are not basic with men, that proletarians have more in common with their fellows in foreign countries than with their bourgeois neighbors. Bombing from the air and huddling in underground shelters have produced fellowships Marx could never imagine.

His class theory is, indeed, one of his most striking errors. This was called a *sine qua non* of the system by Sidney Hook when he was still thoroughly Marxist in 1933. "If the facts of the class struggle can be successfully called into question," Hook admitted, "the whole theoretical construction of Marx crashes to the ground." Now proletarians have proved that they are no more class automata than their employer is Ricardo's Economic Man. Both Proletarian and Economic Man are abstractions that make contact with human beings at only one point — their economic interest.

Marx's Proletarian proved in two world wars that he was also the member of a nation, perhaps of a church, maybe of a locality or a minority group. Moreover, he proved that these other loyalties were often more moving than his class loyalty. He proved he could act from motives that had no economic basis. Marx was wrong in holding economic class divisions the only real divisions in human society. He was wrong in believing either that these divisions were sharp and irreconcilable or that they were not crisscrossed by other equally real divisions. Men can be divided into racial, social, national, religious, political, and many other groups, each one of which has reality but no one of which can claim a human being's sole allegiance.

Marx made such mistakes because he was so thoroughly a child of the nineteenth century, because he accepted uncritically so much of Ricardo's and Bentham's "bourgeois" thought. He approached social problems, not as a social scientist dealing with human relationships, but as a mathematician dealing with abstract entities. His reasoning was always too abstract and mechanical for a social scientist — and he made the fatal blunder of transferring his abstract conclusions to the world of living men. His analysis of the "inner laws" of capitalism, whereby it begets its own negation, for example, are predicated of a capitalism that works out to logical conclusions without any modifications, without any concessions made to the workers, without any government interference. If Marx knew more of human nature, he would never have decided that things work out so logically and inevitably in human relationships. Because he did not know men, he prophesies the end of capitalism simply by transferring his conclusions from his own arbitrary system to the world outside his mind.

To criticize Marx for making such fundamental mistakes as these, however, is to miss his real importance. In some respects his thought had a healthful effect on the capitalistic world. He helped make it conscious of the terrible abuses in the new industrial system, and the threat of revolution made the bourgeois world — and the Marxian too — discover that the iron law of wages had more rubber in it than iron. Marx made a valuable contribution to economic theory by showing that human institutions are not static, that they begin in time, grow strong, decay, and die. More than anyone else, Marx has made us all think historically. His greatest importance was in acting as spokesman for the proletariat. His prophecies may have been wrong, his theory may have been faulty, but he was the voice of the working class. This was both his real importance and his real strength. Jacques Barzun puts it well when he concludes: "The strength of Marx is precisely that he shared the feelings of the downtrodden, that the prejudice of equality was in his very fiber, and joined to it the ambition and jealousy of power, both ready to destroy the present moral order in the name of a higher which he saw." As the Rousseau of the proletariat, then, he was important — and not as the Darwin of the social sciences he thought himself to be. As a symbolic leader in a struggle still being fought throughout the world Marx is even today of tremendous importance.

9

In various degrees and divers ways Marxism is still very much with us. Where would Marx fit in today? Soviet Russia claims him, but would he claim Soviet Russia? Would he rather consider the Weimar Republic, or Labor England, his child, or would he look upon the Spartacists who refused to co-operate with the German government his legitimate descendent? Would he recognize Norman Thomas as his spokesman in America? Or Earl Browder? Perhaps Marx would admit the intellectual paternity of none of these Marxists. He insisted to Paul Lafargue: "*Je ne suis pas un marxiste.*" Whether he was a Marxist or not, however, Karl Marx created the original body of doctrine known as Marxism. He was the creator of a religion that has been, and still is, of tremendous importance in the modern world. His body of doctrine, which pretended to be only a scientific analysis of society, has ironically done something to shape society to the pattern he described, his theory of the class struggle, for example, making the class struggle more of a reality than it would otherwise have been.

Four main schools of exegesis developed to explain "what Marx really meant." One group, led by Kautsky, Hilferding, and others in Germany, accepted Marxian evolution rather than revolution, insisting that capitalism had to be brought to full flower before it would be ripe for decay. Marxism is important to this school for the time being not as a fighting philosophy but as a science for understanding what goes on in the world. They seek to understand world history rather than make it. Kautsky summed up their attitude thus: "The socialist party is a revolutionary party but not a revolution-making party. We know that our goal can be attained only through revolution. We also know that it is just as little in our power to create this revolution as it is in the power of our opponents to prevent it." This school, incidentally, has a strong following in China today.

A second, and somewhat similar, school of exegesis developed around Bernstein in Germany and Jaurès in France. This revisionist school insisted frankly on turning Marxism into a democratic, socialist movement of reform. It stressed expediency, the obtaining of better conditions for labor, shorter hours, and higher pay. It worked for compromise with capitalism, and it entered the arena of party politics to struggle for the proletariat in legal fashion. These are the schools of thought which merged in the Social Democratic party in Germany to take a commanding position at the birth of the Weimar Republic.

As there are two schools of exegesis stressing the evolutionary aspect of Marxism, so there are two schools stressing violent revolution. The first of these in point of time were the syndicalists, led by Sorel, Lagardelle, and Pelloutier, strong chiefly in France, Italy, and Spain. The syndicalists denounced all political activity in favor of spontaneous violence on the part of the workers. Everything, they believe, is to be won by the general strike, whereupon the classless society will be ushered in overnight, springing up with the dawn, as it were, from the ashes of capitalism. Syndicalist zeal soon dissipated itself because it was an emotional rather than a rational application of Marxian doctrine. Syndicalists went off, as one critic described them, like "headless horsemen of the revolution riding furiously in all directions at once."

Finally, there is the revolutionist interpretation of Marxism formulated by Lenin in Russia and Rosa Luxemburg in Germany, and applied in the Bolshevik revolution of 1917. Lenin reproached the syndicalists for renouncing political struggle, for being poetic rather than realistic; he reproached Kautsky for waiting fatalistically for the coming of a revolution he did not try to create. The revolutionists emphasized the conquest of political power rather than theorizing about the future state. They stressed the merging of class struggles with political struggles, and they insisted on the intelligent use of violence to achieve their ends. This school remained in the field to become somewhat more officially Marxist than the others, both by reason of the successful Bolshevik revolution and by reason of their control of the Third International. Kautskyites, anarchists, syndicalists are all treated by the Comintern as Marxian heretics —

and heretics are always more intensely hated than those who are clearly outside the faith.

Marxian doctrine has been important in the twentieth century because there are elements of truth in it and because of the tremendous protest appeal it possesses. Intelligent men everywhere since Marx's day have realized the importance of economic matters in the history of every individual and in the history of the human race. They had formerly been neglected for narrowly political, intellectual, and military affairs. After Marx the swing was to the opposite extreme — following a dialectical pattern, perhaps — in which economics was used to explain everything. History was rewritten according to the pattern of economic determinism; the economic basis was made all important in sociology; politics was seen as the governmental superstructure erected on an economic foundation. Thus the American constitution became the political expression of a certain economic group whose political views were determined by their ownership of considerable property; thus the Civil War was a clash of two economies determined by the very nature of things to meet in struggle to the death.

There is truth in all of this, but it is oversimplification of a single truth — which is error. What, after all, is the Marxian explanation of history but a Freudian explanation of motives without Freud's clinical study? Marx insists in true Freudian fashion that things are not what they seem, that men are not moved by the motives they think they are. Marx and Engels made it a basic point that ideologies, religion, and culture were reflections of economic interests — and they stressed the point that they usually were unconscious reflections. Marx says, for example, that, "as in private life we distinguish between what a man thinks and says about himself, and what he really is and does, still more in historical struggles we must distinguish the phrases and imaginations of parties from their real organism and their real interests."

Engels tells how Marx discovered "the simple fact, heretofore hidden beneath ideological overgrowths, that human beings must have food and drink, clothing and shelter, first of all, before they can interest themselves in politics, science, art, religion, and the like." Again: "The reflection of economic relations in the form of legal principles is accomplished in such a way that this process does not reach the consciousness of the agent. The law-maker imagines that he is acting from *a priori* principles, when in reality it is all a matter of economic reflection . . . and that distortion, when it is not conscious, we call the ideological outlook." Ideology for Marx and Engels, then, is what Freud meant when he spoke of rationalization, substitution, transference, or displacement. The only difference is that Marx pushed it all back to economics, whereas Freud pushed everything back to sex. In their interpretation of human motives, of course, the Marxists were clumsier and cruder than followers of Freud, who at least never presumed to lump the motives of men dead hundreds of years or removed from the psychoanalyst's chamber thousands of miles into the motives of a class. Freudians might animalize men, but at least they treat them individually.

The Marxian explanation of history was a simple one, and it was positive. And men like simple, positive, dogmatic explanations. It appealed to a large portion of humanity because it voiced their feelings and it stressed their wants. Marx has been dismissed as a neurotic whose doctrine is only the expression of his peculiar neurosis. But if Marx was neurotic, so too was the proletariat of his day — a group jealous of the bourgeoisie, harboring resentment in their breasts, feeling inferior deep in their hearts, and blaming the more successful in life for their own lack of success.

Thus Marx was a power in history precisely because he was abnormal. For he spoke for millions of men whom the modern industrial system had condemned to abnormality. His very weakness was therefore his strength. Pointing out his mistakes does not rob him of his place in history — or his influence even today. Marx will continue to be popular in our day whenever there is discontent, economic unrest, or suffering on a wide scale. People who feel cheated by society turn to Marx as the man who tells them why they are cheated, how it is in the nature of the dialectic that they be so cheated — but a day will arrive when they shall come into their own. This was the secret of Marx's importance — his protest appeal to the disinherited of the earth.

That is the reason for Marx's tremendous importance today. His shadow hovers over all of Europe in these years of postwar chaos and unrest. His spirit stalks almost every strike and union election in this country. For Marx remains the symbolical leader of the have-nots in their struggle against the haves. Even today he is the whipping-boy of propertied people who see red Communism behind every worker's demand. He is the object of every witch hunt organized by employers to becloud the issues at stake in their struggle to hold their disintegrating position. The liberalistic, capitalistic world has been crumbling since Marx's time. It would have crumbled had Marx never been born. Born he was, however, and he grew to achieve a symbolical importance out of all proportion to his personal ability or accomplishments. He will continue to be the most important symbolical figure in the world as long as present social and economic dislocation continues. If a measure of world prosperity and a modicum of social justice are achieved in the years to come, Marx's ghost will disappear in the warm rays of content and plenty. Otherwise, it might lead its followers to a hollow victory — to the dictatorship from which no one has yet discovered the road to the classless utopia.

XII
FREUD

EVERYMAN HIS OWN SLAVE

THE last three makers of the modern mind are distinctly contemporary, whereas their eight predecessors are of the past. Today's world belongs to Darwin, Marx, and Sigmund Freud. Although the other eight helped make the modern mind, they would not be at home with the final product of their labors. But Darwin, Marx, and Freud would, for they built bodies of thought which are essentially dynamic, whereas the thought of their predecessors was static. The last three makers of the modern mind offer the reader formless, ever changing systems of thought — like a river of molten lava — whereas the thought of their predecessors had discernible, measurable shape and substance.

The thinking of Darwin, Marx, and Freud is symbolized, in a way, by their smoking. Darwin used to retire to his bedroom after dinner to enjoy a quiet smoke while Emma read to him. Marx smoked so furiously that he complained the royalties from *Das Kapital* could never pay for the cigars he put into it. Freud smoked both furiously and incessantly — about twenty cigars a day — so that his disciples located him by plunging to the center of the smoke cloud in his study. Darwin's body of theory was calm, like his smoking, as compared to Marx's. Both men lived in the same neighborhood at the same time, but Marx thought in twentieth-century tempo, while Darwin remained strictly Victorian in every respect. Marx pushed everyone into vicious struggle for the means of survival, but at least he let him retire home to drink his beer and sleep in peace. Freud denies man even peaceful sleep. His thought rushes past Marx so far that Freudianism compares to Marxism as World War II compares to World War I.

Even more important than the quickened tempo in Freudianism, is the fact that the struggle is pushed down into every man's soul so that no one is allowed a moment of peaceful rest, sleeping or waking. From the time he fights his way blindly into the world until death ends the conflict within his soul — when finally Eros, his life-instinct, has been crushed by irresistible Thanatos, his desire for death — there is no peace. For with Freud there is perpetual conflict within man. At best there can only be an armed truce between the Ego and the Id, a truce which threatens to break out into war within us whenever the Id or the Ego feels well enough armed to tackle its inveterate enemy.

Psychoanalysis was originally a method of medical treatment to cure nervous disorders which seemed to have no organic cause. For a time Freud restricted himself to his medical practice and to clinical research, and here he did invaluable work for psychiatry and psychology. But soon he saw in his discovery a magic key for unlocking every secret held from man. He used it to explain history and prehistory, to tell how religion — and how society itself — originated; he encouraged his followers to apply it to literature and art, to economics and politics, and for the first time, he claimed, Shakespeare was "explained," and children's fairy tales were rightly "understood." Thus Ernest Jones, one of Freud's most competent popularizers, could state that "psychoanalysis has already been applied to sociology, to the study of racial development, and above all, to the psychology of the normal man."

Freud spent the latter part of his lifetime creating his science of "metapsychology" — which came, in his hands and in the hands of his followers, to be a philosophy and a faith. It offered them the last word in regard to man's very nature, in telling him of his hidden motives and of his "unconscious" desires. It explained for them the sexual nature of man's cultural accomplishments: of the music he composed and listened to, the pictures he painted and admired, the literature he wrote and enjoyed. As Newton's experiments with prisms and falling bodies had led him to "legislate for the universe," so Freud's clinical work with neurotics in Vienna led him to create his metapsychology of Freudianism. Floyd Dell can therefore well claim of Freudianism that it is "an idea of the same importance as the Copernican idea, the Darwinian idea, the Marxian idea."

It came to be important because Freud offered it to the world at precisely the right moment. Freudianism fought for its life until World War I, and then, as Freud himself admits, it spread like a forest fire in late summer. It seemed to explain to a war-wracked world what was going on inside of men by telling man how his *psyche* operated. It appealed to the postwar generation because it was hostile to traditional Western culture with its emphasis on reason and with its age-old moral restrictions. Antirationalists like Schopenhauer and Nietzsche had prepared the way in the nineteenth century, and the intelligentsia were ready for Freud to offer them his antirational picture of man. The twentieth-century revolt against tradition was aimed at the formalistic remains of Calvin's puritanism. By the time World War I was over, moral restrictions which were reasonable in days gone by had for many become meaningless, irritating limitations upon man's freedom — and Freud apparently debunked all moral restrictions. Psychoanalysis was daringly new, it appeared shockingly frank, and it seemed wonderfully right in saying what had been hushed up in people's minds since Calvin's day. So young people everywhere, whose spirit was one of revolt, snatched up Freudianism to psychoanalyze each other and to probe into forbidden areas of thought and action.

In the process of popularization Freud's theories were abused, as from the beginning he had feared they would be. Freudian terminology was on every young person's lips: mechanism, complex, fixation, sublimation, transference, repression, displacement are only some of the more common terms coined by Freud and accepted as legal tender in everyday language. Biographers found psychoanalysis an easy device for making a salable book, so the great figures of history from Cleopatra and Caesar down to Darwin an Marx were psychoanalyzed. Thus Kempf explains Darwin's delay in publishing the *Origin* to "anxiety neurosis" caused by sexual irregularity on the *Beagle* (for which the author had no authority other than his imagination), and Rühle explains all Marx's abnormalities by bad metabolism, from which all sorts of neuroses are supposed to derive. For good and for bad — and it was for both, as we shall see — Freudianism won its right to survive as a dominant idea in the contemporary mind, and it came in the years between the wars to permeate everything dealing with men, from religion to pediatrics, from poetry to advertising.

1

Who was this man who created such a powerful body of thought, who made us conscious of our complexes and drove us so disastrously into introspection? It is well to know something of the intellectual history of a man who tells us that the ultimate cause of our shopping for Christmas presents is patricide. Freud has made us conscious of what goes on deep inside ourselves as we were never conscious before; we are naturally curious to discover what went on in his own mind as he organized his practice and theory of psychoanalysis.

Sigmund Freud was born of Jewish parents in 1856 at Freiberg in Moravia. Unlike Marx, he apparently never resented his Jewish origin, though he was bewildered to find it a social handicap later in life. His parents moved to Vienna when he was four, and there he stayed until shortly before his death in 1939. Although he lived almost eighty years in the famous Hapsburg capital, Freud never belonged to the city. Except for his schooling, he may as well have lived in Reno or Kansas City as in Vienna. Nor did Vienna notice him till toward the end of his life. When he had won international fame, a tax collector questioned Freud's declaration of income. Whereupon the then famous psychoanalyst wrote back bitterly: "I note with pleasure this first official recognition which my work has found in Austria."

Freud got more from Vienna than he would admit, for he was educated in the world's leading medical center where he worked under the renowned physiologist, Ernst Brücke. By the time Freud had finished his internship at Vienna's famed *Allgemeine Krankenhaus* he attracted local attention for his work in physiology, neuropathology, and pharmacology. Because of his early publications on his clinical and histological work he was appointed lecturer on neuropathology at the Vienna medical school in the spring of 1885. In the autumn of that same year he went to Paris to watch Charcot use hypnosis in his work on nervous cases. From Charcot, Freud learned that hysteria was not the result of an organic disturbance, as was commonly believed in the 1880's. In his clinic Charcot further demonstrated that by means of hypnosis he could cure some mental disturbances and, further, that he could cause them in the same way.

Young Freud was much impressed both with Charcot's accomplishments and with his simple, scientific bent of mind which inclined him to accept any demonstrable fact, no matter what beautiful theory it might wreck. So when Freud returned to Vienna he reported enthusiastically on Charcot's work, but the doctors there refused to listen. The young neurologist therefore withdrew from Vienna's medical societies, isolated himself from other physicians, and set out to treat nervous diseases independently. Freud had meanwhile married and his family was growing, so, he tells us, he neglected scientific work until 1892 while he concentrated on building up his private practice. In 1889, however, he visited the famous school of psychiatry at Nancy where he saw Bernheim and Liebault prove that suggestion alone, without hypnotism, could cure hysteria. He also saw Bernheim demonstrate how suggestion could be used to help a patient recall forgotten incidents in his life.

A neighboring physician in Vienna furnished Freud with the third and last clue he needed for establishing his infant science of psychoanalysis. A certain Josef Breuer told Freud of an unusual case he had cured by hypnotism some years before. His patient was, in her waking moments, utterly unaware of the causes of her hysterical symptoms, but when hypnotized she recognized the relationship between past events in her life and her present illness. Moreover, the evidence all pointed to the fact that she had forgotten these past events because they were distasteful or painful to her. She had suppressed these memories, rather than forgotten them. Finally, as the case turned out, when Breuer made the patient emotionally conscious of these suppressed memories, the hysterical symptoms from which she was suffering vanished. This was the origin of the highly important psychoanalytic idea of catharsis.

By this time Freud had therefore gathered a number of facts which psychologists did not generally admit at the time: (1) hysteria can have a purely psychic cause, and men have it as well as women; (2) it can be removed by suggestion alone; (3) it can be cured if memories suppressed by the patient and apparently forgotten are brought to light and he experiences them emotionally again; (4) forgetting is a selective process in which the individual "forgets" what he unconsciously desires to.

About this time Freud decided to give up hypnotism in treating his patients. He had found that while "there was something positively seductive in working with hypnotism," it was uncertain and unsatisfactory from a medical point of view. Some patients could not be treated at all; others could not be helped; and those who were cured soon relapsed into the old illness. Moreover, Freud was never particularly adroit in using the hypnotic technique. So he became more and more dissatisfied with the method, which he came to look upon as a dishonest technique that robbed the patient of his integrity and independence.

Freud therefore abandoned hypnosis, retaining only the practice of having the patient lie on a couch without being able to see the analyst. Then, by the psychological device of free association, Freud drew from the patient all the "forgotten" memories which had formerly been recalled in the hypnotic trance. This, Freud tells us, was the beginning of true psychoanalysis. The new method was extremely more difficult for the practitioner, because it demanded untold skill and patience, whereas the hypnotist could accomplish his work easily at a single sitting. But Freud discovered that the new method produced lasting results, since the patient was required to bring his own difficulties to light, analyze them for himself, and propose his own remedy — all under the astute direction of the analyst. Freud contrasts his new method with the old in this way: "The hypnotic therapy endeavours to cover up and as it were to whitewash something going on in the mind, the analytic to lay bare and to remove something."

From his practice in these days Freud was led to form three theories which came to be basic units in the eventual structure of psychoanalysis. He wondered why patients who had apparently forgotten so much could be induced to "remember" these "forgotten" incidents. Observation showed him that everything which had been forgotten "had in some way or other been painful," so he theorized that man's consciousness "debarred the [objectionable] impulse from access to consciousness and to direct motor discharge, but at the same time the impulse retained its full charge of energy. I named this process *repression*. . . . The theory of repression became the foundation-stone of our understanding of the neuroses."

Secondly, Freud's work with his patients led him to the conclusion — which brought such terrible opprobrium on his system — that "in all of these patients [he treated] grave abuses of the sexual function were present. . . . I was thus led into regarding the neurosis as being without exception disturbances of the sexual function." To the day of his death, Freud refused to deviate from this conclusion. He has always insisted that he was led to it inductively, that it was in no way a presupposition on his part, that it was an obvious fact to anyone who would look with open eyes. In his *Autobiography* he protests that his opponents evaded the point when they regarded his theory that all neurosis comes ultimately from sex disturbance as "a product of my speculative imagination and were unwilling to believe in the long, patient and unbiased work which had gone into its making." In 1927, Freud stated rather bitterly that he was still looking for a neurotic who was sexually normal, but that up till then he had not found a single one. By sex, as we shall see, Freud meant something wider, more general, than is commonly connoted by the term.

In these same years Freud's experience as a consultant led him to a third conclusion. He found, he claims, that the study of his patients' unconscious lives led him back eventually to disturbances which occurred in their childhood. These disturbances, moreover, "were always concerned with sexual excitations and the reactions against them." Freud therefore concluded that early childhood is a period of intense sexual activity which reaches its maximum in the fourth or fifth year of the child's life, whereupon a period of sexual latency sets in till puberty. The sexual impulses of early childhood, he decided, are overcome by the child's repressing them when he finds society disapproves of them, and this repression, if done badly, will be the cause of his later neurosis. He further concluded that all children are at least partially neurotic.

By 1898, Freud had arrived at his basic theories of repression, of the sexual etiology of neuroses, of the importance of infantile sexuality. He had become a well-known practitioner, and his income was assured for life. He therefore turned to putting his theories together into the system that has come to be known as Freudianism. Between 1900 and 1905 he turned out his basic — and his best — writings. In 1900, appeared *The Interpretation of Dreams*, which Freud claimed in 1931 was "the most valuable of all the discoveries it has been my good fortune to make. Insight such as this falls to one's lot but once in a lifetime." In this work Freud uses dreams as "the royal road to the unconscious," whereby the analyst can explore that area of a man's soul which the man himself can never know.

His *Psychopathology of Everyday Life*, often called "the psychoanalyst's Bible," appeared in 1901. This work is full of wit and charm and acute observation. Here Freud is at his best — and perhaps most dangerous. For here he erases the line of demarcation between the neurotic and the normal man; here he claims that free will is the illusion of those who do not know that so-called errors are purposeful acts perpetrated by unconscious desires. A somewhat similar work appeared in 1905, *Wit and Its Relation to the Unconscious*, but Freud seems to be straining badly by this time to make all puns and jokes fit into his scheme of psychoanalysis. Here he robs wit of any intellectual content, stressing its function as an emotional safety valve. In the same year he published his account of the part played by sex in the neurotic's life in his *Three Contributions of the Theory of Sex*. These four works contain the basis of Freudianism. A revised terminology and somewhat altered basic concepts appear in his later works, but these are devoted chiefly to popularizing the new philosophy and applying it to all aspects of man's life.

By the turn of the century Freud had attracted the attention of some younger physicians of Vienna. They met with him at seminars in his home — the famous Wednesday evenings when they talked of the new technique and the theories which Freud derived from it. At Freud's house they were served black cigars and coffee — no one dared not to become a cigar smoker and a coffee drinker — over which Freud explained his theories and listened to the reports of followers to whom he had appointed various special subjects for investigation.

2

About 1906, when his books had been on the market long enough to be digested, Freud began to attract attention abroad. Sandor Ferenczi in Budapest had become a follower of the Master in Vienna and his popularizer down the Danube. More important, however, was the interest taken in Freudianism by the well-established, respectable group of psychiatrists at Zurich. There Freud won for a time such capable followers as Bleuler and Jung, Abraham, Eitington, Maeder, and Riklin, all of whom helped immensely in spreading the new theories. In 1908, the young American physician, A. A. Brill, met Freud and arranged to translate his works into English. He and the Canadian, Ernest Jones, who eventually settled in London, became most energetic and effective popularizers of Freudianism in the English-speaking countries.

Freud came to the United States in 1909 to deliver a series of lectures at Clark University. This seems to have been the least successful trip he ever made, and he went back to Europe loaded with dreary impressions of America, impressions which he refused to alter down to the day of his death thirty years later. He summed up his opinion of America by saying it "is the most grandiose experiment the world has seen, but, I am afraid, it is not going to be a success." Americans took to his theories more freely than Europeans, he found, but seemed to understand them only superficially. Freud never thought well of America.

He was worried by the rapid spread of his doctrine in these years, and on the way home from this country he drew up plans with his companions Jung and Ferenczi for perfecting his organization to control the movement and enforce orthodoxy upon all psychoanalysts. By this time Freudianism had become a faith which Freud was anxious to equip with adequate ecclesiastical organization for preserving purity of doctrine. He therefore planned periodic ecumenical councils, international congresses of psychoanalysts where borderline theories would be discussed, where the true teaching would be defined, and where heretics would be expelled. Freud planned to be the Master behind the scenes, in order to control the psychoanalytical movement through young pawns put in office to do his bidding. He also planned to control the movement by maintaining the chief editorship of all psychoanalytic journals.

Four congresses were held before World War I. The first one, meeting at Salzburg in 1908, was all peace and harmony. The new converts were still willing to sit at the Master's feet, marveling at his acute reasoning and his high tobacco tolerance. But at the second congress, which met at Nuremburg in 1910, there began a struggle for power within the psychoanalytic circle. Freud had been very much impressed with the imposing, capable young Swiss, Karl Jung, whom he insisted on making the new international president of the society. Freud's Viennese followers felt themselves slighted, and it was not until some concessions had been made to them that they were willing to let Jung assume office.

Between the second congress and the third, held in 1911 at Weimar, Alfred Adler and his followers were expelled from the organization and forbidden to apply the term "psychoanalysis" to their doctrine. Adler had been one of Freud's first followers, and he was always considered his most apt, most acute pupil. But from 1911, and forever afterward, he and his associates were anathema.

The fourth congress was held at Munich in 1913. Jung, again in the chair, annoyed Freud and shocked his followers by suggesting that all abnormality need not be pushed back to the Oedipus complex — as Freud had decided by that time — and that dreams revealed noble as well as animal impulses in man.

These things smacked of heresy, although the rift was not completed that year. Jung was re-elected president, but before another congress could be held after the war he had cut loose from Freud. The Zurich and Vienna groups separated, never to come together again.

The history of the psychoanalytic movement within Freud's lifetime is the history of its many heresies, of which the two led by Adler and Jung are the most important. After Adler had been expelled from the sacred circle of psychoanalysis in Vienna, the Master pronounced that his former disciple had "entirely repudiated the importance of sexuality, traced back the formation both of character and of the neuroses solely to men's desire for power and to their need to compensate for their constitutional inferiority, and threw all the psychological discoveries of psychoanalysis to the winds." All but the last phrase of the Master's pronouncement is true.

Adler had decided that man's prime driving force was a will-to-power, on the basis of which were to be explained the inferiority complex and all the various mechanisms; Freud, on the other hand, insisted that the will-to-power was only a symbol for the longing to castrate. Adler, moreover, threw out infantile sexuality as the ultimate cause of all psychic disturbances, and he refused to attribute as much importance to unconscious desires as did Freud. He insisted that because all people seek power and are distressed by inferiority, one conscious of his weakness will build up a psychic superstructure to compensate for his weakness. If he is successful, he will have compensated for his lack of power; if not, he will despair and take refuge in real or pretended illness, in a neurosis, or in some other way.

Freud tried to keep Adler within the circle until the spring of 1911. By that time their theories had become so divergent that any layman could see daylight between them. So Freud allotted Adler three successive Wednesday evenings in which to explain his position. On the next Wednesday general discussion began, and on the following Adler was asked to resign. Nine members of the group followed him. (It would be interesting to see a psychoanalyst's account of why they were all socialists, whereas Freud's loyal followers were not.) But whether the cause was a struggle for power, an honest difference of opinion on theory, a personal dispute, or a social cleavage, the rift was final. Adler went his own way, doing good work particularly in educational psychology. Nevertheless, Freud insisted ever afterward that Adler had no claim to the title of "psychoanalyst," that he was a stupid, mean little man — this man whom he had made first president of the psychoanalysts' international — whose ambition was too much for his ability.

Jung's heresy was even more disastrous for the Freudian movement because it cut the whole Zurich school off from the Master, a school which has commanded almost as great a following as Freud himself. Jung broke from Freud, the latter claims, because he "hoped to escape the need for recognizing the importance of infantile sexuality and of the Oedipus complex, as well as the necessity for any analysis of childhood." Jung simply refused to go all the way with Freud in resorting to infantile sexuality as the catch-all explanation of everything in man's later life, whether normal or abnormal, but Freud insisted that "both normal and perverse sexuality are derived from . . . infantile sexuality." Jung believed, moreover, that an unbiased analysis of man's unconscious life revealed something angelic as well as something animalistic, that it was not necessary to interpret all man's cultural accomplishments and all his finer emotions in terms of sublimated sexual energy. The break between Freud and Jung was not as dramatic as Adler's — they drifted apart during the war years — but it was every bit as final, and it left Freud as bitter toward Jung as he was toward Adler.

Other early disciples left Freud from year to year. Most notable of these was Otto Rank, the man who had done such brilliantly erratic work in applying psychoanalysis to mythology and literature, who is accused by Freud's "loyal sons" of deserting the Master because Freud developed cancer of the mouth. The Viennese physician, Stekel, left Freud largely for personal reasons. After having learned the technique and the theory of psychoanalysis, Stekel seems to have shaken off Freud's hypnotic influence and regained his independence. He insisted that the new science should confine itself to the medical treatment of neuroses. So, as Freud abandoned medical work to concentrate on metapsychology, Stekel refused to follow him. He continued to do excellent work as an analyst, but because he did not accept every one of the Master's new ideas unquestioningly he was cut off from the sacred circle forever more.

Freud never even looked over his shoulder at a man on whom he had turned his back. His disciples were always faced with the difficult dilemma either of remaining loyal by being weak, or, by being strong, breaking from the Master. Psychoanalysts explain this difficulty as the inevitable friction between father and son (master and disciple), who are in unconscious deadly strife with each other. The master is bound to hold his disciples tyrannically in check, and they are bound to wish for his death so they can be free to be masters themselves. All this is unconscious, of course, and it reaches consciousness in the form of heresies within the Freudian movement, the disciples thinking they differ on points of doctrine when the real conflict is a struggle-for-power between "father" and "son."

The general postwar instability of the twenties not only guaranteed the survival of Freudianism, but also promoted its growth. An international congress — the first postwar meeting of scholars anywhere — assembled at Budapest late in 1918, and another met at The Hague in 1920. At this last congress Freud gathered together his six most trusted disciples — Rank and Jones, Abraham, Eitington, Ferenczi, and Sachs — to lay plans for controlling this unprecedented, not altogether welcome expansion. Until 1925 Freud was fairly successful in controlling the movement through these six men living in four capitals of Europe. These five years were the period of greatest peace and expansion within the movement.

But Freud was growing old and ill. After 1925 he withdrew into lonely isolation with his dogs and his antiques; only occasionally were such distinguished callers as Thomas Mann or Albert Einstein granted an audience. Freud had withdrawn from the world a friendless old man respected and admired by his loyal disciples. He continued his work in psychoanalysis, or more properly, his metapsychology, which became his only real interest in life. For some time he had been reworking his theory to arrange it into more systematized form, and within a short time he published the two best summaries of his later theory, *The Ego and the Id* and *Beyond the Pleasure Principle*. He also published several popular summaries of this theory under one title or another.

He had meanwhile extended the scope of his metapsychology by applying it to every field of thought. In *Totem and Taboo* and *Moses and Monotheism* he endeavored to explain prehistory as well as history, the origin of society, the beginning and development of religion, the social position of women and children, the meaning of art and literature. These things he did knowingly, for he believed he had the magic key to unlock all social puzzles. He tells us of his *Totem and Taboo*, for example, that it "should lead us directly to the origins of the most important institutions of our civilization, such as state regulations, morality, religion, as well as to the origins of the interdiction of incest and of conscience."

So he labored on, spending his eightieth birthday at home in Vienna working on his last book, *Moses and Monotheism*. Three years longer he lived, long enough to see *Moses and Monotheism* published and call it "quite a worthy exit." He lived long enough to see the Nazis march into Vienna. And he lived long enough to be rescued by Ernest Jones, who came quickly from London, and by Princess Marie of Greece whose little book, *Topsy*, Freud was translating. Freud's rescuers managed to get him to London, but most of his personal property was confiscated. Princess Marie bought back his library and his collections, however, and sent them to London, where Freud could soon be found busily at work — as though he had moved across the street in Vienna.

Freud's end was a happy one for his reputation — for he had the chance to die a persecuted intellectual, a refugee from Nazi tyranny. Freud hardly deserves the apotheosis this accident accorded him. On this score, he deserves sympathy, but little more than that, for in politics he was no more an enemy of the Nazis than he was their friend. As far as he was concerned, all men were fools — and the only difference between Nazis and loyal Austrians was one of degree. It just happened that Freud was a Jew, and Nazis hated Jews. This was the same thing Freud had encountered as a student sixty years before. It had bewildered him then; it could not have done much else in 1938. The doctrine he had created in the intervening time might have helped him understand the Nazis in certain respects, though it probably blinded him to the real cause of their strength. Certainly, though, it gave him no right either to condemn or condone

them. He had himself lectured thus in Vienna: "We can demonstrate with ease that what the world calls its code of morals
demands more sacrifices than it is worth, and that its behavior
is neither dictated by honesty nor instituted with wisdom." The
Nazis had similar opinions.

3

Freud was a strong man who moved deliberately on his course,
oblivious alike of friend and critic. There seem to be only two
important things in Freud's life: himself and his creature, psychoanalysis. Everything else was incidental; everyone else mattered
only in so far as he was related to psychoanalysis. Freud was
strong because he depended on no one, because he needed no
one to satisfy him or make him happy. Freud is indeed the
strongest personality of the eleven men we have discussed in
these chapters. Others were more striking, others more intellectual, others more personable, but none was as strong as Freud.

In typical psychoanalytical fashion one of his "errant" followers, Fritz Wittels, tells how Freud lived in Vienna, the city of
emperors, during his impressionable years and how (by 1924)
he "had become an emperor, . . . who holds enlightened but
absolute sway in his realm, and is animated by a rigid sense of
duty. He has become a despot who will not tolerate the slightest
deviation from his doctrine; holds councils behind closed doors;
and tries to ensure, by a sort of pragmatic sanction, that the
body of psychoanalytical teaching shall remain indivisible and
whole."

The simile is apt. Freud was prouder than any of history's
proud Hapsburgs. Neither disciple nor heretic has denied that
pride was his outstanding characteristic. Even Hans Sachs, one
of the followers who remained unquestioningly loyal to the end,
tells us in his rather pathetic little book, *Freud, Master and
Friend,* that pride was the principal force in Freud's life. He
never posed; he never pretended to be humble; he always admitted quite frankly that he was an unusual sort of person, that
he considered anyone who did not agree with him either stupid
or dishonest. In all relationships he formed throughout life, Freud

insisted on being Master. And Master he was to Sachs, as to all others who remained loyal. But never was he friend. Sachs admits that although Freud called "me his friend, I did not feel that I was; fundamentally he remained as remote as when I first met him in the lecture hall." Freud was always too proud and too self-centered to be anyone's friend. All through life he remained remote from all men.

Freud's success was due largely to his power of concentration and his fixity of purpose. As a young man he discovered the practical advantages of having a fixed idea, in terms of which one viewed everything. While he was an intern he had experimented with cocaine and had written a scholarly article on it. But an acquaintance of his, one Karl Koller, who thought of nothing but the eye — in which he intended to specialize — experimented with cocaine on eyeballs and thus discovered its anesthetic property. Freud always resented his own failure to make the discovery and Koller's success, which he attributed to the latter's "fixed idea" of the eye. So Freud decided to make psychoanalysis his fixed idea, to see nothing, do nothing, read nothing, think nothing except in terms of psychoanalysis. "This is the only way to make important discoveries: have one's ideas exclusively focused on one central interest." He lived out that resolve with unbelievable literalness — never seeing even a play, for example, unless it happened to be such a tragedy as *Hamlet* or *Oedipus Rex*, which he could watch clinically. "In every incident of life that came under discussion," Sachs tells us, "he detected and demonstrated the influence of a particular form of infantile wish-phantasy; of the effects made by its repression, adaptation, distortion, sublimation, or overcompensation; of the ways in which the unconscious disguised itself behind tragic and comic masks."

Thus Freud came to have a closed mind. He frankly confessed that he was annoyed by other men's ideas, that he could not assimilate them, that his was a one-track mind which brooked no interference. Sachs concurs in this opinion the Master offered of himself when he tells us that Freud never listened to his arguments and was never moved by his objections. "After that," Sachs states, "I acquiesced unreservedly with his decisions and

acted in the way he wished, stopping all further remonstrances."
So did everyone else — or else Freud turned his back on them,
never to look back.

Freud would never have reached the absurd theoretical conclusions he ultimately did if he had not been a narrow-minded
man with a fixed idea, a man who listened to no one. For he
would have profited from the observations of his critics and the
criticisms of his opponents. But he never heeded objections to
his doctrine; he considered them beneath his notice, unworthy
of his time. "I did not have to read any of the medical literature,"
he writes, "or listen to any ill-informed opponents." This is the
way the crank works. It is only because of Freud's excellent early
training and the native strength of his mind that he rose above
the level of a mere crank. His method of investigation and
theorizing had become thoroughly unscientific.

It saved him much time, however, for Freud did not proceed
painstakingly as scientists or philosophers do. He jumped to conclusions — and thus he was able to reach many, many conclusions,
many more than even a genius could properly reach in a lifetime.
As far as the world was concerned, he kept within the magic
circle of his devotees, allowing them to argue with his opponents
until he himself was ready to step forth to deliver the crushing
blow. Then he would return again and allow the answers of
his opponents to melt in thin air, or to be dealt with by loyal
followers.

Though such a method saved Freud time, it made him intolerant, a fact he would himself admit, though in different words.
In his history of the psychoanalytic movement he tells us that
"my confidence in the honesty and distinction of my opponents
has always been slight." All this made for strength of mind and
tenaciousness of purpose, but it made for a narrow, confined
sort of strength, for a fixity of purpose that was blind rather
than discerning. Freud's strength was also his weakness. However it enabled him to proceed far along a narrow path obviously
bending in the wrong direction. Freud went far because he
possessed a fixed idea. Others have already come to modify and
correct his obvious errors. But the unconscious would not have
been so deeply explored had Freud not been the narrow-minded,
domineering person he was.

4

To do justice to Freud, one must distinguish between psychoanalysis as a practice and as a philosophy. It has developed in both respects; and though there are some points of contact between practice and theory, neither depends essentially upon the other. Psychoanalysis was originally developed, in fact, as a method for curing hysteria. Only after years of successful clinical work did Freud abandon his practice for the more abtruse realm of philosophizing. In his earlier writings he claimed that "psychoanalysis is a method of medical treatment for those suffering from nervous disorders."

From this method of medical treatment Freud soon deduced the body of theory commonly known as Freudianism. Psychologists, it is well to keep in mind, distinguish three levels of procedure in their work: the scientific, which consists principally in experiment and the immediate conclusions to which it leads them; the theoretical, in which general laws of human behavior are adduced from the experimental work; and the philosophical, where an attempt is made to give ultimate laws of human behavior, and to offer the final explanation of such things as man's nature and the meaning of life. Most psychologists insist that the third level is not a legitimate field for psychological investigation.

In his earlier work Freud worked principally on the first level. Before the nineteenth century ended, however, he moved up the second level of creating theories to explain the phenomena he had discovered in the clinic. Freud was not content to stay on the second level, however, where psychologists even today would like to keep him confined. He went on to build a philosophy and a faith, which he considered his real accomplishment and which he demanded that all those who called themselves Freudian accept uncritically. It is not only valid but absolutely necessary to distinguish these three levels of Freud's work if one is to do him justice and to appreciate the contributions he has made to psychology as a science, as well as to understand the impact he has made on the layman's mind.

As a therapeutic technique, psychoanalysis probes into the unconscious to lay bare hidden conflicts in the patient's soul.

Freud claims that it "aims at and achieves nothing more than the discovery of the unconscious in mental life." It probes into the unconscious, Freud says "to uncover repressions and replace them by acts of judgment which might result either in the acceptance or in the rejection of what had formerly been repudiated." In his later works, after he had revised his theory and changed his terminology, Freud said that "the therapeutic aim of psychoanalysis" is to restore the "Ego" to sovereignty over the "Id." This merely states the same thing in different terms; the significance of the new statement lies in the fact that Freud no longer looks on psychoanalytic practice as the sole aim of the analyst. But he never abandoned it as a legitimate aim. The analyst therefore seeks to cure his neurotic patient by bringing repressed impulses to the light of consciousness, making the patient emotionally aware of the struggle going on within him, thus making it possible for him to reconcile the conflicting claims of his instinctual urges and his conscious self.

The method of treatment, whereby the patient is helped to discover these unconscious or subconscious desires, constitutes Freud's greatest and most lasting accomplishment in the field of psychoanalysis proper. The patient is required to lie down, to put himself in a condition of calm self-observation, to think of nothing, and then to tell the analyst whatever occurs to him: feelings, thoughts, memories, dreams, anything at all. All these things, Freud claims, have meaning, and as they are communicated to the analyst a pattern begins to form.

The analyst must penetrate from the symptoms related to him to the objects for which they stand. Thus Freud knew that the boy who said he was afraid of horses really feared his father, the girl who kept her pillow from touching the head of the bed was jealous of her mother and in love with her father. The analyst must also supply the meaning of dream symbols, something the dreamer can never do. Thus Freud knows that little animals and vermin always stand for brothers and sisters, that clothes and uniforms always stand for nakedness. The analyst must also supply the relationship between his patient's present illness and the past disturbances which he has recalled from the unconscious for the analyst. When he has diagnosed the patient's trouble, the analyst's task is to reveal his difficulties to him so that he can cure himself. That is why Freud sometimes calls psychoanalysis a process of re-education.

Early in the course of treatment, Freud claims, the patient always sets up a strong unconscious resistance to the analyst and to the treatment. This unconscious resistance comes to light in various ways, but it is always "an intense emotional relationship between the patient and the analyst" which can be accounted for, Freud states, only as a transference by the patient of his uncontrolled *libido* from the former object of its attachment to the analyst. This, Freud maintains, is the critical period in the treatment, "the most difficult as well as the most important part of the technique of analysis." How the analyst handles this problem will determine his success or failure in curing the patient. He is now supposed to have concentrated the patient's misdirected "libido" on himself, and he therefore has it temporarily under control. If he can make the patient aware of this fact, and if he can enable him consciously to direct his "libido" to proper outlets, then the conflict within the patient will have been ended and he will be cured. Freud sums it up thus: "The transference is made conscious to the patient by the analyst, and it is resolved by convincing him that in his transference-attitude he is *re-experiencing* emotional relations which had their origin in his earliest object-attachments during the repressed period of his childhood. In this way the transference is changed from the strongest weapon of the resistance into the best instrument of the analytic treatment."

It is obvious, from what we have seen, that psychoanalysis involves interpretation by the analyst. It is so much interpretation, indeed, that the analyst's beliefs seem to play a larger part in the treatment than any other single factor. Freud admits willingly that "the work of analysis involves an *art of interpretation,*" because no one but a trained analyst can know the meaning of the patient's unconscious desires and the devious ways by which they push into consciousness. As an analyst, for example, Freud knew that a president who opened a meeting by mistakenly saying, "the meeting is adjourned," really did not want the meeting to convene. The official thought he did, but unconsciously, if only he knew it, he wished it would not. So too Freud understood that a woman who suspected her husband of going around with younger women did so only because she had herself unknowingly and unconsciously become attached to her son-in-law.

The role played by the analyst's interpretation is therefore necessarily somewhat arbitrary — until rules of interpretation can be established by experimental research. Some general rules have already been established, and certain healthy attitudes can be developed by the analyst. But certainly in Freud's hands interpretation became tyrannically arbitrary — facts were always forced to fit his theories. He insists that no interpretation is valid unless it arrives at a sexual experience and unless it goes back to the patient's infancy. "Every time," he insists, "we should be led by analysis to the sexual experiences and desires of the patient." The roots of all psychic disturbances are in childhood, so every analysis must eventually end up in the patient's infancy — where finally the trouble will be found. Such arbitrary interpretation of the patient's symptoms is bound to support Freud's theories, but it does not make for good scientific procedure. It is based on insufficient clinical study. Analysts who follow Freud closely all tend to overlook the patient's yesterday to study his childhood, but there is no valid reason for believing that yesterday should be ignored. In many later analysts' hands, however, the art of interpreting symbols has been much better developed than it was in Freud's.

Because of Freud's arbitrary insistence on infantile sexuality as the cause of all neuroses, we are apt to deny him credit for what he actually did accomplish. His method was new for its autobiographical attack on mental life, by which the patient freely told his own story, revealing much more to a capable psychologist than if he merely answered routine questions. Freud's method was therefore unique in its directness and fruitful in its results. Valuable insights into the "unconscious" mental life were afforded; light was shed where psychologists had seen only darkness before. Freudian practice was helpful, then, for getting at facts formerly out of reach. It made possible the excellent work now being done in "experimental psychoanalysis" by such men as Erikson, the saner theoretical, as well as practical work of such contemporary psychoanalysts as Karen Horney and Anna Freud. Its interpretation of facts is another matter, however, a matter which led Freud to formulate his body of doctrine which we call Freudianism.

5

Freud is not to be judged principally on the basis of his clinical work. Nor would he want to be. It was the Freudian idea that was his passion, his fixed idea, not the curing of neurotics. It was his theory that he thought important, and on its merits he would willingly rest his reputation. To give an accurate, concise summary of his theory is difficult because he constantly changes the meaning of the terms he uses, and sometimes he seems not to be very sure of what he really means by a term. His earlier theory, completed by 1907, did not melt into obscurity when his revisions appeared. So there have come to be two Freuds, the early and the late, who have much in common but also considerable in opposition to each other.

Throughout all Freud's works, however, runs the fundamental belief that man is not the integrated unit he thinks he is. "Our very own self," he says pointedly, "is not an indivisible unit, as we have always considered it." We are instead several units which Freud treats as though they have a real, independent existence somewhere within us. Certainly, he holds, these units do not flow from a common source. They are not harmonized by any agency, nor do they tend toward a common goal. They are simply heterogeneous. All they have in common is their enmity for each other. Man is thus pictured as a battleground on which is fought a never ending civil war. He is a man divided against himself, and none of his conflicting units can permanently establish sovereignty over the others.

In his earlier works Freud speaks of three psychic areas in man. There is first of all the "unconscious," far and away the largest — and, we get the impression, the most important — of these areas; it remains in the dark, and in no way can happenings in this area be known to us. There is also the "fore-conscious," which contains all that material which can be recalled more or less at will. Finally, there is the "conscious," which Freud complains was the sole concern of psychologists before his time. But this conscious is only a small part of the *psyche*. It is likened to that part of the iceberg which is above water, or again to the skim which forms on the top of a bowl of milk.

In one of his introductory lectures Freud explains this division by an apt simile. He likens the unconscious to a large waiting room in which various "mental excitations" are milling around. Adjoining this is a small room, in the corner of which consciousness sits. Between the two rooms stands as attendant, the censorship, which admits some of these impulses that crowd to the door but refuses to admit many others. Those getting through the doorway enter the smaller room of the fore-conscious system, and they become conscious if they catch the eye of consciousness sitting in the corner. Those turned back at the doorway are "repressed"; they go back into the waiting room of unconsciousness and do devious things.

Freud changes his terminology from spatial concepts to personal ones in his later writings. Here the element of conflict is intensified. Here he divides men into an "Id," an "Ego," and a "Super-Ego." The Id corresponds roughly to the unconscious of the earlier division; it "is much more extensive, impressive and obscure than the Ego." The Id seems to have become a person whose sole aim is pleasure gratification. It knows nothing of the outer world; it is bent on immediate, rash pleasure, and it never reckons the consequences. The Ego differs considerably from the earlier consciousness. Freud calls it "the outer, front layer of the Id." It is "inserted between the reality of the outer world and the Id, the latter constituting the soul proper, the essence of the soul, as it were." The Ego, however, contains both conscious and unconscious elements. It differs from the Id in being more calculating, in following the "reality principle" instead of the "pleasure principle." And it therefore censors the Id's urges, repressing some of them, adapting some to reality, and giving way to others.

The third element in this later division was never nicely defined by Freud. He calls it the "Super-Ego," which he considers an unconscious agent in continual conflict with that other unconscious agent, the Id. Between them the Ego stands as referee, apparently trying to reconcile them by some kind of arbitration. When the Ego takes sides, abdicating as referee, neurosis results. The Super-Ego seems to be pretty close to what most of us call conscience. Brill gives as precise a definition of the Super-Ego as anyone when he says: "The Super-Ego is the highest mental evolution attainable by man, and consists of a precipitate of all prohibitions, all the rules of conduct which are impressed on the child by his parents and parental substitutes. The feeling of conscience depends altogether on the development of the Super-Ego."

Thus each man is made a battleground when Id, Ego, and Super-Ego mill around in mortal, continual conflict. Though it would seem that the conflict between the Super-Ego (conscience) and the Id (animal desire) would be more important from the psychoanalytic point of view, nevertheless the relationship between the Ego and the Id is the critical thing. For neurosis results when the Ego represses the Id's urges and thus leaves them unsatisfied. These urges are conceived by Freud as something like electrical charges which must be spent on an object; when they are repressed they are left fully charged and incapable of finding an object on which to use up, or discharge, this energy. Neurosis results, then, when the Ego fails as referee, taking the side of the outer world and repressing some of the Id's energy instead of finding it another satisfactory outlet.

Freudian theory therefore represents man as an essentially irrational creature powered by instinctive energy alone. The thing we call intelligence comes into play only in censoring these charges of animal energy and in relating them to the demands of the outer world. Reason, no more than part of the "skin on the milk," plays a purely negative role in human activity. Free will, of course, is an illusion to which Freud says he stands "in sharpest opposition." All decisions we seem to make freely come from conflict between the Id and the Ego, the result of which depends in each case upon the relative strength of the two contestants at the time the decision is made — plus, of course, all those battles which have gone on since birth.

This instinctive, irrational, unconscious self called the Id, "the essence of the soul, as it were," is a pan-sexual entity. Freud pushes all its impulses, all its drives, back to the ultimate source of sex-energy. This sex-energy he calls the "libido," defined as "that quantitatively changeable and not at present measurable energy of the sexual instinct." It is simply psychic energy which can be called sexual only in a very loose sense of the word, for it includes such things as thumb-sucking and bottle nursing by babies. Such a thing as loving cats or hating horses is a substitute whose purpose, Freud says, "is either a sexual gratification or a defense against it." So though Freud pushes all energy back to sex, he widens sex to include everything connected with the senses and with instinct.

6

A word must be said about the place errors and wit and especially dreams occupy in Freudian theory, because many amateur psychoanalysts read Freud for no other purpose than to be able to analyze dreams and explain the meaning of errors. This phase of his theory is therefore an important legacy he bequeathed to the modern mind. The error, the joke or pun, and the dream, he concludes, are all essentially similar to neurotic symptoms. They are all compromises resulting from two conflicting tendencies: the Id, which seeks immediate, rash pleasure, and the Ego, which censors the Id's urge, represses it and allows it to focus on a substitute for its original object. This substitute is the error, the joke, or the dream; it can therefore be called the disguised fulfillment of a repressed wish — about which the conscious Ego has no knowledge.

Thus Freud maintains that errors all have meaning. The man who missed his train because he was mixed up on schedules thinks he wanted to catch it, but unconsciously he desired to miss it; the man who said the meeting was closed instead of opened unconsciously wanted the meeting never to open, whether he realized it or not; the maid who knocked over a pitcher really wanted to hurt her employer. Freud therefore concludes: "Mistaking of objects, or erroneous performance of actions, like other errors, is often made use of to fulfill a wish which should be denied; the intention masquerades as a lucky chance." So it is with jokes, "the best safety valve modern man has evolved." They enable us to obtain a satisfaction — lewd or not — which polite society would otherwise deny us.

Dreams are essentially the same as errors and jokes, but they are more important for the psychoanalyst because they lead him into the patient's unconscious, whereas errors and jokes lead only into the foreconscious. Freud tells us that dreams occur because our Ego relaxes its censorship when we go to sleep. The Id takes advantage of this nocturnal relaxation by the Ego to push its way into consciousness. But the Ego is never fully asleep. It therefore censors the "latent dream-thought" by allowing it to reach consciousness as a "manifest dream" in a disguised form agreeable to the Ego. In this way both Id and Ego are satisfied, and the patient does not awaken. The manifest dream must obviously be interpreted by the analyst, for only in this way can he arrive at the latent dream-thought, which is the work of the unconscious Id. The manifest dream therefore corresponds to the neurotic symptom, the latent dream-thought to the repressed desire.

Such, in essence, is the Freudian body of theory which served as the basis for psychoanalysis. This body of Freudian thought, however, should not be confused with psychoanalysis today, for Freud's various theories have been checked and are still being checked by experiment. Some of them have been validated in whole or in part; some have been completely rejected, and some have suggested other lines of investigation which have modified Freud's conclusions. His theories are therefore no more identified by specialists with psychoanalysis today than are Adler's or Jung's. In the popular mind, however, Freudian theory is the same thing as psychoanalysis.

7

The Master himself began to apply his body of theory haphazardly to all fields of human activity. Because he believed it would unlock the secrets of history and religion, literature and art, politics and sociology, because it had such "far-reaching connections," Freud believed that psychoanalysis was "worthy of every educated person's interest." Although he feared what might happen to the purity of his doctrine in the process of popularization, he nevertheless insisted that his doctrine be carried to everyone and applied to every social study.

Freud studies a painting or a poem exactly as he does an error, a dream, or a neurotic symptom. Artists' creations, he writes, are "the imaginary gratifications of unconscious wishes, just as dreams are; and like them they are in the nature of compromises, since they, too, are forced to avoid any open conflict with the forces of repression." The artist, then, satisfies his Id, gives his libido release, and obtains sexual gratification by doing a painting or writing a poem. Like the good wit, Freud says, the artist — poet, painter, musician, choregrapher, and such — is practically a neurotic. "The artist has an introverted disposition and has not far to go to become neurotic. . . . He turns away from reality and transfers all his interest, and all his libido too, into the creation of his wishes in the life of phantasy, from which the way might readily lead to neurosis." Only thus, he believes, can Shakespeare or Da Vinci be understood.

Freud also set himself the task of explaining all history in the light of his wonderful new discovery. He alone could understand history, he believed, because he alone understood man, and "the events of human history, the interactions between human nature, cultural development and the precipitates of primeval experiences are no more than a reflection of the dynamic conflicts between the Ego, the Id and the Super-Ego, which psychoanalysis studies in the individual." Freud accepted uncritically the theory of the primitive horde, whereby the intellectuals of his time were trying to slide man across the chasm between the forest primeval and the civilized village, and from this theory he wrote a highly imaginative account of the beginnings of society, of religion, of all social institutions — which he insisted was not speculation but literal fact.

He tells us how the father of this primitive horde was a tyrant who had seized all the women of the group for himself. His sons came together one day "to overwhelm, kill, and devour their father, who had been their enemy but also their ideal." Conflict among themselves and a sense of guilt prevented them from taking the women for whom they slew their father — whence arises the social disapproval of incest; the patricide was commemorated in time by a totem feast — whence arises religion. And so it goes, on and on, with everything in history eventually explained by this "original sin" of patricide and the sense of guilt which came from it. Freud sums up his contribution to the understanding of history in this way: "Society is now based on complicity in the common crime, religion on the sense of guilt and the consequent remorse, while morality is based partly on the necessities of society and partly on the expiation which this sense of guilt demands."

It is unfortunate that this man of one fixed idea should have tried to bend all the world to it. His reputation would have remained much better had he used that idea to illuminate man's history and his cultural accomplishments — for none can successfully deny that Freud has thrown light on these things, as he did on error, witticisms, and dreams. But he was not content merely to throw light, to offer only partial explanations; he insisted his word was not only the last word on all these things, but the sole word. Instead of using his psychoanalysis for men's welfare and enlightenment, Freud abused men for the prosperity of psychoanalysis.

Psychologists maintain that Freud's application of psychoanalysis to all fields of thought is something that can and should be overlooked in passing judgment on the man. They insist that his philosophy of man and his world view are not essential to the body of his psychoanalytic theory, and therefore it would be well to ignore them. Whether they are right or wrong, the fact remains that Freud did apply his theories to all fields of human speculation, that he insisted his metapsychology was his great contribution to the human knowledge, that it was an integral part of Freudianism, and that it must be so accepted by his followers. Moreover, although psychologists distinguish his theoretical findings from his philosophical conclusions, Freud has influenced the modern mind more with his metapsychology and his popularized, poetized theories about neurosis than he has as a clinical investigator. He must therefore be evaluated as the author of *Totem and Taboo* and *Moses and Monotheism* as well as the discoverer of repression and fixation.

8

It is difficult, nevertheless, to deal with Freudianism fairly, except to evaluate it piece by piece, showing the worth of each theory Freud formulated. A few generalizations, however, can be made. The therapeutic practice introduced by Freud is good in general; on the other hand, although the theory he formulated makes some valuable contributions to our knowledge of man, it is in general an accumulation of absolute dicta unwarranted by the meager evidence upon which they are based. The earlier theory is sounder than the later; after about 1913 Freud seems to have lost his sense of reality as he retreated within himself and ignored the outside world. It is unfortunate that Freud gave up his psychoanalytic practice to philosophize. His earlier discoveries about sex, for example, are revealing; but soon he made unscientific generalizations from his experience in the consultation room; and finally he arrived at fantastic explanations about the role of sex in human life, such as having all cultural accomplishments, all noble acts result from "sublimated libido."

Freud and his followers always insist that his theories are not idle speculation. "I have always felt it as a gross injustice that people always refused to treat psychoanalysis like any other science," Freud has written. He claims that it is not by any means "a speculative system of ideas. On the contrary, it is the result of experience, being founded either on direct observation or on conclusions drawn from observation." But Freud's theories do not all stand up under the tests applied to "any other science." Many of his earlier, better theories are in the process of being checked in the psychologist's laboratory at the present time. Although the evidence is not complete, it already shows that Freud often hit the truth with amazing penetration and insight. At other times he was hopelessly wrong. But right or wrong, he did not arrive at his theories by rigorous scientific methods.

One example will show how he sometimes reached his infallible conclusions in "scientific manner." Freud decided that "birth is the source and prototype of the anxiety effect," and he tells the reader that "speculation had least of all to do with it." He reached this remarkable conclusion by hearing a midwife tell at the dinner table of the hospital how "frightened" an infant had been at birth that morning. Arriving "scientifically" at a theory from a chance remark made by an illiterate midwife is doing strange things to the scientific method. That is why the reader should not feel too much sympathy for a Freud who complains his theories are treated as unwarranted speculation rather than as scientifically established truths. Freud was much more a poet than a scientist. It remains for scientists to check the accuracy of his poetized findings.

That is why medical men and psychologists remained aloof, refused to embrace his theory, condemned it as imaginative meandering rather than sound science. Because many of Freud's fundamental assumptions cannot be tested by techniques now at the disposal of the experimenter, the scientist has reason to demand that they be arrived at only after all evidence available points to their validity. Freud's pages are alive with such phrases as "we may presume," and "we must assume," for which he offers no proof at all. Instead, he hurries along as though what he had assumed is thereby proved. The psychologist, Woodworth, voices the common opinion of his fellow scientists when he says that Freud makes enough dogmatic assumptions on any given page to keep a corps of experimentalists at work for years proving them — and Freud wrote many, many pages. Scientists, therefore, rightly object to Freud's dogmatism. The Unconscious, by its very nature, has not yet been developed as a legitimate field for scientific investigation; whatever is said of it, on the basis of clinical investigation, must be proffered tentatively rather than dogmatically. Freudianism, in this way, can never become a scientific idea like Newtonianism or Darwinism. Freud has demanded that the world accord him more than is his due.

One cannot use the laboratory to prove the nonexistence of such poetized Freudian concepts as the Id, the Super-Ego, or the libido. Inductively it is difficult to prove Freud wrong — just as it is impossible for the Freudian to prove his Master right. Nor can you meet the Freudian on the field of speculation. You simply cannot argue about the unconscious, for Freud holds that you can never know it. Neither can the neurotic know the meaning of his neurosis. "Always and everywhere," Freud has said, "the meaning of the symptoms is unknown to the sufferer." The analyst alone knows the secrets of the soul. Disagreement with his verdict is nicely taken care of by the Freudian theory of "resistance," and explained away as a symptom which in turn is explained as the result of another unconscious drive. Like Marx's dialectic, Freudianism is clothed in an impenetrable armor which no argument can pierce — for every argument is resolved into unconscious, unknown drives of the Id. Only analysts may argue about theories dealing with the unconscious.

So it is with your dreams. They are, Freud says, "a symbolic mode of expression of which he [the dreamer] knows nothing, and does not recognize in his waking life." The dreamer must accept on faith whatever the analyst tells him of his latent dream-thoughts, the unconscious desires of which the remembered dream is only a symbol. So it is with taboos and social customs. The investigator is not to ask the savage what a particular taboo means, for "according to our assumption they must be incapable of telling us anything about it." The analyst alone can supply meaning to the doings of primitive people; what they or anyone else says about their customs is absolutely irrelevant. There is no possibility, then, of meeting Freud on his own terms to criticize his theories and to distinguish what is good in them from what is bad.

His interpretations, however, are certainly strained; his conclusions contradict common sense and the traditional intellectual heritage of the Western World. Either that body of theory known as Freudianism is wrong, or the Western tradition is absurd. A few typical examples will indicate how Freudian interpretation might arrive at unwarranted conclusions. In one of his works he tells of a five-year-old boy who had an abnormal fear of horses. This fear was the symptomatic manifestation of an Oedipus complex — accentuated love by the boy for his mother and desire for his father's death, all unconscious, of course. He feared horses because he had made them substitutes for his father, whom he also feared as well as hated. He was really jealous of his father because of the latter's close relationship to the boy's mother. Now it does not require much persuasion by a terrifying physician in a white coat to make a five-year-old boy admit all these things when the analyst believes them and is ready to force the boy's experiences into his own pattern of thought. Freud fails to prove that the boy was not simply afraid of horses. He may have been correct in his conclusion in this case, but the detached observer is led to suspect that the solution was arrived at with suspicious speed and according to a ready-made pattern.

In similar fashion Freud insists that fear of blindness is always a substitute for fear of castration, which is the basic fear in all patient's lives. Such a theory overlooks the point that one can really fear losing his sight, that such a fear need stand for nothing else. Again, Freud is often correct, but the critic has a right to object to his hasty generalization that fear of blindness is never really fear of blindness. So it is with his explanation of why people curl up in bed. We do this, Freud explains, because of prenatal influence which makes us assume an "intra-uterine" position. All of which overlooks the fact that many people curl up in bed only when they are cold. So it is with almost all Freud's later theories. He explains anti-Semitism by the Gentiles' unconscious opposition to circumcision — which overlooks economic, social, and racial prejudices entirely. Such explanations are at best unnecessarily strained — especially when there is little objective evidence to support them. They can well be right occasionally; but Freud insists they are always right, and nothing else is ever right.

So it is with the interpretation of dreams. If one dreams of riding a canoe, for example, he has an impotence complex, because canoe is a pun for cannot. Again, a female patient of Stekel's dreamt she was flying to Apulia. This meant that she was in love with her analyst, because Apulia is the "heel" of the Italian boot, and in Viennese dialect the heel is called "Stekel." So too the meaning of fairy tales has been discovered for the first time by Freud's interpretation. He tells us, for example, how the wolf in Little Red Riding Hood is "the child-devouring father in disguise," and he concludes that "the world of fairytales can be understood only on the basis of the sex life of the child." These examples could be continued forever, and much more extreme ones abound in Freud's works,* but these are enough to indicate what we are asked to accept on faith if we accept Freudian theory uncritically.

---

* Eventually, Freud came to the conclusion that "the whole chain of reactions characteristic of the female" derived from her "condition of 'Penis Envy.'" On the basis of this Freud thought he could show why women seek or avoid marriage, why they try to be attractive, why they pride themselves on good housekeeping — and so on. With men, he concluded, everything eventually goes back to "Penis Anxiety," or fear of castration. To so simplify everything in a normal person's life is to blind oneself to a thousand things.

The case for the Freudian system is further weakened when we remember that although Freud set out to create a philosophy and a faith, he was by self-admission no philosopher. In his *Autobiography* he states complacently that he always avoided works of philosophy, and that "this avoidance has been greatly facilitated by constitutional incapacity." One therefore has the right to be as suspicious of Freudianism — which is primarily a philosophy of man — as he would be of an historian's theory of how the atomic bomb works, after the historian had expressly stated that he knew nothing of nuclear physics.

Moreover, Freud's later works, in which he applies psychoanalysis to all fields of thought, do not help his case at all. In them he consistently begs the question. He interprets literature and history in the light of psychoanalysis, and concludes from his investigation that he has further proved the validity of psychoanalysis. But no one can prove his point by assuming its truth and using this assumption to interpret all the evidence used to support it. Even the evidence from which Freud proceeds to weave his story of primitive history in *Totem and Taboo* — such as a chance remark of Darwin's, or Frazer's *Golden Bough* — are no longer considered definitive statements on primitive man.

Finally, the case for Freudianism is weakened by the fact that other analysts — many of them as competent as Freud — do not arrive at the same conclusion that all neuroses result from sex disturbances. Why is this? Why should Freud have always found sexual disturbance at the basis of his patients' trouble? No definitive answer can be given, but Freud's tyrannically dominating personality, combined with his preconceptions, seems sufficient to account for this phenomenon. For it certainly should not have been difficult for Freud, without realizing what he was doing, to force one patient after another to admit "unconscious" drives that Freud was certain were in the patient's innermost soul. Freud's experience alone proves nothing about the sexual etiology of neuroses, for if his theories were correct every analyst would arrive at the same conclusions. Some do; some do not. The reason of divergence in their findings lies almost as much with the analysts, it would seem, as with their patients. Freud's dogmatic conclusions, at any rate, are based upon woefully inadequate personal experience which the Master refused to correlate with the findings of others. They cannot pretend to be scientific.

9

Right or wrong, or some of both — as the case seems to be — Freudianism burst upon the world in the postwar years like a volcanic eruption. It caused intellectual furor such as the Western World had not experienced since Darwin published his *Origin of Species* in 1859. Within a few years after World War I, Freudianism was hastily received, widely known, seriously misinterpreted. It filled a want sorely felt by the Western World; Freud was necessary because Calvin's and Kant's puritanism was no longer justifiable. Men were tired of puritan restrictions, for which they saw no justification — nor could defenders of that faith point to any save expediency. And puritan restrictions had not made men happy. Freud's success showed the instability of the modern mind, inasmuch as his system of thought was accepted uncritically, swallowed whole because it tasted good, or it was condemned *in toto* because many saw that it undermined the foundations of their beliefs — and they did not trust themselves to defend these beliefs against the corrosive acid of Freudian doctrine.

The popular acceptance of Freudianism revealed a vacuum in the modern mind and a nervousness in its temper. Attempts, some clumsy and some not, were made to explain the wonderful new thing in Sunday magazine sections of the newspapers, in the respectable popular magazines, and in the slicks that were not always sure their next number would get through the mail. One attempt to "bring Freud down to the people" put his theory thus: "The unconscious would appear to be a region resembling the zoological gardens, with all the keepers on strike. A host of unnoticed and unsuspected desires and passions are constantly roaring and raging in their cages. And the only hope for peace for the unfortunate patient is for the Psychoanalyst to open the cages and set their inhabitants free." This sort of thing was fair neither to Freud nor to the readers for whom it was intended. Hollywood even tried to hire Freud to collaborate with script writers — a pretty good indication of how Freudianism was thought to have taken over the popular mind.

In these days of wild popularization there was little sane criticism. Either men seemed to accept psychoanalysis as a cure-all or embrace it to excuse personal shortcomings, or else they raged against Freud as a nasty Jew who suggested children were sexy. Opponents of Freudian theory would have done a real service to their own cause if they had been more discerning in their criticism, because most young people came to believe that they had to accept Freud intact or else reject everything he said. They preferred to accept him intact. For, without reading him carefully, they thought he justified free love and high living, that he proved marital fidelity to be merely smug and conventional. Puritan standards, they felt, had "repressed" hundreds of urges that Freud had now shown were normal. It was high time, then, to enjoy life and preserve sanity. That is why the London *Times* complained that many people thought Freudianism was a "justification of immorality by science."

For this popularization Freud cannot be held entirely guilty. Neither can he be completely exonerated — since he sought to popularize his doctrines and to apply them to all the fields of knowledge as few scholars have ever done. He had made real contributions to the medical treatment of neuroses, as we have seen, and he had increased mankind's knowledge of the unconscious — but he was not content to stay within these legitimate fields of endeavor. He wanted all men to know the general theory of psychoanalysis, and therefore he went on to create a full-blown philosophy whereby he offered the ultimate explanation for all things.

This is dangerous, as well as useless. Freud's theory is the only one of the eleven we have seen which the average man cannot profitably study. It is essentially introspective (Freud insisted on deep introspection on the part of all analysts), and constant introspection is not good for most people. Reading Freud is enough to make one neurotic. The number of analysts who commit suicide, according even to the estimate of one of them, is disproportionately high. It is a truism that freshmen medical students find themselves catching every disease they study; but eventually they graduate and stay well. In the same way, most people who read much Freud find themselves in constant moral conflict with repressed urges bursting through to consciousness. The urge to stick a pin in the fat man bending over in the bus becomes a horribly serious, worrisome thing when one analyzes it in terms of the Id and the Super-Ego. It is so much easier and simpler to repress the urge until the fat man straightens up — and then forget all about it.

Freud's theory has an unhealthy effect on the modern mind because of what it does to man. Freud tells us that we are all practically neurotics: actors, artists, authors, down the alphabet to punsters and wits and zealots. "The healthy man too," he asserts, "is virtually a neurotic." Many of our social institutions, such as religion, are forms of universal neurosis. Nothing but man's capacity for neurosis distinguishes him from other animals, according to Freud, because man alone is capable of engendering conflict between Id and Ego. Otherwise, man is like the other animals; his Id is "the essence of the soul." Freud's whole bent of thought is anti-intellectual, and he always explains away those motives we think rational in favor of unconscious animal urges of which we are not at all aware. Instinct is the basic thing in man; intelligence is the skin on the surface of the milk of instinct, a thin skin formed by instinct's contact with the atmosphere of reality.

Much has been written about the conflict between Freudianism and traditional Western morality. Freud insisted time and time again that psychoanalysis has "no concern whatever" with morality. Such insistence, however, does not dissolve the fact that Freudianism and morality both deal with man's rational, human activity, that both are concerned with man's soul, or *psyche* — whichever it is called. Freud demanded that morality give way to psychoanalysis, condemning the eminent Harvard psychologist, Putnam, for example, for "yielding too much to the great ethical and philosophical bent of his nature." Freud always insisted that "we have found it impossible to give our support to conventional sexual morality," that the world's code of morals "is neither dictated by honesty nor instituted with wisdom." Psychoanalysis led him no farther than that. It did, however, suggest to uncritical followers that a completely amoral life was the only healthy, normal life.

Freud saw everything dualistically and dynamically. Everything, from errors and dreams to literature and painting, from the first primitive society to modern religion and radio comedians, is the result of conflict between two opposing forces. Within each man a constant raging conflict goes on. And society is only the individual writ large. Every man is then his own little battle-ground, and all society is a big battleground.

Except for terminology and for a dangerous poetizing of the drama, is this business of conflict within man as new as Freud thought it was? Plato saw it. So did the authors of the Old Testament. St. Paul ever talks of the ways of the flesh and the ways of the spirit. The Christian idea of original sin and of a weakened human nature with its inclination to evil accounts more rationally than Freudian theory for those impulses we all feel within us as vicious desires we must strive to refuse.

Freud, it is true, makes the conflict essentially nonintellectual. But has he progressed, in this respect, much past Luther? That first maker of the modern mind treated in these pages was one of the reason's greatest enemies. Freud is another. Both deny the supremacy of the intellect within man, and both deny him free will. In the sixteenth century, we have seen, Luther wrote: "The human will stands like a saddle-horse between the two [God and the devil]. If God mounts into the saddle, man wills and goes forward as God wills. . . . But if the devil is the horseman, then man wills and acts as the devil wills." Freud has not changed things very much by telling us that our apparently free decisions result from a conflict between the Id and the Ego. The terms are changed, the rules of the battle are altered, but man remains a passive, irresponsible instrument whose essential role is that of being a stage on which the living actors — God and the devil, or the Ego and the Id — do battle. The outcome of the conflict is not man's responsibility. He only happens to be the field on which it is fought.

XIII

CONCLUSION

INTELLECTUAL IMPERIALISTS

WE NATURALLY want to know, after discussing eleven makers of the modern mind, what made them outstanding. What essential factors do they have in common to account for their pre-eminence in the history of ideas? How do they differ from less important thinkers? Is it sheer power of mind that raises them above the level of the others? Are they heroes of the intellect, the manipulators of history that Carlyle would have them? Or are they simply fortunate figures selected haphazardly by fate for a role shaped by economic, political, and social circumstances over which they had no control? To answer these questions, even tentatively, we must see what they had in common, and what distinguished them from lesser lights such as Nietzsche or Henry Adams.

Examination of the extrinsic circumstances surrounding these men reveals few hard and fast conditions necessary for becoming a power in intellectual history. One thing they hold in common is their longer than ordinary life spans. Their average age is over seventy, considerably beyond the average for Europeans throughout the past four and a half centuries. Four of them — Kant, Bentham, Newton, and Freud — were more than eighty when they died. Only two of them — Descartes and Calvin — were under sixty. Descartes died at fifty-four, the shortest lived of the eleven. The importance of longevity must not be overstressed, however, for Newton accomplished his greatest work before he was twenty-five, and Calvin wrote the *Institutes* when he was twenty-seven. Kant, on the other hand, was fifty-seven when he published his first *Critique*, and Darwin was fifty when his *Origin* appeared. Some gave great promise as young men, like Newton, Descartes, and Calvin, but others attracted no attention till late in life. Locke, for example, was almost sixty before he published a thing. Some, like Bentham and Descartes, spent an entire lifetime perfecting their systems of thought, whereas others, like Rousseau and Newton, did their great work in a few short years. Some, like Freud and Rousseau, would have better reputations in history had they not lived as long as they did. Longevity, then, enabled some men to cut their niches in history as makers of the modern mind, but it is not essential for success.

There seems little connection between physical health and mental vitality — if we are to judge from the lives of these men. Luther was robust, but Calvin was a bundle of aches and pains. Descartes seems to have enjoyed good health, but Rousseau enjoyed only his debility. Newton's body was so perfectly healthy he could ignore it, but Kant and Locke fussed around with pills and diets all their lives. Darwin's stomach disorder allowed him only a few hours a day for concentrated study — but no other demands than nursing himself and working up his theories were made upon his time. So although good health is not a requisite for good thinking, physical debility must be of such a nature as not to prevent one from intensive study.

At first glance bachelorhood seems an aid to powerful thinking, for half these men lived and died without ever marrying. The fact that five of them did marry, however, shows that a wife is no insuperable handicap to becoming an influential thinker. Neither are children. Luther, Darwin, Marx, and Freud had families that would be accounted large by modern standards. But the fact remains that none of them allowed family affairs to distract him from his intellectual pursuits. Darwin's household, like Freud's, was run by his competent wife. Both men worked in perfect detachment, cut off from household problems and the noise of children. Marx, like Freud, Darwin, and Luther, was a much loved father, but his study was a sanctum which the children dared not violate. All eleven makers of the modern mind managed to obtain long periods of time for concentrated intellectual activity; they did not have to endure frequent distractions of any kind. Descartes moved to Holland so as to enjoy the privacy of a regulated life away from the distractions of his native Paris; Kant never married because he was afraid a wife would upset his scheduled life. No maker of the modern mind picked his ideas up on the run. Long periods of concentrated study were necessary for them all.

The men we have studied took the business of writing seriously. With none of them was it merely an avocation. Either it came directly out of each one's occupation in life — as with Luther, Calvin, Newton, and Kant — or it was made his life's work because he had an independent means of income — as was the case with Descartes and Darwin. This enabled all eleven thinkers to devote full time and all their energies to the task of formulating their systems of thought. They were no more distracted by earning a living than by family cares. Economic security would therefore appear to be essential for one who would think out and present to the world a powerful set of ideas. Certainly he cannot spend most of his time struggling for a livelihood.

One extrinsic circumstance which helps to account for the preeminent position accorded to these men in the history of ideas is the fact that each of them appealed to an enthusiastic young group who devoted their full time and energy to selling the master's bundle of ideas to the world. The last of Freud's immediate followers are now growing old, but they have done their work extraordinarily well. The ideas of great thinkers have always been spread similarly by groups — notably in the case of Marx and Darwin, Bentham and Kant, Newton and Descartes. What the popularizers lacked in critical insight they made up in missionary zeal. Sometimes an official organization was perfected by the master to perpetuate his doctrine, as was the case with Luther and Calvin, Marx and Freud. Whether or not there was machinery for selling the master's idea, there was always a group of enthusiasts who sold it to the next generation.

Moreover, they always sold it to the right people of the next generation, to a rising group who were to control the destinies, the thought, and lives of their associates. Lutheranism was sold to German princes rather than peasants. Calvinism was sold to the rising merchant class, and therefore received even wider circulation. Rousseau's ideas were sold to the up-and-coming bourgeoisie instead of the decadent nobility, Darwin's to the younger generation of naturalists, Marx's to a proletariat that democracy and trade unions were soon to make vociferous. Thus was the master saved from possible oblivion and guaranteed a prominent position in the history of ideas.

Our makers of the modern mind, then, have few extrinsic conditions in common. A long life span is helpful, but not essential; such things as earning a living or managing a household must not occupy so much time as to deny the author long periods of study. A group of popularizers is essential in order to propagate the master's doctrine, even to impose it on subsequent generations, and thus ensure him lasting repute among posterity. But differences among these men are more noticeable than likenesses. Their personalities, for example, do not reveal a common stamp, nor even a general similarity. Locke and Darwin were mild-mannered, easygoing men, whereas Freud and Marx were tyrannical. Luther and Rousseau were all heat and passion, impetuous in their personal lives as in their writing; Bentham, on the other hand, was a mechanically ordered rationalist, unmoved in his thinking by passion or enthusiasm or weakness of the flesh. And Calvin was a block of ice.

Neither did the eleven men we have examined take themselves and their missions with equal seriousness. Descartes thought he was the weightiest man in the history of philosophy since Aristotle, and he was hopeful that posterity would accord him even a higher place than that given to the great Greek. Kant believed himself important — like a fireman who rescues a baby from a burning house. For Kant was convinced that he was the man to rescue philosophy from the eighteenth-century skepticism into which it had fallen. Marx looked upon himself as the Moses of the new dispensation, one who would some day become eminent in history for having seen the promised land and having revealed it to the proletariat. In the same way and with the same conviction, Freud believed that his was the dispensation which would reveal all truth to mankind. It is true he never thought that men would have sense enough to mend their ways, as Marx so optimistically believed, but at least they would be able to understand themselves and the civilization they had patched together.

Darwin thought his discoveries important, but he does not seem to have attached the same overweening importance either to himself or to his work as did Descartes, Kant, Marx, or Freud. Similar importance was given to their doctrines by Bentham, Luther, and Calvin. Newton, Locke, and Rousseau apparently did not think either themselves or their systems of thought particularly important. Rousseau had absolutely no historical sense; he was so interested in his personal peeves and problems that he never had time to consider his ideas as anything more than projections of his own emotions. Locke thought himself only "an under-laborer in clearing ground a little," whose ideas were simply those of common sense, ideas that anyone who followed moderate reason could obtain for himself. Newton was so occupied with making a fortune and achieving a social position for himself that he considered his intellectual achievements important only as a gateway to political and social preferment. Biblical chronology and divinity were his serious studies, he believed, and compared to them science deserved only a nod in passing.

These makers of the modern mind are not eleven intellectual giants beside whom the lesser figures of history shrink in stature as they do in importance. These are not men whose intrinsic merit alone signaled them out for the position they occupy in the history of ideas. Darwin, for example, was absolutely deficient in any kind of abstract reasoning power. Newton was a genius of first rank in physics, it is true, but in the subjects he thought really important he was no more competent than thousands of others who took up biblical chronology or alchemy as hobbies. Freud was a powerful, penetrating thinker in a narrow way, like a shaft of light shot high into the sky from a searchlight. But he was unable to think outside his narrow field of concentration, or even to appreciate what went on outside the ken of his narrow thought. Luther was no thinker at all, though as a younger man he had shown more than average ability in philosophy and theology. Rousseau, again, had never shown intellectual ability of a high order. He felt strongly and he expressed his thoughts in powerful, moving prose. But he did no more than that.

There have, in fact, been greater thinkers in every century than the eleven who deserve to be called makers of the modern mind. Wycliff and Hus had said almost everything Luther was to say a century after them. They said it better and they thought it out more thoroughly — but somehow they did not catch on. Leibniz was a better rounded thinker than Kant. He was as fully aware of scientific, mathematical, and philosophical problems as Kant, and he devised a system to solve all difficulties — but he was not nearly so important in the making of the modern mind as Kant was a century later.

Diderot was superior to Bentham as an eighteenth-century rationalist, but even his editorship of the *Encyclopédie* did not make the citizen of Dijon as influential as Bentham became fifty years later. Lamarck explained evolution even more satisfactorily than Darwin, but Lamarck passed into near oblivion and Darwin became immortal. Many socialists criticized capitalism before Karl Marx wrote *Das Kapital,* and many of them drew plans for a more humane, more enticing utopia than Marx's drab classless society. Many socialists showed a more thorough understanding of economic laws than Marx exhibited in his writings — but Marx is properly looked upon as the founder of Communist doctrine, and the many other socialists are minor figures in history today who are mentioned only as predecessors of the great Marx, or as unimportant heretics who deviated from orthodox Marxian doctrine.

1

Are we then to conclude from our study of these eleven men that they are just ordinary persons whom a conflux of circumstances tossed into the spotlight of history with no regard for their intrinsic merit? Are they only persons who happened to reflect perfectly the popular ideas of a given age, ideas which in turn are a reflection of economic, social, climatic, and political conditions over which man exerts no real influence? In short, are these men makers of the modern mind through any merit of their own, or is it the concatenation of events which makes them great?

Marxists are always faced with that dilemma, as we have seen. They are embarrassed by trying to keep Marx's determinism undefiled while according Marx, Lenin, and Stalin their places as Herculean figures in the historical process. Trotsky's solution of the dilemma is a good statement of the Marxist position: "Of course, of course, of course, we know that the working class will triumph. We sing 'No man will deliver us' and we add 'No hero.' And that is true, but only in the last historical account. That is, in the last account of history the working class would have conquered if there had never been a Marx in the world, if there had never been a Lenin. The working class would work out those ideas which are needful to it, those methods which are needful to it, but more slowly."

Historians who in days gone by tended to emphasize the importance of individual heroic figures would accord the men we have studied a large role in the history of ideas. They would credit them with being heroes of the intellect who singlehanded turned the flow of ideas into new channels. Napoleons of the mind, they would be pictured as individuals whose intellectual power changed the very course of history. More recent historians, on the other hand, would credit their success entirely to the economic, social, and political environment in which they worked. The eleven men we have treated in these pages would be successful, following this interpretation, only because they were in tune with their times.

Neither of these interpretations is the whole truth. Each is an absolute statement of a partial truth. An influential thinker must possess unusual intellectual ability, and must use it to say well what his age feels but has not yet expressed clearly. Kant's doctrine, for example, would fall on barren soil today, because the world does not want an *als ob* philosophy in these times. But it is not enough to be a passive piece of flotsam tossed up by contemporary currents — or else every popular columnist would today be a maker of intellectual history. The thinker must be of more than ordinary proportions, but at the same time he must establish certain relationships to the beliefs and aspirations commonly held by his age. He must be in tune with its thought, sometimes accepting it rather passively and at other times altering it somewhat by changing its temper and by adding his own contribution. But he must accept the age's underlying assumptions; he cannot become important if he contradicts the age's accepted beliefs.

Like Descartes, he must avoid flying in the face of public

opinion. He must trim his doctrine to the winds of the day — as Descartes did in heralding his view on matter as providing a better explanation of transubstantiation than the scholastic provided, or as he did in writing his *Principles* in thesis form with the express purpose of having the Jesuits adopt the work in their schools. Neither can the influential thinker attempt to alter his age's opinions radically. If he tries to, he will appear a revolutionary innovator — and few men ever favor revolutionary change. (There is always the possibility, of course, that a thinker who seems radical to one age will not seem so later on. His works will then be dusted off and he will become a posthumous influence in the history of ideas, as Kierkegaard is today, as Marx has been the past thirty years.)

A maker of intellectual history must offer the world a set of ideas capable of being reduced to a simple formula. He must seem to have discovered the magic key which unlocks all mysteries bothering mankind at the time. Thus Luther solved the economic, religious, moral, and political difficulties irking his fellow Germans by stressing the doctrine of salvation through trust alone. He had them put all their sins on Christ's shoulders, and by a simple act of trust they relieved themselves of all responsibility for anything they did. Descartes's magic key was his infallible method, the use of which guaranteed to a rationalist that his conclusions could not possibly be wrong, no matter how absurd they might seem.

The others had similar key ideas by which they explained everything. With Locke it was the common sense of relatively intelligent Englishmen. No more were logical difficulties to trouble men, no longer were they to follow reason to its rational conclusions, no longer were they to be annoyed by inconsistencies between thought and action, or even between one thought and another. They were simply to follow common sense, even when it arrived at conclusions which could not be balanced in the ledger of right reason. Then there would be no more bitter religious strife or civil war. Rousseau had his magic key too — his heart. Instinctive feeling is infallible, he told his readers. Follow it and you can feel sure that you are right. Its message is God's message, and apparent difficulties are not to worry the good natural man. Darwin explained organic development by struggle for existence and survival of the fittest, and his solution was applied to all facets of life. Marx explained all things in terms of the class struggle, from religion and art to beer and pinochle. And Freud found his magic key in the unconscious. Everything man does or thinks or says or feels is resolved in terms of the unconscious; everything therefore is subject to the same treatment, and nothing is left a puzzle.

It is obvious, then, that an influential thinker must not offer too complex or too profound a set of ideas to the world. Not only his key idea, but also the lesser ideas that cluster around it must be relatively simple. Exactly how simple depends upon the age for which the thinker writes. Locke and Darwin, for example, had to think thinly because the ages in which they lived were superficial intellectually. Luther, Calvin, and Descartes, on the other hand, could probe more deeply, at least into philosophical and theological questions, for their age was able and willing to embrace somewhat profounder ideas. What about Kant, who lived at much the same time as Rousseau? The Genevan thought thinly and felt deeply — and he was influential at once. The Sage of Königsberg, on the other hand, offered the world a complex set of ideas, and for that reason he made almost no impact on the popular contemporary mind. Philosophers after Kant took up one or another of his ideas, simplified it, and passed it on to those who could sell it to the public. Thus Kant's real influence was delayed, and it spread out in the nineteenth century along divergent lines — each one, compared to Kant's original doctrine, an exceedingly simple, all-embracing idea.

Neither can a maker of the modern mind afford to be overly original. The large mass of mankind are essentially conservative, and they will greet original ideas with hostility. New ideas, in fact, crop up in a thousand unsuspected places, and their creators usually remain anonymous. It is only when their ideas survive the test of time and when they no longer appear shockingly new that an influential thinker dare embrace them. In this respect ideas are like party platforms in American history. New planks are put into the platforms of the major parties only when party leaders believe that they are "safe," that they will offend almost no one and will excite universal approbation. Thus it is left to minor parties to introduce new planks — like woman suffrage, or prohibition, or state ownership of public utilities — and to sell them to the public. When the idea is quite generally accepted in the country, either or both parties will warmly claim it as their own.

2

So it is with the makers of the modern mind. They are "intellectual imperialists," to borrow the phrase Barzun so aptly applies to Darwin and Marx. They pick up various ideas propounded by obscure thinkers — sometimes knowingly and sometimes unwittingly — combine these ideas in a new synthesis, and thus stake out a personal claim to intellectual tracts of land which numerous predecessors had explored and developed piece by piece. Influential thinkers, consequently, are not intellectual pioneers. They are rather imperialistic exploiters of the obscure pioneers' discoveries. Their one big contribution almost always lies in combining various ideas into a unified system centering around a master idea. Luther, for example, united such things as German discontent with an Italian papacy, desire for freedom from ecclesiastical control, German mysticism, social and economic discontent, a desire for simplicity in religion, and a strong anti-intellectual feeling. These things had all been developed piecemeal by the sixteenth century, but it remained for Luther to forge them together at the right time and in the right setting. Thus he became important, whereas his predecessors did not.

So it was with Newton. All through the seventeenth century men had groped toward one discovery after another in physics and mathematics. They had formulated the law of falling bodies; they had discovered the law of attraction; they had plotted the course of the planets. From Descartes, Newton learned analytic geometry, from Galileo he learned the fundamental laws of motion, from Kepler he learned how the planets move in their orbits. Newton had read of Descartes's work on lenses and on the telescope; he had read Kepler's treatise on light; he had followed the work on planetary motion done by Bulliadus and Borelli and Hooke. These were the "giants" on whose shoulders Newton admitted he stood in order to see so far. But the fact remains that only Newton could combine these ideas in such fashion as to become "Discoverer of Nature's Laws." These "giants" have been lost in obscurity, but Newton has become immortal because he hit upon the key idea which banished mystery from the universe. The others turned lights on in hallways and closets; Newton seemed to bathe the world in light.

So it was with Kant. The Sage of Königsberg succeeded where Leibniz and Wolff failed because he combined and made his own the two great living ideas of the eighteenth century — Newtonian physics and Rousseauvian morality. So it was with the other makers of the modern mind. Darwin picked up all the accepted ideas and attitudes of his age: Malthus' law of population, Comte's social scientism and worship of Progress, the Hegelian dialectical, evolutionary outlook, the general historical approach of the nineteenth century. All these — and organic evolution too — were explained by his master idea which fitted in so nicely with his generation's assumptions. Marx was successful in the same way and for the same reasons. His combination of static English economics with Hegel's dialectic gave him his master idea of explaining all things in terms of class struggle, an idea which he stated in the language of science.

Our makers of the modern mind cannot be explained, however, simply by concluding that they do nothing but synthesize the age's thought. Otherwise every encyclopedia editor would be a towering figure in the history of ideas. The men we have treated in these pages made an immediate appeal to their readers because they registered strong protest against apparent evils or shortcomings of their age. Usually the protest is vehement, as with Luther and Rousseau, Marx and Freud. But sometimes it is rather by implication, as is the case with Descartes and Kant, Newton and Darwin, whereupon enthusiastic followers of these men point out how woefully inadequate, how thoroughly stupid all thinkers before their heroes had been. This protest appeal had to be nicely timed, however, to condemn what the age had already condemned in its own heart and mind. If it came before the world was ready for it, the thinker's body of thought smouldered for a long time like a delayed-action bomb to burst upon the world posthumously, as was the case with Marx, and in a modified way with Kant.

Freud's popularity was achieved within his own lifetime be-

cause his condemnation of puritan standards came at a time
when these standards were already discredited among intellectuals almost everywhere. Although it appeared radical, therefore,
Freudianism reinforced and justified the twentieth century's basic
beliefs. So it was with Luther's denunciation of Catholic practices, when the Church herself had already begun the needed
reforms in Catholic life, and with Calvin's structures against the
loose living of sixteenth-century Europeans. So it was with
Marx's protest against the abuses of an uncontrolled capitalistic
system, and Locke's quarrel with the extremes to which Cartesian
rationalism had been pushed. The protest appeal is effective,
then, because it is directed against already discredited beliefs or
practices.

Protest alone is not enough. Man is never satisfied with a
purely negative approach. Our makers of the modern mind remained popular because they promised a better life in the future;
the application of their various ideas always ensured a new
world which would be a better world. Luther offered his followers the nice possibility of eating their cake and having it too.
They could enjoy all the pleasures of this world, and by a simple
act of trust assure themselves of happiness also in the next.
Calvin promised to create a city of God on earth where all good
men would be moderately wealthy, where the Elect would remain always in control, where sin would be forever banished
by law. Descartes guaranteed an errorless world where everything would be rationally arranged and ignorance would be next
to impossible.

Locke offered the eighteenth century a cushioned world where
everything would be leisurely, easygoing, where bitterness would
be unknown and contentiousness dissolved into common-sense
compromise. It would be a practical, rule-of-the-thumb world
where a man could follow a few basic rules of decency, do moderately well by his fellow men without being troubled too much
by their misery or their suffering, and he could save his soul by
holding to a couple of fundamental beliefs. He could always
salve his conscience, with Pope, by knowing that "whatever is,
is right." The Benthamites would have a rationally arranged
world where the greatest happiness of the greatest number
would be promoted, where rogues would be ground honest and

misery reduced to a minimum. Everyone would be happy by being selfish in an enlightened way. Darwin's promise was somewhat vaguer — but it appealed strongly to his age. He guaranteed more and more progress, which evidently meant a better world peopled by fitter persons, where everything would be immensely improved both materially and morally. Darwin's generation exulted in the progress they were making — and he assured them ever larger doses of the same thing. And Marx, of course, offered a utopia where each would give according to his abilities and receive according to his needs — a promise which should satisfy anyone.

Makers of the modern mind, then, are men who ride the intellectual tide of their time. They accept the age's fundamental assumptions, protest against what it condemns, promise what it most desires. They articulate the age's thoughts and desires. They are nevertheless important figures in history. For the world is never the same after them as it was before. They act as foci for many ideas which without them would not be combined as strong forces for change in history. They can be likened to a glass which focuses the otherwise harmless, scattered rays of the sun to produce a single burning beam. For they pulled together many scattered ideas and concentrated them in a master idea which became a power in history. It is therefore correct, in a modified way, to speak of pre-Darwinian and post-Darwinian mentalities, or pre-Newtonian and post-Newtonian outlooks. Luther and Calvin and Marx and all the others act as watersheds in the history of ideas. Each played a major role in changing not only the thought but also the social and political institutions of subsequent generations. The world is changed because of them.

Some of them, it is true, do not seem to have played particularly large parts as individual thinkers. Darwin, Locke, and Rousseau, for example, said effectively what others had not expressed so well. There is some likelihood that the world would have gone on pretty much the same if these three men had never lived. Their personal contributions to the history of ideas seem to be chiefly that they put their names on movements already under way — as was the case with Darwin's key idea of struggle for existence and survival of the fittest, a notion which Wallace would probably have supplied if Darwin had not put it forth so successfully. By doing this alone, however, Darwin and others like him crystallized the age's thought with their own personal twist, changed its direction at least slightly, gave it new prestige, and increased its power for change in history.

Other makers of the modern mind change the course of intellectual history more markedly by their personal efforts. Closer to the Carlyle concept of heroes in the history of the human mind are Descartes and Kant, Marx and Freud. Socialism, for example, would most likely not have taken on its bitter, bludgeoning ways had it not been for Marx's personal interpretation of the laws whereby the classless society was to be achieved. Neither was there anything inevitable about the coming of Cartesian rationalism. Some system of thought was needed which would stand the test of late sixteenth-century skepticism, but there is no reason why Aristotle or St. Thomas, or perhaps Bonaventura or Duns Scotus could not have been dusted off and refurbished for the seventeenth century. Descartes chose to build from scratch with his methodic doubt, and his influence on Western man's thinking and living has been continuous. Rationalism became what Descartes made it.

To a lesser extent this is true of Kant and even of Freud. Somehow, someone would have had to reconcile rationalism and empiricism so as to make room for science at the end of the eighteenth century. But there was no special reason why it had to be by cutting reality into two distinct worlds of noumena and phenomena. Kant's solution was largely the product of his personal, peculiar genius. So, too, with Freud. It was certain by the early twentieth century that the unconscious and the instinctive had to be explored, that their relationship with conscious, rational activity had to be examined. Freudianism, however, was not determined by the nature of the problem. Psychoanalysis is what it is today, in great degree, because of the personal equipment of its powerful pioneer.

These are the factors, then, which combine to make a thinker influential on succeeding generations. These are the factors, moreover, which prevented other great, sometimes even greater, thinkers from becoming makers of the modern mind. It is noticeable, for example, that after Luther and Calvin the list of men treated in these pages does not include a single great Christian thinker. Luther and Calvin were influential not because they were Christian, but because they cut men loose from the universal organization of the Catholic Church and because their great appeal was in the direction of the world rather than away from it. Their stress was on this life and on things eminently practical. Newman was certainly a better balanced, more penetrating thinker than either Marx or Darwin, in whose age and whose environment he lived. But Newman disagreed with the age's basic assumptions, condemned its underlying beliefs. He was therefore a dissenter from rather than a maker of the modern mind. So it has been with other Christian thinkers. Modern thought has been increasingly secularistic, going away from theology and religion toward practical sciences and filing cabinets. Christianity has been in retreat. Christian thinkers have therefore been relatively without influence, for they have refused to ride the intellectual tide.

Neither have any literary figures been makers of the modern mind. Dostoyevsky and Tolstoi were independent thinkers as well as able literary craftsmen, but they remained too independent, too romantic to influence the course of ideas and events late in the nineteenth century. So it was with Ruskin in England. He lived almost beside Marx, and he condemned capitalism as strongly as Marx did, often on better grounds and with better logic. But Ruskin failed to strike up real contact with the age's basic assumptions. He was not hard and realistic — so he gets into anthologies today, whereas Marx is in the picket line, the public rostrum, the assembly room. Literary figures, in fact, almost always serve more as mirrors of their age's thought than its makers. Pope is the classic example here. Perhaps he said what "oft was thought, but ne'er so well expressed," but his couplets came too late to have a strong influence on his age's thought. He offered many quotable lines — but only to illustrate a point in Locke or Newton or some other influential eighteenth-century thinker.

3

What can be said, in summary form, of the effect each maker of the modern mind has had on history? How has the world differed because of him? We must remember, of course, that

Luther was not the first maker of the modern mind. The mentality upon which he set to work had been in the making ever since the days of Greek antiquity — and fully to account for the way we think and act today it is necessary to go back to Plato and Aristotle, to work through Zeno and Cicero, through the supreme contribution of the apostolic Church, the contributions of St. Augustine and perhaps Boethius, down to the great synthesis of St. Thomas in the thirteenth century.

From the Greeks, Western man obtained his logical, rational method of thinking, with its faith in the ability of the mind of man to discover truth. From the Romans came an emphasis on law and order. And from Christianity came the strong stress on charity and mercy, on just dealing with one's fellows and with God. From them all came the lofty view of man as a being who is master of all creation, who is lord of all the universe, but who holds all things in trust from the Lord of all, to whom man is responsible for his human actions. From them all came the concept of natural law as that portion of God's law which man can discover by the right use of his reason, a law which is normative and therefore deals with man as a moral person.

The thought of man down till the Renaissance was essentially theocentric. Man was looked upon as a creature of God; he was studied chiefly as a member of the human race whose ultimate destiny was clearly known and whose activity on earth was judged in relation to that destiny. Man's sojourn on earth was a time of trial in which, by rightly using his reason and his freedom, he earned his eternal reward. As an individual, however, man was rather neglected. Certainly such practical subjects as medicine and physics, chemistry and biology made almost no progress from the days of Galen and Aristotle down till the time of Descartes. This was the mind, then, on which Luther set to work, a mind which concentrated on theology and philosophy, viewed man as a person rather than an individual, neglected practical sciences, and tended to accept a great deal on authority instead of learning by experiment. It was philosophical rather than scientific; it was rational and realistic rather than emotional and idealistic. And much that is good in our outlook today can be traced past Luther to the Classical-Christian mentality, a strong residue of which is still with us, having weathered the assaults of modern thinkers through the past four centuries.

Luther's principal contribution to the trend of ideas was his vicious attack on human reason. His is the first successful frontal assault on the power of man's faculty of reason to guide his human actions. Man's moral responsibility for his human actions was consequently weakened, and man himself was reduced to the status of a thoroughly depraved animal who had been saved by Christ if he would trust blindly in His merits — pretty much as a collie trusts its master's decisions. Luther contributed to the justifying and the building of the absolute state, and he promoted the breakup of European unity which, never too solid a thing, was in process of disintegration anyway.

Calvin created a logically organized, legalistically briefed religion, and in doing so he saved the Protestant movement from falling apart before a reviving Catholicism. But Calvin's biggest contribution was his glorification of the puritan virtues, something which was accepted unquestioningly by the most influential groups in Europe and America until recently. Down till Freud's day Calvinistic morality prevailed, except in those countries which remained morally and culturally, as well as doctrinally, Catholic. Calvin's glorification of business, his praise of frugality and high seriousness, his exaltation of diligent labor and social callousness contributed to the formation of the capitalistic mentality and the now crumbling industrial empires of the Western World. Reinforced by Kant in the eighteenth century, Calvin held the field until Marx and Freud led a revolt against his individualist business ethic and his harsh code of personal morality.

Descartes set out to rescue reason from the skeptics, and for a time philosophers felt that he had succeeded in reviving their weakened faith in man's ability to be a rational animal. Descartes came to be identified with rationalism; and because Cartesianism ended up a glorious, tragic failure a century later, it seemed to Western man that reason itself had failed. Descartes's failure is therefore even more important than the positive contributions he made to European thought; for had he successfully rescued reason, Locke, Kant, and Bentham would have been unnecessary, Rousseau and Freud would have been impossible. Because Descartes denied man's senses, his feeling, and his emotion their proper roles in life, men felt faced with a choice between pure reason or no reason, between being angels or animals. Descartes cut man's mind and body apart so decisively that men could no longer reconcile them, as Aristotle and the medievalists had done. They had to choose between them, and in time men voted against their intellects in favor of their bodies. In the long run, therefore, Descartes did reason harm, and he drove it necessarily into practical sciences at the expense of social and theological speculation.

Locke worked out compromises all along the line, compromises which held for a while but in time scattered off in one direction or another, toward one extreme solution or another. He quite properly rejected Cartesian innate ideas in favor of a sensist origin of all knowledge, but his solution was framed in such terms that it could be reduced to a full idealism by Berkeley on one hand, or to an extreme sensism by La Mettrie on the other. In politics, Locke defended the Glorious Revolution as a grand thing, but his defense was used to justify revolution anywhere at any time. His individualism, again, was moderate in his own hands, but it developed into the rugged individualism of the nineteenth century. Moderate in all things, Locke was used as the starting point for contradictory extremes of a later day in philosophy and psychology, in methodology, and the whole field of social sciences. His attitude of common sense and compromise took hold in England and America, however, to influence political and social decisions from his day till ours.

Sir Isaac Newton's fame as a thinker is unequaled in the history of ideas. The goal of every influential thinker in the past two centuries was to become the Newton of some order or other, and the greatest encomium men could devise was to accord this title to their intellectual heroes. Thus Kant flattered Rousseau by calling him the Newton of the moral order — and Kant wished to become the Newton of the philosophical order. Thus Wallace and Huxley eulogized Darwin by calling him the Newton of the biological order.

Newton was influential for his canonization of the inductive, scientific method of arriving at general physical laws. He started with nothing but isolated facts which he compared and systematized and used as data for arriving at general conclusions, whereas

Descartes and Leibniz deduced theories on vortices and vacuums and other things from certain basic philosophical assumptions in order to explain the phenomena of life they encountered. This Newtonian method, valuable in certain fields, came to be *the* method for any kind of reasoning in the eighteenth century; by using it men thought they had banished mystery from the universe. By means of it they learned much, it is true, but certain mysteries eluded them and came in time to plague their children. Newton had made science respectable, however, and he had given the scientist a place of importance alongside the philosopher and the theologian of days gone by.

Rousseau is important chiefly for leading the reaction against decadent Cartesian rationalism. Luther had complained, "Alas, in this life reason is never completely destroyed," and time had proved him right. But rationalists had thoroughly discredited it. In the eighteenth century Rousseau undertook to destroy it, and though he was not completely successful his anti-rational influence was nevertheless both more permanent and more permeating than Luther's had been. After Rousseau, rationalists are on the defensive — largely because of him and because of the partial truths he overemphasized. Rousseau glorified feeling. He said in effect that man would be a good man if he would be more like an animal and less like a man. History since his day is a record of the various ways mankind has tried to put that advice into practice. It is not too happy a story. Rousseau resurrected forgotten virtues and he discovered lost truths, but the romanticism which flowed from his pen into the nineteenth century contained the germs of noxious growths that we tried to kill in this last desperate war. For if man follows infallible feeling he can stray in any direction, and he can go to any extreme. Nothing but brute force can check him. From Rousseau came much good, as well as much that was not, for there are many fine things done under the name of humanitarianism, and the impetus toward democratic living has been a good thing.

Kant tried to do the job Descartes had failed to do more than a century earlier. He tried to rescue philosophy by reconciling it with Newton's universe and Rousseau's heart. His attempt was ingenious, far from superficial, both adroitly and profoundly done. But Kant's solution proved even less stable than Descartes's, for where the latter made our knowledge of the outside world ultimately independent of that world and dependent on God alone, Kant went even further and made the outside world correspond to our ideas. The distinction between the phenomenal and noumenal worlds was kept in balance by Kant himself, but his followers quite naturally tipped the scales in the direction of one world or the other. Those who stressed the phenomenal world came in time to make it the only one, and within a few generations their thought developed into pure materialism. Those who stressed the noumenal world came to deny everything else, and they ended up high in the sky of complete philosophical idealism.

The Benthamites made rationalism's last stand in Western society, and a sad stand it was because Jeremy Bentham had apparently learned nothing from rationalism's failure in the eighteenth century. Considering Rousseau mad, he and his followers looked on man as a creature powered by pleasure and pain alone, and directed by pure reason in seeking his goals. They were important because of the ancient evils they exposed and because of the reforms that followed in their wake. In the history of ideas they are important chiefly as a transitional group between eighteenth-century thought and that of nineteenth-century evolutionists and socialists. Their utilitarian norm for judging the worth and rightness of anything, a typically Anglo-American standard, has lived on in its own right. It has indeed been used, knowingly or unwittingly, by most Englishmen and Americans ever since Bentham's day. With only a few mental twists it developed into the philosophical pragmatism so prevalent in English-speaking countries at the present time.

Darwin, Marx, and Freud remain contemporary figures. Their thought is our thought, our world is cut on their pattern. They are collectively in control of the contemporary mind, for though they have been corrected on various scientific points in their respective fields of biology, social science, and psychology, they are popularly considered *the* thinkers in those respective fields. Darwin stands for evolution and biology; Marx stands for Communism, and for the economic approach to social questions; Freud stands for psychoanalysis, and he is thought to hold the key to the secrets of the soul.

Darwin and Marx are thoroughly materialistic. Both account for everything in terms of matter and motion, Darwin working out a system of biological determinism and Marx a sociological system whereby everything is determined by the forces of production. Darwin reduces thought processes purely and simply to the mechanism of the brain; Marx reduces them ultimately to one's economic position. Both Darwin and Marx tried to explain all things and solve all mysteries of life, then, with matter and motion alone, but their materialism differed from the eighteenth-century variety by stressing motion rather than matter. Theirs is the historical approach. Their emphasis on change and on evolution makes it appear necessary for us to get back to the origin of things properly to understand them.

This is the way of men's minds today. If Descartes was guilty of using the mathematical method universally, if Kant used the Newtonian scientific method outside its proper field, we today are similarly extending the historical approach into fields where it does not rightly belong. Nineteenth-century German historicism is still too much with us. For we use it to answer questions it cannot answer. We believe that knowing the origin and development of a thing gives us full knowledge of its nature when, in fact, it gives us only historical knowledge of its growth. The historical approach throws light on almost any subject, but it cannot solve philosophical problems or unravel psychological and religious puzzles. It cannot replace analysis.

Freud's emphasis, like Marx's and Darwin's, is on the historical approach. For the psychoanalyst must discover the cause of his patient's illness somewhere in the patient's infancy — the earlier, it would seem, the better. Like Marx and Darwin, moreover, Freud puts dynamism and struggle at the core of his system. These three men make struggle for survival, cutthroat competition, jungle warfare among men and nations the only natural, indeed, the inevitable kind of life. Kill or be killed is the lesson one learns from reading them. Freud stressed one point, however, which is to be found only implicitly in Darwin and Marx. This is his frontal attack on human reason, an attack as vicious as Luther's and Rousseau's, one that is more difficult to answer. For Freud resolves all apparently rational activity into compromises resulting from conflict between the Ego and the Id.

Basically man is only an animal for Freud, an animal who has somehow developed a little differently from his fellow animals — so that he can be neurotic. After all, Freud tells us, that is the only real difference between man and the other animals.

The whole course of modern intellectual history has been away from reason. Luther began by attacking it. Various attempts were made to rescue it, especially by Descartes and Kant and Bentham, but these efforts were unavailing. Other influential thinkers concentrated on the more practical matter of studying and controlling the forces of nature — and their work has been progressive. But seeing what man has made of man is the key to understanding the thought of any age. Through the past four centuries man has come, intellectually, to have a lower and lower opinion of himself.

Aristotle defined man as a rational animal, a definition which the medievalists kept intact. But moderns have had trouble with that definition ever since Luther's day. Luther emphasized the animal in man, and Calvin denied it its rightful place. Descartes cut an uncrossable chasm between the rational and the animal in man. And no maker of the modern mind has thrown a bridge across that chasm. Either they have denied the animal in man in order to rescue the rational element, or they deny reason to concentrate on the animal. They never get the two together in proper relation to each other. Ironically, man has used his rational equipment in modern times to prove to himself that he is not rational. So the matter stands today in the Darwinian-Marxian-Freudian world.

4

The men we chose to treat as makers of the modern mind, let us remember, are not solely responsible for the way we think today. There are countless lesser thinkers whose total contribution bulks large in the making of our mind. The full story cannot be told, for example, without including persons like William James and Charles Peirce to account for pragmatism. Fichte, Hegel, Schopenhauer, Nietzsche, Bergson, and Pareto must be included to account for fascism — an important, though we can hope passing, element in the modern mind. Gobineau, H. S. Chamberlain, Günther have to be mentioned for an understanding of racism, and the whole list of German nationalist thinkers from Von Treitschke to Rosenberg must be included to account for nazism.

Nor can the contemporary mind be fully described in terms of its intellectual forebears alone. Time and circumstance, the printing press and the radio, the mechanization of the world with its resulting staccato music and bustling living, have all played a most important part. For they are the environment in which our minds operate, and human beings cannot think calmly — or think at all, perhaps — when a radio commentator is chattering in their ears. The modern world beats at a tempo which militates against rational activity. The Industrial Revolution may not determine precisely what we think, but it has an awful lot to do with the way we think today. It has made calm contemplation almost impossible; it has made self-controlled, rational, objective thought extremely difficult. The modern world, indeed, seems to have conspired this past century against the thinking man.

Men do not seem to want to think today. They would rather have their brains machine-gunned by disjointed words than follow the chain of relationships established between the words of a complete sentence. It is hard for anyone except older persons to realize how faith in human reason has crumbled in the past quarter of a century. All younger men need do, however, is compare a paragraph from Milton with one from Sinclair Lewis or Ernest Hemingway or almost any popular contemporary writer. Or, if he complains that many years have passed since Milton penned his ponderous periodic sentences, let him compare Robert Lewis Stevenson's prose with that found in any slick-paper magazine today. He will find that the sentence has disintegrated, which means that modern thinking has likewise disintegrated, that the business of writing is the disorganization of ideas rather than their organization into complete thoughts.

Ten years ago Wilson Follett observed that "there has always been a striking incidence, never more striking than now, between our conception of the universe and our conception of the sentence." When men viewed the universe as a whole, when they tried to bring order into the world by establishing relationships between its parts, then they wrote in period sentences, then they used principal and dependent clauses. But when thought consists of a series of unrelated impressions, when men's minds operate like kaleidoscopes, then they write in disjointed sentences, one after the other. Today it is not even necessary to write sentences. The fact that Walter Winchell's words and phrases are understood to make sense is an indictment of how we think today. A British general was reported as commenting thus on General Marshall when the latter was appointed Secretary of State: "Good man. Strange though. Reads books." That is the way men's minds operate today, but fortunately it is the way of "intellectuals" rather than the man-in-the-street.

The ordinary man, who culturally tags a generation or two behind the intelligentsia, has thus far stood up pretty well under the concerted attack made upon his mind by the radio, the press, and the school. He might not use Ciceronian sentences, but at least he generally uses sentences. His phlegmatic stand against the current attack on his reason suggests that Luther was correct when he complained that in this life reason can never be completely destroyed. There are little straws in the wind, in fact, which indicate that even "intellectuals" are trying to recover their lost intellects: there seems less emphasis on passion and feeling today than there was a decade ago; there seems to be more discussion than formerly on questions of what is reasonable, what is right, what is prudent, what is possible in world affairs. Such things indicate that we may have passed the nadir of our intellectual history and that we might be recovering rationality.

Any hope for a rationally organized world in the future, for a place where men can live as human beings instead of high-class animals, lies in men's ability again to give the rational part of their human nature its proper place in human activity. It is necessary to recover the Classical-Christian view of man as a rational animal. This view looks on man as a person who possesses a body with its senses, its instincts, its emotions — all of which must be given room for proper satisfaction. But they are all under rational control. It is man's reason, indeed, which distinguishes him from the other animals, which makes him an intelligent creature who can direct his activity according to the light of reason, and who is therefore responsible for his human activity. But there can be no return to the thirteenth or any other century.

One would be foolish indeed simply to revive Aristotle or Cicero or St. Thomas and apply him to the twentieth century as though there had never been a Newton or a Darwin or a Freud. Thinkers of this age cannot be pre-Lutheran, pre-Cartesian, pre-Marxian, pre-anything. The contributions of all these men must be acknowledged, and where they have been proved valid they must be incorporated into any rational system of thought. Thinkers who wish to see the universe as a rationally organized place in the future, then, cannot refuse to accept any established fact, whatever its source might be.

Any hope for reason being given its rightful place again would be blasted by a "rationalist" movement such as Descartes introduced with such disastrous consequences three centuries ago. Such a movement would only discredit reason once again. It would be followed by another reaction, such as Luther's or Rousseau's or Freud's. If man's mind is to start in a new direction in these days and to formulate a successful system of thought, it must effect a synthesis by selecting the various doctrines of its makers which have stood the test of time and have been proved valid. It must synthesize these findings by giving them proper proportion, by realizing that the simple solution is almost necessarily a wrong solution. This was the mistake of Descartes, who cut so cleanly from the past, who considered man pure mind. This was the mistake of Rousseau, who considered man nothing but unadulterated animal feeling; of Darwin, who explained all things by struggle and survival; of Marx, who pushed everything back to methods of production; of Freud, who resolved everything into unconscious drives. Any such simple solution cannot explain the whole of reality. Instead, it contorts everything into its preconceived pattern to give us a caricature of reality.

Not only must the true elements of each man's doctrine be rescued, then, but the danger of applying a single method to all fields of thought must be avoided. This has been the mistake of most modern thinkers. Descartes thought that the mathematical, deductive method would solve all life's problems — when, in fact, it solved only mathematical problems. Kant thought that the method of the physicist would give him certainty in philosophy — and he went astray. Freud thought that the psychoanalytical approach would reveal the secrets of art and literature, history and religion — and he ended up by adding to the confusion already current in those fields.

This is the mistake we must avoid today. Theorists now run the danger of explaining the mysteries of the universe and of man's soul by one of two methods which have been so fruitful of late years in their respective fields: that of the historian, or that of the nuclear physicist. But to tell the story of the origin and development of something is not to reveal its nature. The history of philosophy or of religion can never replace either philosophy or religion. Nor can the laws of splitting atoms be applied to the disintegration of European culture today without arbitrarily creating a picture which is both unnecessary and incorrect. As no one simple law can explain complex social realities, so too no one method can be used outside its proper field without doing violence both to the theorist's mind and to the matter on which he works.

It is the story of the six specialists and the elephant all over again. Like the six men from Indostan, our makers of the modern mind tended to see the whole elephant in terms of their various specialties. Descartes held the tail of mathematics, and tried to describe the whole elephant in terms of that tail. Darwin grabbed the knee of evolution and reduced all things in the universe to struggle for existence and survival of the fittest. So it was with the others. None saw the universe, or even man, for the complex things both are. Each, as a specialist, added to the sum total of our knowledge about the elephant. But none was competent to speak about the animal as a whole, though each tried to do so. Each one told us things we did not know before, but each also added to our confusion. We must appreciate each one's contribution, because it is fatal to condemn them *in toto* in order to preserve our vision of the universe and of man by refusing to learn more about the two.

Those who think on philosophical, historical, or social problems today, those who hope to guide the future course of events by their thinking and their writing, can profit from the mistakes of the makers of the modern mind we have discussed in this book. Thinkers today can profit, too, from the many areas of thought thinkers of the past have explored for us. For they have discovered much. Each one has made a positive contribution to our fund of human knowledge. And each has made his mistakes. Neither their discoveries nor their mistakes need have been made in vain if we utilize their positive contributions to our knowledge, overlooking none of them, and if we are conscious of their errors, repeating none of them in the future.

INDEX